I0135507

Confederate "Tales of the War" in the Trans-Mississippi
Part Three

Area of Operations: Arkansas and Louisiana, 1863

1. Van Buren (Dec. 28, 1862); 2. Arkansas Post (Jan. 9–11, 1863); 3. Operations in Northeast Louisiana (June–August, 1863): A=Milliken's Bend & Young's Point (June 7); B=Lake Providence (June 9); C= Richmond (June 15); D=Mounds or Goodrich Landing (June 29); 4. Helena (July 4, 1863); 5. Little Rock (Aug.–Sept., 1863); 6. Pine Bluff (Oct. 25, 1863)

UNWRITTEN CHAPTERS OF
THE CIVIL WAR
WEST OF THE RIVER

VOLUME VII

Confederate
"Tales of the War"
In the Trans-Mississippi
Part Three: 1863

Author/Editor Michael E. Banasik

Camp Pope Publishing
2012

Copyright ©2012 by Michael E. Banasik

Library of Congress Control Number: 2012952619

ISBN: 978-1-929919-45-1

Camp Pope Publishing
P.O. Box 2232
Iowa City, Iowa 52244
www.camppope.com

Series Dedication:

Dedicated to the forgotten soldiers of both North and South, who fought in the American Civil War west of the Mississippi River; their deeds of perseverance and valor shall not be lost through the ravages of time, but rather recorded for all to remember.

Volume VII, Part Three Dedication:

To my children—Michael Jr. and Marisa. You mean more to me than you will ever know.

CONTENTS

Photographs and Illustrations

Maps

Series Introduction

The Civil War in the Trans-Mississippi region provides a fascinating study of Nineteenth Century warfare under the most severe conditions. Soldiers serving in the region faced an almost complete lack of a railroad net, a decrepit road system, and terrain that varied from arid deserts to rugged mountains. Battles were few, but the constant strain of living under less than ideal conditions wore heavily upon the soldiers serving west of the Mississippi River. Often the stories told by the frontier soldiers were not of great engagements, but of long marches, poor living conditions, or of simple survival. And for each story told there were always two parts, one told by a man in gray and another by one who wore the blue.

Introduction to Volume VII, Part Three

This latest volume of my series comprises an extensive group of reminiscences published by the St. Louis *Missouri Republican* between 1885 and 1887. These pieces were written by the participants in the Civil War and cover the entire conflict from the firing of the first guns until the surrender of the Confederate armies in 1865. The first story appeared on July 4, 1885, and the last one, that I have discovered, on July 2, 1887. In all 94 pieces were published. Typically, in each Saturday issue, the *Republican* printed assorted reminiscences by the lowliest private to the most exalted general, all veterans of the war, covering the Civil War from every aspect, both North and South and from every front of the action, including the high-seas. For this volume, only those pieces not previously published and dealing with the Trans-Mississippi will be presented, while Appendix F will list articles that were previously published or those pieces about the east side of the Mississippi River. Because of the extensive nature of the material, Part Three, of Volume VII, will only deal with the events of 1863, while the final volume of the Confederate Tales will conclude with 1864-1865 and will follow in a short time. The Union material will also be presented in later volumes of this series.

As to why these articles were published, the *Missouri Republican* wrote the following:

> The publication of the official orders and correspondence of the war of the rebellion made it comparatively easy for military writers to get at the exact facts of many disputed questions, and all the campaigns have been discussed by the record in recent years by competent officers of both the contending armies. Probably it is the publication of these numerous volumes, which, as much as anything else, has aroused a renewed interest in all manner of literature based on the incidents of the civil war. In response to what seems a public desire the *Republican* will hereafter publish in its

Saturday edition a series of war papers, either original or selected from the best current sketches in contemporary publications.

It is not desired to make this department especially a medium for criticism of military operations. The incidents of camp life and the experiences of the private soldier will find as ready access to these columns as the history of great campaigns. What ever war reminiscences will interest the thousands of old soldiers and the greater thousands of their children, will gladly be published in the full ballet that these chronicles of personal experiences from both sides, while reviving the memories, will at the same time aid in obliterating the animosities of the great struggle.[1]

The 1863 portion of these *"Tales of the War"* cover the Van Buren, Arkansas, Raid (December 28, 1862) with the subsequent retreat to Little Rock, followed by the Battle of Arkansas Post (January 9–11, 1863). From Arkansas we travel briefly to northeast Louisiana for John G. Walker's efforts to relieve the pressure on Vicksburg, Mississippi, including several raids and skirmishes that took place from May–August 1863. Back in Arkansas, the Battle of Helena (July 4, 1863) and the 1863 Campaign for Little Rock are covered in detail, including the Marmaduke-Walker duel of September 6, 1863. The 1863 version of the *"Confederate Tales"* is completed with the Battle of Pine Bluff, Arkansas, on October 25, 1863. Included in this edition are several appendices, with a detailed Confederate Order of Battle for the Battle of Helena, as well as a lesser, though still significant, Confederate Order of Battle for the Battle of Pine Bluff. As before, selected, detailed biographies are presented, with an assortment of correspondence from the principle personalities of the book, with a detailed index for easy reference. New in this edition, readers will be introduced to an assortment of Confederate poems or songs that were produced during or immediately following the war, as mentioned by one of the authors contained within the Tales. Also included in this edition is the organizational information on Parsons's Missouri Brigade, including brief biographies of all the principle commanders of regiments, battalions, and independent companies, who served in the unit during the war.

I hope you find these pieces as fascinating as I did in researching and preparing them for your reading pleasure.

Michael E. Banasik

---

1. Editorial Comment, *The Missouri Republican* (St. Louis, Missouri), July 4, 1885.

Nameplate which appeared ahead of most of the "Tales of the War" in the *Republican*.

Chapter 1

Winter 1862 to Spring 1863
(December 28, 1862–May 31, 1863):

Van Buren Raid, Retreat to Little Rock, Battle of Arkansas Post, and Winter Quarters In Little Rock

Item: The Early History of Company A, 10th Missouri Infantry, Including the Formation of the Company, the Battle of Prairie Grove, Arkansas (December 7, 1862) and the Retreat to Little Rock (December 28–January 16, 1863), by James L. Grubbs, late Company A, 10th Missouri Infantry.[1] **Published:** January 9, 1886.

[Editor Note: The bulk of this article deals with the 10th Missouri Infantry following the Battle of Prairie Grove, Arkansas, in December 1862. Only that part which covers the period 1861–1863 is presented here, while the remaining parts of the article will be presented later in this series.]

The Last Company That Surrendered.

Canton, Mo., Dec. 12, 1885.

Editor *Republican*

I have been very much interested in "The Tales of the War" that have been published from time to time in the *Republican*, being a member of Co. A, Tenth

---

1. James L. S. Grubbs, a resident of Lewis County, Missouri, initially joined Company A, 1st Cavalry Regiment, 2nd Division Missouri State Guard (MSG). Later he enlisted in Company A, 10th Missouri Infantry, Confederate (CSA) on September 1, 1862, at Camp Mitchell, Arkansas, in Monroe County. Camp Mitchell was about 22 miles southeast of Clarendon near the White River and located on the farm of a "General Mitchell." Grubbs survived the war, being paroled at Camp Allen, in Shreveport, Louisiana, on June 8, 1865. He returned to Missouri and was living in Canton, Lewis County, in 1906. Wade Ankesheiln, *The Last Guardsmen* (Independence, MO, 2008), 92, hereafter cited as Ankesheiln, *Guardsman*; Michael E. Banasik, *Missouri Brothers in Gray: The Reminiscences and Letters of William J. Bull and John P. Bull* (Iowa City, IA, 1998), 35, hereafter cited as Banasik, *Missouri Brothers in Gray*; National Archives, Record Group M322 (roll no. 152), Confederate Compiled Service Records, 10th Missouri Infantry; Wayne H. Schnetzer, *Men of the Tenth: A Roster of the Tenth Missouri Infantry Confederate States of America* (n.p., n.d.), 7, hereafter cites as Schnetzer, *Men of the Tenth*; Wayne Schnetzer, *More Forgotten Men: The Missouri State Guard* (Independence, MO, 2003), 99, hereafter cited as Schnetzer, *More Forgotten Men*.

Regiment, Parsons's Brigade.[2] I noticed that Capt. [James H.] McNamara in regard to the burial of our men in the winter of 1863 says our men were buried in long trenches.[3] I assisted in burying quite a number, and so far as I know they were buried in single graves, and as decently as circumstances would permit. Our company was composed of a remnant of the old Missouri State Guards that had followed Gen. [Sterling] Price east of the Mississippi River after the Battle of "Elk Horn" or Pea Ridge.[4] After making the Campaign of 1862, in Mississippi,

---

2. Mosby M. Parsons's Missouri Brigade was organized on November 9, 1862, and was initially commanded by Colonel Alexander E. Steen. As organized the brigade contained four regiments of infantry which were eventually designated the 10th, 11th, 12th and 16th Missouri Infantries, with Tilden's Missouri Artillery. Prior to the Battle of Prairie Grove the brigade added the 8th Missouri Infantry and Pindall's Missouri Sharpshooter Battalion. The 8th Missouri would later depart the brigade and be formed into a new brigade, commanded by John B. Clark, Jr. Parsons was assigned command of the brigade on November 17, 1862. See Appendix C for the organizational information and biographies of the various commanders of Parsons's Brigade. Janet Hewett, ed. *Supplement to the Official Records of the Union and Confederate Armies*, 100 vols. (Wilmington, NC, 1994-2001), pt. 2, vol. 38:596–597, hereafter cited as *O.R.S.*; Letter (November 9, 1862), Newton to Parsons, Copy Letter Book (June 1–December 18, 1862), Hindman's Command, Peter W. Alexander Collection, hereafter cited as Copy Letter Book No. 1; Special Orders No. 38 (November 9, 1862) and No. 44 (November 17, 1862), Special Orders Letter Book (June 1–Dec. 18, 1862), Hindman's command, Peter W. Alexander Collection, Columbia University, hereafter cited as Special Orders Book No. 1.
3. James H. McNamara was born in Ireland in 1837, emigrated to the United States in 1852, and settled in St. Louis. An Architect by profession, McNamara was a member of the St. Louis Militia, the Emmett Guards, and was captured at Camp Jackson on May 10, 1861. After his parole McNamara journeyed to north Missouri where he engaged in farming until October 1861, when he joined the 6th Division, MSG. He served initially as an orderly sergeant to A. M. Standish, and then as a volunteer in Gorham's, MSG Battery at the Battle of Pea Ridge, in March 1862. Following a short stint on the east side of the Mississippi River, McNamara returned to the west side of the river, where General M. M. Parsons appointed him Division Paymaster, replacing Colonel H. A. Parmales, who had died. McNamara remained on General Parsons's Staff until the Battle of Helena, when he volunteered to serve in Tilden's Battery. Severely wounded at Helena, McNamara recovered and returned to duty with Colonel Standish. In January 1865 he joined the engineers, and in May 1865 McNamara was appointed a captain. Following the war he returned to St. Louis, where he resumed his profession, including a period where he was a professor at what is now St. Louis University. Clement A. Evans and Robert S. Bridgers, gen. eds., *Confederate Military History, Extended Edition*, 19 vols. (Atlanta, 1899; reprint ed., Wilmington, NC, 1987), vol. 12: *Missouri* by John C. Moore, 258–259, hereafter cited as Moore, *Missouri, Confederate Military History, Extended*; Richard C. Peterson, et al., *Sterling Price's Lieutenants: A Guide to the Officers and Organization of the Missouri State Guard* (Jefferson City, MO, 1995), 173, hereafter cited as Peterson.
4. Sterling Price was born in September 1809 in Virginia and moved to Missouri in 1831. He served in the U.S. Congress, was governor of Missouri (1852), and became a brigadier general during the Mexican War. At the beginning of the Civil War he cast his lot with Missouri and subsequently the Confederacy. Price was one of the principle Confederate commanders at the Battle of Pea Ridge. He died in St. Louis in 1867. For a complete biography see *Missouri Brothers in Gray* of this series. The Battle of Pea Ridge was fought on March 6–8, 1862, in northwest Arkansas. Earl Van Dorn commanded the Confederate forces, while Samuel R. Curtis led the Federals. After a three day battle, a disorganized Confederate Army fled the area, having suffered as few as 1,000 casualties or as many as 2,000. Curtis reported 203 killed, 980 wounded and 201 captured or missing on the Federal side. United States War Department, *The War of the Rebellion: A Compilation of the Official Records of the Union and Confederate Armies*, 70 vols. in 128 (Washington, D. C. 1880-1901), Series 1, vol. 8:206, 282, hereafter cited as *O.R.* All citations of *O.R.* refer to Series 1 unless indicated otherwise; Banasik,

we returned with Gen. [Mosby M.] Parsons[5] west of the river for the purpose of bringing a large quartermaster's train, which we crossed near the mouth of the Arkansas River. After camping a short time at Arkansas Post,[6] Gen. Parsons started north for the purpose of recruiting his brigade. We went as far north as Yellville, Ark. There we received quite a large number of recruits.[7] From Yellville

---

Missouri Brothers in Gray, 148–150; Mark Mayo Boatner III, *The Civil War Dictionary* (New York, 1959), 669, hereafter cited as Boatner; William L. Shea and Earl J. Hess, *Pea Ridge Civil War Campaign in the West* (Chapel Hill, NC, 1992), 271.

5. Mosby M. Parsons, a resident of Jefferson City, Missouri, was born in Virginia in 1822, moved to Missouri at age thirteen, and served in the Mexican War. Parsons was appointed a brigadier general on May 17, 1861, commanding the 6th Division, MSG. Parsons led his command in all the 1861 battles of his division, but was not present at the Battle of Pea Ridge, being at the time in Richmond, Virginia. On April 8, 1862, Parsons succeeded Price as commander of the MSG, and on November 5, 1862, he was commissioned a brigadier general in the Confederate Army. Parsons commanded a brigade at Prairie Grove, and later a division during the Red River and Camden Campaigns. Parsons spent his Civil War years, except for three months, in the Trans-Mississippi Department. At war's end he went to Mexico, where he was killed on August 16, 1865. See Banasik, *Missouri Brothers in Gray*, 146-148, for biography and photo. Michael E. Banasik, *Missouri In 1861: The Civil War Letters of Franc B. Wilkie Newspaper Correspondent* (Iowa City, IA, 2001), 380-381; Peterson, 34; Thomas L. Snead, *The Fight For Missouri From the Election of Lincoln to the Death of Lyon* (New York, 1866), 313, hereafter cited as Snead, *Fight For Missouri*.

6. In describing Arkansas Post, General John A. McClernand, who captured the Post in January 1863, wrote:

Post [of] Arkansas, a small village, the capital of Arkansas County, is situated on elevated ground, above the reach of floods, and defining for some miles the left bank of the river. It was settled by the French in 1685 [actually June 1686]; is 50 miles above the mouth of the river, 117 miles below Little Rock, and is surrounded by a fruitful country abounding in cattle, corn, and cotton.

Arkansas Post was the first white settlement west of the Mississippi River and served as a major trading center for years in competition with New Orleans. Before being sold to the United States in 1804, the Post was first controlled by the French (1686–1782), then the Spanish (1763–1803). In its time, the Post served as the capital of Arkansas from July 1819 to 1821, until the capital was moved to Little Rock. By the time of the Civil War its importance had virtually disappeared, with a pre-war population of 500, the Post boasted a courthouse, church, a few stores, some brick houses, a school and a "printing house." A doctor serving at the Post simply called it a "*vile* place" and unhealthy, even to the snakes that resided in the area. Following the capture of Fort Hindman the Post was utterly destroyed and never rebuilt. Banasik, *Missouri Brothers in Gray*, 33–34; Edwin C. Bearss, "The Battle Of The Post Of Arkansas," *Arkansas Historical Quarterly* 18 (Autumn 1959), 237, hereafter cited as Bearss, "Post of Arkansas"; John L. Ferguson and J. H. Arkinson, *Historic Arkansas* (Little Rock, AR, 1966), 15, 27, 124, hereafter cited as Ferguson; Mark K. Christ, *Civil War Arkansas 1863: The Battle for a State* (Norman, OK, 2010), 39-40, hereafter cited as Christ; T. J. Gaughan, *Letters of a Confederate Surgeon* (Camden, 1960), 102, hereafter cited as Gaughan; "Victory At Arkansas Post," *Chicago Daily Tribune* (Chicago, IL), January 20, 1863; War Department, *The War of the Rebellion: Official Record of the Union and Confederate Navies*, 31 volumes (Washington, DC, 1894-1922), Series 1, vol. 24: 124, hereafter cited as *O.R.N.* All citations of *O.R.N.* refer to Series 1 unless indicated otherwise.

7. The remnant of the MSG left Abbeville, Mississippi, on July 18, 1862. They crossed the Mississippi River near Bolivar Lake in northern Mississippi, reaching the Arkansas shore at Cypress Creek, Desha County, on the night of July 30–31, and went into camp. After waiting six days for their commissary train to cross, Parsons's command moved to Arkansas Post, where they arrived on August 12. Six days later Parsons marched to Clarendon on the White River, then to Camp Mitchell, twenty-four miles to the southwest, in Monroe County. Between August 30 and September 7, 1862, the remnants of the

we marched west near Van Buren, where we met Gen. [Thomas C.] Hindman,[8] who was then in command of the Trans-Mississippi Department. A few days after our arrival the different squads were marched out and formed in line, which were immediately organized into two companies.[9] W. M. Moore,[10] who had been a lieutenant-colonel in the State Guard, was made captain of Co. A and E. Magofflin[11] captain of Co. B. and immediately ordered to report to Col. Stein [Steen] for

---

MSG transferred to Confederate Service. They departed Camp Mitchell on September 8, en route to Yellville, Arkansas, via Des Arc, Searcy and Clinton. Arriving at Yellville on October 4, Parsons remained there until October 29 and then completed his march to General Hindman's camp on Mulberry River on November 7, thus completing their trek to join the Trans-Mississippi Army. *O.R.S.*, pt. 2, vol. 38:600–601; Banasik, *Missouri Brothers in Gray*, 31–43; William N. Hoskin Civil War diary (1862–1865), Western Historical Manuscript Collection, State Historical Society of Missouri, July 18, 30–August 6, 12, 18, 24 , 30, September 8, October 4, 29 and November 7, 1862, hereafter cited as Hoskin; National Archives, Record Group 109, Confederate Muster Rolls, 10th Missouri Infantry; S. C. Turnbo, "History of the Twenty-seventh Arkansas Confederate Infantry With Many Interesting Accounts of the Counties Through Which it Passed During the Civil War and Accurate Accounts of the Battles in which it Engaged," S. C. Turnbo Collection, University of Arkansas (Little Rock), 128, 143, hereafter cited as Turnbo.

8. Thomas C. Hindman was born in Tennessee in 1828, fought in the Mexican War, and settled in Helena, Arkansas, in 1856. At the beginning of the Civil War he commanded an Arkansas Infantry Regiment and was promoted to general officer in November 1861. After the Battle of Shiloh, Hindman was again promoted and returned to Arkansas to command the Trans-Mississippi District. He went on to command the army at Fort Smith, fought and lost the Battle of Prairie Grove, after which he departed the Trans-Mississippi for the east side of the river. Following the war Hindman moved to Mexico where became a coffee grower. He later returned to Helena, became involved in Reconstruction politics, and was assassinated on September 28, 1868. One source described Hindman as "'A dapper little man, five feet one inch tall, who dressed in tight-fitting clothes, ruffled shirts, and patent-leather boots.'" For a biography and photograph see Banasik, *Missouri Brothers in Gray*, 139–141; Boatner, 402.

9. Two days after Parsons's command arrived at Hindman's camp, Hindman organized what became the First Corps, Trans-Mississippi Army. The old MSG troops were incorporated into the 10th Missouri Infantry (CSA) and placed into what became Parsons's Brigade on the same day, where they would remain for the rest of the war. Michael E. Banasik, *Embattled Arkansas: The Prairie Grove Campaign of 1862* (Wilmington, NC, 1996), 253–255, hereafter cited as Banasik, *Embattled Arkansas*; Banasik, *Missouri Brothers in Gray*, 43; Special Orders No. 38 (November 9, 1862), Special Orders Book No. 1.

10. See Appendix C for a biography of William M. Moore.

11. Elliah or Elijah H. Magoffin was born about 1838, and lived in Georgetown, Pettus County, Missouri, at the beginning of the Civil War. He joined the MSG in May 1861, was captured on January 3, 1862, while on recruiting service, and was sent to Alton, Illinois Prison. He escaped on July 25, 1862, with his father and thirty other inmates. Magoffin later rejoined the MSG. After transferring to the Confederate service on September 7, 1862, Magoffin was elected captain of Company B, 10th Missouri Infantry (CSA). He was promoted to major on December 2, 1863, with an effective date of December 7, 1862, and served throughout the war. Upon his father's death in the latter part of the war, at Rocky Comfort, Arkansas, the young Magoffin followed his father's killer for six hundred miles to Texas, staked out his house for several days and finally caught the murderer. The next morning, Magoffin, gave the killer the option of how he wanted to die—the killer wanted to be shot; instead Magoffin hanged him. He returned to camp carrying the same knife that had been used to kill his father. Following the war Magoffin was killed in a train wreck. *O.R.*, Series 2, vol. 1:344, 347–348; Joanne C. Eakin and Donald R. Hale, *Branded as Rebels: A List of Bushwhackers, Guerrillas, Partisan Rangers, Confederates and Southern Sympathizers from Missouri During the War Years* (Independence,

duty.[12] They were attached to his regiment. Capt. Moore was made senior captain. By this wholesale order quite a number of colonels, lieutenant-colonels, majors, captains and lieutenants were reduced to the rank of high privates. About December 1 we headed north again. On the 7th we fought at Prairie Grove, where we had twenty-seven men killed and wounded out of our company, Cols. Steen and Chappell both being killed.[13] Capt. Moore was promoted to lieutenant-colonel of the regiment. George W. McChristy became captain of Company A. We continued to receive new recruits until our company numbered 125 men.[14] We had been regularly drilled by Col. [Joseph] Kelly[15] and our company officers until we were quite

---

MO, 1993), 280, hereafter cited as Eakin & Hale; Joanne C. Eakin, *Missouri Prisoners of War From Gratiot Prison & Myrtle Street Prison, St. Louis, Mo. and Alton Prison, Alton Illinois Including Citizens, Confederates, Bushwhackers and Guerrillas* (Independence, MO, 1995), "Magoffin, Ebenezer H." entry, hereafter cited as Eakin, *Missouri Prisoners of War*; Michael Flanagan, "The Memoirs of Dr. Robert J. Christie," http://flanaganfamily.net/genealo/memoirs.htm, hereafter cited as Flanagan; National Archives, Record Group 109, Confederate Muster Rolls, 10th Missouri Infantry; National Archives, Record Group M322 (roll no. 153), Confederate Compiled Service Records, 10th Missouri Infantry; Schnetzer, *Men of the Tenth*, 1, 16.

Note: Most sources have Magoffin's first name as Elliah, some as Ebenezer or Elliah, Jr. The National Archives has the name as Elijah.

12. See Appendix C for biography of Colonel Alexander Steen.

13. The Battle of Prairie Grove was fought in northwest Arkansas on Sunday, December 7, 1862. It began just before dawn and lasted the entire day. Initially successful, the Confederates failed to hold the initiative, allowing the out-maneuvered Federals time to concentrate. By 3:15 p.m. the two wings of the Federal Army, commanded by James G. Blunt and Francis Herron, were united on the battlefield and managed to survive the day. During the night, General Thomas C. Hindman, believing he faced insurmountable odds, and being short of ammunition, ordered his command to retreat, giving the field and the victory to the Unionists. Company A, 10th Missouri carried 88 men into the battle and lost 20 in killed and wounded, according the *Supplement to the Official Records*; the Muster Rolls in the National Archives listed 19 wounded (4 mortally) with 3 killed; the *Missouri Republican* listed 4 killed and 16 wounded. For a complete account of this battle of Prairie Grove see *Embattled Arkansas. O.R.S.*, pt. 2, vol. 38:601; Banasik, *Embattled Arkansas*, 338–339, 428–429, 431, 458–459; R. J. Bell (Brigade Surgeon), Letter to the Editor, By Name Loss in Parson's Brigade, *The Daily Missouri Republican* (St. Louis, MO), February 11, 1863; National Archives, Record Group 109, Confederate Muster Rolls, 10th Missouri Infantry.

14. When Company A was first organized on November 10, 1862, it listed 104 men on its rolls. National Archives, Record Group 109, Confederate Muster Rolls, Company A, 10th Missouri Infantry. George W. McChristy was born about 1833 in Missouri and lived in Palmyra at the beginning of the Civil War. He joined the MSG in 1862 and transferred to the Confederate service on September 1, 1862, at Camp Mitchell, Arkansas, where he was elected first lieutenant of his company. Following the Battle of Prairie Grove he was elected captain of his unit on December 19, 1862, was captured at Helena on July 4, 1863, sent first to Alton, Illinois, then to Johnson Island, on Lake Erie on August 6, 1863. McChristy was forwarded to Fort Delaware, for exchange in January 1865 and on to New Orleans on January 9. He was exchanged on February 26, 1865, at the Red River Landing, Louisiana, returned to his company, where he was paroled at war's end on June 8, 1865, at Shreveport, Louisiana. Eakin, *Missouri Prisoners of War*, "McChristy, G. W.," entry; W. M. Moore letter (May 10, 1915), Skaggs Collection, Arkansas History Commission, hereafter cited as Moore, Skaggs Collection; National Archives, Record Group M322 (roll no. 153), Confederate Compiled Service Records, 10th Missouri Infantry; Schnetzer, *Men of the Tenth*, 3.

15. This was probably Colonel Joseph M. Kelly, a member of General Parsons's staff. Colonel Kelly, a resident of St. Louis, had been a solider in the British army before coming to America. He commanded

proficient in marching and the manual of arms, so much so that Capt. [Moses J.] Bradford[16] of the Tenth Regiment offered to resign and offered to elect one of our men captain of his company. But the offer was declined as they

Preferred to Remain Together.

After the retreat from Prairie Grove we fell back to Camp Mazzard, the camp from which we started. We remained there until Christmas, '62, and we had made grand preparations for a Christmas dinner.[17] Our dinner was about ready when we were fired upon by "Yanks" from the opposite side of the Arkansas River.[18] About

---

the Washington Blues, a St. Louis Volunteer Militia Company prior to the Civil War. At the Battle of Wilson's Creek (August 10, 1861), Kelly, then colonel of his regiment, commanded 142 men and was wounded in the hand "which partially disabled it for life, and he would have lost it if he had not... put his pistol under his pillow and threaten to shoot any doctor who should attempt to amputate it." While still in the Guard, Mosby M. Parsons appointed Kelly commander of the 6th Division, MSG on April 9, 1862. Later, Kelly joined the staff of General Parsons, being appointed Adjutant General of the brigade and later the division. During the war one veteran recalled that Kelly "was a good officer and a man of deep religious sentiment, but he had a habit of swearing with almost every sentence." *O.R.*, vol. 8:815; Banasik, *Missouri In 1861*, 380; Flanagan, 58; Joseph A. Mudd, "What I Saw At Wilson's Creek," *Missouri Historical Review* 7 (October, 1912–July, 1913), 98; National Archives, Record Group 109, Confederate Records, Chapter 7, vol. 394, Parsons's staff; Peterson, 172, 181.

16. Moses J. Bradford commanded Company G, 10th Missouri Infantry (CSA). He was born in 1833, on Spring Creek, in what became Relfe, Phelps County, Missouri. A businessman, Bradford operated saw mills in Phelps County with his four brothers and his father. He married in 1859, joined the 6th Division, MSG in 1861, and was appointed a quartermaster by General James McBride. After his service in the Guard, Bradford returned home and operated with Col. William Coleman for a time. He was captured near Rolla, Missouri, in June 1862. He later escaped or was paroled and joined the Confederate service on August 6, 1862, at Batesville, Arkansas. His company was later organized as Company G, 10th Missouri Infantry (CSA). Bradford was captured at Helena on July 4, 1863, and did not survive the war, dying of scurvy and malnutrition at a prison at Fort Pulaski, Georgia, on February 13, 1865. He was listed as one of "The Immortal Six Hundred" who were imprisoned in Charleston harbor, under Confederate fire and fed "starvation rations." *O.R.*, Series 2, vol. 4:61; Joanne C. Eakin, *Confederate Records From the United Daughters of the Confederacy Files, Volume One*, 8 vols. (Independence, MO, 1995–2001), 1:135, hereafter cited as Eakin, *Confederate Records*; "Information Sheet," Moses Jasper Bradford Letters (1861–1865), Missouri State Historical Society (Rolla); Joseph A. Mudd, *With Porter in North Missouri: A Chapter In the History of the War Between the States* (Washington, DC, 1909), 444–445; Schnetzer, *Men of the Tenth*, 69.

17. Normal rations for the men of Hindman's command, according to an Arkansan, consisted of "cornbread mixed with part of the bran, cornmeal bran coffee and a very limited supply of exceedingly poor beef." Christmas dinner for December 1862, was normally a scant affair for those in the First Corps Trans-Mississippi Army, though there were exceptions. William Bull, from Parsons's Brigade recorded: "Contrary to all expectations, we had a very good dinner today. Provisions are very scarce but somebody in the mess has been doing some good foraging. We had chicken, pork and beans, potatoes (slightly frosted), corn bread, molasses, and Lincoln coffee." Another from the same brigade noted that he was going to feast on "Hog, Hominy, and Corn Bread." Banasik, *Missouri Brothers in Gray*, 49; Michael E. Banasik, *Serving With Honor: The Diary of Captain Eathan Allen Pinnell of the Eight Missouri Infantry (Confederate)* (Iowa City, IA, 1999), 41, hereafter cited as Banasik, *Serving With Honor*; Turnbo, 160.

18. Not true. The attack occurred on December 28, 1862, in what became known as the "Capture of Van Buren, Arkansas." By the time of the attack most of Hindman's army had already departed the area en route for Little Rock, via Lewisburg, Arkansas. *O.R.*, vol. 22, pt. 1:167–173.

the same time Col. Edwards[19] came riding across the ridge at full speed with orders to be ready to move in an hour. Of course, we did not get to enjoy our dinner we had worked so hard to prepare. Our company was ordered to take charge of the commissary stores that were near the river with Lieut.-Col. Moore in command.[20] We assisted loading the wagons until late at night when the enemy commenced shelling us from the opposite side of the river. Fortunately no one was hurt, one of our men lost his gun, knapsack or haversack (or "habitsack" as we called it).[21] By this time everything, except for one hogshead of sugar, had gone. We put as much of that as we could in our haversacks and immediately took up the line of march for Little Rock. We overtook our regiment about daylight the next morning. That day the new recruits learned of our having so much sugar and would come along and propose buying some. The boys told them they had none to sell, but that if they would come around to Lieut. [Pleasant E.] Chesnut's[22] that evening when we

---

19. This was probably James F. Edwards, Aid-de-Camp on General Parsons's staff. Edwards was born on January 31, 1838, at Pauldingsville, Warren County, Missouri. In June 1861 he enlisted in the MSG at Boonville and subsequently fought in the Battles of Carthage (July 5, 1861), Wilson's Creek (August 10, 1861), Siege of Lexington (September 18–20, 1861) and Pea Ridge (March 6–8, 1862). He later transferred to the Confederate Service as an officer on General Mosby M. Parsons's staff and fought at Prairie Grove, Helena, and Jenkins' Ferry (April 30, 1864) in Arkansas and Pleasant Hill (April 9, 1864) in Louisiana. During the course of the war he was wounded three times and rose to the rank of major, and it also appears he served as a lieutenant colonel in the MSG. At the time of the incident described by Grubbs, Edwards was a captain. Edwards survived the war and returned to the Foristell area, where he raised tobacco and died at home on April 10, 1923. *O.R.*, vol. 22, pt. 1:423; *O.R.*, 53:461; Eakin, *Confederate Records*, 3:6; Donald R. Hale, *Branded as Rebels Volume 2* (Independence, MO, 2003), 93, hereafter cited as Hale; National Archives, Record Group 109, Confederate Records, Chapter 7, vol. 394, Parsons's staff.
20. At the time of the Van Buren raid, Frost's Division, of which the 10th Missouri Infantry was part, was located ten miles below Van Buren on the march to Little Rock. Hindman ordered Parsons to protect the Arkansas River crossing at Stain's Landing, about four miles from his current location. At 3:00 p.m., Parsons broke camp, sending a detachment of 225 men with a section of artillery from Tilden's Battery to protect the crossing while another detachment with the remaining guns of Tilden's command were ordered three miles closer to Van Buren to observe the enemy. Additionally, Hindman directed that Frost remove what supplies he could from the area, which task fell upon Company A, 10th Missouri Infantry. *O.R.*, vol. 22, pt. 1:172; Banasik, *Missouri Brother in Gray*, 50; Banasik, *Serving With Honor*, 42; John P. Quesenberry manuscript diary, December 28–29, 1862, Western Historical Manuscript Collection, State Historical Society of Missouri (Columbia, MO), hereafter cited as Quesenberry.
21. The attack by the 1st and 2nd Kansas Cavalries began a little after dark and wounded two men in Tilden's Battery, though apparently none in any of Parsons's infantry. At about midnight Parsons's detachment withdrew from the area to join the retreat to Little Rock. Banasik, *Missouri Brothers in Gray*, 50; Edwin Bearss, "The Federals Raid Van Buren and Threaten Fort Smith," *Arkansas Historical Quarterly* 26 (Summer, 1967), 141, hereafter cited as Bearss, "Van Buren"; Quesenberry, December 29, 1862.
22. Pleasant E. Chesnut was born on April 4, 1840, in London, Laurel County, Kentucky, and moved to Platte County, Missouri in 1859. At the beginning of the Civil War, he was living in Platte City, Missouri, and joined the MSG in the summer of 1861. Elected second lieutenant of Company G, 2nd Infantry Regiment, 5th Division MSG, Chesnut joined the Confederate service on September 1, 1862, at Camp Mitchell, Arkansas. Chesnut was elected lieutenant of Company A, 10th Missouri Infantry on December 19, 1862, and served in that capacity throughout the war. Chesnut settled in St. Joseph after

Mosby M. Parsons

camped they could be supplied. The gallant lieutenant was soon beset with customers on all sides. He, however, soon took in the situation, and told them to call the next evening, as his trains had not yet arrived. Nothing of further interest happened for a day or two. One morning we were marched into line for the purpose of witnessing the shooting of three Arkansas men for desertion.[23] When we reached within fourteen miles of Little Rock we were caught in a severe rain and snow storm, which our men were poorly prepared for, many of them being bare-footed and poorly clad. It was here that many of our men contracted pneumonia, of which so many died during the Winter of 1863, my only brother being one of the number. The mud was so deep after the storm, we had to abandon our wagons, and take our camp equipage on our backs and proceed to the river where we took boats for Little Rock. We went into camp a mile south of the statehouse with a beautiful open field in front, which we used as a drill-ground four hours each day, until about the 20th of April.[24] While in this camp we only lost one man while others lost heavily.

Jas. L. Grubbs,
Late of Co. A, Tenth Regiment, Parsons's Brigade.

[Editor Note: Grubbs's article will continue in the next chapter: "The Summer of 1863: Battle of Helena, Campaign for Little Rock and Campaigning in Louisiana."]

---

the war, where he open a grocery store (1865) and later owned a livery stable (1871). Chesnut married in 1877, had one son, and died in St. Joseph on November 6, 1907. Eakin, *Confederate Records*, 2:47–48; Eakin & Hale, 68; *History of Buchanan County, Missouri, Containing a History of the County, Its Cities, Towns, Etc.* (St. Joseph, MO, 1881), 705–706; Peterson, 163; Schnetzer, *Men of the Tenth*, 3.

23. While the remnants of Hindman's command moved toward Little Rock, desertions increased, causing Hindman to order that two men be shot in the presence of the command as a warning to others. The two were selected from a party of the "5 worst men," and they were executed before they broke camp on December 31, 1862. The two men came from W. C. Adams's 38th Arkansas Infantry (also known as Shaver's Infantry). A detail of twenty-four men from the deserters' regiment were selected to perform the task led by a Lieutenant Langford of the same command. Banasik, *Missouri Brother in Gray*, 50; Banasik, *Serving With Honor*, 43; Hoskin, December 31, 1862; Letter (December 31, 1862), Newton to Roane, Copy Letter Book (June 11–Dec. 30, 1862), Hindman's Command, Peter W. Alexander Collection, Columbia University, hereafter cited as Copy Letter Book No. 2; Quesenberry, December 31, 1862; Turnbo, 181–182.

24. Details of the march to Little Rock will be presented in the letters following by Silas Turnbo of the 27th Arkansas Infantry.

Item: Retreat from Ft. Smith to Little Rock in December 1862, by Silas C. Turnbo, Company A, 27th Arkansas Infantry.[25]
Published: September 19, 1885.

A Hard March

We can think back over twenty-seven years ago when the Arkansas, Missouri, Louisiana and Texas troops marched on the same road and endured the wearisome march together and unhesitatingly shared each other's hardships, and many times half starved and half naked. But, all the same, we were soldiers and must do our duty without faltering. We all remember well, what few of us are yet alive, of the terrible toilsome march from Van Buren to Little Rock, evacuating camps on Sunday evening the 28th of December, 1862. It is nearly impossible to give an accurate account of the sufferings the soldiers underwent during the tedious march of days and nights, many of us at times living on parched corn until we could draw our scanty rations. We can distinctively recollect the night before we arrived at Little Rock, a heavy rain having overtaken us during the late afternoon, and struck camp under a downpour of water. Our train mired in the swamp and could not possibly reach us that night. We were without any rations, no tents, and but few of us had blankets. In a few hours our camping place was covered with a sheet of water, in places over shoe-mouth deep. But we maintained our position the best we could. Some were actually compelled to stand up all night in the water, while others stretched themselves on bags, and we all whiled away the hours of that long and dreary winter night as only an army could under the circumstances. In fact this was the most terrible night our regiment experienced during the war, as far as the inclemency of the weather was concerned. The following day was the 14th of January, 1863, and we were probably about seven miles from Little Rock. The march to town was extremely slow and tedious. No attempt whatsoever was made by the regimental and company commanders to march their men in regular order. On the level flats of ground there was a perfect sheet of water, and the small streams were very high, and frequently while crossing we found the water to be nearly waist deep. Sometimes the water course would obstruct our march in such a manner that we would have to make wide circuits through the woods to keep from getting into swimming water. But onward in this miserable and exhaustive style the march continued. Many of the men even while dragging their feet through the mud and water showed remarkable signs of cheerfulness, whistling tunes, singing songs and passing many jokes at each other's expense. About 12 o'clock it ceased raining, turned severely cold and began to snowing in the evening. Near night we crossed over to Little Rock on the steamboats, cold, wet and hungry. How we suffered afterwards on the trip to Pine Bluff and back again to

---

25. Turnbo wrote two pieces concerning the retreat to Little Rock in late December 1862, and early January 1863. This first piece is short on details and presented without comment as a lead in to his more extensive segment which immediately follows.

Little Rock on steamers from the effects of the bitter cold is known only to the survivors, and how rapidly the poor soldiers were sent to their long homes in the hospitals and in camp from the exposed condition to the severity of the weather during that remarkably cold winter, will never be half told. Hundreds were buried and our ranks greatly reduced.

Silas C. Turnbo.

* * * * * *

Item: The Van Buren, Arkansas Raid (December 28, 1862) and Retreat to Little Rock (December 28–January 14, 1863),[26] by Silas C. Turnbo, 27th Arkansas Infantry.
Published: May 8, 1886.

Twenty-Seventh Arkansas Infantry

Pro Tem, Taney Co., Mo.
Editor *Republican*

I will follow the old Twenty-seventh Arkansas a little farther.[27] Sunday, December 28th, 1862, just three weeks after the Battle of Prairie Grove, our regiment was with the brigade a few miles from Van Buren.[28] We had crossed the river to be nearer supplies of fuel and to occupy a better camp for winter quarters. It was a beautiful day. The men were generally laying out plans for the erection of log cabins, which work was to begin the next day. Some were cooking and some were reading or gaming. Everyone supposed we were to remain there all winter.[29] For-

---

26. This is an abbreviated version of a similar piece that appeared in an undated typescript manuscript that Turnbo wrote following the war. Turnbo, 160–210.
27. Turnbo had previously written a piece on the Battle of Prairie Grove, Arkansas, that was published in the April 3, 1886, edition of the *Republican*. See Volume 7, Part Two of this series for this article.
28. At the time of the Battle of Prairie Grove, Turnbo's regiment was part of Colonel Robert G. Shaver's Brigade which fought at Prairie Grove, though the 27th did not take part in the engagement. The 27th had been left behind in the Ft. Smith-Van Buren area, serving as Provost Guard. The 27th, according to its commander Colonel John R. Shaler, was ill equipped to participate in the any battle; as such Hindman replaced Shaler's command with John B. Clark's Missouri Regiment, which had been serving as Provost for the area. Banasik, *Embattled Arkansas*, 291, 515; Special Orders No. 58 (December 1, 1862), Special Orders Book No. 1; Turnbo, 152.
29. Even as the Confederate troops prepared for a winter at Ft. Smith, General Hindman was already organizing a withdrawal from the area, in part due to the lack of forage. On December 12, 1862, John S. Marmaduke's cavalry division, departed Ft. Smith for Point Provence, near Lewisburg, Arkansas, to recoup for an expected campaign into Missouri. On the same day, in a telegraphic conversation with the department commander, General T. H. Holmes, Hindman queried about the rest of his command: "When shall I commence retiring?" to which Holmes replied, "You had better fall back at once." Hindman first withdrew his command to the south side of the Arkansas River, leaving only a small picket force on the north side to warn of any Union movements. On December 21, General Holmes visted Hindman at Ft. Smith and directed that the remainder of his command move immediately to Lewisburg, leaving only John S. Roane's First Division to protect the Indian Territory and western Arkansas. The sick, who could be moved, were dispatched on December 23, Francis Shoup's Division, now commanded by James F. Fagan, left on December 26, and Mosby M. Parsons's Division on December 28.

age wagons were arriving with corn, which was dumped in a heap for the use of the horses. About 1 o'clock P.M., however, a courier brought orders from Gen. Hindman to march in half an hour.[30] At first the men thought there was some mistake, but then the news spread that the Federal Army was advancing and his head column in sight of town. The astonishment was so great that much confusion resulted. Everybody made haste to obey the order and there was much rattling of wagons, yelling of teamsters and rushing about of men as the tents were struck and camp traps loaded. As soon as this was done troops began to have time to ask each other, "Will we fight or run for it?" We had not long to remain in doubt. Orders came to disable the three steamers and the ferryboat lying at the wharf.[31]

The last scheduled brigade to leave the area was Shaver's 1,000-man brigade of Parsons's Division, which prepared to march even as the Federal troops were marching into Van Buren. Also in the area, located four miles southeast of Ft. Smith was Roane's Texas Brigade, which joined the march eastward to Spadra Bluff, on the Arkansas River. *O.R.*, vol. 22, pt. 1:171–172, 905; Telegraphic conversation between Hindman and Holmes (December 12, 1862), Telegrams, Peter W. Alexander Collection, Columbia University, hereafter cited as Telegrams; Robert S. Weddle, *Plow-Horse Cavalry: The Caney Creek Boys of the Thirty-fourth Texas* (Austin, TX, 1974), 78, 84; John C. Williams Memoirs, *Civil War Times Illustrated* Collection, U.S. Army Military History Institute, Carlisle Barracks, PA., 26–27, hereafter cited as Williams Memoirs.

30. At 10:00 a.m. Federal cavalry, hit the outlying Confederate picket at Olivers, nine miles from Van Buren. Lieutenant Colonel R. P. Crump, commanding the Confederate advance immediately sent word to Hindman's headquarters informing him of the Union attack. With his army on the march eastward there was little Hindman could do, except save his army. Even as Hindman organized for the retreat, the Federals entered Van Buren at 11:05 (Federal sources place the arrival at 12:00 noon). Shaler's Regiment and two 12-pound howitzers from Henry West's battery of Shraver's Brigade were ordered to Van Buren to contest a possible Unionist crossing. About 2:30 p.m. West and Shaler were in place and the shelling began, scattering the Federal troops who were milling about the city. Reacting quickly to the rebel guns, Blunt ordered up his artillery. Two small 12-pound mountain howitzers from the 6th Kansas Cavalry started the action followed by four guns each from the 1st Kansas Artillery and the 2nd Indiana; in all ten guns. Hopkins's Trophy Battery (2nd Kansas) and Stockton's Battery (became the 25th Ohio Artillery) arrived on the scene next having whipped their horses from Dripping Springs, but the shelling had stooped after one hour. According to one period writer, "Gen. Blunt had sent word to Hindman across the river, that if he fired another shot on the city it would be laid in ashes." *O.R.*, vol. 22, pt. 1:169–172; Michael E. Banasik, *Reluctant Cannoneer: The Diary of Robert T. McMahan of the Twenty-fifth Independent Ohio Light Artillery* (Iowa City, IA, 2000), 96–97, hereafter cited as Banasik, *Reluctant Cannoneer*; Bearss, "Van Buren," 136–137; Camp Follower, "The War In Western Arkansas," *The Quincy Herald* (Quincy, IL), January 21, 1863; "Capture of Van Buren," *Freedoms Champion* (Atchison, KS), January 3, 1863; "The Raid Upon Van Buren," *Missouri Democrat*, January 15, 1863.

31. There were several rebel boats in the area scattered from Ft. Smith to Van Buren. According to both rebel and Union accounts there were two steamers at Ft. Smith, the *Arkansas* and the *Era* (several of the Federal sources called these vessels the *Van Buren* and the *Erie No. 6*, which was not correct). At the city of Van Buren the *Frederick Norte*, the *Key West* and the *Rose Douglas* were docked when the Federals arrived and attempted to escape, but were pursued by Federal troops and forced to surrender. Additionally, the *Violet* was also in Van Buren, but being disabled was not able to flee. Also present in the area was a horse pulled ferry, that Federal sources stated was at Van Buren while rebel accounts placed it at or near Ft. Smith. The three Van Buren boats, that had escaped, were subsequently returned to Van Buren where they were burned the next day along with the *Violet*. The two boats and ferry at Ft. Smith were ordered burned by General Hindman to prevent their capture or as one rebel commentator noted, "our men only did what the 'Abies' would have done the next day, and saved them that much

Then a section of two 12-pound guns was detailed to keep the enemy from cross-ing and our regiment was left to support the guns.[32] We moved to the river op-posite Van Buren and were posted in a depression that afforded cover. The guns were prepared for action on an open field next to us. The Federals could be seen across in the streets of Van Buren. The guns soon opened and the Federal troopers were seen scampering away. We had about concluded that they had no artillery with them, but in a few minutes a

A Puff of Smoke

rose from a hill back of town. Then after the brief interval occupied by a shell in its flight there was grand crash in the top of a tree about seventy-five yards to our right and a big branch came down to the ground.[33] The next shell buried itself in the ground not more than fifteen feet in front of where our men were standing in line. It threw sand and gravel in every direction. The third one passed a little above our heads. Then it seemed more guns opened on us and they kept feeling for us very closely. Our two guns were over-matched and soon as we heard Col. [James R.] Shaler[34] sing out: "Boys, this is no place for us. Let's git," and we

---

trouble." As an added note, the *Arkansas* appears to have been subsequently recovered and was back in service by February 1863. *O.R.*, vol 22, pt. 1:172; Banasik, *Reluctant Cannoneer*, 98; Banasik, *Serving With Honor*, 53; Bearss, "Van Buren," 141; Wiley Britton, *The Civil War on the Border A Narrative of Military Operations in Missouri, Kansas, Arkansas, and the Indian Territory* (New York, 1899), 437, 439; "The Expedition Into Arkansas," *The Indianapolis Daily Journal* (Indianapolis, IN), Janu-ary 1, 1863; "From Arkansas," *The Memphis Daily Appeal* (Jackson, MS), March 4, 1863; "The Raid Into Van Buren," *The Daily Gate City* (Keokuk, IA), January 6, 1863; "The Raid Upon Van Buren," *Missouri Democrat*, January 15, 1863; Wau–Cas–Sie, "Letter From Arkansas," *Tri-Weekly Telegraph* (Houston, TX), January 30, 1863.

32. The guns belonged to Henry C. West's Arkansas Battery. In addition to the two 12-pound howit-zers the battery contained two 6-pound smoothbores, which remained back in their camp. Bearss, in his account of the Van Buren Raid, has West's Battery containing four 6-pound smoothbores, which were all engaged at Van Buren. This was not correct. Banasik, *Embattled Arkansas*, 517; Bearss, "Van Buren," 140.

33. Federal sources at the time recorded that the first rebel shot "struck near the levee, and the next near" a rebel hospital. In all West's two guns fired about one hundred rounds and then withdrew. The artillery duel lasted about an hour, and by the time the shelling had stopped two small children were dead, as were two Union soldiers, with another eight wounded. The Confederates suffered no losses during the exchange of fire; however, Federal sources reported leaving seven dead rebels, with a num-ber of wounded near Dripping Springs and capturing about one hundred more when they took Van Buren. Camp Follower, "The War In Western Arkansas," *Quincy Herald*, January 21, 1863; F. H. Dyer, *A Compendium of the War of the Rebellion* (Des Moines, IA, 1908; reprint ed., Dayton, OH, 1978), 677; "From Arkansas," *Mobile Advertiser and Register* (Mobile, AL), February 26, 1863; "Gen. Blunt Accomplishes a Daring Raid," *Daily Conservative* (Leavenworth, KS), December 31, 1861; Letter (December 29, 1862), *Leavenworth Daily Times* (Leavenworth, KS), December 31, 1862; "The Raid Upon Van Buren Arkansas," *Missouri Democrat*, January 15, 1863.

34. James Riddle Shaler was born on December 23, 1830, in Pennsylvania. Settling in St. Louis, Shaler was a merchant by profession and an agent for the Pennsylvania Railroad. As a major in the St. Louis Volunteer Militia, Shaler was captured at Camp Jackson and exchanged on October 26, 1861. Shaler fought with the 7th Division, MSG at Pea Ridge, where he earned the praise of General Daniel M. Frost. When Thomas C. Hindman rebuilt the Trans-Mississippi Army, in the summer of 1862, he ap-

got. Our artillery galloped away and Col. Shaler led us back through the brush on the double-quick. They kept shelling us, but we were soon out of danger and out of breath. Counting noses we found that neither man nor horse had been hurt. Marching leisurely back to camp we found everything gone but the pile of corn which was burning. We pulled out ears and parched them over the blazing heap and that was all the supper we had. At dusk we started on our memorable retreat to Little Rock. The train was reported to be two hours ahead. The night was clear and the moon was bright. On reaching the Mazzard Prairie, while posting rear pickets for the night we could hear the enemy again shelling the woods back of our old camp. After a short halt we pushed on, occasionally passing exhausted men who lay by the fires they had kindled near the road. We overtook the main force at 11 o'clock, but continued on well into the morning. The men began to straggle and lay down in bunches of four and five. The rear guard would rout them up and make them keep on the road. Finally the straggling was so bad that Gen. Hindman

Ordered A Halt.

Nearly everyone except the guards quickly lay down to snatch a few hours' sleep. The hungry mules were left hitched to the wagons ready for a quick start. Some of the boys got some fires started and baked some bread. In a short time a courier came in with a report that the Federals had crossed the river and were coming right after us. The camp was at once aroused and the train moved off.[35] The brigade marched about a quarter of a mile and formed a line of battle across the road, remaining in ranks until daylight, when it was found the report was nearly all false. We also heard that the Federal force that had given us such a scare only amounted to 2,800 cavalry and eight guns.[36] Whether this was true or not I

pointed Shaler colonel of the 27th Arkansas Infantry Regiment on July 2, 1862. Shaler took command of his regiment on July 10, making a poor impression on his troops; many considered him a tyrant and openly questioned why Hindman appointed a Missourian to command an Arkansas regiment. Many of his men branded him an "old hellion" or the "old devil." In the latter part of 1863, Shaler was voted out as colonel of the 27th. Sterling Price subsequently appointed him major and inspector general of his command. During Price's 1864 Missouri Raid, Shaler was credited by one veteran of "getting" Price "out of tight places on the return of his shattered army" back to Arkansas. After the war, Shaler moved briefly to British Honduras, then to Chattanooga, Tennessee, and to Panama in 1896, where he played a role in the Panamanian Revolution of 1903. Shaler died at his summer home, in Ocean City, New Jersey on September 7, 1910 and was buried in Bellefontaine Cemetery in St. Louis. *O.R.*, vol. 41, pt. 1:719; *O.R.*, Series 2, vol. 1:117, 554; *O.R.S.*, pt. 2, vol. 2:712; Bruce S. Allardice, *Confederate Colonels A Biographical Register* (Columbia, MO, 2008), 337, hereafter cited as Allardice, *Confederate Colonels*; Turnbo, 81–82, 98, 306, 380–381.

35. The camp was roused about 11:00 p.m. and Hindman's command, essentially Frost's Division and Roane's Texas Brigade, moved out on the road to Little Rock. The troops halted briefly between 4–5:00 a.m. to eat what breakfast, if any, that they had, and then resumed their march near sunrise. Shaver's Brigade continued as the rear guard for the army, and would remain so until they again crossed the Arkansas River at Spadra Bluff. Banasik, *Missouri Brother in Gray*, 50; Banasik, *Serving With Honor*, 42–43; Quesenberry December 28–29, 1862; Turnbo, 167.

36. The Federal force that attacked Van Buren consisted of 8,000 troops with thirty pieces of artillery. The cavalry portion of Blunt's Unionists contained 3,000 cavalry with four 12-pound mountain how-

never knew. Here we also heard that Gen. [Thomas J.] Churchill's force at Arkansas Post was hard pressed.[37]

Soon after daylight we again pushed on toward Little Rock, passing Charleston at 10 o'clock, and camping with the train five miles beyond that village. Tuesday the 30th, was pleasant, and we marched as far as the Six-Mile Creek.[38] Next day we camped at night by a steam sawmill, fifteen miles from the Arkansas River, and at New Year's Day at noon we once more reached the river opposite Spadra Bluff, where three steamers were waiting to take us across. It was toward evening on the next day before we were well over, and camped on the bluff.[39] Here the rickety wagons were repaired and the sick sent forward by steamboat. Among the latter was my mess mate Jas. L. Holt, with whom I have parted for the last time, as he died in the hospital at Little Rock. We moved again on the 4th, passing through Clarksville to the tune of "Homespun Dress," while the ladies cheered us on. The retreat was a dreary affair, and such little incidents were the only pleasant spots in it.[40] There were always

---

itzers. *O.R.*, vol. 22 pt. 1:167.

37. Thomas James Churchill was from Kentucky and studied law until he volunteered for service during the Mexican War. He was captured in January 1847, and not released until Mexico surrendered. At the beginning of the Civil War, Churchill, now living in Arkansas, organized the 1st Arkansas Mounted Rifles and was elected the unit's colonel. He fought at Wilson's Creek and Pea Ridge and for gallant service was promoted to brigadier general, to rank from March 6, 1862. He surrendered Arkansas Post in January 1863, and was later exchanged. After a short stay with the Army of Tennessee, Churchill returned to Arkansas, where he commanded an Arkansas division. He participated in the Red River and Camden Campaigns and was promoted to major general on March 18, 1865. After the war he became the governor of Arkansas in 1880 and died in 1905. See Appendix B for a complete biography. *O.R.*, vol. 22, pt. 1:902; *O.R.*, vol. 34, pt. 1:785; Anne Bailey, "Thomas James Churchill," in *The Confederate General* (William C. Davis, ed.; 6 vols.; Harrisburg, PA, 1991), vol. 1, 186–187; Clement A. Evans, gen. ed. *Confederate Military History*, 13 vols. (Atlanta, 1899; reprint ed., Secaucus, NJ, 1974), vol. 10: *Arkansas* by John M. Harrell, 394–396, hereafter cited as Harrell, *Arkansas, Confederate Military History*; Ezra J. Warner, *Generals in Gray: Lives of the Confederate Commanders* (Baton Rouge, LA, 1959), 49–50, hereafter cited as Warner, *Generals in Gray*.

38. On the 30th, the command made about eight miles before they camped, with one soldier remarking that six Mile Creek should be "christened 'Muddy'" Creek." Even though the march to Little Rock had just begun it was obvious to the common soldier of the command that the army was in no condition to fight. John P. Quesenberry recorded, "Our army is in a bad condition, and I hope they [Federals] will not pursue us now. We have no cavalry here, and the majority of the infantry was sent off several days ago. What move is in contemplation no one seems to know…I was as broken down last night as I have ever been since the war began, having traveled all night and day without anything to eat." Banasik, *Missouri Brothers in Gray*, 50; Banasik, *Serving With Honor*, 43; Quesenberry, December 29–30, 1862.

39. The command crossed the Arkansas River, to the north side, at Spadra Bluff, on the steamboats *Alamo*, *Tahlequah* and the *Lady Walton*. The Missouri troops of Parsons's Division began crossing the Arkansas River on January 1, followed by the division trains on January 2, closely followed by Shaver's Brigade. By January 3 the army had crossed the river joining Fagan's Division which was already on the other side awaiting orders. Banasik, *Missouri Brother in Gray*, 50; Banasik, *Serving With Honor*, 43; Circular (January 3, 1863), Copy Letter Book No. 2; Quesenberry, December 31, 1862; Turnbo, 177.

40. After Hindman's command crossed the Arkansas River, they rested until January 4, allowing the men to receive some scanty rations and dispose of those too sick to continue. On January 3, the sick

Some Gay Spirits

who could raise a laugh and make the boys forget their misery under the most wretched circumstances. Lieut. Albert G. Cravens was one of them—"Gen. Miller" we called him. He could almost raise a smile on a dead man's face and as a rule our company officers were always ready to take part. Their lively sallies would often freshen us up when we were ready to drop down with fatigue. Few who haven't been through it can understand the terrible strain of forced marches over bad roads with poor supplies and the demoralizing, depressing knowledge that you are retreating from a superior force of the enemy. It is miserable business at best. We camped this night ten miles from Clarksville, where a sign board said "To Little Rock 102 miles."[41] On the 5th we had to construct pontoons for a bridge over the Big Piney. A short distance beyond it we camped, expecting to stay a week and collect supplies, but on the 8th we were off again and after a hard day's march reached Illinois Bayou.[42] The pioneers made a bridge and we crossed over. Next day two or three deserters were shot.[43] This was not approved by the troops, and instead of diminishing the evil it increased the dissatisfaction and the desertions. At Russelville we halted for orders and were directed forward on the Lewisburg Road, it was said by Gen. [T. H.] Holmes.[44] That day, a crazy man, who

---

boarded boats for the hundred mile trip to Little Rock—many of them, as detailed by Turnbo, never to return to the army. Quesenberry, January 1–4, 1863; Turnbo, 178–179.

41. Clarksville was the county seat of Johnson County, Arkansas, and the concentration point for Hindman's Army prior to resuming their march to Little Rock. Hindman, for his part, made his headquarters in the city. At 11:00 p.m. that night, the long roll sounded in Parsons's Brigade and the men were ordered to immediately march back toward Clarksville to protect the city from an expected Union raid. Hindman had received word that a Federal raiding party, from the 2nd Kansas Cavalry Regiment, was in Ozark and might be moving on Clarksville. Having little desire to be surprised again as he was at Van Buren, Hindman ordered the nightime march. With little cavalry available to resist the Union move, Hindman decided to use Parsons's Brigade to block the potential Union advance into Clarksville. Breaking camp, Parsons's Brigade marched back through Clarksville and planted themselves one and a half miles west of the city, awaiting a Union attack that never materialized. Parsons's Brigade remained in place, just west of Clarksville, until the remainder of the army had successfully left the area. On January 8, they would move to rejoin the army, now camped at the Big Piney River. Banasik, *Missouri Brothers in Gray*, 52–52; Bearss, "Van Buren," 142; Letters, Newton to Frost and Thompson (January 4, 1863), Copy Letter Book No. 2; Quesenberry, January 4–7, 1863.

42. With the march resuming on the 8th, Roane's Texas Brigade departed the army and moved back to Fort Smith. En route, the Texans met Parsons's Brigade which was returning from picketing Clarksville to the west. Quesenberry, January 8, 1863; Williams Memoirs, 26–27.

43. In both this portrayal and in Turnbo's extended version he has the deserters being shot on January 9; however in all the other diaries the event occurred on December 31, with nothing out of the ordinary occurring on the 9th. Banasik, *Missouri Brothers in Gray*, 52; Banasik, *Serving With Honor*, 46; Quesenberry, December 31, 1862–January 9, 1863; Turnbo, 181.

44. Major General Theophilus H. Holmes was born in 1804, graduated from West Point in 1829 (number 44 of 46) and served with distinction during the Mexican War. In April 1861, he resigned from the army and cast his lot with the Confederacy. Initially serving in the East, Holmes was made the commander of the Trans-Mississippi Department on July 16, 1862, and was promoted to lieutenant general to rank from October 10, 1862. On March 7, 1863, Holmes was relieved of the Department command and placed in control of the District of Arkansas. Following the debacle at Helena, Arkansas, on July

was under guard, caused endless trouble and some little fun.[45] He broke away and, as he was running, came face-to-face with Gen. Hindman, who happened to be alone. The general halted and so did the man. They stared at each other, neither saying a word, till the guard came up. All the men were laughing, and as soon as the general knew that the fellow was crazy he ordered his release. The man then went straight to a bunch of officer's horses and was

About to Mount One

when the guard caught him.[46] We never saw him after that day. On the 10th we passed a swamp where it took a detail of 600 men to get the wagons through the ten miles of mud, water and rotten corduroy. It was a terrible task. On Sunday we reached Lewisburg and drew ample rations of turnips. With plenty to eat we felt saucy once more. Here we learned of the capture of Arkansas Post and Gen. Churchill's command. We were then hurried on faster than ever for fear an attack would be made on Pine Bluff to threaten Little Rock. Monday, 12th, we started an hour before daylight and camped at night twenty miles from Little Rock. Next day the line of march was through a big swamp, traversed by a stream of good size. The road was in horrible condition. The rain began to pour down; the stream rose rapidly. It was all the men could do to get through. A few wagons were pulled through by the strongest teams, but most of the train, having got well into the swamp, could be moved neither one way nor the other and had to be abandoned there. Much of our marching was done in mud and water from shoe mouth to half leg deep. At dark we halted. Rations, tents and most of the blankets were back in the abandoned train. The rain continued to pour down and our camping place was flooded here and there to a depth of several inches. A man who could find a log to sleep on was lucky. It was absolutely impossible to keep fires going. Many had to

---

4, 1863, Holmes was relegated to a minor role in the Trans-Mississippi and finally resigned his position in 1864. Returning to North Carolina, Holmes completed his military service. Following the war, Holmes remained in North Carolina as a "small-scale" farmer. He died in Fayette, North Carolina on June 20, 1880. For biography and photo see Banasik, *Missouri Brothers in Gray*, 141–143; Boatner, 406; Francis B. Heitman, *Historical Register and Dictionary of the United States Army From Its Organization, September 29, 1789, to March 2, 1903*, 2 vols (Washington, 1903; reprint ed., Gaitherburg, MD, 1988), 1:539, hereafter cited as Heitman; Stewart Sifakis, *Who Was Who in the Confederacy: A Comprehensive, Illustrated Biographical Reference to More Than 1,000 of the Principal Confederacy Participants in the Civil War* (New York, 1988), 133, 261, hereafter cited as Sifakis, *Who Was Who in the Confederacy*.

45. Turnbo identified the man as John Archibald McNeil (or McNeal). Born in Lawrence County, Missouri, in about 1837, McNeal enlisted in Company F, 11th Missouri Infantry on October 4, 1862, at Elkhorn Tavern. He was discharged from the army on March 3, 1863: "for insanity." Wayne H. Schnetzer, *Men of the Eleventh: A Roster of the Eleventh Missouri Infantry Confederate States of America* (Independence, MO, 1999), 69, hereafter cited as Schnetzer, *Men of the Eleventh*; Turnbo, 186.

46. In his extended version of this incident, Turnbo has Hindman riding with some of his staff officers and not alone as stated in this article. Additionally, when McNeal ran for the horses he was pursued by Colonel Shaler, commander of the 27th Arkansas, who caught the horse before McNeal could escape. Turnbo, 185–186.

stand up in the water all night and it was mid-winter, too. It was the worst night's experience our regiment had during the war. Morning dawned with the rains still falling. News came from the train that several wagons had been washed away and some mules drowned. The rest of the outfit was safe but stuck in the mud. The seven miles distance to Little Rock was covered somehow that day. There was no pretense of keeping the men in their places. About 100 of our regiment left to hunt shelter for themselves wherever they could. Nearly all of them came back to us when the severe weather was ended, but it was more than any but the very toughest flesh could stand—this kind of campaigning.[47] The last miles of our march were often

Through Water.

The streams were all up, and long detours had to be made to find crossing places. Still we struggled on, some of the men whistling and singing songs as if to mock their own wretchedness. At noon it quit raining, turned cold, and began to snow. This added to our suffering. Finally we reached the river bank opposite Little Rock. The remains of our regiment crossed on a steamer, passed through the city and camped in a grove, making shelter of pine boughs.[48] The snow fell to the depth of six inches, and how the wind did whistle through our brush walls. We had not had food for twenty-four hours. Next morning our brigade found shelter in the penitentiary buildings and arsenal.[49] Our regiment was quartered on

---

47. When the march resumed to Little Rock on January 9, it was marked by intermittent rain, cold weather and the continued deterioration of the army. It would not end until the army staggered into Little Rock between January 14–16. William Bull, of Parsons's Brigade, stopped writing in his diary and didn't resume it till days later. He simply recorded: "Since making the last note we have had a very hard time...It rained for several days until the ground became so soft it was impossible for artillery or wagons to move; then it turned very cold, colder than has been here for years. Snow fell 6 inches deep." A South Carolinian, serving on General Hindman's staff noted of the last days of the tramp to Little Rock: "It became one of the most dreadful marches on record. Many of the men were barefooted, even the soles of their feet were upon the ground. At night we had no tents, and many no blankets. Men died on the march, some died at their fires at night, some died on the bank of the river and hundreds deserted, and returning became drovers and in many places became murderers. My God what a condition of affairs. The men remaining (not more than 5,000) reached here [Little Rock] in groups, emaciated, frozen and exhausted." As to why they endured the march, Captain Eathan Allen Pinnell recorded: "None but patriots could have endured what you have and none but the most devoted would do it." Banasik, *Missouri Brothers in Gray*, 52; Banasik, *Serving with Honor*, 47; "From Arkansas," *Memphis Daily Appeal*, March 4, 1863; Quesenberry, January 9–16, 1863.
48. On January 14, the 27th Arkansas boarded a steamboat and crossed over to Little Rock, while the other units of the brigade took some of the other five boats that were waiting for them. The brigade reformed on the south shore and marched though Little Rock, in a snowstorm, to the grounds of the state prison where they camped. Turnbo, 202–203.
49. The Little Rock Arsenal was located just southeast of the city on the road to Pine Bluff (currently the site of MacArthur Park). Captain James Totten surrendered the arsenal, at the request of Governor Henry Rector on February 8, 1861, removing his command to St. Louis on February 12. Both the arsenal and the penitentiary manufactured or repaired military goods for the Confederacy during the war. The penitentiary had been established in 1842, while the arsenal was established in the late 1830's in response to the Indian migration to modern-day Oklahoma. With the fall of Little Rock, in September

the second floor of a brick building, and it must be said that Col. Shaler did all a man could do for our comfort. We had one stove and soon drew plenty of rations. The weather continued cold, and great as had been our sufferings we were lucky compared with some of the Missouri troops who were caught back in the swamps and unable to get through.

On the 17th The regiment went on board the steamer *Arkansas* for Pine Bluff to intercept a Federal force.[50] The wind was piercing cold and some of us crawled down the fore hatch and went to sleep on a pile of corn. During the night the boat struck a log with such a shock that the captain thought it prudent to tie up on the bank. We in the hold were pretty badly scared and didn't stand on the order of our getting out. Arriving at Pine Bluff we found no Federal force had appeared there, so we were ordered back to Little Rock. A few days after reaching there we went into those winter quarters two miles south of the city that were marked by so much sickness and death in the command.

Silas C. Turnbo,
Twenty-seventh Arkansas Infantry

* * * * * *

1863, the two facilities would be reoccupied by Federal troops. *O.R.*, 1:645–646; Ferguson, 76, 115, 137, 180.

50. On January 14, 1863, even as the troops began to arrive in Little Rock, General Holmes ordered them hurried to Pine Bluff as he expected a Federal attack against the city was imminent. General Hindman subsequently sent officers from Little Rock to inspect the road, which they found impassable. Informed of the road's condition, Holmes ordered the troops be carried to Pine Bluff by boat. On January 17, Shaver's Brigade boarded boats and headed to Pine Bluff. The 27th Arkansas was the last regiment to board at 3:00 p.m. as the fife and drum corps played the "Bonnie Blue Flag." The troops arrived at Pine Bluff the next day and were informed that the threat was not real, so they returned to Little Rock the following day where they entered winter quarters. Letters, Hindman to Frost (January 14,1863) and Hindman to Anderson (January 15 and 16, 1863), Copy Letter Book No. 2; Quesenberry, January 17, 1863; Turnbo, 212, 214–215.

Item: The Battle of Arkansas Post, by Leon Fremon, Company E, 6th
Texas Infantry.[51]
Published: April 17, 1886.

Battle of Arkansas Post

Vineland, Mo., April 4.

Editor *Republican*

I have waited a long time for someone to write a description on the Battle of
Arkansas Post[52] for your interesting "Tales of the War," but as no one will do so,
have determined to try my hand myself. Early in the Winter of 1862-3 our brigade
(Granberry's), at that time commanded by Gen. Churchill, went into winter quarters at Arkansas Post on the Arkansas River.[53] Pine and cypress being plentiful we
built excellent buildings of pine logs covered with cypress boards. The houses
were the best I saw during the war, and as we were very comfortably situated we
had anticipated spending a very pleasant winter, but as the sequel will show in
this instance the rebs proposed and the Yanks disposed. Some two weeks before
the battle a party of our men captured a steamboat, the *Blue Wing No. 2*,[54] on the

51. Leon A. Fremon or Freman was born about 1845, enlisting in the 6th Texas Infantry at the age of
sixteen. Following his capture at Arkansas Post, he was paroled and later exchanged. Fremon continued in service of the 6th Texas until he was wounded and captured at the Battle of Atlanta on July 21,
1864. He survived the war. "Leon Freman" entry at "Co 'K', 6th TX Infantry: 'Alamo Guards'", http://
www. www.6thtx.org, hereafter cited as www.6thtx.org.

52. On January 9, 1863, Federal forces under General John A. McClernand landed near Arkansas
Post, which was located on the northern bank of the Arkansas River, about twenty-five miles from the
Mississippi River. To secure their advance on Vicksburg, the Unionists reasoned that they first needed
to secure their flank by taking Fort Hindman on the Arkansas River. General Thomas J. Churchill,
who assumed command of the Post on December 10, 1862, commanded the Confederates, who were
outnumbered six–to–one. McClernand's command secured Arkansas Post two days later, capturing the
entire rebel garrison. Boatner, 24–25; Christ, 44.

53. The 6th Texas Infantry was part of Robert A. Garland's Texas Brigade while stationed at Arkansas
Post. It would not become part of Granberry's Brigade until March of 1864, when Granberry was
promoted to general officer and given command of the 6th's brigade. At Arkansas Post the 6th was
brigaded with the 24th and 25th Texas Cavalries (Dismounted), William Hart's Arkansas Battery of
six pieces of artillery and W. B. Denson's Louisiana Cavalry; in all Garland reported 1,797 effectives. *O.R.*, 17, pt. 1:783, 800; Ralph A. Wooster, *Lone Star Regiments In Gray* (Austin, TX, 2002),
124–125, hereafter cited as Wooster.

54. The *Blue Wing* was a 170 ton steamer, serving as an army transport for the Federal forces operating
on the Mississippi River. It had been previously seized by Federal authorities for suspected smuggling
in early November 1862, but released on December 10. The vessel had been authorized by the Treasury Department to trade salt for cotton, leading uninformed Federal officials to believe that it was a
smuggler. On the evening of December 26, 1862, it departed from Helena, Arkansas, towing two coal
barges and carrying military supplies for the fleet operating against Vicksburg. On December 28, the
boat was attacked by a "guerrilla force" employing artillery and small arms, at Cypress Point, eight
miles below Napoleon. The rebel force was a company of Louisiana cavalry commanded by L. M.
Nutt, which was stationed at Arkansas Post. The vessel promptly surrendered, according to two crew
members, because they had "no guard or escort or other defense." On December 29, at 2:00 p.m., the
boat docked at Arkansas Post where it were off-loaded. The loss of the *Blue Wing* was subsequently
blamed on the treachery of the ship's captain, though there was no evidence to support the charge.

Mississippi River, and brought it up to Arkansas Post. This boat, with the stone coal on it, was a great curiosity to our men, the greater portion of them having seen neither, and it was musing to see them pick up the lumps of coal, examine them critically and then wonder "how in thunder they managed to burn the stuff anyhow." The officers captured on the boat were something of a curiosity to all of us, for they were the first we had seen since the beginning of the war.[55] They were paroled the next day. It was said that there would have been no battle at Arkansas Post at that time had it not been for the capture of this boat, for the Yankees were under the impression that the water was too low to admit the passage of gunboats until we convinced them of their error by bringing the boat up to the Post.[56] About noon of Friday, January 9, 1863, news reached us that the Federal Army of Vicksburg was coming up the river on transports accompanied by gunboats.[57] A few

---

Generals W. T. Sherman and John A. McClernand would ultimately use the capture of the *Blue Wing* as one of several reasons to support their expedition against Arkansas Post. Following the capture of Arkansas Post, McClernand sent several boats to the White River in pursuit of the *Blue Wing* but the vessel managed to elude the Union expedition. The *Blue Wing's* final disposition was not known, though it was probably destroyed by General Price when he evacuated Little Rock in September 1863. *O.R.*, vol. 17, pt. 1:613, 709; *O.R.*, vol. 17, pt 2:522, 570; *O.R.*, vol. 22, pt. 1:886; *O.R.N.*, vol. 23:436, 528, 623; *O.R.N.*, vol. 24:93, 154, 163, 209; Bas, "From Helena," *Missouri Democrat*, January 5, 1863; Christ, 44, 262; Gaughan, 105; Naval History Division, Navy Department, *Civil War Naval Chronology* (Washington, DC, 1971), VI–206, hereafter cited as *Civil War Naval Chronology*; Don R. Simons, *In Their Words: A Chronology of the Civil War in Chicot County, Arkansas and Adjacent Waters of the Mississippi River* (Sulphur, LA, 1999), 27, hereafter cited as Simons; Harold B. Simpson, ed., *The Bugle Softly Blows: The Confederate Diary of Benjamin M. Seaton* (Waco, TX, 1965), 29–30, hereafter cited as Simpson, *Bugle Softly Blows*; Bell Irwin Wiley, *Fourteen Hundred and 91 Days in the Confederate Army* (Wilmington, NC, 1987), 89–90, hereafter cited as Wiley.

55. The *Blue Wing* also carried according to one period commentator, "Flour and Coffee, Whisky, Salt, Apples and…some few Pr. [*sic*] cotton cards and Ammunition, Guns and Pistols and several other tricks too numerous to mention." Also included in the catch was a supply of the latest newspapers, personal letters and military correspondence. Christ, 44–45.

56. General McClernand gave eight reasons as to why he attacked Arkansas Post:
  1. To secure communications between Memphis and Vicksburg.
  2. The capture of the *Blue Wing* showed that flank was not protected.
  3. General Gorman, at Helena, Arkansas had not taken the Post.
  4. The failed Yazoo River Expedition showed that any assault on Vicksburg required support or cooperation from other quarters.
  5. With Grant's retreat to Holly Springs, the garrison at Vicksburg could be easily reinforced by rebels from Grenada, Mississippi.
  6. General Banks could not support Vicksburg Expedition.
  7. Nothing better for McClernand's command to do.
  8. The Arkansas Post Expedition would provide the support needed to take Vicksburg.
Of all the reasons provided by General McClernand, the only two that seem plausible were the first two and they were weak at best. McClernand considered his an independent command and acted as he saw fit. In his mind, the best way to take Vicksburg was to first take Arkansas Post. *O.R.*, vol. 17, pt. 1:709; Thomas L. Snead, "The Conquest of Arkansas," *Battles and Leaders of the Civil War*, 4 vols. (New York, 1887–1888), 3:451, hereafter cited as Snead, "Conquest of Arkansas."

57. The naval portion of the expedition consisted of three ironclads, nine gunboats or tinclads (some sources have the number as five, six or seven), with a supporting transport fleet of 105 vessels—ironclads: *Baron de Kakb*, *Cincinnati*, *Louisville*; gunboats or tinclads: *Forest Rose* (tinclad), *Glide* (tinclad), *Juliet* (tinclad), *Lexington* (gunboat—also known as a timberclad), *Marmora* (tinclad), *New*

Arkansas Post

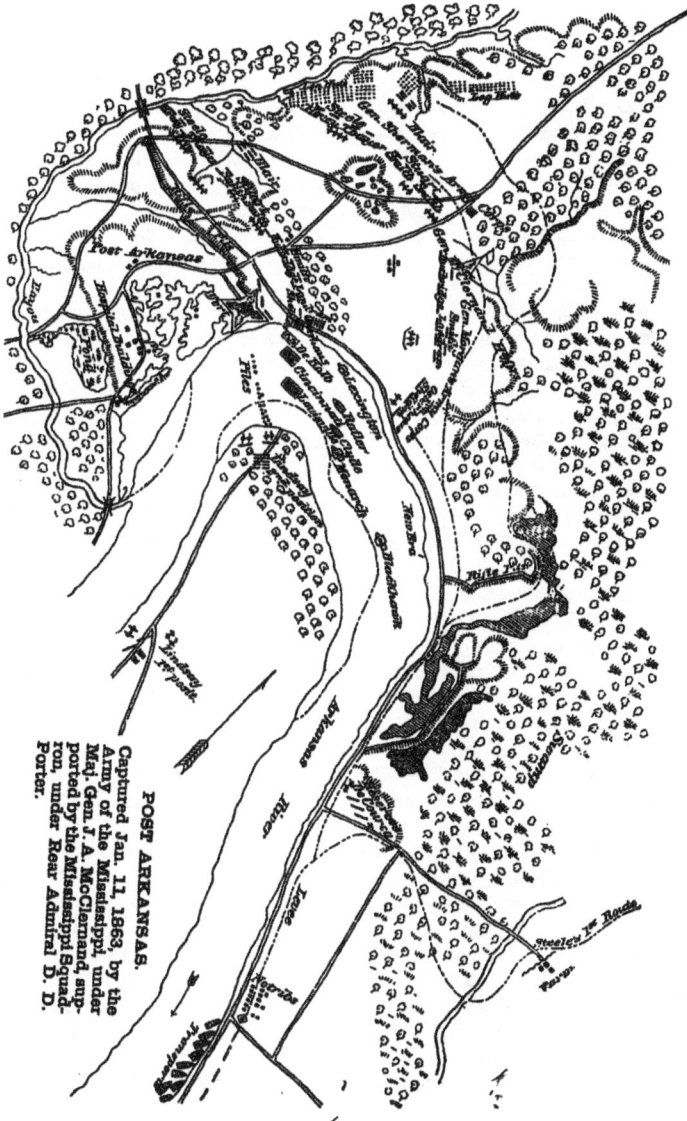

POST ARKANSAS.

Captured Jan. 11, 1863, by the Army of the Mississippi, under Maj. Gen. J. A. McClernand, supported by the Mississippi Squadron, under Rear Admiral D. D. Porter.

minutes after the news reached us we were ordered to prepare three day's rations and be ready to march at a moment's notice. Then all was hustle and excitement, and the men were in high spirits. It was to be their first battle, and everyone expected and was anxious to distinguish himself. No thought of defeat entered our minds, no matter how great the numbers of enemy might prove.[58] About the middle of the afternoon[59] we were ordered to

---

Era (tinclad), *Rattler* (tinclad), *Romeo* (tinclad), *Signal* (tinclad), and the *Springfield* (tinclad). *O.R.*, vol. 17, pt. 1:780; *O.R.N.*, vol. 24:99, 103, 107; *O.R.N.*, Series 2, vol. 1:85, 96, 116, 159, 189, 194, 208–209, 213; "Capture of Arkansas Post," *Waukegan Weekly Gazette* (Waukegan, IL), January 31, 1863; *Civil War Naval Chronology*, III–5; Thomas Jefferson Chambers, "Arkansas Post Civil War Memorandum For 1863: Jan. 1–13, With Map," Typescript copy, Sam Houston Regional Library & Research Center (Liberty, TX), 27, hereafter cited as Chambers; Christ, 52; Patricia L. Faust, ed. *Historical Times Illustrated Encyclopedia of the Civil War* (New York, 1986), 757, hereafter cited as Faust; Chester G. Hearn, *Ellet's Brigade: The Strangest Outfit Of All* (Baton Rouge, LA 2000), 83, 89, 124; Snead, "Conquest of Arkansas," 452; Wiley, 89.

NOTE: Tinclads were actually 4th Class, light draft vessels meant for operations on the shallow rivers and bayous that permeated the South. In all, more than sixty vessels were so designated. They were generally armed with either 32-pound smoothbore or 24-pound guns, while gunboats or timberclads carried the heavier guns like the 8" Dahlgren naval gun.

58. The Union forces were placed at 32,000 infantry (Christ has the number as 30,000), 1,000 cavalry, with 40 or more pieces of artillery. The Confederates surrendered, according to Federal sources 4,791 prisoners coupled with their losses of 103, as reported by the Houston *Tri-Weekly Telegraph*, which would place the Confederate strength at about 4,894. However, in his official report of the affair Confederate General Thomas J. Churchill reported that he had "about 3,000 effective men," which upon closer review cannot be correct. Robert Garland placed his brigade strength at 1,797; James Deshler at about 1,500 to 1,600 (allow about 1,500); John Dunnington's Brigade was not stated. However one can piece together the bulk of the command: it contained 37 naval officers and men plus, three cavalry companies (Richardson's Texas Company had 52 effectives—the other two companies estimated at 43 men each as follows: 120 less Denson 33 men leaves 87 men for Alf Johnson's and Nutt's command or 43.5 men each; the Nineteen Arkansas Infantry (estimated at 460 men—the average of all the other regiments in the battle) and a detachment of the Twenty-fourth Arkansas Infantry (190 men)—Total estimated for Dunnington's Brigade 826; Total for Chrurchill's Command estimated at between 4,173 and 4,223 effectives. *O.R.*, vol. 17, pt. 1:757, 780–781, 783, 791; *O.R.*, vol. 17, pt. 2:553; Christ, 52, 63; "The Conflict At Arkansas Post," *Tri-Weekly Telegraph*, February 4, 1863; Wiley, 93; Wm. J. Oliphant, "Arkansas Post," *Southern Bivouac*, 6 vols. (reprint ed., Wilmington, NC, 1993), 4:737, hereafter cited as Oliphant.

59. At 1:00 p.m., according to Thomas J. Chambers of the 25th Texas Cavalry (dismounted), there was "great excitement in camp. Genl. Churchill has just been informed by Scouts from the mouth of the [White] River that a large number of the enemy's Gun Boats & Transports have entered the river & are coming up." Between 2–3:00 p.m., on the afternoon of January 9, Colonel Robert A. Garland, received word that his command should be in readiness to move at a moment's notice. Upon hearing the bugle call for assembly, the men moved at a leisurely pace, "reluctant to answer the call," as no one could imagine that the enemy was near. Deshler's Brigade was ordered to cook three days' rations, but before the task was completed the "long roll" was sounded about 3:00 p.m., calling the men to arms. Just before dark, Churchill's command moved out and occupied their assigned positions; Deshler's Brigade occupied the upper rifle pits about one and a quarter miles from the fort with his right resting on the Arkansas River, to his immediate left Dunnington's Brigade continued the line to a pond. Garland's command was held in reserve just behind the other two brigades with ten companies of his brigade being sent out several hundred yards in front of the rifle pits to serve as the skirmishers for the division. Hart's Battery was positioned in the rifle pits on the right of Deshler's Brigade. *O.R.*, vol. 17, pt. 1:780, 783, 790; "Arkansas Post Affair," *Tri-Weekly Telegraph*, February 6, 1863; Chambers, 5–7; R.

Fall In.

Our captain's name was [Samuel W.] McAllister. He was a magnificent look-ing man, and was armed with a sword, a six-shooter, a rifle, and a double-barreled shotgun. When we were ordered to fall in he buckled on his sword and six-shoot-er, shouldered his double-barreled shotgun, and made a stirring little speech, in which he stated that one rebel was equal to any fifty Yankees, and closed with: "Now, boys, when you see me run it's time for you to run."[60] After listening to this speech of our gallant captain we felt as though with him at our head, we could lick a whole regiment of Yankees. We were then ordered to march down to the river. After marching about a mile one of the boys pointed down the river and yelled out, "Look! there's the smoke of the gunboats!" We cast our eyes in the direction indicated, and sure enough there was the smoke in plain view, though a considerable distance below us. By a strange coincident just as the smoke of a gunboats was discovered our captain turned deathly pale and leaned against a tree for support. He told us he was suddenly taken with severe cramps, but that a glass of whiskey would set him all right, and that he would be with us again in an hour or so. This sudden stroke was a great blow as well as a surprise to us, but Lieut. [Henry] Burns[61] immediately took command of us and we managed to bear up un-der it and proceed on our march. That night we lay on our arms, every man having his gun besides him, and I doubt if twenty men in the brigade slept a wink.[62] Early

---

R. Garland, "Arkansas Post," *Southern Historical Society Papers*, (R. A. Brock, gen. ed.; Richmond, VA, 1876–1859; reprint ed, Wilmington, NC, 1990–1992), 22:10, hereafter cited as Garland; Oliphant, 4:736; Simpson, *Bugle Softly Blows*, 31.

60. Samuel William McAllister was born in Danville, Kentucky, on April 8, 1831, moved to Texas and settled in San Antonio in 1847. A business owner and skilled mechanic, McAllister was married in 1855, and subsequently had five children. At the beginning of the Civil War, he was elected captain of Company K, 6th Texas Infantry. The unit was organized at Camp McCulloch near Victoria, Texas, and was mustered into the service on March 31, 1862. McAllister had difficulty raising his company and even requested that he be given permission to obtain recruits from Federal prisoners. Major Sack-field Maclin recommended to P. O. Hebert, commanding the Department of Texas, that the request be turned down. After his company had been organized, McAllister led his command to Arkansas, where it was captured at Arkansas Post. However, McAllister's name was never listed among the captured or the paroled prisoners, leading one to believe that he escaped from the fort. Returning to San Anto-nio, McAllister completed his military service as the "Drill Officer" for the 30th Battery [NOTE: No such battery listing has ever been found with this designation]. On August 17, 1865, McAllister was paroled in San Antonio as the captain of Company K, 6th Texas Infantry. Returning to civilian life, he was elected as an Alderman for the city, served on off in that position throughout most of his life. By the time of his death on May 18, 1893, McAllister was a retired judge. *O.R.*, vol. 4:136; *O.R.S.*, pt. 2, vol. 68:655; Daniel E. Snell, "Captain Samuel William McAllister," www.6thtx.org; Wooster, 123.
61. Henry Burns was born in about 1817 and was Company K's first lieutenant. Captured at Arkansas Post, Burns was paroled, after which his name disappears from all official records. Burns, at age 46, probably was unable too return to duty or simply had had enough of military service. "Henry Burns" entry at www.6thtx.org.
62. When the units were originally called to arms the weather was warm for the month of January and the men left any heavy clothing or coats in their quarters. They would never have time to recover any personal items from their quarters as the camp was captured on January 10 and later burned by the

the next morning the smoke of the gunboats was seen pretty close to us, and as we had never seen one, quite a number of us concluded that we would run down to the river bank and see what they looked like. As it happened just as we got sight of the gunboats they got sight of us, and by way of greeting sent us a shell. This shell burst before it reached us, but it was the first shell that we had even seen exploded, and besides we had no idea at that time that if a shell from a gunboat exploded anywhere within half a mile of you, you were a goner, and so we unanimously and instantaneously concluded that a gunboat was not much of a sight anyhow, and instantly acting on that conclusion, we precipitately withdrew to the shelter of the woods, and paid very little attention to the order of our going.[63] We had hardly got to our places in the ranks when a second shell exploded with a tremendous report, a short distance in the rear of our company. About half the regiment broke ranks,

Myself Among the Liveliest

and jumped behind trees. Lieut.-Col. [Thomas S.] Anderson,[64] who commanded

---

Federal troops. However, at least two members of the 25th Texas Cavalry (dismounted) sneaked into their abandoned camp during the night of January 10, under the very eyes of the Federal occupiers and successfully secured their belongs. Chambers, 17; Oliphant, 736.

63. According to Confederate sources, the Union boats began their attack between 8–9:00 a.m. on January 10, initially concentrating their fire on the outlying pickets and troops (Federal sources have the boats moving at 8:00 a.m., but not firing until between 9:30–10:10 a.m.). In the afternoon, at about 3:30 p.m., the boats prepared to engage Fort Hindman, and at 5:30 they moved forward and opened fire, which continued until about 9:00 p.m. (Federal sources have the fight ending at 7:00–7:15 p.m.). Overall the bombardment did little more than take the Confederate garrison's attention away from the Federal landings, which were taking place one mile below the fort. Confederate casualties were apparently very light. *O.R.*, vol. 17, pt. 1:783–784; *O.R.N.*, vol. 24:104, 685–686, 697; "Arkansas Post Affair," *Tri-Weekly Telegraph*, February 6, 1863; "Capture of Arkansas Post," *Waukegan Weekly Gazette*, January 31, 1863; Christ, 59–61; Samuel C. Foster, "We Are Prisoners of War," *Civil War Times Illustrated* 16 (May 1977), 27, hereafter cited as Foster; Garland, 10–11; Oliphant, 737; Simpson, *Bugle Softly Blows*, 31; "The Victory At Arkansas Point," *Home Journal* (Mount Pleasant, IA), January 24, 1863; Wiley, 92, 94.

64. Thomas Scott Anderson was born 1827 in Tennessee and migrated to Texas in 1854, settling at Eagle Lake, Colorado County, just outside of Houston. A lawyer by profession Anderson served as the Texas Secretary of State (1857–1858) under Governor Hardin Runnels and was a member of the Texas Secession Convention in February 1861. Prior to the Civil War, Anderson served as a sergeant in the Mexican War. Anderson was appointed lieutenant colonel of the 6th Texas Infantry, on September 3, 1861, and served in that position through the Battle of Chickamauga, Georgia, in September 1863, where he earned the praise of his brigade commander for his actions during the battle. Anderson was later reassigned to the Trans-Mississippi commanding the prisoner of war camp outside of Tyler, Texas. On April 23, 1864, he was appointed colonel of what was known as Anderson's Texas Cavalry and served as either the unit's commander or commanding a brigade in Texas until he was appointed Inspector General of the District of Texas (February 23, 1865). Anderson returned home following the war and died in Eagle Lake on September 26 (or 25), 1868. *O.R*, vol. 26, pt. 2:514; *O.R.*, vol. 30, pt. 2:190; *O.R.*, Series 2, vol. 7:208; *O.R.S.*, pt. 2, vol. 80:344; Allardice, *Confederate Colonels*, 44; Harold B. Simpson, *Texas in the War 1861–1865* (Hillsboro, TX, 1965), 122, 175; Wooster, 123, 213, 311. NOTE: In Simpson's book there was conflicting data as to when Anderson migrated to Texas as well as where he settled. In one case Simpson has him in Eagle Lake outside Houston and in another in Austin, while migrating to the state in either 1852 or 1854.

us, ordered us back into line and gave us a sharp lecture, and that was the first and last time our regiment ever showed trepidation under fire. The gunboats continued shelling the woods during the day, and there was some lively skirmishing in our front, but no general engagement. The shells from the gunboats made a tremendous noise, but as they did no harm we soon got used to them, and some of the boys even went so far to laugh and joke at them. Still we didn't like that style of fighting—it didn't give us any chance to distinguish ourselves. About an hour before sundown we were ordered to fall back to our works.[65] Our works consisted of a fort (a poor affair) on the north bank of the Arkansas River, with rifle pits running from the fort in a northerly direction.[66] The armament of the fort consisted of three large smooth-bore cannon, I believe 12-pounders.[67] The only artillery

---

65. Once the initial Federal troops were ashore the 290-man 8th Missouri Infantry (Union) was sent forward as skirmishers at about 1:00 p.m., to allow time for the remainder of the command to form and land. They actively skirmished with the three cavalry companies of the Post, commanded by Captains L. M. Nutt, W. B. Denson and Samuel J. Richardson, "advancing from tree to tree." The 120 grayclads were no match for the better armed and more numerous Federals, who forced the skirmishers back time and time again until they had retired into their main line. W. W. Heartsill, of Richardson's command, noted of the predicament that cavalry faced: "It is impossible for cavalry to compete successfully with infantry even were numbers equal and arms the same." Mounted they simply made an easy target and dismounted their strength was diminished by one quarter. Even as the skirmishers advanced, General Churchill received word that he was being flanked on the left and ordered a withdrawal to the main works. Between noon and 1:00 p.m. the withdrawal began, covered by the "skill & coolness" of the cavalry under Captain L. M. Nutt of Louisiana. *O.R.*, vol. 17, pt. 1:775, 780, 792; Chambers, 10; W.E.W., "The Capture of Arkansas Post, *The Chicago Times* (Chicago, IL), February 22, 1863; Wiley, 94.

66. Following the capture of Fort Hindman, General McClernand provided this description of the fort: Fort Hindman, a square, full-bastioned fort, was erected within this village, upon the bank of the river, at the head of a bend resembling a horseshoe. The exterior sides of the fort, between the salient angles, were 300 feet in length; the faces of the bastions two-sevenths of an exterior side and perpendiculars one-eighth. The parapet was 18 feet wide on the top, the ditch 20 feet wide on the ground level, and 8 feet deep with a slope of 4 feet base. A banquette for infantry was constructed around the interior slope of the parapet; also three platforms for artillery in each bastion and one in the curtain facing north. On the southern face of the northeastern bastion was a casemate 18 by 15 feet wide and 7 1/2 feet high in the clear, the walls of which were constructed of three thicknesses of oak timber 16 inches square, and so the roof with additional revetment of iron bars. One of the shorter sides of the casemate was inserted in the parapet and was pierced by an embrasure 3 feet 8 inches on the inside and 4 feet 6 inches on the outside, the entrance being in the opposite wall...A similar casemate was constructed in the curtain facing the river...The entrance to the fort, secured by traverse, was on its northwestern side, and from the salient angle of the northwestern bastion extended a broken line of rifle–pits westerly for 720 yards toward the bayou, intersected by wooden traverses. Along the line of rifle–pits six field pieces were mounted, of which three were rifled.

Admiral David D. Porter wrote that the fort was "well constructed...with the best engineering skill.... There was nothing known to the military art," Porter continued, "that had been neglected in constructing these works, and to look at them one would suppose they could defy a naval force three times as strong as that now about to be brought against them." *O.R.*, vol. 17, pt. 1:705; Bearss, "Post of Arkansas," 239; David D. Porter, *Naval History of the Civil War* (New York, 1986; reprint ed., Secaucus, NJ, 1884), 289, hereafter cited as Porter.

67. The main guns of the fort were one 9-inch Columbiads and two 8-inch Columbiads (Bearss has the battery as two 9-inch and one 8-inch guns). One of the 9-inch and the 8-inch guns were protected by a casemate, while the other 8-inch piece was mounted in the southeast bastion of the fort. Addition-

we had besides these cannon was one battery of six-pounders of six pieces.[68] There were obstructions placed in the river a short distance below the fort, but it seemed that the officers captured on the *Blue Wing No. 2* knew the opening, and the obstructions did not amount to anything.[69] Our regiment being the right of the brigade took position next to the fort.[70] About 9 o'clock p.m. the gunboats came within range and opened a tremendous fire upon us. With the exception of the next day we were never under as heavy a cannonade. There were seven ironclads and two wooden gunboats playing upon us. The sight was grand and magnificent be-

---

ally, the fort also contained four 10-pound parrot rifles and four 6-pound smoothbore (iron) cannon which were placed at various locations within the fort's bastion. *O.R.*, vol. 17, pt. 1:705; *O.R.*, 53:867; Bearss, "Post of Arkansas," 239.

68. Not true. There has been a lot of speculation as to the composition of Hart's Arkansas Battery. According to Alyn Barr, the battery contained three 6-pound smoothbores, two 10-pound rifled Parrots and one 12-pound howitzer. General McClernand has Hart's Battery consisting of six guns with three rifled pieces—this would suggest that Hart's Battery had three 10-pound Parrots with three other smoothbore pieces. This is further supported by a correspondent of the *Chicago Times*, who noted that Hart's Battery contained "three…twenty-pound Parrots." General Churchill in his official report has Hart's Battery containing only 6-pound and 12-pound guns, but this was clearly incorrect as seen in Colonel Deshler's report which reported a section of 10-pound Parrots in Hart's Battery. At the Battle of Pea Ridge, in March 1862, Hart's Battery had four 6-pound guns. Additionally, when the battery ended up in Little Rock, during the summer of 1862, the command was noted as still having the light guns, just prior to its assignment to Pine Bluff in August 1862, and finally to Arkansas Post. The Chief of Ordnance, Trans-Mississippi Department, settled the argument, by recording the loss of "three 6-pounder iron guns and carriages; one 12-pounder bronze howitzer;…[and] two 3-inch Parrot rifles (iron)" at Arkansas Post, in addition to the guns lost in the fort. *O.R.*, vol. 8:776, 788; *O.R.*, vol. 17, pt. 1:705, 780, 792; *O.R.*, 53:866–867; *O.R.S.*, pt. 2, vol. 14:262; Michael E. Banasik, *Confederate "Tales of the War" In the Trans-Mississippi Part Two: 1862* (Iowa City, IA, 2011), 153; Alyn Barr, "Confederate Artillery in Arkansas," *Arkansas Historical Quarterly* 22 (Autumn, 1963), 260; Letter, Hindman to Roane (August 8, 1862), Copy Letter Book No. 2; Letter, Wilson to Dunnington (July 11, 1862), Copy Letter Book No. 2; Special Orders No. 56 (August 4, 1862), Special Orders Copy Book (June 11–August 19, 1862), Army of the Southwest, Peter W. Alexander Collection, Columbia University, hereafter cited as Special Orders Book No. 2; W.E.W., "Capture of Arkansas Post," *Chicago Times*, February 22, 1863.

69. The river obstructions consisted of piles, linked with chains, driven into the bed of the river opposite Fort Hindman to restrict boat movement on the Arkansas River. Additionally, ranging sticks were placed in the river to allow better targeting by the fort's guns. By all accounts, the obstruction were little better than an annoyance, while the ranging sticks had limited value on the crucial second day, as the naval action took place at about 400 yards, well inside the range markers. *O.R.*, vol. 17, pt 1:211, 213; Bearss, "Post of Arkansas," 248; Porter, 289–290.

70. By the morning of January 11, the Confederate command was positioned as follows. Dunnington's Brigade held the fort with four companies of the 19th Arkansas Infantry, Crawford's Arkansas Battalion and the 37-man detachment of sailors from the rebel gunboat *Pontchartrain*. Immediately adjacent to the fort came the remaining companies of the 19th Arkansas. Next in line were the men of Garland's Brigade—first came Hart's Arkansas Battery, then the 6th Texas Infantry, followed by the 24th and 25th Texas Cavalries (dismounted). Deshler's command made up the final units of Churchill's defenses, being positioned next to Garland's Brigade. The 15th Texas Cavalry (dismounted) held the left, next to the 10th Texas Infantry, while the 18th Texas Cavalry (dismounted) took its place adjacent to Garland's Brigade and the 17th Texas Cavalry (dismounted) held the right center of Deshler's Brigade sandwiched between the 10th and 17th Texas. As the day progressed, Chruchill's cavalry companies would occupy the far left of the rebel line, being dismounted and serving as infantry. *O.R.*, vol. 17, pt. 1:783, 791; Bearss, "Post of Arkansas," 257.

Fort Hindman

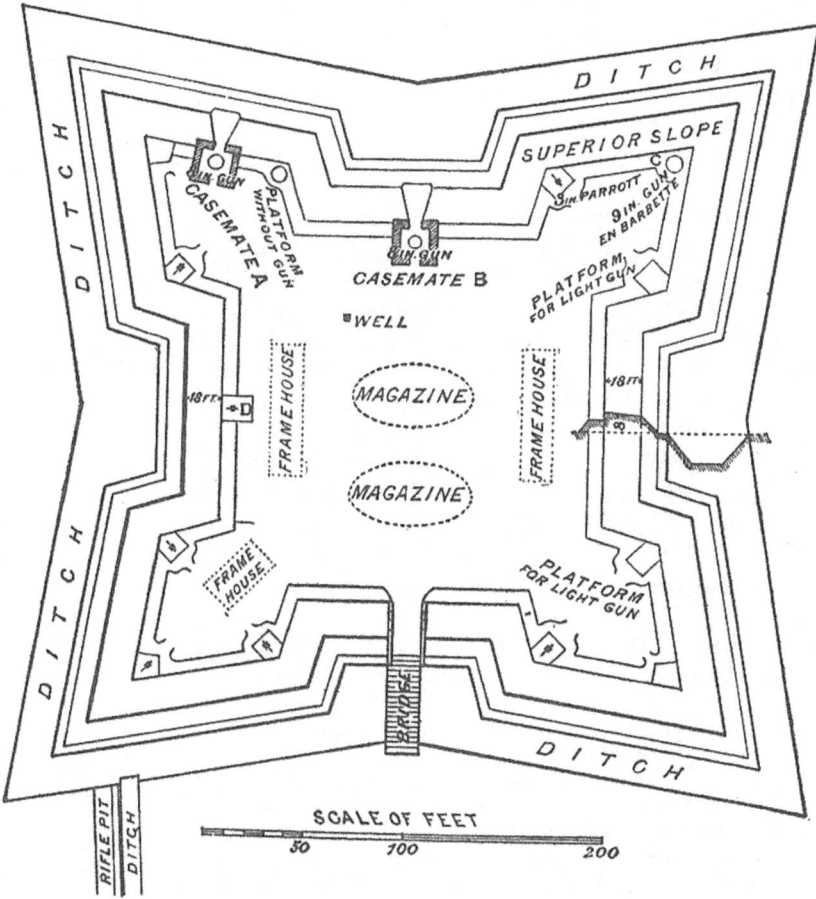

yond description. There was no moon, and, the night being dark, the burning fuses of the shells as they flashed over us, left in their wake streams of light, giving the appearance as though the heavens were filled with flying meteors, and climaxed by the magnificent spectacle of the bursting shells, the whole accompanied by the grand, yet terrible music of the booming cannon. It was a scene never to be forgotten, but it was one in which "distance would have lent enchantment to the view." I have no doubt that, had I been on an eminence some ten or twenty miles away, I would have appreciated it as it deserved, but under the circumstances, I was not yearning after grand views, my principal anxiety being to keep my body as close as possible to the

Bottom of the Ditch.

This dreadful artillery fire resulted in the killing of most of our artillery horses, but did no other damage that I know of. Our fort of course returned the fire of the gunboats. In about two hours the gunboats withdrew and we were jubilant, thinking our fort had knocked the daylights out of them. After congratulating ourselves over our victory without firing of a shot or the loss of a man, we lay down and had a good night's sleep.[71] The next morning (Sunday) bright and early, our captain made his appearance. He made us another little speech in which he said that he had entirely recovered and ending with "And now boys, I'm with you." The speech fell rather flat, for we thought the Federal already whipped. However, [illegible] to dispel that illusion [illegible] of three and four discussing our victory when we were electrified by a voice exclaiming: "Look! there's the smoke of the gunboats again!" and sure enough there it was coming up he river.[72] In about

---

71. The bombardment on January 10 had ended near 8:00 p.m. after about three hours. "But little damage had been done," according to William Oliphant of the 6th Texas Infantry, and "considering the extent of the bombardment... only a few men and horses had been killed or wounded." Robert Garland and James Deshler, brigade commanders, both support Oliphant's claims. As to the losses in horse flesh, by the time the battle had ended 81 of 83 horses (another source has the number 83 killed out of 85, while yet another put the loss of 80 out of 86) in Hart's Arkansas Battery would be dead—only two survived with one of those being wounded. The main losses during the 10th, to personnel, appear to have been in the fort, where two shells penetrated one of the casemates, killing three and wounding yet another three. Injuries to the troops in the trenches appear to have been limited, with only a few wounded in the two primary brigades. *O.R.*, vol. 17, pt. 1:781, 784, 791; *O.R.N.*, vol. 24:697; "Arkansas Post Affair," *Tri-Weekly Telegraph*, February 6, 1863; Bearss, "Post of Arkansas," 258; Chambers, 14, 27; Foster, 27; Garland, 11; Harrell, *Arkansas, Confederate Military History*, 159; Oliphant, 737; Wiley, 95; Udolpho Wolfe, "The Fight At Arkansas Post," *Tri-Weekly Telegraph*, July 1, 1863.

72. During the night, the rebels strengthened their entrenchments and prepared for the morning to come. General Churchill, for his part, received a telegram from General Holmes which said in part: "Hold out till help arrives or until all are dead." Trooping the line, the next morning, Churchill told the troops in Garland's Brigade: "He had made his last stand. Dug his last entrenchment and would retreat no further." He further elicited a "solemn pledge," according to one participant "to never surrender, but to hold the fort until *all*, all! should die." By 8:00 a.m. it was light enough for scattered firing to begin, even as the Federals continued to move into position for the final assault. Four guns from Hart's Arkansas Battery and six companies from the 19th Arkansas Infantry were moved from the Confederate right to bolster the left, which had a two hundred yard gap on their far left. The post's cavalry,

half hour a big blaze in the direction of the winter quarters—which were in our front—attracted our attention and this was almost instantly followed by the sharp rattle of musketry in the same direction. We then knew that fight had not yet begun and cast our eyes sufficiently around in search of our redoubtable captain, but he had disappeared, without even so much as an explanation and we never saw him afterwards. We heard after we joined the army in Tennessee that he was in Texas drilling conscripts.[73] As soon as the gunboats got within range they opened on us, our fort returning their fire. Again the shells commenced flying over us and exploding all around us again and we thought it expedient to explore the bottom of our ditches. The Yankee infantry then drove in our skirmishers and formed in line of battle and planted their artillery in the woods about 300 yards in our front. The gunboats then paid their attention to the fort, and the land batteries opened with solid shot and shell on the rifle pits, but we being next to the fort got the benefit

Of Both Fires.

The fire of the land batteries was terrible—the balls came faster than you could count them and every one seemed to strike the works.[74] Our works were of

including Alf Johnson's Texas cavalry company, which arrived about 10:00 p.m. the previous night, were also ordered to the far left to further secure that quarter. By 9:00 a.m. Hart's Battery began to fire and periodically engaged the Union columns, whenever they could get a clear shot. The gunboats remained silent through all these preparations and not until about noon (most Federal sources have the time as 1:00 p.m., though at least one correspondent and one brigade commander put the time at noon) did the gunboats appear to begin their simultaneous attack with the Federal ground forces. *O.R.*, vol. 17, pt. 1:706, 723, 726, 730, 733, 756 781, 784, 792; *O.R.N.*, vol. 24:697; Bearss, "Post of Arkansas," 260, 265; Chambers, 15–17; Christ, 63; Garland, 11; Harrell, *Arkansas, Confederate Military History*, 159; Oliphant, 737; R. H. F., "A Rebel Narrative," Frank Moore, ed., *The Rebellion Record A Diary of American Events*, 12 vols. (NY, 1861–1868; reprint ed., New York, 1977), 6: Doc–373, hereafter cited as *Rebellion Record*; Simpson, *Bugle Softly Blows*, 31; W.E.W., "The Capture of Arkansas Post, *Chicago Times*, February 22, 1863.

73. Following the Battle of Arkansas Post the prisoners were sent north to Union prisons in Chicago (Camp Douglas) and Springfield (Camp Butler), Illinois and to Camp Chase near Columbus, Ohio. The officers were paroled from Camp Chase on April 10, 1863, and sent by rail to Philadelphia, thence by boat to Fort Delaware to await exchange. On May 18, they were forwarded to Fortress Monroe, in Virginia, held for two days and exchanged at City Point, Virginia on May 20, 1863. The first batch of enlisted men began leaving their camps on April 7, winding their way to Washington, D.C., where they arrived on April 10 at midnight. On April 11 they boarded a steamer for Fortress Monroe and thence on to City Point where they are exchanged on April 14. Other enlisted men arrived on April 18. Eventually, the troops comprising those captured at Arkansas Post, were later consolidated forming but three regiments; the remaining men had either died in prison or had taken the Federal oath of allegiance. "The Fight At Arkansas Post," *Tri-Weekly Telegraph*, July 1, 1863; Foster, 31–32; Wiley, 102, 106, 118–123; Wooster, 129–130.

74. According to plans, as soon as the Federal boats began their bombardment of the fort the land batteries were to join in and after 30 minutes the land forces were supposed to "advance to the charge." At 1:30, William T. Sherman's Corps began their attack, on the rebel left, but were quickly halted at about 300 yards by severe fire from Hart's Arkansas Battery with support from the light guns of the fort. To the left of Sherman, George W. Morgan's Corps opened upon the Confederate fort and works at 1:00 p.m. and were to continue their fire until the fort's guns were silenced, at which time they would also advance. The spearhead of Morgan's Corps was Stephen G. Burbridge's Brigade, which began

earth and whenever a ball would strike the bank those in the rear were covered with dirt. I am certain that I was not covered with less than twenty times during the day. When a shell would strike the bank and explode and then fragments of shell and dirt would fly in all directions, accompanied by that whirring, shrieking, dreaded sound, always produced by the flying fragments of shells. The fire was the most terrible we ever experienced and all we had to oppose it was six little six-pounders scattered along our line. Then would come a lull in the firing, and a cheer from the Yankees would announce to us that a charge was in progress. this was the style of fighting that suited us. Up we would rise and pour volley after volley into them. Their line would first waver and then stop; then turn and rush back, pell mell, to the shelter of the woods and of their batteries, always leaving a considerable number behind, and their batteries would again open their terrible fire upon us. These assaults were repeated time and again during the day and always with the same result, their columns never getting within fifty yards of our entrenchments. Their losses in these charges, so they told us after the fight, were terrible, their killed alone almost equaling our entire numbers.[75] Strange as it may appear, their terrible cannonading did us but very little damage, we losing but sixty-five killed and wounded during the engagement, in our company we had one man struck and knocked down by a nearly spent fragment of a shell, but no one else was touched.[76] Our company [K] and Co. G, were the center companies of

its assault about one hour after the bombardment had begun. They slowly drove back the skirmishers from Garland's Brigade, before launching the first of three assaults on the Confederate right. Garland's Brigade, on the rebel right received fire from both its front and rear, which eventually led to the surrender of the Confederate command. *O.R.*, vol. 17, pt. 1:706–707, 723, 730; Christ, 67, 69; Foster, 28; W.E.F., "The Capture of Arkansas Post, *Chicago Times*, February 22, 1863.

75. During the course of the day, Morgan's Federals made three charges on the rebel trenches and were repulsed each time. On the Confederate left and center, Sherman's Corps made eight charges and like Morgan's troops were also repulsed—Recalled one soldier in the 25th Texas Cavalry (dismounted), who was opposite Sherman's command: "The last charge they were in solid column of eight deep...Finding they could not carry our works by assault their infantry retired beyond the range of our muskets." In all McClernand reported the loss of 134 killed, 898 wounded with 29 missing or captured—Total 1,061. *O.R.*, vol. 17, pt. 1, 719; Chambers, 23; "Conflict At Arkansas Post," *Tri-Weekly Telegraph*, February 4, 1863; "The Fight At Arkansas Post," *Tri-Weekly Telegraph*, July 1. 1863.

76. When the battle was over Colonel Garland reported the loss of 25 killed, 64 wounded with 68 missing; Colonel Deshler reported the loss of just 3 killed and 17 wounded. There was no report from Dunnington's Brigade. Total known losses in Churchill's Division were 109—excluding the missing. However, one period newspaper reported "the official report" of killed and wounded, in Chruchill's Division as 103. As to the missing and the difference in the total numbers, including the lack of Dunnington's report there were several accounts of the battle that talked about the men who escaped from the fort, including some wounded. Even as the battle raged the surgeons removed the wounded from the hospitals as they were receiving artillery fire. Slightly wounded men and shirkers began to filter their way from Arkansas Post and made good their escape. Additionally, other rebels, including at least two companies from the 17th Texas Cavalry (dismounted), departed the area following the surrender not desiring to be sent into captivity. The estimated number of escapees ran from a low of 300 to 1,500. In the case of the 17th Texas, it appears that about forty percent of the command escaped capture, as the rolls showed 366 men on the rolls even as the remainder of the regiment was being exchanged. *O.R.*, vol. 17, pt. 1:785, 795; *O.R.*, Series 2, vol. 5:937–938; "Arkansas Post Affair," *Tri-Weekly Telegraph*, February 6, 1863; Chambers, 26; Christ, 81; "Conflict At Arkansas Post," *Tri-*

the regiment, Co. G, being the color company. Just between these two companies and immediately behind the ditches there stood a small tree. Lieut.-Col. Anderson took up his position immediately in front of and under this tree. There he stood

During the Entire Engagement,

as cool as though on dress parade, the entire upper portion of his body being in full view of the Yankees and exposed to their fire. We expected every minute to see him fall, but he passed through it unscathed. When the Yankees would charge he would hallo out to us: "Up boys, they're coming!" and when we would drive them back he would wave his sword over his head and give three cheers for Texas. Truly we could have said of him, as was said of [Thomas H.] Jackson,[77] "There stands Anderson like a column of granite."

About 2 o'clock in the afternoon news reached us that one of the gunboats, had passed the fort.[78] This surprised but did not daunt us. The flag on the gunboat had become blackened by the smoke, and the men in the fort sent word down the line that the Yankees had raised the black flag; but we did not mind that, for we were certain that we could lick them out of their boats. About an hour after the gunboat passed the fort an order came down the line to raise the white flag. We at first thought it was a mistake, and it was the Yankees who were raising the white flag. But casting our eyes toward the fort we saw the white flag run up; but it had hardly been raised before someone tore it down. The fighting then continued a short time longer, when an order again came down the line to raise the white flag.

Weekly Telegraph, February 4, 1863; "The Fall of Arkansas Post," *The Dallas Herald* (Dallas, TX), February 4, 1863; Martin M. Kenny, "Letter From Arkansas," *Bellville Countryman* (Bellville, TX), March 21, 1863.

77. Thomas J. Jackson, better known as "Stonewall" Jackson, received his moniker, at the Battle of Manassas (or Bull Run), in July 1861. During the course of the battle Confederate General Barnard Bee, attempting to rally his brigade and seeing Jackson's command shouted: "Look at Jackson's brigade standing like a stone wall! Rally on the Virginians!" Jackson was born in 1824, graduated from the U.S. Military Academy (number 17 of 59) in 1846, and fought in the Mexican War. A Virginian by birth, he was an instructor at the Virginia Military Institute when the Civil War began. He rose quickly in rank, from a militia major to lieutenant general by October 1862. Jackson was known for his military brilliance and considered "as [General Robert E.] Lee's strong right arm." He was wounded by friendly fire at the Battle of Chancellorsville on May 2, 1863, and died on May 10. Boatner, 432, 808; Faust, 391–392.

78. Just before 4:00 p.m. (3:00 p.m. rebel time), the fort's guns were silenced by the naval force under Admiral David Porter. With no risk to his lighter boats Porter directed the tinclads *Rattler* and *Glide*, with the ram *Monarch*, to run past the fort to block the enemy's retreat. The three boats also managed to dismantle some of the piles blocking the river bed allowing passage up river. With the passage of the fort secured, the *Blackhawk*, carrying Admiral Porter also passed the fort and took on board the 3rd Kentucky Infantry Regiment for the purpose of taking the fort by naval landing. Meanwhile, with the fort's guns silent on the river side, Colonel D. W. Lindsey moved up two 20-pound rifled Parrots and two 3-inch rifled guns (Christ has the battery with 10-pound parrots) to the river bank to bombard the fort from the rear quarter and enfilade Garland's Brigade. Within a short time of Lindsey's guns opening on the fort, the Confederate command ran up the white flag ending the engagement. *O.R.*, vol. 17, pt. 1:748, 752–753; *O.R.N.*, vol. 24: 108, 686, 697; Bearss, "Post of Arkansas," 264, 271; Christ, 54–55; Foster, 28; Porter, 291.

This time it was raised and left over the fort, and the men in the ditches seeing it, also raised it.[79] Miller of our company had a white pocket handkerchief, with which he was wiping his face at the moment of the surrender, and a lieutenant of another company ordered him to affix the handkerchief to his ramrod and raise it. [Armstead] Miller was

About to Execute the Order

when Martin Braden cocked and drew his gun on him, at the same time exclaiming: "I'll kill any man in Co. K that raises his white flag."[80] The lieutenant then took the handkerchief and raised it himself. When the Yankees saw our white flag they gave a cheer and rushed up to us, an officer on horseback leading them. The officer rode direct for Col. Anderson, and when he got up to us he cast his eyes up and down the trenches and then in a tone of surprise said to Col. Anderson: "Colonel, where's your dead?" "In the ditches," replied Col. Anderson. The Yankees, knowing it was impossible for us to remove them, expected to find our ditches filled with killed and wounded. We then marched out of our works and staked our arms, and thus ended the Battle of Arkansas Post.

The ending was a great humiliation to us, yet we had nothing to be ashamed of.[81] We had 3,100 men, the Yankees, so they told us, 10,000. We had one battery

---

79. With the fort guns silent and pressure mounting on the rebel rear, Admiral Porter moved the *Blackhawk* into position to assault the fort. Following a final fury of firing by the gunboats, that were now firing at about 50 yards distance, the fort surrendered. However, General Churchill commanding the Confederate garrison had not surrendered his command, but would do so only after a period of quick negotiations with the Federal land forces, following an unauthorized act of capitulation that apparently started in Garland's Brigade. Even while the fort was preparing to surrender, at about 4:30 p.m., Colonel Garland heard a cry being raised: "*Raise the white flag, by order of General Chruchill; pass the word up the line.*" General Chruchill had not ordered a surrender, but according to one period Federal correspondent, a Colonel Porter came forth from the 24th Texas Cavalry Regiment (dismounted) and made the following statement to General David Stuart, commanding the 2nd Division, Fifteenth Corps: "General, I surrender my regiment to you without any orders, on my own responsibility." (There was no such rebel colonel in the battle; Colonel F. C. Wilkes, who was wounded the night before, commanded the 24th Texas, though at the time of the surrender Lieutenant Colonel C. C. Gillespie, commanded the 24th.) Federal troops took advantage of the lull in the battle and crowded into Garland's lines and the fort proper, forcing Garland to reluctantly accept the situation and surrender his brigade. Under the circumstances, General Churchill had no choice but to surrender. *O.R.*, vol. 17, pt. 1:781; *O.R.N.*, vol. 24:108; Bears, "Post of Arkansas," 273–274; "Capture of Arkansas Post, *Waukegan Weekly Gazette*, January 31, 1863; Chambers, 16, 25; Christ, 82; Foster, 29; Garland, 12; R.H.F., "A Rebel Narrative," *Rebellion Record*, 6:Doc–374.
80. Private Armstead Miller was born in about 1838, while Private Martin Braden was born about 1842. Both men were captured at Arkansas Post and sent to Camp Butler, near Springfield, Illinois where they were held as prisoners of war. Braden was later paroled, while Miller died at Camp Butler. www.6thtx.org.
81. In Deshler's Brigade, the firing continued on for several more minutes, even as Garland's command surrendered. On the Union right, General Sherman ordered a cease fire and sent an aid forward to determine what the white flags meant. Shortly thereafter Colonel Deshler met General Frederick Steele in front of his lines to discuss the situation. Steele pointed out that the rest of the garrison had surrendered and only his command still remained unbowed. Deshler refused to capitulate without a

Bombardment of Arkansas Post

of six-pounders, the Yankees a number of twelve and I believe twenty-four pound batteries, while our fort with its three old smooth-bore cannon, was matched against the nine gunboats with their splendid armaments and superior rifled cannon.[82] At the time of the surrender we had but one serviceable gun left—a six-pounder. I cannot understand why Gen. Churchill made the fight at Arkansas Post, as he must have known the superiority of the enemy.[83] The following story was

direct order from General Churchill. Further, as the Federal troops were moving up even closer, while under the cease fire, Deshler told Steele, "If you do not command 'Halt,' I will command fire." Steele ordered his men to halt and awaited an order from General Churchill, which arrived thirty minutes later. The battle was over. *O.R.*, vol. 17, pt. 1:793–794; Bearss, "Post of Arkansas," 273–274; Harrell, *Arkansas, Confederate Military History*, 159–160.

82. At the time of the battle, Morgan's 13th Corps contained four batteries of artillery, with 24 guns, including 2 heavy guns; while Sherman's 15th Corps contained seven batteries of artillery, with 32 guns, including 4 heavy guns—total 56 pieces. The six heavy pieces were 20-pound Parrot rifles, which did terrible execution on the fort and garrison of Fort Hindman. The lighter guns consisted of 6-pound smoothbores, 3-inch rifles and 12-pound howitzers. *O.R.*, vol. 17, pt. 1:700–701, 705–706, 728, 753, 755, 767, 774; *O.R.*, vol. 17, pt. 2:576; Bearss, "Post of Arkansas," 269–270.

83. Churchill had no choice but to defend Fort Hindman, having been ordered by General Holmes to "hold out until help arrived or all were dead." As for Arkansas Post, it was systematically destroyed by the Federal forces, never to be rebuilt. McClernand abandoned the Post on January 17 and returned for the Vicksburg Campaign. The battle itself accomplished nothing for the Vicksburg Expedition, according to Edwin Bearss, though it did boost the morale of the Union troops, having captured the fort and almost 5,000 men. General U.S. Grant would admit in his later years that removal of the garrison and the loss of the rebel property actually prevented interference in his Vicksburg Campaign, though at the time he gave McClernand no such credit. *O.R.*, vol. 17, pt. 1:708, 781; Bearss, "Post of Arkansas," 278–279; *Civil War Naval Chronology*, III–8; Harrell, *Arkansas, Confederate Military History*, 155–156; Ferguson, 124; Porter, 292–293.

told at the time: It was said that Gen. Holmes, commanding the department, was engaged to be married to a widow who owned a very fine plantation just above Arkansas Post, and as he was anxious to prevent this plantation from being pillaged by the Yankees, he ordered Gen. Churchill to hold at all hazards. The marriage, so the story went, was to have taken place at Pine Bluff on the Sunday morning of the battle, but the widow, hearing the guns at Arkansas Post, informed the general that his duty demanded that he should be at the front fighting with his men, instead of at the rear making love to the women, and then refused to marry him. Of course this story was not true, but it was pretty generally believed at the time.[84]

Leon Fremon,
Co. K, Sixth Texas Infantry

* * * * * *

---

84. Following their capture at Arkansas Post, the Confederate prisoners stacked arms and were gathered up on the banks of the Arkansas River to await transport to prisoner of war camps in the north. The rebel prisoners remained unbowed following their capture and during the night on March 12–13 "one of the prisoners started the song, 'The Bonnie Blue Flag,' others caught up the refrain, and for more than an hour hundreds joined in the song, and made the woods, which had so recently echoed far different sounds, ring with the rich melody." During the same night the prisoners began loading unto the transports *Sam Gatty*, the *Nebraska* and the *John J. Roe*. In the afternoon of January 14, the prisoners headed north with the gunboat *Lexington* as an escort. At the mouth of the White River the captive fleet was joined by the tinclad *New Era* and continued their journey northward. Snow greeted the prisoners on January 15, as the weather turned very cold, and at 4:00 p.m. on January 16 they reached Memphis. Following a two day rest at Memphis, the fleet continued northward, arriving at Cairo on January 21, where they halted for a time to parole General Churchill and staff. Continuing northward on January 22, the *Nebraska* ran aground, causing a delay while she was freed with the help of the other two craft. On January 24, they reached St. Louis, where the sick were off-loaded and the officers transferred to rail cars for movement to Camp Chase, near Columbus, Ohio (Mark Christ has the officers going to Johnson Island, while the enlisted men were carried off to Camp Douglas in Chicago). The *Nebraska* and the *Sam Gatty* departed for the north on January 28, while the *Roe* moved out the next day. Landing at Alton, Illinois, the remainder of the captives were deposited for their final journey by rail to Camp Douglas in Chicago and Camp Butler in Springfield, Illinois. On January 31, the last of the prisoners reached their destination as they entered Camp Butler, in Springfield. *O.R.*, Series 2, vol. 5:241, 257, 311; *O.R.N.*, vol. 24:122; Foster, 31–32; Christ, 89; Oliphant, 738–739; Wiley, 99–106; Wooster, 129.

Item: Sickness in Little Rock During the Winter of 1863, by Silas C. Turnbo, 27th Arkansas Infantry.[85]
Published: June 12, 1886

Twenty-Seventh Arkansas Infantry

Pro Tem, Taney Co., Mo. June 3
Editor *Republican*

Capt. McNamara in his paper on the Arkansas campaigns mentions the sad scenes in winter quarters at Little Rock and the soldiers who died "were buried in long trenches." James L. Grubbs of the Tenth Missouri Infantry, commenting on this in your war tales, states that he saw nothing of the kind but assisted at many burials, and so far as he knew the dead were buried in single graves. That was my own experience, too, yet there is no doubt many were buried in trenches. It was the common talk of our brigade. Of course when a man died in camp there were always comrades to dig a grave and bury him as decently as circumstances would permit though owing to the heavy rains the grave would often fill up with seep water before the corpse was placed in it. It was at the hospitals in Little Rock that the mortality was so great that it was reported to be impossible to bury them singly in coffins. They were accordingly buried in trenches like soldiers who had fallen in battle. Some of the trenches were too shallow. I passed through this portion of the burying-ground with our brigade in August following. The sight was sickening. Bones protruded through the thin covering of earth and the stench was almost unendurable.[86] It was sad to think of men who had left home as volunteers soldiers being

Dumped Away

with so little honor. The diseases which caused so great mortality were pneumo-

---

85. This piece is an abbreviated presentation of what Turnbo wrote in his history of his regiment. Turnbo, 221–233.

86. The march to Little Rock and the subsequent hurry-up race to Pine Bluff took a terrible toll on the army. The diet of "poor beef and cornbread" and lack of medicines also added to the medical problems of the Little Rock army. Overall, according to period soldiers, pneumonia was the main cause of death, with measles and diarrhea apparently also playing a role in the high death rate. Turnbo in his expanded version of this article also attributed the deaths to "the want of attention, for the nurses were insufficient." Even as the winter wore on one soldier recorded: "This will be the last winter for a great many." Another simply wrote: "There was a great deal of sickness and many deaths among our soldiers at Little Rock, the result no doubt of our hard march from Van Buren." One soldier in the 10th Missouri was given up for dead by his doctors, with pneumonia, but survived to later record his memoirs. As to the number of deaths during the winter of 1862–1863, one doctor serving in the army, noted that the cemetery of "about six acres" was "nearly all taken up" by soldiers, which he estimated at 500. "The horrors are indescribable" wrote John P. Quesenberry, with "hundreds on the brink of the grave...The graveyard at Little Rock is...filling up very fast with soldiers." Banasik, *Missouri Brothers in Gray*, 53; John C. Dwyer Memoirs, Missouri Historical Society, 3; Gaughan, 127; Quesenberry, February 4–5, 11, 15 and 16, 1863; Turnbo, 224.

nia and camp diarrhoea caused by the severe weather and unwholesome food. The physicians were powerless for want of proper medicines and nourishing diet. Prudent men exercised great care with their diet and chewed white oak bark with good results. When the sickness was worst our regiment established a hospital of its own with its own surgeon and nurses, and by this means the death rate was materially reduced. Among the nurses was my relative, Harvey Laughlin of Taney County, orderly sergeant of our company, but he grew sick, was furloughed and died at Yellville, on his way home.[87] Our company lost several of its best men. During the worst sickness drilling was light, but in March and April, as the health of the troops improved drill was resumed and there were several fine division parades. Our regiment became expert and lest it be doubtful if any army in the Confederacy was more proficient in the Manual of Arms than the forces at Little Rock. Prize drills were common and the men were stimulated by rivalry between organizations as well as by prizes. A common reward for the best drilled man was a twenty-four hour pass.[88]

Early in March, Gen. Hindman was ordered east of the Mississippi, having been removed from command.[89] He had his final review March 5.[90] He had en-

---

87. Harvey Laughlin was the son of Mat Laughlin and lived on Beaver Creek, in Taney County, Missouri. He was marked at a young age with a dented forehead, from a severe kick by a horse that almost killed him. He was buried in the cemetery west of Yellville, and, according to Turnbo, Laughlin "was a true soldier and our company regretted to hear of his death." Turnbo, 224–225.

88. As the winter progressed, drilling began anew in the army when the weather moderated. On February 2, the 16th Missouri Infantry began to drill again, which did little to relieve the "great monotony" of camp life. On occasion there were drill competitions as noted by Turnbo, with the most noteworthy occurring on March 21, 1863. The Arkansas regiments of Asa S. Morgan and John E. Glen squared off "for a fine stand of colors, costing the sum of $400…Glen's Regiment got the prize." C. B. Lotspeich typescript diary, Arkansas History Commission, February 2 and 13 and March 21, 1863, hereafter cited as Lotspeich; Gaughan, 130; Hoskin, March 21, 1863.

89. Following the Battle of Prairie Grove, General Hindman blamed himself for the defeat, admitting to General Holmes that he was better at organizing an army than leading one in the field. In a later conversation, Hindman asked to be relieved of command. The Confederate War Department approved his request on January 30, 1863, but left the ultimate decision up to General Holmes. After repeated requests by General Hindman, Holmes relented and approved Hindman's request, effective March 2, 1863. When the Missouri Brigade heard of Hindman's departure they wrote a series of resolutions praising their departing commander (See Appendix A) on March 3 and went "en masses," the same day, to serenade the general at his residence. With Hindman's departure, General Daniel M. Frost assumed temporary command of "Hindman's Division," until such time as General Sterling Price arrived in the area to assume command. O.R., vol. 22, pt. 2:784–786, 794, 808; S. P. Burns, Letter (March 3, 1863), The Arkansas True Democrat (Little Rock, AR), March 18, 1863; Gaughan, 124; Lotspeich, March 7, 1863; Telegraphic conversation between Hindman and Holmes (December 12, 1862), Telegram collection.

90. Of Hindman's final review one soldier in the 16th Missouri Infantry (CSA) recorded of the day: Hindman "is really a better man than we have ever taken him to be. He seemed very much affected as we were passing in review he sat on his horse with his cap off and he was too full to speak." Another, from Tilden's Battery, simply recorded that it was "nicely done." On March 10, Hindman followed up his farewell review by throwing a party for all the officers of his command. The following day the Arkansas officers "administered unto Gen. Hindman, a serenade," with General James Fagan serving as master of ceremonies. On March 13, 1863, Hindman departed Little Rock en route for the East.

emies who declared him unfit for command, but I believe he was a true officer who did all he could for his troops.[91] He was kind-hearted and sociable.[92] The old Twenty-seventh will remember that he once got off his horse and walked to let one of the sick boys ride, and also, that he was out to and ate a corn-bread supper with a mess of private soldiers.[93] Later, Gen. Price took command of the division. He was the pride of the Missouri troops, and was highly esteemed by the Arkansas men. His arrival undoubtedly had a great effect in appeasing the dissatisfaction existing.[94] Gen. John [James] C. Tappan[95] was assigned to our brigade as com-

---

Gaughan, 122; Diane Neal and Thomas W. Kremm, *Lion of the South General Thomas C. Hindman* (Macon, GA, 1993), 158; Hoskin, March 10, 1863; Lotspeich, March 5, 1863; Quesenberry, March 5, 1863.

91. Of those who disliked Hindman, Arkansas Captain F. E. Earle wrote—Hindman's "exit will be hailed with delight. He seems to have the unanimous consent of the army to depart." A surgeon from the 33rd Arkansas Infantry, upon hearing a speech praising Hindman, following a serenade, on March 12, recorded that he found the whole affair "abominably disgusting," and was glad when the event was over. Gaughan, 123; Robert E. Waterman and Thomas Rothrock, eds., "The Earle–Buchanan Letters of 1861–1876," *Arkansas Historical Quarterly* 33 (Summer, 1974), 139, hereafter cited as Waterman.

92. Turnbo was not alone in his belief that Hindman was a good commander. The men of Parsons's Missouri Brigade were particularly saddened at his departure and held a meeting on March 3, 1863, to record resolutions of support for the old commander, which they forwarded to the Little Rock *True Democrat* for publication (See Appendix A for a copy of the letter). Others also expressed dismay at Hindman's departure, with a Texan stationed at Pine Bluff providing probably the best description of Hindman's effect on the Trans-Mississippi. Captain Elijah Petty wrote:

> Genl Hindman has been relieved of his command here and ordered to report for duty at Vicksburg. Genl H though somewhat severe is one of the best officers that we have ever had here and to his efforts more than any other man do we owe for the safety of Arkansas. He has been one of the most slandered man in the Confederate Government and is worst sinned against than sinning. He is an able and efficient though unfortunate officer—I hope he may be properly appreciated.

Norman D. Brown, *Journey to Pleasant Hill: The Civil War Letters of Elijah P. Petty Walker's Texas Division C.S.A.* (San Antonio, TX, 1982), 150, hereafter cited as Brown; S. P. Burns, Letter (March 3, 1863), *True Democrat*. 150.

93. In his expanded version of these stories, Turnbo related that on one occasion Hindman gave his horse to a sick soldier, on the march to Little Rock, allowing him to ride "some distance," while the general walked along with the ailing soldier. In the other incident, General Hindman visited their camp in Little Rock one night and queried as to if they had prepared dinner. A soldier replied that they hadn't, and proceeded to invite the general to supper. Hindman waited as the men prepared the meal that consisted of "poor beef and poor cornbread." After eating the general departed and returned to his headquarters. Turnbo, 233.

94. General Price was assigned to duty in the Trans-Mississippi on February 27, 1863, crossed the Mississippi River on March 18, and arrived in Little Rock on March 25. When word reached the Missourians that Price had arrived in Little Rock "some of the boys went down to see him…He came out of the Anthony house and shook hands with them and they commenced hollowing for a speech. The General told them that he did not come to make a speech, but to 'fight.'" The following day the army had a "Grand Review" in honor of Generals Price and E. Kirby Smith. On March 30, General Holmes assigned Price to duty commanding Hindman's old division. *O.R.*, vol. 22, pt. 1:3; *O.R.*, vol. 22, vol. 22, pt. 2:808; Albert Castel, *General Sterling Price and the Civil War In The West* (Baton Rouge, 1968), 139; Lotspeich, March 25 and 26, 1863; Quesenberry, March 31, 1863.

95. James Camp Tappan was born in Franklin, Tennessee, on September 9, 1825. He was educated in New Hampshire, then at Yale University, and studied law in Vicksburg, Mississippi. After passing the bar, Tappan relocated to Helena, Arkansas, where he resided at the out break of the Civil War. Even

mander, and his brother Capt. Amos Tappan, as Adjutant-general.[96] The brigade soon learned to

Esteem Its New Commander

who was brave, courteous and competent. Capt. Beal Galttier [Gaither][97] of Co. D was promoted to major of the regiment, in consequence of the death of Maj. John Methwin.[98] Ben Griever, our Commissary Sergeant, was a jovial fellow, well liked, and always with a word of fun as he issued out rations. Sometimes the boys, however, would get on a high and bury his beef with the honors of war as being too poor to eat. Poor Ben died in Lead Hill, Ark., in 1872.

---

though he possessed no military training Tappan was elected colonel of the 13th Arkansas Infantry. He fought at Belmont, Missouri (November 7, 1861), moved his regiment east of the Mississippi and fought gallantly at Shiloh. After Bragg's Kentucky invasion, Tappan was promoted to brigadier general on November 5, 1862, and returned to the Trans-Mississippi Department. General Holmes assigned Tappan to command a brigade in Hindman's Division, on February 28, 1863. He fought at Pleasant Hill, Jenkins' Ferry, and was part of Price's 1864 Missouri Raid. After the war Tappan return to Helena to practice law. He died on March 19, 1906. See Appendix B for a complete biography. *O.R.*, vol. 22, pt. 2:793; Harrell, *Arkansas, Confederate Military History*, 416–417; Warner, *Generals in Gray*, 298, 299.

96. Little is known of Amos Tappan, save he was the brother of General Tappan and served on his staff as his Adjutant General. General Tappan did note that his brother served him well both during the Red River Campaign and the Camden Expedition, recording that Amos bore himself "with distinguished gallantry" while rendering "great assistance." *O.R.*, vol. 34, pt. 1:606, 802.

97. Beal Gaither was born on August 22, 1833, in Tennessee, and at the beginning of the Civil War was a farmer in Carroll County, Arkansas. He was mustered into the Confederate Service on February 15, 1862, and was elected captain of a cavalry company. He was captured in Carroll County, Missouri, on April 4, 1862, and sent to St. Louis where he was imprisoned at the Gratiot Street and Myrtle Street Prisons. He was exchanged on July 24. Meanwhile, on July 15, Gaither was elected captain of his reorganized company, which formed the core of what became Company D, 27th Arkansas Infantry. The newly reorganized unit was dismounted on July 29, and Gaither rejoined his command sometime after his exchange. On April 27, 1863, (Allardice has the date as April 21), Gaither was promoted to major, then to lieutenant colonel and completed his military service as the colonel of his regiment, having been promoted on November 27, 1863. Following the war, Gaither resided in Boone County, Arkansas, and moved to Oregon in 1887, where he was the Indian agent at the Siletz Reservation. Later he moved to Washington state, where he died on July 8, 1915, in Kalama. *O.R.*, vol. 34, pt. 2:933; *O.R.S.*, pt. 2, vol. 2:711, 713, 718; Allardice, *Confederate Colonels*, 156–157; Eakin, *Missouri Prisoners of War*, "Gaither, Beal" entry; National Archives, Record Group M317, Confederate Complied Service Records, 27th Arkansas Infantry; National Archives, Record Group 109, Confederate Muster Rolls, 27th Arkansas Infantry.

98. John W. Methwen or Methwin, a resident of Yellville, Arkansas, and County Clerk of Marion County, was the first lieutenant in Company A, 27th Arkansas Infantry. James R. Shaler appointed Methwen major of the regiment when the command was organized on July 31, 1862. The *Supplement to the Official Records* indicates that Methwen declined the promotion; however, later events would seem to show that he was the major of the regiment. Methwen was captured on October 17, during a night attack on a Union train near Mountain Home, Arkansas. He was sent to St. Louis where he died at Jefferson Barracks on December 8, 1863 (Turnbo has Methwen dying in Rolla, Missouri). According to Turnbo, Methwen "was a much respected citizen before war times and the soldiers held him in great esteem." *O.R.*, 13:318; *O.R.S.*, pt. 2, vol. 2:711; Eakin, *Confederate Records*, 5:178; Turnbo, 95, 122–123.

Silas C. Turnbo
Twenty-seventh Arkansas Infantry, Tappan's Brigade

[Editor Note: This article is continued in the next chapter: "The Summer of 1863: Battle of Helena, Campaign for Little Rock and Campaigning in Louisiana."]

* * * * * * *

Item: Winter quarters in Little Rock (January–April 1863), by Captain James H. McNamara, Confederate Engineer.
Published: December 5, 1885.

Missouri Confederates

The following was read by Capt. McNamara before the Southern Historical Society:

Winter quarters at Little Rock in 1863 was the graveyard of hundreds of our men who died of hardships endured on the retreat from Prairie Grove. They were buried in long trenches.

One of Gen. Parsons's first orders, after getting into camp, was to detail a captain and lieutenant and recruiting officers from each regiment to collect all the absentees of their commands and also to take by conscription all men between the ages of 18 and 40 years. Within certain described districts in Missouri the duty was a hazardous one, and was but indifferently successful.

January 22, 1863, found all the infantry and artillery, by special orders from Lieut.-Gen. Holmes, formed into Hindman's Division.[99] In this reorganization changes occurred which made Parsons's the Fourth Brigade instead of the First. Cols. [DeWitt C.] Hunter and [Josiah H.] Caldwell retired from command of their regiments and were succeeded by Cols. [Simon P.] Burns and [Levin M.] Lewis.[100] These with [Alexander C.] Picket's (Steen's old regiment) and [James D.] White's regiments of infantry, [L. A.] Pindall's Battalion of sharpshooters, Capt. [L. D.] Roberts' Company of cavalry and [Charles B.] Tilden's Battery of light artillery, composed the brigade.[101]

---

99. On January 22, 1863, General T. H. Holmes held "a council of war," according to one Missourian. The following day the infantry of Hindman's First Corps, Trans-Mississippi Army was reorganized forming five brigades and was known as Hindman's Division. The brigades were commanded by Daniel M. Frost, Dandridge McRae, Robert G. Shaver, James F. Fagan, and Mosby M. Parsons. On February 7, 1863, Frost's Brigade was detached from the division, being ordered to duty first at White's Bluff, on the Arkansas River, and finally to Fort Pleasant on February 20, at Day's Bluff, near Pine Bluff, where they would be quartered on and off until the 1863 Campaign for Little Rock. *O.R.*, vol. 22, pt. 2:781; Banasik, *Serving With Honor*, 53, 55; Letter (January 23, 1863), Hindman to Anderson, Copy Letter Book No. 2; Circular (January 24, 1863), Copy Letter Book No. 2; Lotspeich, January 22, 1863.

100. See Appendix B for a complete biography and Appendix C for Lewis's connection with the 16th Missouri Infantry and Parsons's Missouri Brigade.

101. When the various regiments of Parsons's Missouri Infantry Brigade received their official designation they were known as:

Roberts Cavalry Company (General Parsons's Escort, Company I, 4th Missouri Cavalry)
10th Missouri Infantry (Steen's, Picket's or Moore's)
11th Missouri (7th Missouri, Hunter's, Gunter's, or Burn's)
12th Missouri (9th Missouri, White's or Ponder's)
16th Missouri (8th Missouri, Jackman's, Caldwell's, or Lewis')
9th Battalion Missouri Sharpshooters (Pindall's)
3rd Missouri Field Artillery (Gorham's, Tilden's, Leseuer's)

The discipline of this camp was admirable. Each morning at "guard-mounting," the soldier whose arms and equipments were in the best order, and whose person and clothing were the cleanest, and whose appearance was the most soldier like, was awarded by being relieved of duty for the day, and received a pass to Little Rock. The daily contests in drill, and the Friday drills of the commissioned officers, had a most beneficial effect. They were witnessed by crowds of men and officers. Gen. Parsons always made it a point to be present on those occasions. Col. Joseph Kelly, the father, in drill and discipline of every officer and private in the brigade, conducted this impromptu school of the soldier which resulted in bringing "drill" in the Fourth Brigade to a state of perfection.

Life at Headquarters

was as pleasant as could possibly be in camp. All of the general's military family were social, and some of them convivial souls. "Muggins"[102] was the favorite game every night, after the labors of the day, because all could take a hand in it. And the great enjoyment was to see either the general, Col. Kelly or Col. [Austin M.] Standish[103] "mugginsed." It was not always though, that some of the staff confined themselves to "muggins." Parsons was strongly opposed to gambling in his command. He once caught some of his officers

Theophilus H. Holmes

NOTE: Alternate names for the various units are listed in parentheses
See Appendix C for the organizational information on the units that composed Parsons's Brigade, including biographies of the principle regimental, battalion and battery commanders. *O.R.*, vol. 34, pt. 2:933; Joseph H. Crute, *Units of the Confederate States Army* (Midlothian, VA, 1987), 202–205, 207; National Archives, Record Group 109, Confederate Muster Rolls, 10th, 11th, 12th and 16th Missouri Infantries, 9th Battalion Missouri Sharpshooters, and 3rd Missouri Battery.

102. Muggins: "A variation of the game dominoes," though in this case it was probably a "card game in which players try to match exposed cards." Jean L. McKechnie, *Webster's New Universal Unabridged Dictionary Deluxe Second Edition* (New York, 1979), 1179.

103. Austin M. Standish was the brother-in-law of General Mosby M. Parsons. A civil engineer by profession, Standish helped "locate the first railroads constructed in Missouri." Standish was a "protestant Irishman," and he was appointed a colonel and Adjutant General of Parsons's 6th Division, MSG on June 12, 1861. He later transferred to the Confederate Service, remaining on Parsons's staff as his Adjutant General and served throughout the war. He was captured, but later escaped, at Wilson's Creek on August 10, 1861. Standish was praised for his actions at the Battle of Prairie Grove and during the Red River Campaign of 1864. Following the war, he left for Mexico, with General Parsons, and was murdered in the early morning hours of August 16, 1865, with Parsons, near the town of China, Mexico. *O.R.*, vol. 34, pt. 1:603; *O.R.*, vol. 53:434, 461; Flanagan, 58–59; R. H. Musser, "Murder of Gen. Parsons," *The Daily Missouri Republican* (St. Louis, MO), January 23, 1886; Peterson, 172.

in camp on Grand Prairie, playing poker by moonlight in a hollow of the prairie, and lectured them severely, promising to put them under arrest if he ever again found them at such work. Many times when the general was supposed to be asleep in his tent, would he be out questioning the sentries on the subject. One such occasion, long after midnight, he approached Dr. [Caleb Dorsey] Baer's[104] tent in which were Maj. [John B.] Ruthven,[105] Capt. [A. F.] Cake[106], Lieut. Morrison[107]

---

104. Caleb Dorsey Baer was born in Maryland in about 1828, moved to Missouri, and at the beginning of the Civil War was living near Dover, Lafayette County. He was appointed the Regimental Surgeon, 2nd Infantry Regiment, 8th Division, MSG on July 6, 1861. Baer continued in the service, serving under General M. M. Parsons and later joined the Confederate Service as surgeon of the 12th Missouri Infantry (CSA). With the organization of the 1st Corps, Trans-Mississippi Army, Baer was appointed the chief surgeon of the 3rd Division, under General Parsons a position he would hold throughout the remainder of the war. Following the Battle of Helena, Arkansas, Baer was left behind with the Confederate wounded in Helena and died of an apparent heart attack on August 30, 1863. *O.R.*, vol. 22, pt. 1:423; Carolyn O. Bartels, *The Forgotten Men Missouri State Guard* (Shawnee Mission, KS, 1995), 9, hereafter cited as Bartels, *Forgotten Men*; Hale, 11; Letter (November 16, 1862), Baer, etc. to Newton, Miscellaneous Correspondence, Peter W. Alexander Collection, Columbia University (New York), hereafter cited as Miscellaneous Correspondence; Letter (October 7, 1862), Parsons to Hindman, Parsons's Letters, Peter W. Alexander Collection, Columbia University (New York), hereafter cited as Parsons Letters; Peterson, 222; Cythia Dehaven Pitcock and Bill J. Gurly, *I Acted Out of Principle: The Civil War Diary of Dr. William M. McPheeters, Confederate Surgeon in the Trans-Mississippi* (Fayetteville, AR, 2002), 39, 344 n. 11, hereafter cited as Pitcock.
105. John Ruthven joined the MSG early in the war and served under General Mosby M. Parsons as his Brigade Commissary. He was present at both the Battles of Prairie Grove and Helena, Arkansas after which his name disappears from all known records. *O.R.*, vol. 22, pt. 1:423; *O.R.*, 53:459; Letter (October 7, 1862), Parsons Letters; National Archives, Record Group 109, chapter VIII, vol. 394, Parsons's Division.
106. Captain Amos F. Cake was born in December 1837, in Deerfield, New Jersey, and later moved to Missouri, where he was a resident of Jefferson City at the beginning of the war. During the Civil War, he was elected captain of Company C, 9th Battalion of Missouri Sharpshooters (CSA), also known as Pindall's Sharpshooters, on November 29, 1862. He was wounded at Helena, on July 4, 1863, recovered and later he became an Aid-de-Camp to Sterling Price. Cake survived the war and lived for a time in Shreveport, Louisiana, dying at the home of his brother in Lincoln County, Missouri, in February 1870. He was buried next to his wife in Howard County, Missouri. *O.R.S.*, pt. 2, vol. 38:594; Eakin & Hale, 57; National Archives, Record Group 109, Confederate Muster Rolls, 9th Battalion Missouri Sharpshooters; National Archives, Record Group M322 (roll no. 149), Confederate Compiled Service Records, 9th Battalion Missouri Sharpshooters; Pitcock, 344 n. 9.
107. This was probably Samuel M. Morrison. Morrison was born about 1839, in Fayette, Howard County, Missouri, and was living in Jefferson City at the beginning of the Civil War. He was elected second lieutenant of Company C, 1st Infantry Regiment, 3rd Division, MSG on July 2, 1861. Morrison was wounded at the Battle of Wilson's Creek on August 10, 1861, but recovered and joined the MSG Quartermaster Department. In the latter part of 1862, Morrison joined the Confederate Service as a first lieutenant and adjutant in Pindall's Sharpshooters, to rank from December 15, 1862. He later served as an Assistant Adjutant General in Parsons's Brigade, and on December 14, 1864, was appointed the captain, commanding the newly organized Company F of Pindall's command. On June 7, 1865, he was paroled at Shreveport, Louisiana, where he settled. Later, Morrison became the editor of the *Daily Standard* newspaper of Shreveport. *O.R.*, vol. 34, pt. 1:815; Carolyn O. Bartels, *The Bravest of the Brave Pindall's 9th Missouri Battalion of Sharpshooters* (Independence, MO, 2001), 86, hereafter cited as Bartels, *Bravest of the Brave*; Bartels, *Forgotten Men*, 263; Carolyn O. Bartels, *Trans-Mississippi Men at War, Volume I: Missouri C.S.A.* (Independence, MO. 1998), 25–26, hereafter cited as Bartels, *Trans-Mississippi Men*; Eakin, *Confederate Records*, 6: 21; Moore, Skaggs Collec-

and Jim Bannerman,[108] playing a game of "force blind." The tent door was closed with a "fly" and they went their "betters" in low voices. The major had drawn "three kings" and "a pair" and had just "gone his $50 better," when a when a deep slow voice at the door said, "You hold a good hand, major!" and the general stepped into the light of the tallow candle. There was slight coughing, shuffling of feet and redding of faces at the appearance of the unwelcome visitor. But the veteran major spoke up with, "This is 'Boston'[109] general." "That pile over at your elbow, sir, doesn't look like it. I never saw 'Boston' played with such results," retorted the general. His shaggy eyebrows met; he left the tent biting his mustache. The game was finished some other time.

A Pathetic Incident

One day, in this encampment, the widow of Lieut.-Col. Chappel[110], who was killed in a charge at Prairie Grove, accompanied by another lady on horseback

tion; *History of Howard and Cooper Counties, Missouri, Written and Complied From the Most Authentic Official and Private Sources, Etc.* (St. Louis, 1883), 461–462; Peterson, 115; Schnetzer, *More Forgotten Men*, 168; Diary of James T. Wallace (1862–1865), Manuscript Department (Collection #3059), Southern Historical Collection, University of North Carolina (Chapel Hill, NC), June 7, 1863 and December 15, 1864, hereafter cited as Wallace dairy.

108. James P. (or H.) Bannerman was born November 20, 1840, in Bradford, Ontario, Canada, and moved to Jefferson City, Missouri, in 1850. He joined the Governor's Guards, Missouri Militia, in 1857, and was captured at Camp Jackson in May 1861. Following his release in June 1861, he joined the staff of the 6th Division, MSG, and later the Confederate Service. Bannerman served primarily in the Quartermaster Department and was present at the Battles of Carthage and Pea Ridge while in the MSG. While in the CSA service he fought at Pleasant Hill in Louisiana and in the Arkansas Battles of Marks Mill and Jenkins' Ferry. Surviving the war, Bannerman moved to St. Louis in 1866, and with a partner, formed the Meyer-Bannerman Company "one the world's largest manufacturers of saddlery and harness." In post-war St. Louis, Bannerman was elected to several local political positions, but lost his bid for mayor in 1893. He was also the president of a local Confederate association that built the Confederate Soldiers Home in Higginsville, Missouri. Bannerman was found dead in his home on August 10, 1911—an apparent suicide—and was buried in Bellefontaine Cemetery in St. Louis. Ankesheiln, *Guardsman*, 23–24; Hale, 15.

109. "Boston" was a card game, using two decks of cards, that was associated with the Siege of Boston, Massachusetts (1775–1776). David B. Guralnik, ed., *Second College Edition Webster's New World Dictionary of the American Language* (New York, 1972), 165.

110. Lieutenant Colonel William C. Chappel was a private in the St. Louis Legion during the Mexican War. He joined the 1st Division, MSG in July 1861, and became an aide-de-camp to General M. Jeff Thompson. He was wounded at Fredericktown, Missouri, on October 21, 1861, but recovered sufficiently to assist in the capture of the river transport *Platte Valley* on November 18, 1861, at Price's Landing, Missouri. Thompson's command was at the Battle of Memphis (June 6, 1862) and there is every reason to believe that Chappell, as Thompson's aide, was also present. Chappell departed Thompson's staff in June 1862, while at Grenada, Mississippi. He returned to Missouri during the summer of 1862, and helped organize Steen's Missouri Regiment (10th Missouri Infantry), in which he was second in command. On December 7, 1862, Chappell was killed at the Battle of Prairie Grove, in the same charge that felled his commander Colonel A. E. Steen. *O.R.*, vol. 3:367, 368; *O.R.*, Series 2, vol. 1:137; Banasik, *Embattled Arkansas*, 449; Peterson, 43; Donal J. Stanton, Goodwin F. Berquist, and Paul C. Bowers, eds., *The Civil War Reminiscences of General M. Jeff Thompson* (Dayton, OH, 1988), 125, 126, 165.

visited headquarters, expressing a desire to see her husband's regiment, before she left the country. Parsons ordered the old regiment to assemble on the color-line; and gallantly mounting his black charger, escorted the ladies to the regiment. Mrs. Chappel sobbed bitterly when she was saluted by the veterans. Once before at Van Buren, immediately after the battle, this regiment was assembled to receive the wife and child of its gallant commander, Steen.[111]

Now and then on a warm sunny day, bright faces would appear at the head-quarters and for a wile make the general forget to bite his mustache, thinking of the next "move;" Col. Standish, his horse and those "infernal orders;" Col. Edwards, his Mexican spurs and his "widow." (It is proper, that I should explain that the "widow" was his little black mare.) Dr. Baer, the last joke and his last patient; Col. [Thomas] Monroe,[112] "the nigger teamsters." But those sunny faces would have to have wings attached to their shoulders—as well as their hats—before they could make Col. Kelly forget the daily battalion drill; or Maj. Ruthven the six days rations ahead.

The soldier who never forget his duty deserves great praise, and the soldier who forgets a great deal, in the presence of a pretty woman in camp, deserves no censure.

The smallest and prettiest of these fair visitants—the wife of a Missouri colonel, and I believe a St. Louis lady—was the author of the following address, which Gen. Hindman in compliment to "his Missouri comrades," he said, had printed and distributed in Parsons's Brigade:

> To the Missouri Army.
> Brothers—brave brothers; never despair—
> Tokens are brightening—the future is fair;
> Shouts of the victor, on the valley and plain,
> Tells that the hordes of the tyrant are slain,
> Virginia has borne down the insolent foe,
> His capital trembles, expecting the blow;
> Kentucky has spoken from mountain and glen,
> And marshalled the hosts of her true-hearted men.
> And bold Tennessee, with the sword at her breast,
> Still shouts the defiance of all the brave West.
> The storms may rage and the lightening be hurried.

111. See Appendix A for the last known letter that Colonel A. E. Steen wrote to a cousin, who was living in Van Buren, Arkansas.
112. This was probably Thomas Monroe, who was born in Tennessee in about 1820, and a lawyer by profession. As a resident of Morgan County, Missouri, he was elected the Circuit and County Clerk in 1842, and in 1860, ran for the State Senate. With the beginning of the Civil War, M. M. Parsons appointed him as Assistant Division Quartermaster of the 6th Division, MSG on May 20, 1861. He later transferred to the Confederate Service, as a major and Parsons's Brigade Quartermaster and later as his Division Quartermaster. O.R., vol. 22, pt.1:422; O.R., vol. 22, pt. 2:1050–1051; O.R., vol 34, pt. 1:603; Bartels, Forgotten Men, 259; History of Cole, Moniteau, Morgan, Benton, Miller, Maries and Osage Counties, Missouri, Etc. (Chicago, 1886), 336, 446, 984; Peterson, 173; Pitcock, 355.

But the Southerners, united, can challenge the world!
While our war-cry is "Freedom," our trust is in God!
The tyrant can never enslave our free sod.
Brothers, dear brothers, never despair.
The signs of deliverance beam bright in the air.
Turn the gloom that the present may fling;
Think of the blessings the future must bring.
We know that the trials are hard to be borne.
We think of your toils and privations, and mourn;
But oh, when the battle for freedom shall end
And you stand 'mid the radiance its glory shall lead—
When you think thro' your sufferings the victory has won
And feel that your duty so nobly was done—
That Missouri, borne down by a conqueror's might,
Has rived her fetters and led in the fight—
That through insult and shame you stood firm by her side;
Ah, well may your hearts swell with patriot's pride,
For no name in the long, bloody annals shall shine
With effulgence more growing or lasting than thine.
Our Price—with what reverences we write the dear name—
The heart of the South throbs with pride of his fame.
Frost, Bowen and Parsons, Green, Burbridge and Hull,
Clark, Little, McDonald, the list is too full[113]
To stamp all the stars, save in infinite space,
And their splendor no future can ever erase.
Brothers, farewell, till the good time shall come,
When all shall be welcomed to freedom and his home.
Think of that meeting and strike down the foe;
Think of that meeting and double the blow;
And remember, amid all darkness and gloom,
That friends, warm and faithful, are praying at home.
Friends who will suffer in all of your pain—
Friends who will aid you, in spite of their chains.
A Sister

How Calmly, Now,

veterans can listen to the spirited words of our talented "Sister," but in the days it was written, it was a fire-brand thrown among the young soldiers. About the middle of February, 1863, Parsons made application at district headquarters to

---

113. The writer was referring to D. M. Frost, John Bowen, M. M Parsons, Martin Green, John Q. Burbridge, John B. Clark, Sr., Henry Little, and Emmett MacDonald. There was no "Hull" of note that could be discerned from the various sources I searched.

take his own and Hawthorn's Arkansas Brigade [114]and attack Helena, where it was reported that there was a large quantity of stores and a light garrison. His application was refused. He next endeavored to mount his brigade and make a raid into Missouri.[115] In this he was also unsuccessful. He used to say that the Missourians were kept making "clearing" in Arkansas.

Unfavorable reports from Vicksburg and east of the Mississippi, together with the inactivity of the troops, spread a gloom over the army.[116]

---

114. On February 28, 1863, "Hawthorn's Brigade" was still commanded by General James F. Fagan and consisted of the 22nd, 29th, 34th and Hawthorn's Arkansas Infantry Regiments, with Blocher's Arkansas Battery. The brigade would not become Hawthorn's until February 1864. Alexander Travis Hawthorn was born on January 10, 1825, in Alabama. He was educated at Mercer University in Macon, Georgia, and studied law at Yale University. Relocating to Camden, Arkansas, in the late 1840s, Hawthorn established a law practice. At the beginning of the Civil War, he helped organize the 6th Arkansas Infantry in 1861, of which he was elected the lieutenant colonel on June 7. As colonel (appointed October 15, 1861) of the 6th, he fought at Shiloh in April 1862. After the battle he failed to be reelected colonel of his regiment and returned to Arkansas. In Arkansas, General Hindman appointed Hawthorn a major and assigned him to command a battalion of Arkansas infantry on October 9, 1862. On November 3, 1862, Hindman appointed Hawthorn a colonel, commanding an Arkansas regiment known as "Hawthorn's Regiment." Hawthorn led his regiment at Prairie Grove and Helena and later commanded a brigade as a brigadier general (February 18, 1864) during the Camden and Red River Expeditions of 1864. Following the war, Hawthorn moved to Brazil and did not return to the United States until 1874, locating first at Atlanta, Georgia, where he was a businessman. He was ordained a Baptist minister in 1880 and moved to Dallas, Texas, a short time later, where he died on May 31, 1899. *O.R.*, vol. 22, pt. 1:903; *O.R.*, vol. 22, pt. 2:781, 793; *O.R.S.*, pt. 2, vol. 2:383, 389; Letter, Newton to Brooks (November 3, 1862), Copy Letter Book No. 1, 310; Special Orders No. 18 (October 19, 1862) and No. 30 (November 3, 1862), Special Order Book No. 1; Faust, 352–353; Sifakis, *Who Was Who in the Confederacy*, 123; Warner, *Generals in Gray*, 129, 130.

115. The rumor of Parsons's proposed movement came to camp on March 24, 1863. Quesenberry, March 24, 1863.

116. If there was any great gloom in the army, it was not related to events from the east side of the Mississippi River. One Missourian, from Parsons's Brigade noted on February 18: "Nothing new today only that prospects are brightening for the South. At least everything says so." All attempts by Grant to flank or take Vicksburg from October 1862, to March 31, 1863, had proven unsuccessful, with the exception of the taking of Arkansas Post. I suspect that the gloom that the writer mentioned was linked more to the condition of the army, than war news. When the command first arrived in Little Rock it was in a sad condition as previously described. By mid-February, conditions were little improved, causing one surgeon to record that "the troops here would be in a bad fix if the enemy were to come. The mules could barely pull the wagons away. I doubt whether they could even do that." But despite the problems the "spirit" of the troops was noted as "good." By March 1863 things had improved significantly, causing the same surgeon to write: "The health of the troops is rapidly improving. If the enemy should come, they could manage to march away without the necessity of surrendering the spot." An Arkansas captain supported the surgeon's comments, noting that "the health of the troops is improving, and we all seem to have become more spirited." By April 9, 1863, the hospital contained only seventy-five patients—the army had been mended. Though morale had been down following the retreat to Little Rock, Missourians as a group seemed to be less affected by any reversals, leading one to record that the men would be "willing to fight till death" to again secure their home state. They were anxious to move north, and with General Price's return, they had every reason to expect that they would. Boatner, 871–873; Gaughan, 112, 124, 132; Letters (February 13, 1863), McRae to Wife, Samuel Spotts Wassell Collection, Arkansas History Commission, hereafter cited as McRae Letters; Lotspeich, February 18 and 26, March 19 and 20, 1863; Quesenberry, February 27, 1863; Waterman, 129.

On the 4th of March Gen. Hindman relinquished the command of his division. He was ordered east of the Mississippi. Gen. D. M. Frost[117] succeeded him. The arrival of Lieut. Gen. E. Kirby Smith[118] on the 18th of March to take command of the department, followed on the 25th by Maj.-Gen. Sterling Price, at once dispelled the gloom that had settled over Hindman's Division. Price's presence filled the camps of the Missouri troops with the wildest joy.

On the 26th the division was reviewed by Gens. Smith, Holmes and Price. The display made was very impressive. The troops appeared in excellent condition.

After the review Parsons marched his brigade into Little Rock, forming in front of the Anthony House[119] to welcome "Old Pap." Gen Price made a short speech, thanking them heartily, saying, he "came to them to fight, not to make speeches."[120]

---

117. Daniel M. Frost was born on August 9, 1823, in New York, graduated from West Point (number 4 of 25) in 1844, served in the Mexican War, being breveted a first lieutenant "for gallantry and meritorious conduct in the Battle of Cerro Gordo, Mexico." On May 31, 1853, Frost resigned from the army and moved to St. Louis. At the beginning of the Civil War, Frost ran a "planing mill," in St. Louis, and was a general in the Missouri State Militia. He was captured at Camp Jackson, Missouri, on May 10, 1861, and was exchanged in November 1861. As a general in the MSG, Frost was at the Battle of Pea Ridge in March 1862, and was promoted to a Confederate brigadier generalship in October 1862, effective March 3. At the Battle of Prairie Grove, Frost commanded a Confederate division, and Price's infantry at Little Rock in September 1863, after which he submitted his resignation and escorted his wife to Canada via Mexico. Unfortunately, Frost's resignation was never accepted and he was listed as a deserter, the only Confederate general officer so listed at the end of the war. Frost later returned to St. Louis and became a farmer. He died on October 29, 1900, and was buried in St. Louis. For additional information on Frost see Banasik, *Missouri Brothers in Gray*, 138; Boatner, 318; Heitman, 1:438; Warner, *Generals in Gray*, 94–95.
118. The Confederate War Department assigned Edmund Kirby Smith to command the Southwestern Army, embracing Louisiana and Texas, on January 14, 1863. Later, the command was expanded on February 9 to include all troops west of the Mississippi River. Smith assumed his new post on March 7, 1863, and eleven days later was appointed the commander of the Trans-Mississippi Department. For a biography and photo see Banasik, *Missouri Brothers in Gray*, 152–153; *O.R.*, vol. 22, pt. 1:3; Harrell, *Arkansas, Confederate Military History*, 173.
119. The Anthony House was the leading hotel in Little Rock, located on Markham Street about two blocks from the State House and from the Arkansas River. It was the scene of frequent military balls and political meetings. During the Civil War it served as a local boarding house. One Confederate resident of the house wrote of it: "They serve the coffee in little pitchers, and have little plates to drink it out of. It is the nearest played out of any house I have seen. The desert generally consists of a piece of ginger cake done up in gravy, and one servant to every eighteen boarders. I have counted them." Gaughan, 133–134; Margaret Ross, *Arkansas Gazette: The Early Years 1819–1866* (Little Rock, AR, 1969), 12, 214, 283, hereafter cited as Ross.
120. Another soldier present at the event recorded in his diary what occurred at the Anthony house after they arrived. C. B. Lotspeich wrote:
Gen. Parsons got up and told the old chief that we had come to pay him a compliment, which was due him and the c—— and c——. After which Gen Price got up and thanked us for the compliment which we had bestowed upon him. He [talked about] the troop that had followed him to the other side of the Mississippi a great deal and bragged upon the name they bore in these states and said as fighting men, the world could not produce better ones. He hopes that we would be as careful of our reputations as his troop on the other side of the river. He at length said that he did not get up to make a speech for the time of speech making was past and that if we were "true grit" he would not leave here until the crisis was past at Vicksburg and the troops on the other side of the river would have time to arrive here. He

Price Takes Command.

It was not till April 1 that Gen. Price, in the following order, took command of the division:

Headquarters Price's Division, Little Rock, April 1, 1863—

(General Order No. 1.)

1. In compliance with orders from District Headquarters the undersigned assumes command of the division, lately commanded by Brig.-Gen. Frost. The occasions affords him an opportunity of which he gladly avails himself, to express the gratification with which he returned to the department; and the proud satisfaction which he places himself at the head of the troops— the excellence of whose drill and discipline he has himself witnessed, and whose courage, constancy and endurance have become historical.

(signed)Sterling Price,
Major-General Commanding Division.
Official: Maclean, A.A.G.

Gen. Price had brought with him to the Department some beautiful battle flags, presented him by the ladies of New Orleans, a red cross on a white field. He had them distributed to the Missouri troops. The troops of Parsons's Brigade refused to use them, they alleging that they were Catholic flags. Gen. Price learning of their objection to the flags came over to Gen. Parsons's quarters and both rode out to the color line, where the troops were assembled. After they had been soundly lectured by Gen. Price—he telling them that the colors were those of the crusaders and Missourians were the crusaders of this age. After that the flags were used.[121]

April the 21st Parsons's Brigade was reviewed by Gens. Holmes and Price, who expressed themselves to the highest sense of satisfaction at the appearance and spirit of the troops. A General Order from Gen. Parsons announced to the troops the satisfaction of the District and Division Commander.[122]

The excitement of the review had scarcely died away when marching orders came to the brigade, Gen. Parsons had all his sick sent to St. John's Hospital in Little Rock where they were well cared for.[123]

On the 27th of April winter quarters were broken up and the brigade marched

---

closed by again thanking us for our compliment. After he sat down, his band played a beautiful hymn after which we marched to quarters." Lotspeich, March 26, 1863.

121. The flag presentation occurred on the morning of April 18, 1863, following yet another grand review of the army. Ibid., April 18, 1863.

122. Three days after the grand review General Holmes and Price inspected the "guns and camp" of Parsons's Brigade at 1:00 p.m.. The inspection "was very satisfactory" according to the commander of Company H, 11th Missouri Infantry (CSA). The 16th was "thought very well" of according to another in that command. Ibid., April 21, 1863; Quesenberry, April 21, 1863.

123. St. John's College was founded by the Masonic order as a military school in 1859. When the war began the college closed and became a military hospital. After the war, the college reverted back to a military school. Ferguson, 97, 136, 167.

across the river and pitched tents in "Camp Anderson," three miles from Little Rock, where it remained in daily anticipation of a move till the 31st of May.[124]

Small-Pox.

Whilst in this camp small-pox broke out in the brigade which caused some alarm. But by the great precaution and skill of our surgeons it was confined to the regiment in which it appeared.

It was in this camp that news of [Joseph] Hooker's defeat by [Robert E.] Lee, the shooting of Gen. Van Dorn by Dr. [George B.] Peterson, and the depressing intelligence of the death of Stonewall Jackson had reached us.[125] Also came gloomy news from Dick Taylor in the District of Louisiana.[126]

---

124. On April 26, 1863, Parsons's Brigade was paid and the following day they crossed to the north side of the Arkansas River and established themselves at Camp Anderson: "a very pleasant camp" with plenty of good water, that was "much nicer" than their previous one. In the meantime, the remaining elements of Price's Division also departed winter quarters. McRea's Brigade crossed the Arkansas River on May 4 and joined the Missourians in preparations for an anticipated movement northward. They were followed by Fagan's Brigade which crossed on May 7. Tilden's Battery, which was temporarily assigned to the Artillery Brigade, remained on the south side of the Arkansas and did not rejoin Parsons's command until May 26. Tappan's Arkansas Brigade did not cross the Arkansas River, but instead, moved south five miles on the Arkadelphia road, on May 12, encamping at "Camp Texas," where they remained until the summer campaign began. *O.R.*, vol. 22, pt 2:849; *O.R.S.*, pt. 2, vol. 38:622, 642; Gaughan, 135; Hoskin, May 5 and 26, 1863; Lotspeich, April 27, 1863; Quesenberry, April 26–27, 1863; Turnbo, 230–231.

125. The writer was referring to the Chancellorsville Campaign in Virginia, which was conducted between April 27–May 8, 1863. Joseph Hooker commanded the Federals while Robert E. Lee led the Confederates. The most prominent engagements were the Battles of Chancellorsville (May 1–3), Second Fredericksburg or Marye's Heights (May 3), Salem Church (May 3) and Banks Ford (May 4). The Federals lost 1,694 killed, 9,672 wounded, and 5,938 captured; 17,304 total. The Confederates lost 1,724 killed, 9,233 wounded and 2,503 missing; 13,460 total. Stonewall Jackson was wounded on May 2 by his own men while scouting forward and died on May 10 from his wounds. Stephen W. Sears, *Chancellorsville* (Boston, 1996), 293–295, 448, 492, 501. Earl Van Dorn was killed on May 8, 1863 at Spring Hill, Tennessee by Dr. George B. Peters, a respected physician and previously a Tennessee State Senator, who accused Van Dorn of sexual improprieties with his wife. See Van Dorn's biography and photo in Banasik, *Missouri Brothers in Gray*, 157, 159–160; Sifakis, *Who Was Who in the Confederacy*, 288–289; "The Van Dorn Tragedy," *Tri-Weekly Telegraph*, June 13, 1863.

126. Richard Taylor was born on January 17, 1826, near Louisville, Kentucky. His father was President Zachary Taylor. Educated in France, then at Harvard University, Taylor graduated from Yale University in 1845. He served as his father's secretary during the Mexican War, and in 1850, following his father's death, he inherited the family plantation in Louisiana. Taylor was elected to the Louisiana Senate in 1855, a position he held until the outbreak of the Civil War. Elected colonel of the 9th Louisiana Infantry, Taylor led the command in Virginia, and though lacking military experience he was appointed a brigadier general in October 1861, in part because his brother-in-law was Jefferson Davis. Taylor proved to be a natural leader, serving successfully during Stonewall Jackson's Valley Campaign of 1862. He was promoted to major general in July 1862, and was transferred to Louisiana to command the District of Louisiana. He successfully parried Union efforts in Louisiana during 1863, despite the writer's comments to the contrary, and achieved his greatest success in 1864, by defeating Nathaniel Banks's Red River Campaign. Because of a disagreement with his superior, General E. Kirby Smith, Taylor left the Trans-Mississippi and assumed command of the Department of Alabama and Mississippi in July 1864. He was appointed a lieutenant general, to rank from April 8, 1864, mak-

The brigade enjoyed the delightful summer weather in this camp. And next to that enjoyed, was the "cleaning out" of an unlucky sutler, who established his whiskey and tobacco quarters in sight of camp.[127] [To be continued]
Editor Note: The rest of this article will be presented in the Chapter 3.

* * * * * * *

ing him one of only three non-West Pointers to hold the rank in the Confederacy. Taylor completed his military service east of the Mississippi River. He died unexpectedly in 1879, at age fifty-three, while visiting a friend in New York City. *O.R.*, vol. 13:877; Boatner, 827–828; T. Michael Parrish, "Richard Taylor," in *Confederate General*, 6:29–31; Warner, *Generals in Gray*, 299–300.
127. Parsons's Brigade, with McRea's and Fagan's Brigades, would remain in Camp Anderson until May 31, when they would start their movement northward, that would eventually result in the Battle of Helena, in east Arkansas on July 4, 1863. McNamara's article will continue in the next chapter. *O.R.S.*, pt. 2, vol. 38:600, 615, 631; Hoskin, May 31, 1863; Lotspeich, May 31, 1863.

Chapter 2

Spring–Summer 1863 (May–August 1863):

Campaigning in Louisiana

Item: Campaigning in Louisiana with Walker's Texas Division (continued from previous chapter: "Sickness in Little Rock During the Winter of 1863"), by Silas C. Turnbo, 27th Arkansas Infantry.[1]
Published: June 12, 1886

Twenty-Seventh Arkansas Infantry

Pro Tem, Taney Co., Mo. June 3
Editor *Republican*

On the 12th of May our regiment broke camp and was soon ordered on detached service with Gen. Walker's Texas Division in Louisiana.[2] Thus we did not take part in the disastrous assault on Helena.[3] We were then running the enemy down near the Mississippi, but the great trouble was that we generally led the way with the Feds after us. The spring was the most backward ever known. Up to the

---

1. This version of the 27th's exploits in Louisiana is a shortened version of Turnbo's extensive history of the 27th Arkansas Regiment. Turnbo, 230–238, 246–283.
2. John G. Walker was born in Missouri on July 22, 1822, attended school in St. Louis and received an appointment from President Polk to a lieutenancy in the U.S. Army in 1846. He served in the Mexican War and resigned his commission in July 1861. During the Civil War, Walker served in Virginia and North Carolina, where he earned his promotion to major general on November 8, 1862, and then transferred to the Trans-Mississippi. General Holmes assigned Walker to command of a Texas division on December 23, 1862, which he led throughout the Red River and Camden Campaigns. Walker replaced General Richard Taylor as commander of the District of Western Louisiana in June 1864 and completed his Civil War service commanding the District of Texas, New Mexico, and Arizona. Following the war Walker moved briefly to Mexico and later served as a diplomat in South America. He died on July 20, 1893, in Washington, D.C. See Appendix B for a complete biography; also, see Appendix C for the Organization of Walker's Texas Division. *O.R.*, vol. 34, pt. 1:7; Joseph Palmer Blessington, *The Campaigns of Walker's Texas Division* (New York, 1875), 65, 72, hereafter cited as Blessington; Brown, 188 (n. 79); Warner, *Generals in Gray*, 224, 319–320.
3. General Holmes attacked Helena on July 4, 1863, the same day Vicksburg surrendered and a day after the Battle of Gettysburg. Holmes's command consisted of 7,646 men from Price's, Marmaduke's, and L. Marsh Walker's divisions. The Confederates lost 173 killed, 645 wounded, and 772 missing or captured; total 1590 (Note: A corrected total will show 1594 total losses, with 8,146 effectives. See Appendix C.). The Federal forces were well prepared for the attack, losing only 57 killed 146 wounded and 36 missing or captured; total of 239. Detailed accounts of the battle will follow later in this chapter. *O.R.*, vol. 22, pt. 1:391, 411, 412; Boatner, 331–340, 877.

middle of May vegetation on the trees at Little Rock was not fully developed. The cold storms delayed the movements of troops, but after this time the weather grew pleasant. Our regiment was intended to harass outlying parties of Grant's army operating against Vicksburg.[4] The year 1863, however, was a gloomy one in our department. It seemed that no matter what fatigue in march or bravery in battle the Confederates displayed they were doomed to nothing but defeat.[5] We started May 18 for Camden, going only eight miles the first day.[6] We passed Benton, Saline County, the second day, and on the 21st camped on a pine ridge where there was no water to cook with. At Tulip a lot of Col. Grinstead's men were furloughed to go home.[7] We passed to Princeton on the 23rd, and the ladies of the town lined the

---

4. On April 19, even as Banks's Western Louisiana Campaign was moving forward, Kirby Smith cautioned General Holmes, "that if the enemy should reach Monroe they may by steamers make a raid to destroy the depot at Camden." Smith further "desired" that if Holmes should "receive information of the advance of the enemy on Monroe," he should "send a portion of...[his] force to protect that depot." With Monroe threatened, Holmes dispatched Tappan's Brigade on May 18 to march to Camden to protect the depot. By June 5, with Monroe now secure, Tappan's Brigade was ordered forward from Camden, to be temporarily assigned to General Taylor, then to operate with Walker's Division. O.R., 15:1046, 1054; O.R., vol. 22, pt. 2:856–857.

5. The year 1863 was truly a gloomy one for the Confederate fortunes throughout the various battle fronts, with major losses occurring at Gettysburg in the east, Vicksburg in the west, and the loss of Little Rock in the Trans-Mississippi. However, there were also great successes that occurred for the rebel cause during the same year. Lee won what historians have called his "masterpiece" victory at Chancellorsville (May 1863), while Confederate fortunes in the west were revived at the Battle of Chickamauga in September. In the Trans-Mississippi, Banks's operations were seen as largely unsuccessful, highlighted by Richard Taylor's skillful handling of his rebel army at Irish Bend and Fort Brisband (April 12–14, 1863), and the embarrassing Federal loss at Sabine Pass (September 8, 1863). Taylor's actions at the Battle of Irish Bend or Franklin were called "one of the most brilliant holding actions of the entire war" by one writer. Overall, despite Confederate successes, 1863, was still a disastrous year for the rebel cause. Boatner, 138, 426, 716; Edwin Adams Davis, *Heroic Years Louisiana in the War for Southern Independence* (Baton Rouge, LA, 1964), 45, hereafter cited as Davis, *Heroic Years*; Donald S. Frazier, "Louisiana," in *Encyclopedia of the American Civil War A Political, Social, and Military History* (David S. and Jeane T. Heidler, eds; New York, 2000), 1222–1224, hereafter cited as *Encyclopedia of the Civil War*.

6. Even while the 27th Arkansas began its march southward, operations in Western Louisiana had already prompted General Holmes to send support to that beleaguered front. On April 14, General E. Kirby Smith, had directed Walker's Texas Division to Richard Taylor's support. On April 24, Walker's command broke camp at Pine Bluff and headed south, being directed to Monroe, Louisiana, via Camden, Arkansas, where they were to join Taylor's army to resist General Nathaniel P. Banks's Federals. While on the march southward, the roads proved to be in a "wretched" condition, prompting Walker to deviate from his initial march to Camden and move directly to Monroe. On April 28, Walker received two dispatches from Smith, directing him at first to march to Alexandria, Louisiana, which Smith quickly canceled in the second dispatch, but instead directed him to Shreveport. Taylor's small army was simply no match for the superior numbers that Banks had, forcing Smith to order a concentration of the forces at Shreveport. Subsequent orders and directives eventually placed Walker's Division into Alexandria on May 27 and joining Taylor the following day. O.R., 15:1041–1043, 1048, 1051, 1054, 1057–1058; Brown, 203–204, 206, 224, 228, 341–343; Richard Taylor, *Destruction and Reconstruction Personal Experiences of the Late War* (New York, 1879; reprint ed. Nashville, TN, 1998), 138.

7. Colonel Hiram Lane Grinstead was born in Lexington, Kentucky, in 1829. He studied law at Transylvania University and practiced law in Lexington before moving to Texas in 1854, where he was elected district judge at age twenty-five. In 1859 Grinstead relocated to Camden, Arkansas, where he

main street to wave us welcome and God-speed and give us banquets, our bands doing their best for the occasion. At Camden, which we reached on the 25th, there were more

Ladies With Bouquets,

drums, fifes and cheers.[8] While waiting here for supplies we heard the news of Stonewall Jackson's death. June 3 we started again for Monroe, La., and in the night fifty-four men deserted from the brigade, fourteen being from our regiment. This was a surprise.[9] Many of the villages which we passed through were now visited by troops for the first time, and the inhabitants were enthusiastic in greeting us. On Sunday, the 7th, we crossed the Louisiana state line, camping at night in a black oak grove near Marion. The second day after this we struck a region where all the trees were covered from root to the highest twig with mosses, which

---

practiced law until the beginning of the Civil War. On July 11, 1862, Grinstead organized the 33rd Arkansas Infantry, at Camden, being appointed colonel of the regiment by General T. C. Hindman. The regiment was raised primarily from Montgomery, Pike, Polk and Sevier Counties, Arkansas. After its organization, Grinstead led his regiment to Little Rock and then to Ft. Smith where they were placed in Shaver's Arkansas Brigade (later Tappan's Brigade). At Prairie Grove Grinstead led his regiment with "gallantry and zeal." During the 1863 Campaign, the 33rd, with Grinstead, played a limited role, operating for a time with Walker's Texas Division in Louisiana. In 1864, during the Red River Campaign, Grinstead "commanded the brigade to which his regiment belonged and at Jenkins' Ferry he was not found wanting." He died on April 30, 1864, while leading a charge at the Battle of Jenkins' Ferry, being among those "who fell nearest the enemy. In noting the loss of Colonel Grinstead, General Tappan recorded: "The army has lost a brave and gallant officer, the country a good and loyal citizen." *O.R.*, vol. 34, pt. 1:802; Allardice, *Confederate Colonels*, 176; Crute, 57; Lula Grinstead Smart, "H. L. Grinstead," in Confederate Scrapbook, 548–550, Camden Public Library; Special Order No. 28 (July 11, 1862), Special Orders Book No. 1.

8. In Turnbo's detailed account, he provided more information on the march to Camden. On the first day they made Eight Mile Creek, the next day they were in Saline County on Rock Creek, then through Benton, after which they waded the Saline River, which was knee-deep and went into camp after a 28 mile march. The third day they camped at Fransways Creek in Hot Springs County and on the 21st they marched through a thinly populated area, where "they had no water to cook with [and] barely enough to drink and had to do without anything to eat." They made 14 miles on the 22nd and passed through Tulip. Tappan's Brigade marched through Princeton on the 23rd and reached the banks of the Ouchita River on the 24th and crossed over to Camden on the 25th, where they went into camp. When the brigade passed through both Tulip and Princeton, many of the men from the 33rd Arkansas were allowed to go home for two days, but many lingered, according to Turnbo, for three or four days. Over all, the last 32 mile march from Princeton to Camden "was a very pleasant one for the men," according to Turnbo, "for large numbers of people would gather at the side of the road in places and wave their handkerchiefs and give bouquets to the soldiers." Note—In his original account of the march to Camden, Turnbo recorded that he was ill at the time and the events of the march were given to him by those who participated in the trek. Though ailing with "bronchitis, and a serious cough," Turnbo left St. John's hospital, in Little Rock, and rejoined his regiment the day after they had camped in Camden. Turnbo, 235–237, 243, 245.

9. In addition to the 14 men, who deserted from the 27th Arkansas, 10 deserted from the 38th Arkansas and 30 from Grinstead's 33rd Arkansas. One of the men who stayed behind and did not desert was Surgeon Junius Bragg of the 33rd Arkansas, who was married on the evening on June 4. Bragg would spend a couple of weeks with his new bride Anna Josephine Goddard and not rejoin his command until mid-June. Ibid., 248; Gaughan, 137, 139–140.

also hung in long strings from the branches.[10] At Ouachita City we took boats and amused ourselves watching the alligators during a slow run of forty miles to Monroe. After one day's rest we moved forward by train to Delhi, thirty miles from Vicksburg.[11] The place was surrounded by swamps and marshes, with deserted farms here and there. Mosquitoes, frogs, alligators, centipedes and snakes were the enemies which here disputed the country with us. The soldiers and villagers fell out because troops insisted on drawing water from wells in town, and we had a pretty dismal time of it. Here Tappan's Brigade was united to Walker's Division, composed of three small brigades and some cavalry.[12] One of the Texas brigades was commanded by Brig. Gen. Henry McCulloch,[13] brother of Ben. McCulloch.

---

10. The 120 mile march from Camden to Monroe City, Louisiana, was marked with assorted joys and problems. On the evening of June 3–4, 54 men deserted. On June 4, Colonel Shaler, of the 27th, challenged any disaffected men to leave "immediately," but none did and that evening they camped on Big Beaver Pond in Union County. June 5, brought the brigade to El Dorado, where the brigade closed up to parade through the town, which had never witnessed troops passing though in that part of Arkansas. To the tune "Dixie," the brigade moved through El Dorado, greeted by young ladies waving handkerchiefs and giving out bouquets of flowers. The brigade made Hillsboro, about 15 miles from El Dorado on June 6, where it was discovered that one of the men of the 33rd Arkansas had smallpox. The affected man was stricken from the march and later recovered with no apparent ill effect on the brigade. At 10:00 a.m., on June 7, Tappan's command crossed into Louisiana. June 8 was marked by the lack of water, prompting General Tappan to order out parties from each regiment to find water and return with it to the brigade. The following day, at 10:00 a.m., Tappan's Brigade reached Ouchita City, where they boarded boats for the last 40 miles (by water; 22 miles by land) to Monroe City. Turnbo, 247–251.
11. When Tappan's Brigade reached Ouchita City, they found two boats waiting for them; The 27th Arkansas boarded the *Vigo*, while the 33rd and 38th Arkansas boarded the *Judge Fletcher*. The wagon train crossed the river on a ferry and proceeded by land to Monroe. The men arrived at Monroe the same day while the trains arrived at Monroe on June 10. The following day the brigade boarded the train to Delphi, where they arrived the same day and went into camp, awaiting the arrival of Walker's Texas Division. Ibid., 252–252, 254–255.
12. In addition to Walker's Texas Division (previously addressed), the cavalry referred to by Turnbo consisted of Colonel Frank A. Bartlett's 13th Louisiana Cavalry Battalion (200 men), Major Isaac F. Harrison's 15th Louisiana Cavalry Battalion (500 men) and A. F. Crawford's 13th Texas Cavalry Regiment (300 men)—in all about 1,000 mounted men. Even while Walker prepared for his assault on Milliken's Bend and Young's Point, Bartlett was ordered on the morning of June 4 to conduct an operation against Lake Providence, leaving 100 men from Harrison's Battalion behind with Walker's command to serve as guides for Walker's upcoming movements on the Mississippi River. Bartlett reached Floyd on the evening of June 5, built a bridge across Bayou Macon, but did not cross. Moving northward to Caledonia, they built another bridge over the Macon on June 8, and crossed at seven the next morning. They met two companies from the 1st Kansas Infantry (Mounted) at Bayou Baxter, 6 miles from Providence, drove them back in a running fight to the Tensas River where General Hugh T. Reid had deployed his 800-man command to resist the Confederate raid. Unable to cross the Tensas, Bartlett withdrew his troops. Overall Bartlett captured "a large amount of stores and a number of prisoners, 9 army wagons and 36 mules, besides destroying much of the enemy property. Bartlett's loss was 3 killed and 7 wounded." The Federals reported the loss of just one man wounded, though that seems unlikely given the running battle from Bayou Baxter to the Tensas River and the loss of their pickets at Bunch Bend. *O.R.*, vol. 24, pt. 2:448–449, 457, 460; Napier Bartlett, *Military Record of Louisiana Including Biographical and Historical Papers Relating to the Military Organizations of the State* (New Orleans, 1875; reprint ed., Baton Rouge, 1964), pt. 3:34–36; Thomas Reid, *Spartan Band Burnett's 13th Texas Cavalry in the Civil War* (Denton, TX, 2005), 96–98.
13. Henry Eustace McCulloch was born on December 6, 1816, in Rutherford County, Tennessee,

He wore a brown jeans suit and could not be distinguished from a private, but he was considered a fine commander. We were now close to the enemy, and the regiments took turns doing outpost duty. On the 15th our brigade was ordered forward to relieve some Texans. We advanced though bayous, over ridges and across swamps twenty feet below high water mark of two years before. After pushing ahead many miles

We Heard Firing

and learned that McCulloch's Texans were engaged near Richmond.[14] We were hurried up and the firing increased, but finally ceased as we drew near the Tensas

---

moved to Guadalupe County, Texas, in 1837, and commanded a company during the Mexican War. Following the war, McCulloch entered Texas politics and prior to the Civil War was appointed the U.S. Marshal for Eastern District of Texas by President Buchanan. On April 15, 1861, he was appointed colonel of the 1st Texas Mounted Riflemen and played a leading role in the surrender of Federal troops in Texas in 1861. McCulloch was made a brigadier general on March 14, 1862, and continued to serve in Texas during most of his Civil War career, though he served for a time in Walker's Texas Division. McCulloch's one battle of note was Milliken's Bend, Louisiana (June 7, 1863), during the relief efforts for Vicksburg. On July 25, 1863, McCulloch was relived of command in Walker's Division and ordered to General John B. Magruder, in Texas, where he served until the end of the war. Following the war, McCulloch returned to farming in Texas and died in Rockport, Texas on March 12, 1895. See Appendix B for a complete biography. *O.R.*, vol. 26, pt. 2:121; Heitman, 2:60; Roberts, *Texas, Confederate Military History*, 36, 244–245; Sifakis, *Who Was Who in the Confederacy*, 183; Warner, *Generals in Gray*, 201.

14. Following the engagements at Young's Point and Milliken's Bend on June 7, 1863, Walker's Division fell back to Richmond, Louisiana on Roundaway Bayou, about 18 miles from Delphi. The following day General U.S. Grant ordered General Joseph A. Mower's Brigade to reinforce E. S. Dennis's command at Young's Point. Grant further directed Dennis that "if the enemy is in the neighborhood of Richmond, he should be driven from there, and our troops pushed on to Monroe." Having determined the location of the rebel force at Richmond, Dennis ordered Mower, in conjunction with Alfred W. Ellet's Marine Brigade, to drive the rebels from Richmond. On the morning of June 14, Ellet landed his 2,000-man brigade (Richard Lowe has the brigade at 1,300 men) at Milliken's Bend and moved toward Richmond. Ellet linked up with Mowers' Brigade of 1,200 men, coming from Young's Point, at 10:00 a.m. on the morning of June 15, about 3 miles from Richmond. With the 5th Minnesota leading, the expedition moved on to Richmond. Nearing Richmond, the Federals discovered Walker's command deployed in a grove of trees, fronting an open field. With skirmishers in front, the 5th Minnesota moved forward, only to be met by rebel skirmishers from the 18th Texas Infantry, who were hidden in a brush covered ditch, about half a mile from Walker's main body. Delivering a "heavy volley" at point blank range, the Minnesotan's hit the ground and began to return fire the best they could. After 20 minutes, the 500-man, 18th Texas charged the Federals pushing the skirmishers back to their main body which was forming in a line of battle. A quick volley by Mower's Brigade sent the rebels back to their lines, after which an artillery duel commenced. Within two hours the battle was over, Walker withdrew from the area and burned the bridge over the bayou to prevent a rapid pursuit. Rebuilding a portion of the bridge, Mower crossed over about 200 men from Ellet's Brigade, who then burned Richmond to the ground. Mower did a limited pursuit with some cavalry capturing some prisoners before departing the area. *O.R.*, vol. 24, pt. 2:451–455; *O.R.*, vol. 24, pt. 3:390; *O.R.N.*, vol. 25:175–177; Blessington, 110–111, 123–124; Brown, 239–240; George B. Davis and Leslie J. Perry and Joseph W. Kirkley, *Atlas to Accompany the Official Records of the Union and Confederate Armies* (Washington, DC, 1891–1895), plt. 135, hereafter cited as Davis, *Civil War Atlas*; Hearn, 168–169; Richard Lowe, *Walker's Texas Division C.S.A. Greyhounds of the Trans-Mississippi* (Baton Rouge, LA, 2004),105, hereafter cited as Lowe.

Operations in Northeast Louisiana
(June–August 1863)

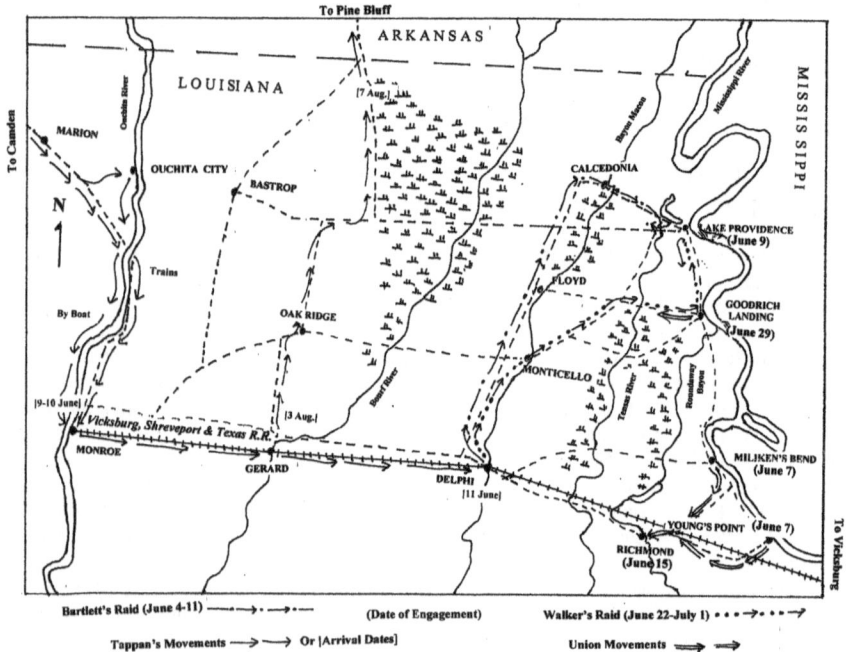

River. We were posted behind a levee to check a force that was forcing the Texans back. In a few minutes McCulloch's small force appeared, crossed the bridge and formed on our left. We awaited the attack but soon learned form our videttes that the enemy had withdrawn.[15] We then broke ranks and mingled with McCulloch's men. One of the men who had been in the Battle of Pea Ridge caught sight of

---

15. As soon as Tappan's command heard that the Texans were in trouble, they immediately broke camp, leaving all their baggage, save a few wagons, and marched off to support the Texans. After 6 miles they reached the Tensas River, where they established a line behind the levee, some 14 miles from the battlefield. About sundown they were joined by McCulloch's Brigade. With no Unionists in pursuit the engagement ended. The rebel command at Richmond consisted of McCulloch's and Hawes' Brigades of Walker's Division, while Randal's Brigade had departed the area for Alexandria following its engagement at Young's Point. In all Walker reported that he had no more than 1,500 effective men, though with Tappan's command it boosted his total to 2,800 men. At Richmond the Federals lost 8 wounded, from the 5th Minnesota, while Ellet lost 2 wounded with 1 killed. Federal sources put rebel losses at 5 dead, 11 prisoners with another 25 stragglers bagged as the Confederates retreated. Walker, for his part, recorded that his command lost 15 killed wounded and missing, while his division "looked like a vast moving hospital" when it retreated from Richmond. As for the city of Richmond, it became a permanent casualty of war as it was never rebuilt. *O.R.*, vol. 24, pt. 2:451–453; *O.R.N.*, vol. 25:175–176; Blessington, 123–124; Brown, 240; Davis, *Civil War Atlas*, plt. 135; Davis, *Heroic Years*, 100; Lowe, 104, 106; Turnbo, 257–258.

Gen. McCulloch's horse and said that it resembled the one Gen. Ben McCulloch rode when he was killed. It turned out that it was the same horse. On the 16th we burned the bridge across the Tensas and withdrew to Delhi.[16] A few days later we made a reconnaissance toward the Mississippi,[17] and on the 29th our brigade was sent against a small fortified post, which proved to be so slightly garrisoned that the cavalry took it before the infantry came up. Here we found a large number of negroes said to have been in the employ of the Federals.[18] They were all sent back to Delhi. What use the Federals or our own government had for them is a mystery. It was said that many of the children died in Delhi from being too closely crowded.[19] The Federal gunboats came up the river and shelled the woods, but we only

---

16. After a meager breakfast of boiled meat, Tappan's Brigade broke camp and marched back to Delphi, where they arrived that same afternoon. Turnbo, 258–259.

17. On June 20, orders were issued for Walker's command to march into northeast Louisiana for the purpose, according to one participant, "to break up a nest of federals who were cultivating cotton and corn in the valley of Bayou Macon [Mason] and on the Mississippi." However, the march was delayed until the 22nd, at which time they moved northeast to Monticello. On the 23rd the command made camp on the Tensas River, rested a day, and then moved toward Milliken's Bend, where they attempted to draw the Unionists into an ambush. The cavalry, under Colonel Harrison came within a few hundred yards of the fortifications of Milliken's Bend, but were unable to draw out the Federal garrison. Returning to Monticello on June 26, Walker's command moved up the Mason Bayou the next day at 8:00 p.m., camped at 10:00 p.m. and rested on June 28, awaiting the arrival of Colonel Parsons's Texas Cavalry Brigade and the expected operations against the Federal plantations between Goodrich Landing and Lake Providence. Gaughan, 141–142; J.E.T., "Letter From Burford's Regiment," *Dallas Herald*, August 5, 1863, hereafter cited as J.E.T., "Letter From Burford's Regiment,"

18. On June 28, William H. Parsons's Texas Cavalry Brigade, which was coming from southeast Arkansas and Pine Bluff, broke camp in Morehouse Parish, Louisiana, and arrived at Walker's camp at 3:00 a.m. on June 29. An hour later, Parsons's boys were on the march toward the Mississippi River, overtaking Tappan's Brigade and Randal's Texans a short time latter. "Dashing" ahead, Parsons's Brigade came upon "Desoto Mound," or "Mound Farm," which one Texan labeled "Nigger Mound," and deployed for combat. The 12th and 19th Texas Cavalry, with the support of a Mississippi Battery, deployed 800 yards from the elevated mound, while the Randal's Texas Brigade, with Shaver's Arkansas Regiment debouched from the woods and filed in behind the cavalry. Meanwhile, following an abortive assault, Colonel Parsons sent in a flag of truce, demanding an unconditional surrender. A short time later the fort surrendered, with two companies (113 men) of Negroes, who were "officered each by three white men." The surrender was made under the condition that the officers be treated as prisoners of war while the armed black troops could be treated "unconditionally" or at the "discretion" of the captors. *O.R.*, vol. 24, pt. 2:4, 446, 466; *O.R.N.*. vol. 25: 215; Anne J. Bailey, *Between the Enemy and Texas: Parsons's Texas Cavalry in the Civil War* (Fort Worth, TX, 1989), 138–140, hereafter cited as Bailey; Gaughan, 143, 160; J.E.T., "Letter From Burford's Regiment"; Turnbo, 260; Soldat, "Col. Parsons's Cavalry Raid in the Valley of the Mississippi, Nearly Opposite Vicksburg," *Tri-Weekly Telegraph*, August 4, 1863, hereafter cited as Soldat, "Parsons's Cavalry Raid."

19. Within months of Federal forces occupying New Orleans in April 1862, the U.S. Congress passed the Confiscation Act (July 12, 1862), which allowed army commanders the right to appropriate property, of all types, that belong to disloyal Confederate officers or civilian officials. Ben Butler, in New Orleans, used the opportunity to begin the work of confiscation in September 1862, and yet again in November. Thousands of properties were taken and sold at auction or leased to cotton or sugar speculators, raising over a million dollars for the Union treasury. "Free" Negro labor was recruited to work the plantations along the Mississippi River and into lower Louisiana. Following the implementation of the Emancipation Act (See Appendix A) in January 1863, General Nathaniel Banks, now in command of the Department of the Gulf, issued General Orders No. 12 (See Appendix A) which defined the role

fell back a short distance and remained in line. No one was killed or wounded by the shells. At nightfall we marched back over the road by which we approached, and in the morning were just ready to start for Lake Providence when we learned that a force of Federals was approaching, having pushed forward in pursuit during the night. Line was formed, and skirmishers soon met the enemy's advance. The skirmish lines met in heavy timber, and the developments soon convinced Gen. Tappan that it would be wiser to withdraw than fight.[20] We accordingly marched away, the skirmish line covering the withdrawal. He only had one man of our regiment wounded, but our retreat was so rapid than many of the men were

Overcome by Sunstroke.

The writer was so badly overheated that he never fails to feel the effects of that march now in the summer time. In two days we were back in Delhi, where the hospitals were soon filled with men who had broken down under the hot summer marching in swamp miasmas and from drinking the filthy slough water.[21] The

and use of Negro labor to work the confiscated lands. One biographer of Banks recorded the following on the new system under the heading of the "necessity of toil":

If a negro had no job in town, he was required to do plantation work. He could choose his master, but having chosen, was bound for a year. Workers were promised just treatment, healthy rations, comfortable clothing, quarters, fuel, medical attendance, and instruction for the children. Also pay, graded by ability, and running up to ten dollars per month...Each worker was to have a private garden plot, up to an acre apiece, for "encouragement" of independent industry [which] will...prepare for the time when he can render so much labor for so much money, which is the great end to be obtained.

Those planters, who still held slaves in occupied territory, and cooperated with the Federal authorities, would not have their lands confiscated. Though not happy with Banks's order it was better than the total loss of all that they owned. At its peak 50,000 workers, operating on 1,500 plantations, brought in thousands of dollars for the Union speculators, who purchased, leased or operated the farms, with the support of the Northern Armies. *O.R.*, vol. 15:666–669; Gaughan, 153; Fred Harvey Harrington, *Fighting Politician Major General N. P. Banks* (Philadelphia, 1948), 105–106; John D. Winters, *The Civil War In Louisiana* (Baton Rouge, 1963), 140–141, 146, 208.

20. Following the engagement at the Desoto Mound or the "Mounds," Parsons pushed on to the town of Lake Providence, with the 12th Texas leading the way, while the infantry remained behind to guard the captured Negroes. About 6 miles from the town of Providence, the column was ambushed in a skirt of timber by the 1st Kansas Mounted Infantry. Dismounting all but one squadron of the 12th Texas, Parsons ordered his battery to deploy and shell the enemy out of their "lair." The Kansans took to their heels and retreated rapidly to Providence, hoping to "coax" their enemy into the town, where the remainder of the garrison was entrenched behind cotton bales and earthworks. Considering the condition of their horses, the lack of sleep (8 hours in the last 60), and with night falling Parsons pulled his command back from Lake Providence and retreated the way they had come. During the night, the Marine Brigade under General Ellet arrived at Goodrichs Landing and in the morning began their pursuit of Parsons's Brigade. Ellet's command found the rebel raiders located on the west bank of the Tensas River a little after noon on June 30. Following a short engagement of 2 hours, marked by long range skirmishing, Parsons burned the bridge over the Tensas and moved off without further interference. *O.R.*, vol. 24, pt. 2:450; *O.R.S.*, pt. 2, vol. 21:533; *O.R.N.*, vol. 25:215–216; Bailey, 138; Davis, *Civil War Atlas*, plt. 35; Hearn, 174–176; Soldat, "Parsons's Cavalry Raid."

21. The bulk of Walker's command returned to Delphi on June 30, with Parsons's Cavalry coming in the next day. The Confederate raid in the Lake Providence area netted from 1,400 to 2,000 former slaves, about 450 horses or mules, 200 stands of arms and assorted camp and garrison equipment. Ad-

news of the fall of Vicksburg and Port Hudson and unsuccessful attack on Helena found us still sweating among the alligators and turtles of this wretched swamp region and we were discouraged to the last degree.[22] A convalescent camp was established near Monroe and while there I had the pleasure of meeting the Fourteenth Arkansas on parole from Port Hudson.[23] Among them were Tom Stallings, now well known as a steamboat captain on Upper White River, and W. A. Tumphreys or [Pumphry], now a merchant in Lead Hill, Ark. The boys all reported that they were well treated as prisoners of war. They rested over night with us and then went on home. Near the convalescent camp was large field of corn just in roasting ear and we all hoped the owner will forgive us. As we recovered strength we returned to Delhi and then moved to Gerard where yellow fever broke out and we lost several men.[24] Two of our company died one morning.[25] About the 3d of Au-

---

ditionally, it was estimated by one participant that "several million dollars worth of property" had been destroyed, much of it willingly, by the owners of the assorted plantations. The raid cost the Confederates 4 dead (all from the 19th Texas Cavalry), 8 wounded including 1 from the 27th Arkansas, 5 from the 12th Texas Cavalry and 2 from the 19th Texas. The Federals for their part reported 1 killed and 3 wounded in the 1st Kansas, with an additional 1 killed and 2 wounded in Ellet's Brigade. However, the *Supplement to the Official Records* also noted that the 1st Kansas lost 3 men missing. Further, a Lieutenant S. F. Cole of Ellet's "horse marines came across the bodies of several white officers who had commanded black companies. They had been nailed to trees, crucified, and set on fire. Other men had been nailed to slabs and roasted alive."—A dreadful end for the white officers of the Desoto Mound engagement. *O.R.*, vol. 24, pt. 2:466; *O.R.S.*, pt. 2, vol. 21:533; *O.N.R*, vol. 25:215–216; Gaughan, 141, 144; Hearn, 175; J.E.T, "Letter From Buford's Regiment;" Soldat, "Parsons's Cavalry Raid."

22. The surrender of Vicksburg happened on July 4 as did the Confederate defeat at Helena. Port Hudson, Louisiana, surrendered on July 9. Boatner, 392–393, 663, 877.

23. When Port Hudson surrendered it gave up 10 Arkansas regiments, either in whole or part, including the 14th Arkansas. The 14th Arkansas was organized on September 23, 1861, under Colonel John McCarver for a term of 12 months. The men came primarily from northwestern Arkansas. William C. Mitchell later became the colonel of the regiment, but was dropped upon reorganization in May 1862, in favor of Eli Dodson. The unit fought at Pea Ridge in March 1862, but then transferred to the east side of the Mississippi River, where they completed their military service. When the unit surrendered at Port Hudson, they were commanded by Lieutenant Colonel Pleasant Fowler, whose rank dated from May 8, 1862. The unit was never reconstituted following its exchange. *O.R.*, vol. 26, pt. 1:143; *O.R.S.*, pt. 2, vol. 2:512, 519–520; Crute, 50.

24. While stationed at Delphi, sickness ran rampant in the units located there. One doctor serving in Tappan's Brigade noted that Delphi was "certainly one of the most unhealthy places" that he had ever seen. "Billious fever" seems to have been the main culprit, which was easily treated with quinine; however, quinine seemed to be in short supply, and several died for the lack of it. General Walker blamed the sickness on malaria and the "stagnant and unwholesome water," while a doctor in the 14th Texas added diarrhea to the list. To assist in the recovery rate, as soon as a solider got sick, he was sent out of the swampy region, back to Monroe. This in turn necessitated larger garrisons of troops on the Vicksburg-Shreveport Railroad, to secure Monroe. In the case of the 33rd Arkansas, two thirds of the regiment were used to guard either Monroe or Gerard Station, about 20 miles from Monroe on the railroad; only companies B, D, G and H remained with the brigade at Delphi. Turnbo, the writer of the article, was himself sent to Monroe, to recover, after which he was sent to a convalescent camp near Monroe, where he met the men of the 14th Arkansas Infantry. On July 22, Tappan's Brigade was moved back to Gerard Station, on the Boeuf River. The encampment was dubbed "Camp Taylor" in honor of General Richard Taylor. *O.R.S.*, pt. 2, vol. 2:763, 765, 767–768, 821, 823–824; Davis, *Civil War Atlas*, plt. 135; Gaughan, 147, 155–156, 160, 165; Lowe, 105, 111; Turnbo, 172.

25. Despite the better conditions of their camp, yellow fever visited Tappan's Brigade, with "several"

gust we were ordered back to Little Rock. The march was a tiresome one, lasting twenty days. One night, near the Arkansas line, we camped close to a distillery, and about two-thirds of the brigade, officers included, were very drunk. Of all the nights I ever experienced that was the worst. Gen. Tappan evidently thought that the whiskey would drive the malaria out of us, and so he let us go for it. Anyhow, it seemed to have that effect, for we all had better health afterwards. When we reached Little Rock Col. Shaler was made commander of the post and we did post duty.[26] These details are given to show what a hard time we had of it in Louisiana fighting the fever and the swamp reptiles.

Silas C. Turnbo
Twenty-seventh Arkansas Infantry, Tappan's Brigade

---

men dying from the disease. To combat the sickness, a church was made into the yellow fever ward and was located a short distance from the 27th Arkansas Camp near Steep Bayou. The two men, who died, were originally part of Charles W. Adams's Arkansas Regiment and were named Jim Strange and Charley Smith. Davis, *Civil War Atlas*, plt. 135; Turnbo, 275.

26. On August 1, 1863, Kirby Smith issued orders, directing Tappan's brigade to Pine Bluff, Arkansas. On August 3, the brigade departed Gerard Station and headed north. The second day, the brigade camped near a distillery and by morning nearly "two thirds of the brigade, officers included," were drunk. General Tappan had allowed the drinking in an effort to combat the ills that infected his brigade. The next morning all efforts to stir the camp failed, but finally at 11:00 a.m. the brigade moved off, only to make camp a short time later, there to remain until August 7. The brigade made it into Arkansas on the 7th and camped at Berlin on August 9th. The following day they made it to Hamburg (Turnbo has it as the 8th). Even while the brigade moved northward, more and more men were left behind sick at the various towns as they passed through; by the time the 33rd Arkansas made Pine Bluff, Dr. J. N. Bragg reported that the regiment had only 100 men present for duty—still, on they marched. On August 12, they marched to Monticello, where the 33rd left 32 men sick, and on August 18 (Turnbo says August 19) the brigade entered Pine Bluff. No boats were available for conveying Tappan's men to Little Rock and so the march continued the following day. Finally on August 22, Tappan's Brigade returned to Little Rock, entering the town in the middle of the afternoon, with their band playing. *O.R.*, vol. 22, pt. 2:951; Gaughan, 165–167, 169–170, 173–175; Turnbo, 277.

Chapter 3

Summer 1863
(July-September 1863):

Battle of Helena and
Campaign for Little Rock

Item: A short account of the Battle of Helena (July 4, 1863), by W. H. Wood, Company G, 10th Missouri Infantry (CSA).[1]
Published: January 16, 1886.

The Battle of Helena.

Fyan, Laclede Co., Mo., Jan. 1
Editor, *Republican*

I see in your paper an account by J. T. [L.] Bright of the Battle of Helena.[2] I do not want to criticize nor hurt anyone's feelings, for I well remember John Bright[3] of our old regiment with every feeling of love and respect for an old comrade. I was one of the men that cut their way out of that place where he says Col. [William M.] Moore got himself and eighteen of his men out, one being wounded by

---

1. William H. Wood was a resident of Pulaski County, Missouri, when he enlisted at West Plains on July 29, 1862, in what became Company G, 10th Missouri Infantry. He was left sick at Pocahontas, Arkansas, in September 1862, and was considered a deserter by April 1863. Wood later returned to the army, was reinstated, his record cleared and then fought at Helena. On June 8, 1865, he was paroled at Shreveport, Louisiana, as a member of Company K. National Archives, Record Group M322, (roll no. 155), Confederate Compiled Service Records, 10th Missouri Infantry; Schnetzer, *Men of the Tenth*, 80.
2. J. L. Bright's account of Helena was not found, though he did do a piece in November 1885, on the Red River Campaign. However, James L. Grubbs, Company A, Tenth Missouri Infantry, did a short history on his regiment that did include an account of the breakout of the remnants of Moore's Regiment at the Battle of Helena (See "The History of Company A, Tenth Missouri Infantry," by James L. Grubbs) in this volume, that was published on January 9, 1886. Additionally, James H. McNamara, of Parsons's Brigade, also wrote an account of the Battle of Helena that was published on December 5, 1885 (See "M. M. Parsons's Missouri Brigade (CSA) in 1863" in this volume.)
3. John L. Bright was a resident of Worth County, Missouri, when he enlisted in Company B, 10th Missouri Infantry. He had served in Priest's MSG Regiment, prior to transferring to the regular Confederate service on September 1, 1862, at Camp Mitchell, Arkansas. Bright surrendered at Shreveport, Louisiana on June 8, 1865. Following the war he lived in Linkville, Missouri. Eakin, *Confederate Records*, 1:148; Moore, Skaggs Collection; National Archives, Record Group 109, Confederate Muster Rolls, 10th Missouri Infantry; National Archives, Record Group M322 (roll no. 150), Confederate Complied Service Records, 10th Missouri Infantry; Schnetzer, *Men of the Tenth*, 18; Schnetzer, *More Forgotten Men*, 31.

a shot through the shoulder.[4] Frank Hollinsworth[5] was the man that was wounded in our little charge. We were called in line of battle that morning before daylight, near the enemy. Pindall's Sharpshooters surprised and captured the picket.[6] We were then ordered forward, [James F.] Fagan's Arkansas troops on our right and

---

4. In the course of the battle, Parsons's Brigade took Graveyard Hill, in the center of the Helena defenses. While its troops were consolidating their position, General Holmes arrived on the scene and directed Colonel S. P. Burns to assault and capture Fort Curtis. Burns related the order to Colonel Levin Lewis and the two regiments moved out on the assault, followed shortly by J. D. White's and A. C. Pickett's regiments. The assault was a complete disaster for the Confederates. "Not more than half of those who went in that direction returned," reported General M. M. Parsons while "the remainder were killed, wounded and taken prisoner." For the day, Parsons's Brigade lost 365 prisoners, including Colonel Levin Lewis commanding the 11th Missouri Infantry—Lewis had collapsed during the assault from sheer exhaustion. The 10th Missouri lost the most prisoners, with 220 out of roughly 500 men engaged. *O.R.*, vol. 22, pt. 1:412, 421; *O.R.S.*, pt. 2, vol. 38:607; Christ, 131–132; J. F. H., Letter (July 18, 1863), *Arkansas Patriot* (Little Rock, AR), July 28, 1862, hereafter cited as J. F. H. Letter; Wallace diary, July 4, 1863.
5. This was probably James F. "Frank" Hollensworth or Hollinsworth, who was a resident of Washington County, Missouri, at the beginning of the Civil War. Hollensworth joined what became Company G, 10th Missouri Infantry (CSA) on July 29, 1862, at West Plains, Missouri, and was promoted to sergeant on September 19, 1862. Left as sick at Van Buren, Arkansas, on December 28, 1862, when the city was raided, it's assumed that he was paroled, but later exchanged. He was wounded "slightly" in the shoulder at Helena and again in the shoulder at Pleasant Hill, Louisiana, on April 9, 1864. For his actions at Pleasant Hill, Hollensworth was noted on the "Confederate Roll of Honor" as published by the Confederate Inspector General, Samuel Cooper. Hollensworth survived the war, being paroled out of the service on June 8, 1865 at Shreveport, Louisiana. *O.R.*, vol. 34, pt 1:637–638; National Archives, Record Group, M322 (roll No. 152), Confederate Compiled Service Record, 10th Missouri Infantry; Schnetzer, *Men of the Tenth*, 75.
6. Prior to the attack on Helena, Confederate forces had stopped about five miles from the city, at the Polk Plantation where preparations were made for the attack. About midnight, the command was broken down into three elements and moved out, with orders to make a simultaneous attack at dawn. James F. Fagan's Arkansas Brigade was on the rebel right, Price's two brigades in the center, with the cavalry under L. M. Walker and J. S. Marmaduke assaulting the Union right. Parsons's Brigade reached its destination about a mile and a half from Helena and waited for dawn to break before resuming the advance at sunrise. In his report on the battle T. H. Holmes stated that Sterling Price's Division, of which Parsons was part, did not commence its attack until an hour after the appointed time. Price in his report of the battle, has Holmes waiting with his command and makes no mention of Holmes ordering an immediate advance or objecting to where Price had halted to make his assault. With a "signal gun" fired on the brigade's right, General Parsons's Brigade began advancing at dawn, as ordered, but not "first light as Holmes wanted," with Pindall's Missouri Sharpshooters leading the way. Other accounts from the men of Parsons's Brigade also indicate that they moved out at dawn to assault Helena. It appears, from General Holmes's official report of the battle, that he expected Price to be engaging the Unionists at "first light," which occurred an hour earlier. Pindall's command made contact first, shortly after the advance began, as they took long range artillery fire; finally, when still half a mile from Graveyard Hill, Pindall's men began to pepper the Federal troops to their front. *O.R.*, vol. 22, pt. 1:409–410, 413; Banasik, *Missouri Brothers in Gray*, 55, 57; Edwin Bearss, "The Battle of Helena, July 4, 1863," *Arkansas Historical Quarterly* 20 (Autumn, 1961), 265, 275, hereafter cited as Bearss, "Battle of Helena"; Thomas A. DeBlack, "1863: 'We Must Stand or Fall Alone,'" in *Rugged and Sublime: The Civil War In Arkansas* (Mark K. Christ, ed.; Fayetteville, AR, 1994), 81, hereafter cited as DeBlack; Harrell, *Arkansas, Confederate Military History*, 182; J. F. H., Letter; Wallace diary, July 4, 1863.

[John S.] Marmaduke on our left.[7] Just as we got under a galling fire we were halted for the men on our right to get up in line. We then charged and carried a line of rifle pits without much trouble, crowding the Feds back to town and to the very water's edge. We held on until the Federals reinforced, had driven Fagan's men back and concentrated against Marmaduke.[8] Then Parsons, seeing the situation, ordered a retreat, but some of our regiment did not get the order and held place until surrounded and called on to surrender.[9] Col. [William M.] Moore then told us to direct our fire to one place, cut a gap in their line and break through at point of bayonet. Only eighteen men obeyed the order. We did as directed, and after the third round made the break

James F. Fagan

---

7. John S. Marmaduke was born in 1833, graduated from West Point (number 30 of 38) in 1857, and served on the frontier until the beginning of the Civil War. After resigning from the army on April 17, 1861, he was appointed a colonel in the MSG. Marmaduke commanded the MSG troops at Boonville, Missouri, and later entered the Confederate service. On November 15, 1862, he was promoted to brigadier general and major general on March 15, 1865. Following the war he was elected Governor of Missouri in 1884, and died while in office in 1887. For complete biography see Banasik, *Missouri Brothers in Gray, 143–146.*

James F. Fagan was born on March 1, 1828, near Louisville, Kentucky, and moved to Arkansas in 1839. At the beginning of the Civil War, Fagan organized the 1st Arkansas infantry, and was elected its colonel on May 6, 1861. Fagan resigned from his regiment on July 11, 1862, returned to Arkansas, and raised a regiment of cavalry. Appointed colonel of the 1st Arkansas Cavalry on August 5, 1862, Fagan was subsequently promoted to brigadier general on September 12. He commanded a brigade at the Battles of Prairie Grove and Helena in Arkansas and led a division during the Camden Expedition. On May 13, 1864, Fagan was promoted to major general to rank from April 25. After the war, Fagan return to farming. He died in Little Rock on September 1, 1893. For a complete biography see Banasik, *Serving With Honor, 386–388. O.R.,* vol. 22, pt. 1:409–410; *O.R.S.,* pt. 2, vol. 2:271: Boatner, 513; Christ, 112–113; Heidler, "Fagan, James Flemming," *Encyclopedia of the Civil War,* 673; J. F. H., Letter.

8. Fagan's Brigade began the assault on Helena, at "first light," which came about an hour before daylight. Advancing under heavy Federal fire, they managed to take five lines of rifle pits, but were stopped cold when they made the final assault on Hindman Hill. Price's Division, in the center, proved to have launched the most successful of the rebel attacks, by taking their stated objective—Graveyard Hill. Walker and Marmaduke, on the rebel left, were equally unsuccessful as Fagan. By 10:30 a.m. the attack on Helena had failed and General Holmes ordered his forces to withdraw. Fagan's Brigade on the right and the cavalry on the left, received their orders about 11:00 a.m. and withdrew from the battlefield. Price's command, which was located with General Holmes received the orders to withdraw first, being informed almost immediately after Holmes made his decision to call off the attack. The battlefield and the victory belonged to the Federal forces. *O.R.,* vol. 22, pt. 1:410–411, 429, 437; Bearss, "Battle of Helena," 286; DeBlack, 81-82; Harrell, *Arkansas, Confederate Military History,* 182.

9. Parsons's Brigade began their withdrawal from the battlefield, according to Parsons at 10:30 a.m. When the losses were totaled in the Missouri Brigade, 365 men were listed as missing. *O.R.,* vol. 22, pt. 1:412; J. F. H., Letter.

and went through. We then had one mile to run up as far as Graveyard Ridge. The timber had all been cut off, so there was not even a twig to turn a bullet. We made the trip under a shower of balls, from the size of a minnie to a 32-pound cannon-shot, with only one man wounded. Col. Moore had his saber shot off about twelve inches from his hand and I had my gun shot in two at the small part of the stock, just behind the lock. Several bullets passed through my clothes.

W. H. Wood, M.D.

* * * * * *

Item: Battle of Helena, Arkansas (July 4, 1863), by John C. Moore, Private, Company G, 16th Missouri Infantry (CSA).[10]
Published: April 10, 1886.

The Battle of Helena.

Memphis, Mo.

While the soldiers, Federal and Confederate, are writing accounts of the different engagements, it is not inappropriate that the Battle of Helena be written. The engagement took place the same day as the Battle of Gettysburg and the surrender of Vicksburg, and its importance was eclipsed by the greatness of those affairs, so but little of the public attention has been directed that way; yet no engagement west of the river was so important in its results upon the Trans-Mississippi Department as this battle.[11]

The army under command of Gen. Holmes consisted of the cavalry brigade under Marmaduke, McCrae's [McRae's] and Fagan's Arkansas Brigades and a brigade of Missouri infantry under Brig.-Gen. Monroe [Mosby] M. Parsons.[12]

The attack was upon the forces of Gen. [Benjamin M.] Prentiss, the hero of the Hornet's Nest at Shiloh, and commenced at day-break on the morning of the

10. John Cassius Moore was born on August 18, 1831, and was living in Ray County, Missouri, when he joined what became Company G, 16th Missouri Infantry on July 18, 1862, at Van Buren. He was slightly wounded at Helena on July, 4, 1863, was captured and sent to Alton Prison, where he arrived on July 9, 1863. Forwarded to Camp Douglas, in Chicago on August 23, 1864, he escaped. Following the war, he lived for a time in Memphis, Missouri, and later moved to Excelsior Spring, where he died on October 27, 1915. Eakin, *Missouri Prisoners of War*, "Moore, John C." entry; Eakin & Hale, 313; James E. McGhee, *Missouri Confederates A Guide to Sources for Confederate Soldiers and Units 1861–1865* (Independence, MO, n.d.), 108, hereafter cited as McGhee, *Missouri Confederates*; National Archives, Record Group M322 (roll no. 169), Confederate Compiled Service Records, 16th Missouri Infantry.

11. Few secondary sources have addressed the importance of the Battle of Helena, and most of these comment on "the severe loss of confidence" in the Confederate command structure west of the Mississippi. Thomas L. Snead, an ex-Confederate recorded that the loss at Helena "opened the way for the Union armies for active operations in Arkansas." Mark K. Christ, author of *Civil War Arkansas*, probably provided the best analysis of the effect of the Confederate defeat. He wrote: "The successful defense of Helena emboldened the Federals, and the sudden freeing of thousands of Union troops following the capture of Vicksburg did not bode well for Confederate Arkansas. As one rebel engineer concluded, 'Little Rock was lost at the Battle of Helena.'"
Christ, 144; Snead, "Conquest of Arkansas," 3:456; George J. W. Urwin, "Helena, Battle of," in *Encyclopedia of the Civil War*, 962-963.

12. Dandridge McRae was born on October 10, 1829, in Alabama, graduated from the University of South Carolina in 1849, and moved to Arkansas to manage the family plantation. At the beginning of the Civil War, he was living in Searcy, Arkansas, where he practiced law. McRae fought at the Battle of Wilson's Creek, the Arkansas battles of Prairie Grove, Helena, the Camden Expedition, and the Red River Campaign. By war's end, he had been promoted to brigadier general. After the war, McRae returned to Searcy, resumed his law practice, and in 1881 was elected the Arkansas Secretary of State. He died on April 23, 1899, at Searcy, where he was buried. See Appendix B for a complete biography. The other named individuals have been previously addressed. For the organization of the Confederates at Helena, see Appendix C. *O.R.*, 3:112–113; Warner, *General in Gray*, 206.

4th of July, 1863.[13] The battle was commenced by a simultaneous attack with Gen. Marmaduke's cavalry dismounted on the extreme left. Next followed McRae's Brigade on the left center, Parsons's Brigade in the center and Fagan's on the right. Your correspondent was a member of Co. G, Seventh Missouri, in Parsons's Brigade.

In the very earliest of the dawning, when the command had halted for the purpose of forming in order of battle, a shell came screaming through the tree-tops and fell among some of the men of the brigade, and exploded, the fragments striking five men and wounding them. The attack then commenced in column by divisions,[14] our duty being to charge upon a battery and some rifle pits designated as the Graveyard Fort. Fagan in the meantime commenced an attack upon the enemy's left, McRae upon our left, and Marmaduke was deployed up to the river to direct the enemy's attention in that quarter.

As the sun rose over the eastern hills the "rebel yell" commenced with

---

13. Benjamin M. Prentiss was born on November 23, 1819, in Bellville, Virginia (now West Virginia), moved to Missouri in 1836, and to Quincy, Illinois, in 1841. During the Mexican War he commanded a company in the 1st Illinois Infantry, and upon war's end he took up the study of law and later ran an unsuccessful campaign for the U.S. Congress in 1860. At the beginning of the Civil War, Prentiss was elected colonel of the 10th Illinois Infantry, and on August 9, 1861, he was appointed brigadier general to rank from May 17. Prentiss served in Missouri for a short time until appointed commander of the 6th Division, Army of the Tennessee, on March 26, 1862. At the Battle of Shiloh, Prentiss commanded at the "Hornet's Nest" which resulted in his capture. Exchanged in October 1862, Prentiss served on the court martial of Fitz-John Porter, and then was assigned to eastern Arkansas in February 1863. Prentiss won the Battle of Helena on July 4, 1863, but resigned from the army on October 28, 1863, citing health concerns. He returned to Quincy and the law and eventually moved to Bethany, Missouri, where he died on February 8, 1901. Boatner, *Civil War Dictionary*, 667–668; Stewart Sifakis, *Who Was Who in the Union: A Comprehensive, Illustrated Biographical Reference to More Than 1,500 of the Principal Union Participants in the Civil War* (New York, 1988), 322, hereafter cited as Sifakis, *Who Was Who in the Union*; Ezra J. Warner, *Generals in Blue: Lives of the Union Commanders* (Baton Rouge, LA, 1964), 385–386, hereafter cited as Warner, *Generals in Blue*.
The Battle of Shiloh (Union name) or Pittsburg Landing took place on April 6–7, 1862, on the Tennessee River near the Mississippi and Tennessee border. General U. S. Grant commanded the Federals while Albert S. Johnston led the rebels. The initial, surprise attack, sent the Unionists reeling, but they rallied and stemmed the Confederate tide toward nightfall on the first day. Having received reinforcements during the latter part of April 6 and into the night, Grant counterattacked the following day and drove the rebels from the field. A total of 62,682 Union troops had engaged 40,335 rebels, losing in the process 13,047 men, while the Confederates suffered 10,694 killed, wounded or missing men. Boatner, *Civil War Dictionary*, 754–757.
14. When Parsons's Brigade was formed for the attack they were organized as "columns of divisions," of which Parsons's Brigade had three. Each division had "one or two regiments each;" and within the individual regiments, companies were "divided into two equal parts and one placed directly in front of the other." The "first Division," on the far left, was led by Pindall's Sharpshooters, then Tilden's Battery boys, commanded by L. L. Lesueur. They were followed by the 10th Missouri Infantry and finally the 16th Missouri Infantry. The 12th Missouri, comprised the right division of the brigade, while the 11th Missouri took the center position of Parsons's Brigade. *O.R.*, vol. 22, pt. 1:420; Banasik, *Missouri Brothers in Gray*, 57; Dr. R. E. Young, *Pioneers of High, Water and Main: Reflections of Jefferson City* (Jefferson City, MO, 1997), 116, hereafter cited as Young.

A Charge

by the three brigades and Parsons was soon in possession of the Graveyard Fort.[15]

By this time Fagan and McRae had failed and had retreated out of range.[16] Gen. Price then ordered Fagan to form a new attempt and directed Gen. Parsons to advance obliquely to the right and engage the Federal works in the rear while Fagan would renew the attack in the front.[17] The ground was exceedingly rough, being cut by precipitous gullies, and the hillsides in many places were very steep. Parsons moved to the rear attack while about fifty men, who misunderstood the order made a ruinous charge directly against Fort Curtis, a large work built near the riverbank and armed with heavy siege guns.[18] These men arrived at an old

---

15. Of the three main elements in the rebel assault, Fagan's Brigade on the right began their attack a little after 4:00 a.m., when the first light was seen in the eastern sky—Colonel A. T. Hawthorn, who led off Fagan's Brigade, reported contacting Union pickets at 4:05 and led an immediate assault. On the far left of the rebel line, John S. Marmaduke's Cavalry Division, making up another element of the main assault, began his attack on Fort Rightor at almost the same time, according to Mark Christ; however, Marmaduke noted that his command held their position "from 4:30 a.m. till 11 a.m.," though his advance made contact with the Union pickets at about 3:00 a.m. Price's Division, in the center of the Confederate line, did not make contact until 5:00 a.m., as Pindall's Sharpshooters engaged the Union pickets in that quarter. Edwin Bearss in his account of the battle has Price's assault taking place at 7:00 a.m. *O.R.*, vol. 22, pt. 1:392, 398, 421, 428, 437; Bearss, "Battle of Helena," 280; DeBlack, 81; "The Battle of Helena," *Tri-Weekly Telegraph*, August 12, 1863; "The Battle of Helena," *Washington Telegraph* (Washington, AR), July 15, 1863; Christ, 118, 121; Hoskin, July 4, 1863.

16. Not true. Fagan's Brigade had indeed failed to take the fort on Hindman Hill, also known as "Battery D," but remained in place confronting the enemy until ordered to withdraw at the end of the battle. McRae's Brigade was ordered, with Parsons's Brigade to take Graveyard Hill, or Battery C, which they did. According to most accounts, the 36th Arkansas Infantry, commanded by Colonel John E. Glenn, entered Battery C almost simultaneously with the 12th Missouri Infantry, led by Colonel James D. White. "Each brigade," according to General Price, "had done its allotted duty with equal zeal, devotion and gallantry and is entitled to an equal share of the honor." And like Fagan's Brigade, McRae's command did not withdraw until ordered to do so by General Holmes. *O.R.*, vol. 22, pt. 1:414, 421, 425–426; "Attack On Helena," *Arkansas State Gazette* (Little Rock, AR), July 11, 1863; "The Battle of Helena," *Washington Telegraph*, July 15, 1863; "Helena Battle," *Tri-Weekly Telegraph*, July 27, 1863.

17. Price never issued any orders to Fagan during the battle but did communicate with him. After Price took Graveyard Hill, his command was in general confusion, with all the regiments badly decimated from taking the center position. General Holmes then arrived on the scene and directed Colonel S. P. Burns to take Fort Curtis, causing Lewis to move on toward the town, followed by the rest of Parsons's Brigade. After this follow-on attack proved a failure, Parsons re-established control of his scattered brigade and continued to hold Graveyard Hill, under increased fire from every quarter. Perceiving that the best way to relieve the pressure on Graveyard Hill was to assist General Fagan, Price directed Parsons to assault the rear of Hindman Hill. When Parsons received the order by courier, General McRae was with him and suggested that Parsons hold Graveyard Hill, since his was the larger of the two commands; meanwhile, McRae would assault Hindman Hill. Parsons agreed and sent word to General Price to that effect. Gathering up what men he had, about 200, McRae led a futile attempt to assist Fagan's command, which quickly collapsed. In his account of the battle, Mark Christ has Parsons's assault on Fort Curtis occurring just before the battle ended and not immediately following the taking of Graveyard Hill as indicated by the *Official Records* and other accounts. *O.R.*, vol. 22, pt. 1:414-115, 418, 422; Bearss, "Battle of Helena," 283-284, 287; Christ, 131-135; J. F. H., Letter.

18. Fort Curtis was named after General Samuel R. Curtis. The Federals began construction of the fort on the northwestern side of Helena on August 21, 1862, after they first occupied the city in July. A

Interior of Fort Curtis, Helena

building at the outskirts of town, and finding themselves unsupported stopped. The fort at once commenced throwing grape among them at about 200 yards distance and they were soon compelled to surrender. In the meantime Fagan's second attempt failed and left Parsons unsupported. A portion of the brigade escaped by way of a ravine and by running a gauntlet of hot fire,[19] but the remainder

---

grand review of the troops on October 29, 1862, marked the completion of the fort. The battery of the fort initially consisted of 6 pieces, comprising 32 and 64 pound smoothbore guns, though at the time of the battle one Confederate recorded that "Fort Curtis was the best fortified of all, with high walls and dirt dug down perendiculary [sic] 8 feet below them. It had 9 heavy guns supported by a large body of infantry." However, a Union correspondent at the time noted that Fort Curtis contained only 6 heavy guns; "five twenty-four pound siege guns, and one thirty-two pound columbiad." Edwin Bearss has the fort armed with only 3 30-pound parrot guns. Bearss, "Battle of Helena," 295; S. C. Bishop Letters, Indiana Historical Society, October 29, 1862; Christ, 109; Gilbert H. Denny Letters, Indiana Historical Society, August 24, 1862; J. F. H. Letter; James H. Hougland Civil War Diary, Indiana Historical Society (Indianapolis, IN), August 21, 1862; Deryl P. Sellmeyer, *Jo Shelby's Iron Brigade* (Gretna, LA, 2007), 106, hereafter cited as Sellmeyer; "St. Louis 'Democrat Account,'" *Rebellion Record*, 7:140.

19. Immediately following the capture of Graveyard Hill, General Holmes ordered Colonel S. P. Burns of Parsons's Brigade to assault Fort Curtis. Unknown to either General Price or General Parsons, Burns, per his orders from Holmes, led Parsons's Brigade off toward the Union fort on the outskirts of Helena. Colonels Lewis and Picket followed suit while White's 12th Missouri charged toward the town and some Federal tents, which were located at the bottom of Graveyard Hill. Burns's, Lewis's and Pickett's regiments got to within 200–300 yards of Fort Curtis, when the combined fire on their front and both flanks caused them to halt. For about 20 minutes Parsons's Brigade endured the ranking fire and then retreated back to the Graveyard Hill. In the process of the retreat, portions of the 1st Indiana Cavalry, 33rd Iowa and 35th Missouri Infantries surged forward, capturing about 350 men of the brigade, who had taken shelter in a ravine, having found it was impossible to retreat. *O.R.*, vol. 22, pt. 1:421–422; Bearss, "Battle of Helena," 286; Christ, 132–134; J. F. H. Letter; "The Victory At

Were Surrounded

in a deep gorge which put down to the river. A gunboat [U.S.S. *Tyler*][20] lying in the river dropped down until in range and then sent broadside after broadside up the ravine, while the Federal forces, being unengaged elsewhere, congregated in great numbers, about the devoted band of men, who now, unaided, sustained the conflict; and the officers seeing nothing but destruction in further fighting surrendered. So ended at about 10 o'clock in the day, the engagement that resulted in giving to the Federal forces control over the most of the state of Arkansas and very materially weakened the Confederate military power in the Trans-Mississippi.[21]

Gen. Price in council had declaimed against a battle, and the troops knew he was unwilling to risk an engagement.[22] They loved "Old Pap" and placed more reli-

Helena," *Chicago Tribune*, July 12, 1863.

20. The 180 foot, 575 ton, *U.S.S. Tyler* was built in 1857, and purchased by the War Department in June 1861. It was a side-wheel steamer, mounting eight guns by the Battle of Belmont, "6 8-inch shell guns and 2 32-pounders." During the war the *Tyler* served on the western waters at Belmont, Forts Henry and Donelson, and engaged the rebel ran *Arkansas* on the Yazoo River. The *Tyler* was part of the Western Flotilla and played an important role in defeating the Confederate attack on Helena on July 4, 1863. At Helena the *Tyler* was armed with 10 guns; one 12-pound; one 30-pound on stern; on broadside, two 30-pound Parrot rifles and six 8-inch guns. *O.R.*, vol. 22, 1:385–386; *O.N.R.*, Series 2, 1:227, 229; Tony Gibbons, *Warships and Naval Battles of the Civil War* (New York, 1989), 73.

21. In addition to the Missourians, who surrendered in the abortive attack on Fort Curtis, another group of Arkansas soldiers, from Fagan's Brigade, were also cut off and forced to surrender. In all, according to official Confederate reports, Holmes lost 772 men as captured or missing. However, Union sources, immediately following the battle, listed the numbers of prisoners sent north as follows: "The *Tycoon* took up north 612, including 68 commissioned officers. The *R. C. Wood* 212, including 20 commissioned officers, and the *Silver Moon* 114 including 5 commissioned officers and 75 prisoners," still at Helena, awaiting shipment north—Total 1,013 prisoners of war. General Prentiss, commander of the Federal forces reported that of those men sent north, 212 were wounded and these were deposited at Memphis by the *R. C. Wood*, a hospital steamer. The other boats that carried the unwounded prisoners north to Alton, Illinois, where the post commander reported the arrival of "725 from Helena, Ark. captured...on the 4th instant." Overall, Holmes reported the loss of 772 missing, but makes no mention of any of the wounded who were captured, though clearly several hundred were. *O.R.*, Vol. 22, pt. 1:387, 389, 412, 432-433; *O.R.*, series 2, vol. 6:96; National archives, Record Group M322 (roll. no. 163), Confederate Complied Service Records, 12th Missouri Infantry; "The Victory At Helena," *The State Record* (Topeka, KS), July 22, 1863.

22. Not true, according to Thomas C. Reynolds, the Confederate Governor of Missouri, who assumed his position upon the death of C. F. Jackson in December 1862. In his reminiscences, Reynolds recorded "that ill judged, ill planned, and ill conducted campaign originated with Gen. Price...Gen. Holmes vacillated as to its propriety and did not finally decide on it until he came to Jacksonport, and held a consultation with Generals Price and Marmaduke, who both advised it." Holmes subsequently agreed on the attack, but only after Price agreed to "sustain the action taken in ordering" the attack, if it failed. However, according to Edward Pollard, on the eve of the attack Price changed his mind and "argued that the enemy was doubtless expecting them, and had concentrated as many troops as he deemed sufficient to defend the place, and that, if it had been necessary to call troops from Vicksburg for this purpose, the object of the expedition had already been accomplished." Price further supported interdicting the supplies into Helena, believing that even if Helena should be taken that it could not be held. Bearss, "Battle of Helena," 258–259; Edward A. Pollard, *The Lost Cause: A New Southern History of the War of the Confederates, etc.* (New York, 1867; reprint ed., New York, 1970), 397; Robert G. Schultz, ed., *General Sterling Price and the Confederacy* (St. Louis, 2009), 85, hereafter cited as Schultz.

Frederick Steele

ance in his judgement than in the judgement of "Granny Holmes." And it is our humble opinion that had the view of Gen. Price prevailed Little Rock would never have fallen a prey to Gen. [Frederick] Steele, nor would the battles on the Ouachita have ever been fought.[23]

The war would have been practically over so far as regards the Trans-Mississippi Department, and the country would have come out of the conflict with much less loss of life and property. I was wounded and taken prisoner in the battle.

John C. Moore.

* * * * * * *

---

23. Frederick Steele was born on January 14, 1819, in New York, and attended West Point, where he graduated in 1843 (number 30 of 39). During Mexican War, Steele received two brevets for gallantry at the Battles of Contreras and Chapultepec. At the beginning of the Civil War, he was a captain stationed at Fort Leavenworth, Kansas. He rose quickly in rank, first appointed the colonel of the 8th Iowa Infantry on September 23, 1861, a brigadier general on January 29, 1862, and a major general on November 29, 1862. Steele was best remembered for capturing Little Rock in September 1863, and leading the Camden Expedition in 1864. Following the war, he remained in the Regular Army, but died by a freak accident on January 12, 1868, when he fell from a buggy he was driving. For a complete biography see Banasik, *Missouri Brothers in Gray*, 152–155.

In referring to "the battles on the Ouchita," the writer was commenting on the Camden Expedition of 1864. Steele's Federals left Little Rock on March 23, 1864, occupied Arkadelphia on March 29, crossed the Little Missouri River April 3, and occupied Camden on April 15. During the expedition numerous engagements took place with the most prominent ones being Poison Springs (April 18), Mark's Mill (April 25), and Jenkins' Ferry (April 30, 1864). The bulk of Steele's command arrived back in Little Rock on May 2, 1864, having failed in the purpose of the expedition, which was to support General Nathaniel Banks's Red River Expedition. *O.R.*, vol. 34, pt. 1:779–780; Banasik, *Reluctant Cannoneer*, 234, 238-239; Boatner, 23-24, 794-795; Heitman, 1:918; Warner, *Generals in Blue*, 474-475.

Item: The History of Company A, Tenth Missouri Infantry, including the march to Helena (June 1863), the Defense and Retreat from Little Rock (August–September, 1863), by James L. Grubbs, Company A, 10th Missouri Infantry.
Note: This article is continued from Chapter 1: "Winter 1862–1863," by the same author.
Published: January 9, 1886.

The Last Company That Surrendered.

Canton, Mo., Dec. 12, 1885
Editor *Republican*
I have been very much interested in "The Tales of the War" that have been published from time to time in the *Republican*, being a member of Co. A, Tenth Regiment, Parsons's Brigade...
We went into camp a mile south of the [Little Rock] statehouse with a beautiful open field in front, which we used as a drill-ground four hours each day, until about the 20th of April...From there we crossed the river to Camp Anderson. We remained there until the 1st of June, when we were ordered North.[24] We arrived at Jacksonport about the 10th of June.[25] This camp was called Camp Stonewall in honor of that distinguished general. We remained here a few days, when we were ordered East to Helena, where a battle was fought July the 4th, 1863. Our company went into that battle with about eighty men. We lost one killed, but our loss in prisoners was terrible, being three commissioned officers and sixty men.[26] The remainder of the company was brought out by Orderly Sergt. J. W. Williams,[27] who was known throughout the brigade as the "tall sergeant." Fortu-

24. Parsons's Brigade, less their artillery company, broke camp on April 27 and crossed to the north side of the Arkansas River. They remained there until May 31, when they moved northward to Jacksonport, Arkansas on the White River, where they were directed to recruit for their command and prepare for a possible invasion of Missouri. *O.R.*, Vol. 22, pt. 2:849; Hoskin, May 31, 1862; Lotspeich, April 27 and May 31, 1863; Quesenberry, April 27 and May 31, 1863.
25. Price's Division, led by Parsons's Brigade, arrived at Jacksonport on June 7, and went into camp on the south side of the river. On June 18, 1863, General Holmes arrived at Price's headquarters to discuss the up coming operations against Helena. Holmes had previously written Kirby Smith, the Department Commander, on June 15: "I believe I can take Helena. Please let me attack it." On June 16, Smith replied: "Most certainly do it." Following the consultations at Jacksonport, and, with the support of Generals Price and Marmaduke, Holmes decided to attack Helena. On June 18, Holmes issued orders for the attack, and two days later, Price's Division broke camp and headed to Helena. As part of their initial moves Price was to meet Marmaduke's command, which was scattered in northeast Arkansas, at Cotton Plant on June 26. *O.R.*, vol. 22, pt. 1:407; *O.R.*, vol. 22, pt. 2:863, 868, 873–874, 877; Bearss, "Battle of Helena," 259; Hoskin, June 7 and 20, 1863; Schultz, 85; Wallace, June 7 and 20, 1863.
26. Lieutenant Pleasant E. Chestnut, who took command of Company A, 10th Missouri Infantry following the defeat at Helena, reported that the unit took 80 men into the battle, of which 2 were killed and 58 captured. *O.R.S*, pt. 2, vol. 38:600; Schnetzer, *Men of the Tenth*, 3.
27. John William Williams, of Lewis County, Missouri, was a member of the MSG, probably Winston's or Priest's unit, when he enlisted in what became Company A, 10th Missouri Infantry at Camp

nately Lieut. [Pleasant E.] Chesnut, who was acting as aid-de-camp to Gen. Parsons took command of the company. He was a very popular officer and was proud of his company. He had his company well disciplined and drilled. At the defense of Little Rock our company occupied a position where the fortifications cross the railroad.[28] After the evacuation of Little Rock nothing of interest occurred until we reached Arkadelphia;[29] there we drew new Austria Rifles (the guns were issued to the whole regiment).[30] Then it was to be seen who had the nicest gun, as a premium was offered for that. The prize was awarded to David Daggs.[31] There were quite a number of very fine guns shown. The guns were inspected by Gen. Price. He also gave Mr. Daggs a leave of absence for fifteen days, but he did not accept this offer, as he did not care to leave his company. From Arkadelphia we went to Camp Bragg, where went into winter quarters.[32] There we enjoyed ourselves

Mitchell, Monroe County, Arkansas. Williams, the 1st sergeant or orderly sergeant of his company, was "severely" wounded at Prairie Grove on December 7, 1862, in the "right leg, and groin," but recovered. He was again wounded at Pleasant Hill on April 9, 1864, but again survived. He was later promoted to first lieutenant and transferred to Company E on January 31, 1865. R. J. Bell, Losses in Parsons's Brigade at Prairie Grove, "First Regiment," *Missouri Republican*, February 11, 1863; Hoskin, August 22-24, 1862; National Archives, Record Group M322 (roll no. 155), Confederate Compiled Service Records, 10th Missouri Infantry; Schnetzer, *Men of the 10th*, 15.

28. After the Battle of Helena, the army leisurely returned to Little Rock, first stopping at Bayou Meto on July 27, where they encamped at Camp Green—named in honor of General Martin E. Green, who was killed at Vicksburg on July 3, 1863. The command then began work on the main Confederate defenses, north of Little Rock on August 9 and continued to improve upon them until the evacuation of the city. "The works extended from the river about five miles back to an impassable swamp. They were well constructed with an extensive open space cleared in front." The division then moved its camp on August 23, and relocated opposite Little Rock. The new camp was designated Camp Price, after Sterling Price. *O.R.*, vol. 22, pt.2:973; Banasik, *Missouri Brothers in Gray*, 62; Hoskin, July 27 and August 23, 1863; Wallace, July 27 and August 9, and 23, 1863.

29. The Confederates evacuated Little Rock on September 10, 1863, as the final action in the Little Rock Campaign of 1863. They reached Arkadelphia on September 15, where they went into camp. Banasik, *Missouri Brothers in Gray*, 62; Banasik, *Serving With Honor*, 104; Hoskin, September 15, 1863; Lotspeich, September 13-19, 1863.

30. In January 1864, the Confederate Ordnance Department supplied 976 Austrian Rifles (.54 caliber) to the Trans-Mississippi Department—the only Austrian guns they provided for that time period. The Austrian Rifle, also known as the Austrian Lorenz, "were all of a pattern" rifle adopted by the Austrian government in 1854. It was the "second in importance" to other imported rifles, the first being the British Enfield Rifle. The U.S. Government considered them to be a second class weapon. The barrel was 37 1/2 inches, while the overall length was 53 inches. The weapon mounted a "quadrangular bayonet." *O.R.*, vol. 41, pt. 2:1058; William B. Edwards, *Civil War Guns: The Complete Story of Federal and Confederate Small Arms: Design, Manufacture, Identification, Issue, Employment, Effectiveness, and Postwar Disposal* (Secaucus, NJ, 1962), 256–258.

31. David Daggs, a resident of Lewis County, Missouri, enlisted in Company A, 10th Missouri Infantry at Camp Mitchell, Monroe County, Arkansas, on September 1, 1862. He had previously served in Winston's MSG Regiment. Daggs also supposedly served under Colonel Joseph Porter, circumstances unknown. Daggs survived the war and was paroled at Shreveport, Louisiana on June 8, 1865. Eakin, *Confederate Records*, 2:141; National Archives, Record Group M322 (roll no. 151), Confederate Compiled Service Records, 10th Missouri Infantry; Schnetzer, *Men of the Tenth*, 5; Schnetzer, *More Forgotten Men*, 60.

32. Frost's and McRae's Brigades departed Arkadelphia on October 1, 1863, followed by the rest of the command on October 2. On October 3, the first contingent of Confederates crossed the Little Mis-

hugely, living on the best the country had offered, and making love to Arkansas girls and occasionally young widows. "Old Sam's" girls were great toasts with us, especially with Lieut. Chestnut, Col. Moore and Gus Turner.[33]

Jas. L. Grubbs,
Late of Co. A, Tenth Regiment, Parsons's Brigade.

[Editor's Note: The remainder of the article deals with events that occurred in 1864–1865 and will be included in *Confederate Tales, Part Four: 1864–1865*.]

* * * * * * *

---

souri River, where they went into camp, just north of Camden, which they called Camp Mitchell. The remainder of the troops came in the following day. On October 16, Parsons's Brigade headed south and then west, followed by the rest of the command on October 18. Parsons's Brigade made camp the same day the rest of the army marched, naming the area Camp Reynolds, after the Confederate Missouri Governor. Finally, the remainder of the army arrived at the new encampment on October 21, which was about 20 miles, southwest of Camden, in Ouchita County and near Leaks Store. The camp's name was officially changed to Camp Bragg by October 26, and would be the winter quarters for the command until January 29, 1864, when they moved west toward the Red River, where they made their final camp for the winter—dubbed Camp Sumter. The last camp was in Lafayette County, Arkansas, about 4 miles from the Red River and 6 miles south of Spring Hill. Banasik, *Missouri Brothers in Gray*, 64; Banasik, *Serving With Honor*, 109, 114–115, 136; Quesenberry, October 2, 16, 18, 23, 1863 and February 1, 1864; Wallace, September 26–27, October 2–3, 16-18, 1863, January 29 and February 4, 1864.

33. Ferdinand G. "Gus" Turner was a resident of Marion County, Missouri, when he enlisted in Company A, 10th Missouri Infantry on September 1, 1862, at Camp Mitchell, Arkansas. He had previously served in Winston's MSG prior to his transfer to the Confederate service in September 1862. Turner was captured at Helena, sent to Alton Prison and forwarded to Fort Delaware on February 24, 1864. He was finally exchanged on February 27, 1865, but was recaptured again at Bruinsburg, Mississippi, on April 23, 1865. Sent back to Alton, Turner was released for the final time on June 16, 1865, after he took the Oath of Allegiance to the United States. Eakin, *Missouri Prisoners of War*, "Turner, F. G." entry; National Archives, Record Group M322, (roll no. 155), Confederate Compiled Service Records, 10th Missouri Infantry; Schnetzer, *Men of the Tenth*, 14; Schnetzer, *More Forgotten Men*, 231.

Item: Movement to Helena, Arkansas (May–June 1863); Battle of Helena (July 4, 1863); and the Campaign for Little Rock (August–September 1863), by Captain James H. McNamara.
Published: December 5, 1885.
[Continued from Chapter 1]

Missouri Confederates.

The following was read by Capt. McNamara before the Southern Historical Society:

The long anticipated move was near at hand, and the Campaign of 1863 was begun by breaking up of Camp Anderson. General Order No. 62, I, from Parsons's headquarters, ordered the brigade to be "prepared to take the line of march on Sunday next, at 4 o'clock a.m." Transportation was very scarce. All surplus clothing was ordered stored at Little Rock. All blankets, knapsacks, haversacks, arms and ammunition issued to the troops were allowed to be carried in wagons. The only wagons allowed were just sufficient to carry fifteen days' rations. No further leaves of absences, except on Surgeon's Certificates were to be allowed. All others, except those countersigned by division commanders, were countermanded. Surgeon [Eugene W.] Herndon[34] was placed in charge of the small-pox and convalescent hospitals.

On Sunday, May 31, 1863, the Fourth Brigade [Parsons's], light and active, accompanied by McRae's, Fagan's and Tappan's Arkansas Brigades and [L. M.] Walker's Cavalry,[35] marched out of Camp Anderson. The other two brigades of

---

34. Eugene W. Herndon was a resident of Clarksville, Missouri, when he joined 2nd Division, MSG as the regimental surgeon for Dorsey's command that was destroyed at Mt. Zion Church on December 28, 1861. Later, Herndon joined Priest's 5th Cavalry Battalion and subsequently transferred to the Confederate Service, being commissioned a captain and surgeon, on September 24, 1862, in the 11th Missouri Infantry (CSA). Before war's end Herndon had become the senior surgeon in Parsons's Missouri Brigade. *O.R.*, vol. 22, pt. 2:1125–1126; Harrell, *Arkansas, Confederate Military History*, 381; Peterson, 94, 102–103; Schnetzer, *Men of the Eleventh*, 7.

35. Lucius Marsh or Marshall Walker, born in Columbia, Tennessee, on October 18, 1829, was the nephew of President James Polk, and graduated from West Point in 1850 (no. 15 of 44). He served two years in the army and then resigned to pursue the mercantile trade in Memphis. He returned to military service in November 1861, being elected colonel of the 40th Tennessee Infantry. After an unsuccessful career east of the Mississippi River, Braxton Bragg transferred Walker to the Trans-Mississippi, noting that Walker could not be trusted with a command. Walker was assigned to duty on June 2, 1863, and commanded a brigade of cavalry at Helena, after which he had a falling out with John S. Marmaduke over Walker's lack of support. The feud between Walker and Marmaduke escalated during the Little Rock Campaign, when Walker refused to communicate with Marmaduke during an engagement on August 27 at Reed's Bridge on Bayou Meto. On September 6, the feud boiled over and the near-sighted Marmaduke mortally wounded Walker in a duel near Little Rock. Walker died the next day. Walker's Brigade consisted of two regiments—5th Arkansas Cavalry and Dobbin's Arkansas Cavalry Regiments—with a four-gun battery of artillery. *O.R.*, vol. 22, pt. 1:412, 433, 435; Anne Bailey, "Lucius Marshall Walker," in *Confederate General*, 6:92–93; Boatner, 885; Timothy Wayne Burford and Stephanie Gail McBride, *The Division. Defending Little Rock: August 25–September 10, 1863* (Jacksonville, AR, 1999), 3, hereafter cited as Burford; Crute, 60; Harrell, *Arkansas, Confederate Military*

Price's Division, Frost's and Hawthorn's were on outpost duty—Frost fighting gunboats along the Mississippi and Hawthorne watching the enemy at Fort Smith.[36]

The troops were ignorant of their destination; but the joyful shouting and yelling of the men when the head of the column turned north showed that their hearts led to Missouri.

Their Vision

overlooked all distance and danger that lay between them and their homes. [Mosby M.] Parsons knew that this was the expedition that he, a few months previous, had hoped to command.

Gen. Price commanded the division, and the expedition was under the immediate command of Gen. Holmes.

Lucius M. Walker

For the first few days of the march the weather was delightful.[37] We passed through the towns of Austin, Stony Point and Searcy. We crossed the Little Red River during a violent thunder storm. It caught nearly all the brigade in the river bathing; where they had to remain, with only their heads above water. Paradoxical as it may sound—those who were caught on the river banks were wetter than those in the river. Crossing the "deadening" on the opposite side of the river, one of the teamsters was killed by a stroke of lightening.

History, 210; Leo E. Huff, "The Marmaduke-Walker Duel: The Last Duel in Arkansas," *Missouri Historical Review* 58 (Winter 1964), 453–454, hereafter cited as Huff, "Last Duel"; Moore, *Missouri, Confederate Military History*, 137–138; Warner, *Generals in Gray*, 321–322; J. Carter Watts, "A Duel of Generals," *Confederate Veteran* (Houston, TX, 1988), vol. 36, no. 1, 35, hereafter cited as Watts.

36. Not exactly accurate. Frost's Brigade had been taken over by James Tappan on April 20, 1863. At the time that Tappan assumed command of Frost's Brigade, Frost was in command of the "Defenses of Lower Arkansas" with his headquarters at Pine Bluff, which included Tappan's Brigade and several unattached units. Frost never took part in any of the operations described by the writer, until the Campaign for Little Rock began. However, Frost did order Colonel John B. Clark's and Richard Musser's units, with artillery, to operate against Federal boats on the Mississippi in mid June 1863. Clark subsequently began his operations about June 20, when he attacked a Federal landing party at Cypress Bend, Arkansas. Additionally, Tappan's Brigade, as previously shown, departed the Pine Bluff on May 18, 1863, and eventually joined with Walker's Texas Division for operations in Northeast Louisiana. Hawthorn's Brigade, on the other hand, did not exist at this time, though A. T. Hawthorn would later command a brigade during the 1864 Campaign. The unit in the Indian Territory was a division commanded by William Steele, and based in Fort Smith, Arkansas, in the western part of the state. *O.R.*, vol. 22, pt. 2:794, 832, 851, 866; Boatner, 388; Simons, 87–88; Turnbo, 221.

37. Parsons's Brigade left Little Rock, on May 31, to the tune of "The Girl I Left Behind Me"; and every day on the march northward, the command would start out with the same song repeated as the men anticipated a return to Missouri. However, Helena would be their eventual destination. Hoskin, May 31, 1863; Lotspeich, May 31, 1863; Young, 113.

We reached White River at Grand Glaze, and kept up that stream to Jacksonport, on the opposite bank, where we went into "Camp Stonewall Jackson," in the "Oil Through Bottom."[38] This was the turn-table of the expedition, whether it turn south or north—as the fortunes of Vicksburg would dictate.

Pneumonia and dysentery became epidemic in this camp for the two weeks we remained there, holding ourselves ready to march at a moment's notice.[39]

The troops enjoyed themselves bathing in its clear water and catching fish.

The situation of the Confederate forces at Vicksburg called for relief; so Price's Division took up the line of march for Helena on the 20th of June, the object being

To Draw Off

some of the Federal forces from in front of Vicksburg. It was slow work crossing White River, that stream being swollen to overflowing by the recent rains, and the pontoon constructed for our use was swept away. The troops crossed on flats, passed through Jacksonport and camped in the little village of Elizabeth, where our brigade was addressed by Gov. Reynolds of Missouri. The accomplished Governor delivered an eloquent speech—to his "fellow exiles."[40]

---

38. After making 10 miles the first day, the march continued as they made 18 miles the second day, arriving in Austin on June 2. As they marched along they passed through a wheat growing area, where an abundance of wheat was being harvested. A surgeon with the 10th Missouri noted that the people they met on the march "exhibited but little taste and intelligence. Their houses were all made out of logs, and their fences were out of repair." The weather, another declared, was "very warm." On June 3, they made 17 miles, traveling through a "better neighborhood" that was "principally cotton plantations, though now planted in wheat and corn." The next day they marched through Searcy and were greeted by the ladies of the town who waved handkerchiefs "for as long as they could see" the passing column. Crossing the Little Red River amid a rainstorm, the troops made camp on the evening of June 4 just north of the river. Another 18 miles on June 5 brought Price's command to Grand Glaze Creek, where they camped for the night. The command passed through Grand Glaze, "a beautiful village," on June 6, making another 15 miles. On June 7, Price's Division completed the last 15 miles of their march, arriving on south bank of the White River just below Jacksonport. R. J. Bell Diary, M. M. Parsons's Collection, Missouri Historical Society, June 1–June 7, 1863, hereafter cited as Bell; Hoskin, June 2–7, 1863; Lotspeich, June 1–6, 1863; Young, 113–114.

39. The day after Price's command arrived in the Jacksonport area, Surgeon R. J. Bell, of the 10th Missouri Infantry, noted that he anticipated "some sickness in the regiment," recording on June 9: "The situation of our camp is unfavorable to health." The troops were camped in the low lands of the White River, being both marshy and a breeding ground for malaria. Within days of arriving in Jacksonport, dysentery and pneumonia appeared in the command. To alleviate the problems in the 10th Missouri, Surgeon Bell recommended that the troops build "pole beds" to get the men off the ground and away from the cold and moisture. However, the longer the Confederates remained in the Jacksonport area the more it affected the men of the command. When the 10th Missouri finally departed Jacksonport on June 20, they left 40 men behind in the local hospital. Bell, June 8–10, 12, 14 and 20, 1863.

40. Parsons's Brigade crossed the White River first followed on June 21 by McRae's Brigade. Overall the crossing was a slow process, there being but three small boats to ferry the troops, baggage, and artillery across. After Price's Division crossed the White River, they went into camp at Elizabethtown and remained in the area until June 22 when they continued their march southward. While at Elizabethtown, Governor Thomas C. Reynolds addressed the troops on June 21. Surgeon Bell of the 10th Missouri recorded that Reynolds was an "accomplished gentleman," who delivered a "very appropriate speech." Lieutenant James T. Wallace, of Pindall's Sharpshooters noted that Reynolds was a fine

On the 22nd the long weary march for Helena was resumed. None of the soldiers who participated in that march can forget its hardships. The crossing of the Cache River, Bayou de View, Candy and Big Creeks, with their attendant six days' wading through mud and water, from ankle to waist high, whether in timber or prairie, it was "splash" after "splash" from one to four feet deep, and creeks two miles wide. Some of the nights following these weary days were spent without rations or shelter, for the wagons could not reach camp. Yet, through all this disheartening hardships the troops bore themselves with heroic fortitude.[41]

The 3rd of July brought the division within five miles of Helena, where we were furnished with ammunition and two days' cooked rations that many who grumbled at their allowance were fated to never eat.[42]

That night, under guide, we marched to Helena, approaching it from the west.[43] The artillery was left behind, the cannoneers going into the fight as infantry. Pindall's Sharpshooters were thrown out as flankers between the column and

---

speaker and told the gathered troops "some windy tales." A private in Tilden's Battery simply recorded that the speech "was good for what it was intended—it was in regard to the affairs of the Mo. troops." Ibid., June 20–22, 1863; Hoskin, June 20–22, 1863; Wallace, June 20–22, 1863.

41. The first two days of the march toward Helena were without problems, as the command made 25 miles and camped 4 miles north of Augusta. Up at 2:00 a.m., Price's Division resumed its march at 4:00 a.m. on June 24, having been subjected to an all-night rain. The rain continued through the day on June 24 as they marched through Augusta, a town of about 1,000 inhabitants, and camped on the banks of the Cache River. Despite the all day rain, one soldier noted that the women still turned out to greet the soldiers and declared them to be "the most handsome, the most lovely and the most accomplished" that he had seen since he had left his home state. The Cache River required a bridge be built before the division could cross. The troops crossed on June 25 and were followed the next day by the baggage train. On June 27, they made 7 miles and camped 2 miles east of Cotton Plant by the Bayou DeView. The skies finally cleared on June 27, but the mud prevailed. They crossed Bayou DeView the next day and made but two miles having to pass through a connected swamp area. To buoy the spirits of the passing troops, drummers and fifers were placed upon a floating flat boat. June 29, Caney Creek was crossed after a makeshift bridge was constructed. Ellis Creek and Big Creek were crossed on the 30th. On July 1 the command finally reached a dry area, passing through Moro, in Phillips County. July 2–3 were without incident as Price's Division finally made it to Polk's Plantation, about five miles from Helena. Lieutenant James T. Wallace probably summed up the feeling of Price's Division best: "This was about the most disagreeable time, that I have ever spent in my life." Bearss, "Battle of Helena," 260–261; Bell, June 23-July 3, 1863; Hoskin, June 23-July 3, 1863; Wallace, June 23-July 3, 1863.

42. After Holmes's command made camp on July 3, final preparations began for the up-oming battle. Of the activity one observer recorded: "All through the camp were seen preparations for battle—officers were instructing their men—surgeons, with professional nonchalance, discussing future amputations; while the men collected in little groups, where some engaged in filling cartridge boxes or haversacks, some of the most sanguine were talking over the good things in commissary or quartermaster's stores they would draw at Helena, while others of a more serious turn of mind—men whose piety had stood the test of camps, were singing religious hymns. Here and there some old campaigner was trying to get a little sleep, before the march commenced, but all felt serious and earnest." J. F. H. Letter.

43. When the various columns broke camp, for the final trek to Helena, they were led off by 5 local guides; 3 accompanied Parsons's Brigade and 2 went with McRae. Before Parson's Brigade reached their stopping point they had lost all their guides, prompting McRae to send one of his two guides to assist Parsons in finding his assembly point. Parsons and McRae both eventually lost their last guide; still both brigades arrived at their destinations as ordered. *O.R.*, vol. 22, pt. 1, 417 Bearss, "Battle of Helena," 274.

the enemy. The night was pitch dark, the timber was heavy, and the ground cut up into gullies.[44]

Battle of Helena.

It was a tedious march; I have performed more agreeable duty than acting as "right flanker" that night. When we got within a mile of the enemy's works we halted for a rest and the final disposition of forces. Parsons's and McRae's Brigades in the center, Fagan's and Tappan's on the right and Walker's cavalry on the left.[45] Helena's batteries opened before day with a shell from the Graveyard Fort. It came cutting angrily through the calm air, passing over Parsons's and McRae's Brigades. Daylight followed in the wake of the shell and lighted our division into line of battle.

The line advanced slowly and noiselessly, the men climbed up the steep and rugged approaches, now crowding down in the deep and narrow ravines; out of which they emerged on each other's shoulders, the last man being drawn up by the butt of his musket and again entangled in the thickly felled timber. Slowly and cautiously Pindall's Battalion and Capt. [Cameron N.] Balcoe's [Biscoe] Company of Sharpshooters deployed in front of Parsons's and McRae's Brigade.[46] Steadily they advanced, skirmishing with the enemy. Sharply the minies came slipping about the logs and stumps (sharpshooters breast works). Anxiously the quick cry, "look out," "lie down," often came too late. Sadly the "Enfield"[47] was

44. When Price's Division began their march on Helena, they followed in the rear of James F. Fagan's Brigade for 2 miles, when the two commands separated; Fagan's command veered to the right toward Battery D, while Price's Division moved to the left to confront Graveyard Hill, in the center. Price's Division was led by Parsons's Brigade, with Pindall's Sharpshooters leading, followed by the 12th Missouri, 11th Missouri, 16th Missouri and the 10th Missouri Infantry. Immediately behind Parsons's command came the boys of McRae's Brigade. *O.R.*, vol. 22, pt. 1:420–421; Bearss, "Battle of Helena," 274; Christ, 126.
45. Tappan's Brigade was not present at Helena. It was campaigning in northeast Louisiana with Walker's Texas Division and would not return to Little Rock until August 1863. See Chapter 2 of this book for details.
46. For the Battle of Helena, Company B, 30th Arkansas Infantry (C. N. Biscoe's Company) was detached from McRae's Brigade and attached to Pindall's Sharpshooters. Biscoe's Company had previously served as skirmishers during the Battle of Prairie Grove and were perfectly suited for their assignment at Helena. Biscoe was originally a lieutenant in Company B, 2nd Arkansas Infantry and later moved back to Arkansas, where he became the Adjutant of the 30th Arkansas Infantry. Company B was organized on June 19, 1862, with Captain I. N. Deaderick elected to command the unit. On July 28, Biscoe was appointed captain of Company B, which he successfully led at the Battle of Prairie Grove, where his unit earned the praise of his division commander. With the formation of McGhee's Arkansas Cavalry Battalion in the fall of 1863, Biscoe transferred to Company I and later to Dobbin's Arkansas Cavalry. Final disposition unknown. *O.R.*, vol. 41, pt. 2:1002; *O.R.S.*, pt. 1, vol. 4:61; *O.R.S.*, pt. 2, vol 2:294, 724; Crute, 62.
47. The Enfield Rifle was the standard issue for the British Army in 1855, and widely used by both sides during our Civil War. The official Enfield was manufactured at the Royal Small Arms Factory in Enfield, England, while the exported models were produced by private contractors throughout England. The weapon weighed 9 pounds, 3 ounces and was .577 caliber. It was very accurate to 800 yards and effective to 1,100 yards. About 400,000–500,000 were imported during the war and it was consid-

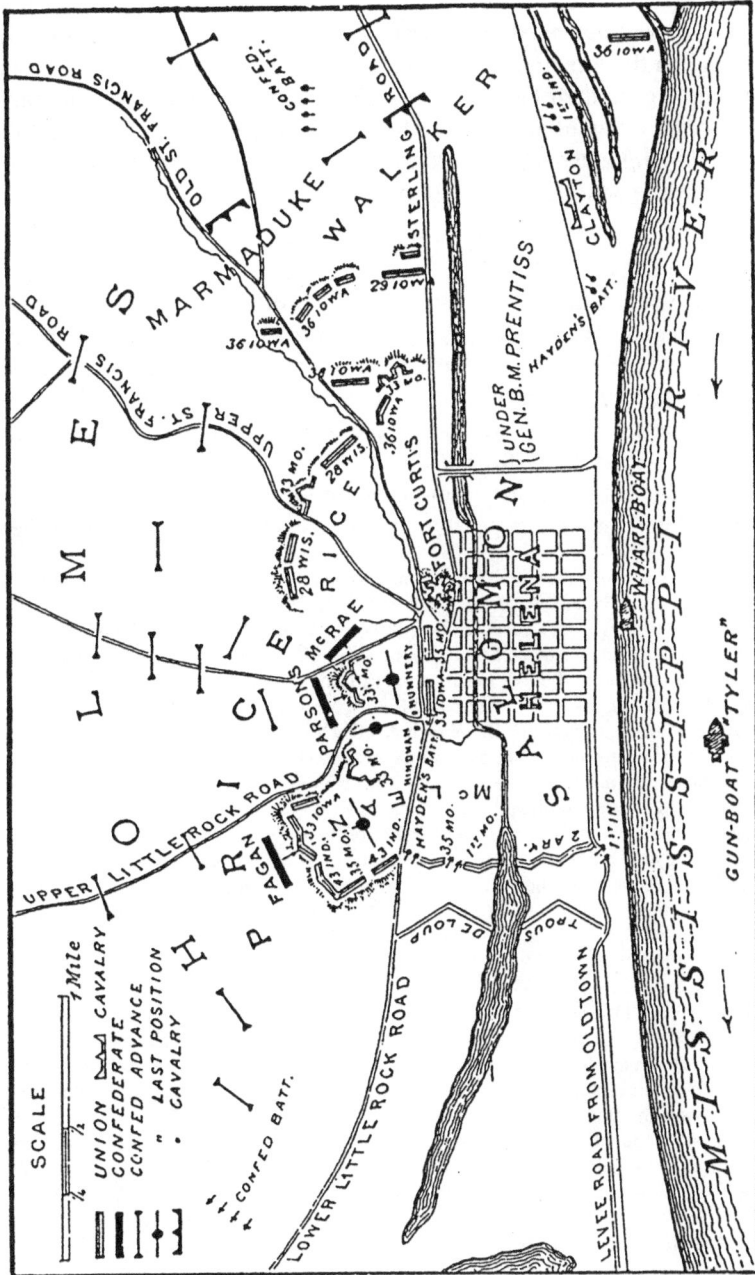

Battle of Helena (July 4, 1863)

rested across the body of a comrade, and a message sent to avenge his death.

Many a deadly ball was sent and received along the rough slope. But the slope was won, and its well defended brow occupied. Then a few minutes flat on the ground to bring up the infantry. On they came in a swaying zig-zag line, scrambling and stumbling till their heavy breathing fell on the quick ears of the sharpshooters. A halt for a few minutes on the field to allow the officers to correct the lines. All ready! a firm grasping of muskets, at "trail arms," a hurried glance along the line, all the while batteries are thundering in the front.

The Charge

from Parsons is echoed along the line by the field officers. The sharpshooters spring to their feet and dash at the battery in their front, followed closely by the infantry.[48] The outside ditch is gained, the crest of the works passed, and Parsons's and McRae's Brigades are charging down "Graveyard Hill," through the graves and abandoned batteries. Capt. Amos F. Cake, Co. C, Pindall's Sharpshooters, was the first man to top the fortifications.

Fagan is vainly struggling for an entrance on the right, and Walker is fighting hard on the left.[49] In the charge, two brigades swept the enemy before them

---

ered the most popular weapon in the Confederate Army, while the Springfield Rifle was the preferred weapon in the Union Army. Boatner, *Civil War Dictionary*, 266; Faust, 243–244.

48. In the charge upon Battery C, or Graveyard Hill, General Parsons rested his command on two occasions before making the final assault on the battery. In both Union reports and secondary accounts of the battle, Parsons's command is repulsed twice before carrying the hill—however, that was not true. The exceedingly hot day, rugged terrain, and felled trees were more than the charging Confederates could handle. James Wallace, of Pindall's Battalion noted that his unit was "completely exhausted" by the time they even came within sight of the enemy on Graveyard Hill, causing many to drop out of the attack. These conditions in turn caused Parsons to rest his command momentarily before continuing the charge. Recalling the charge, William Bull, of Tilden's Battery recorded:
At the command to charge we made a rush over the top of the first hill, down the opposite side and on the near side of the next hill where we were halted, in comparative safety, to rest and correct our formation, which had become disordered in getting over the felled timber and by the shots of the enemy...After a few minutes rest we were ordered to rush the next hill and then the third and then the fort which was captured." *O.R.*, vol. 22, pt. 1:, 388, 392, 414, 421; Banasik, *Missouri Brothers in Gray*, 57; Bearss, "Battle of Helena," 275; Christ, 229; DeBlack, 82; Hoskin, July 4, 1863; "The Victory At Helena," *Chicago Tribune*, July 12, 1863; "The Victory At Helena," *State Record*, July 22, 1863; Wallace, July 4, 1863; Young, 115–116.

49. At about 7:00 a.m. Parsons made his final assault on Graveyard Hill. Fagan, seeing Parsons's assault ordered his command forward in yet another attempt to capture Battery D. Where Price's Division was successful in capturing Graveyard Hill, Fagan's Brigade failed in taking Hindman Hill, but did manage to take the fifth and last line of rifle pits that guarded Battery D. It was the farthest that Fagan's Brigade would advance during the battle. However, Bearss in his account of the Battle of Helena, has Fagan's Brigade taking the last line of rifle pits well after Graveyard Hill had fallen and not during the assault as depicted in Christ's account of the battle. Meanwhile, L. M. Walker's Brigade on the far left of the rebel line was doing little more than skirmishing with the enemy. Walker, according to orders was supposed to cover the left flank of Marmaduke's Division in its assault on Rightor Hill. However, following the battle Marmaduke would complain bitterly that he could have taken Rightor "had it not been for the force on my left and rear,...which could and should have been prevented from taking that position...by General Walker's Brigade, which did not come to my support

down to the very streets of the town. But the lack of support compelled us to fall back. Slowly and shatteringly we moved up the steep hill, loading and turning and firing at will. Many a man dropped on the hill-side, never to rise. All the while heavy shell came after us, singing through the air from the gunboats and faster and deadlier they came from the forts on our right and left, tearing up graves from over the peaceful dead, shattering tombstones, stretching many a man across graves already tenanted, and sending others into graves newly made for other tenants.

When the troops came back scrambling over the breastworks into the outer ditch they were ordered by Parsons there to remain till Fagan could capture the fort on the right.

All the brigade commanders went into battle on foot.

Pindall's Sharpshooters were deployed in our front—in the inner ditch and along some ravine running down the hill, keeping up a fire on a few isolated brick buildings, behind which were bodies of enemy. Behind several of the monuments were groups of our sharpshooters—exchanging shots with the Federal sharpshooters on our right.

When Graveyard Fort was captured our cannoneers, who went into battle as infantry, threw down their muskets and rushed for the guns—every man to his own position on the piece—intending to turn them on the enemy, but they were found spiked. The men sadly picked up their muskets again.[50] One of them, seeing a few Federal gunners emerging out of a deep ravine, where they had run when they had abandoned their battery, rested his Enfield along a caisson and sent a ball through one of them, who was seen to fall back again into the ravine.

While we lay in this outer ditch waiting for Fagan to capture his fort, Gen. Holmes came over from Price, who had his position between the center and right of our line, to consult with Parsons. The consultation was interrupted several times by shells dropping around them. Holmes dismounted and the two generals walked to the right to reconnoiter.[51] Garrett Scott of Kelly's old infantry was called out of

---

of my left till after 7 a.m...Walker's Brigade not only did not prevent re-enforcements from going to Fort Rightor, but the enemy after sunrise actually passed to my left and a half mile to my rear, and held that position during the day." *O.R.*, vol. 22, pt. 1:425, 428–429, 437; Bearss, "Battle of Helena,"285; Christ, 130–131.

50. After the Confederates captured Graveyard Hill, both General McRae and Parsons directed their musket-armed artillerymen to man the captured guns. However the guns were found shotted with balls rammed into the barrels and no powder. Finding that the retreating Federals had taken their "worms" (a tool to clear the shotted artillery pieces) with them, there was little the Confederates could do to use the captured artillery, which numbered 4 guns. (In Bearss's account, as in most accounts, he has the battery with only 2 guns.) Undaunted, nine men from Lesueur's detachment of Tilden's Battery tried to make one of the guns serviceable. Unfortunately the gunboat *Tyler* got their range and exploded a shell under the gun. Of the nine men who were working the gun, according to Robert E. Young, 2 were killed, 5 wounded with only himself and "John Walker of St. Charles," Missouri, were not injured. In another account of the same incident another soldier claimed that worms were available and that he had lost both his arms while working the worm. *O.R.*, vol. 22, pt. 1: 414, 418, 421; "The Attack On Helena," in *Southern Historical Society Papers*, 24:199; Banasik, *Missouri Brothers in Gray*, 58; "The Battle of Helena," *Washington Telegraph*, July 15, 1863; Bearss, "Battle of Helena," 282, 295; Christ, 130; "Helena Battle," *Tri-Weekly Telegraph*, July 27, 1863; Hoskin, July 4, 1863; Young, 117.

51. In the conversation between Holmes and Parsons, Holmes directed Parsons to assist Fagan in

the ditch to hold the horse. Garrett soon discovered a well-filled canteen hanging on the pommel of the saddle. Soon all three—Garrett, the horse and the canteen—disappeared in the timber. The horse was picked up on the retreat, Garrett turned up in camp a few weeks afterwards, but nothing was ever seen

Of the Canteen.

While lying in the ditch, the cry, "The enemy advancing!" was raised; the men sprang out of the ditch, clambered up the parapet, and again—contrary to Parsons's orders—charged down the hill and into heavy masses of the enemy, who swarmed out of the streets to meet us. Again had we to fall back, loading and firing as we slowly moved up the hill. Again the gunboats sent their massive missiles and the forts their smaller, but deadlier ones, through the retreating brigades.[52]

In this last charge the two brigades lost 800 men killed, wounded and prisoner, and 300 men were surrounded and captured. Col. Wm. M. Moore, Parsons's Brigade, with 200 men, was also surrounded, but through an abatis of bayonets he cut his way and brought off his men.[53]

At 11 o'clock, Holmes giving up all hopes of success on our right, ordered a retreat. The infantry, covered by sharp-shooters, moved out of the works, held five hours, down same rough steps and bivouacked for the night five miles from the battlefield.[54]

Twice the enemy tried to flank our column, but the well handled sharp-shooters frustrated the design, repulsing the enemy's charge both times.[55]

---

taking Hindman Hill, by attacking Battery D from the north face of the Hill. After giving Parsons the order, Holmes retired to his headquarters, which was about 250 yards to the rear of Graveyard Hill. Meanwhile, even as Holmes departed the area a courier arrived from General Price directing Parsons to accomplish the same objective that General Holmes had directed. Prior to launching any assault, Parsons consulted with General McRae, who had just arrived on the scene. The two generals agreed that as Parsons's command was the larger of the two, with about 400 men remaining after the disastrous assault on Fort Curtis, that McRae would take whatever men he had to lead the assault. In all McRae had about 200 men to come to Fagan's aid. When McRae finally launched his attack, according the Edwin Bearss, the "attack collapsed almost before it started, the men taking cover in the timber-strewn ravine." And there they would remain until ordered to retreat from the battlefield. *O.R.*, vol. 22, pt. 1:411, 414–415, 418, 422; Bearss, "Battle of Helena," 284–285; Christ, 131; J. F. H. Letter.
52. This is the incident where General Holmes directed Colonel S. P. Burns to assault Fort Curtis. Burns in turn was followed by the entire brigade, which met with disastrous results as previously discussed. J. F. H. Letter.
53. See W. H. Wood's letter, which was previously presented on this incident.
54. Following the Battle of Helena, Holmes's army fell back to the Polk Plantation where it licked its wounds prior to retreating to Little Rock. To those who survived, the rest was a welcome relief, giving them time reflect upon the battle. Recalled one soldier: "It made our hearts sad though thankful we had been spared. It was a sad thought to think how many brave noble soldiers had been foolishly sacrificed. We may say needlessly or foolishly done by a dupe." Bell, July 4, 1863; Hoskin, July 4, 1863; Pitcock, 39; Wallace, July 4, 1863.
55. Pindall's Sharpshooter covered the retreat, "which was rather precipitate," according to one member of the battalion. In recording the retreat from the battlefield James T. Wallace, further noted:
The regiments were soon forced to retreat out as hastily as they went in at least as many as could being heavily flanked. We still held our position holding the enemy in check, covering the retreat…We

Our entire force was less than 5,000 men. Parsons's Brigade was only 1,364 muskets. Our loss, according to Dr. R. J. Bell[56] of Parsons's Brigade, who remained on the field after the battle, was 1,000 in all. One hundred killed, 500 wounded and 400 prisoners.[57] Gen. Holmes in person commanded the right and Gen. Price the center. We supposed that Gen. Prentiss commanded the Federal forces.[58]

At the Council of War

held by Gen. Holmes the night of the 3d, he assigned Gen. Price to the center, saying: "Gen. Price, I'll leave you to take Graveyard Fort tomorrow." Price assured him that "As sure as the sun rises, that fort will be ours." Holmes accepted the assurance rather warmly, saying: "That's the way I like to hear a general talk…"[59]

Among those who fell mortally wounded was the chivalrous Lieut. James A. Kelly, son of the "old colonel." He fell in the midst of his company in the second charge on Graveyard Hill. We were companions on many a weary march and cheerless bivouac.[60] We were together in the charge and fell about the same

passed out very swiftly ourselves after the rest were out of danger. The Yankees emboldened by our retreat followed us a short distance and firing with their artillery made it rather warm for comfort to us until we were out of range of their guns which was done as soon as our weary legs could do it urged on by the dread of being shot in the *back* which to me felt as broad as a barn door. By the time we had got out we were so exhausted we could hardly stand." Wallace, July 4, 1863.

56. Robert Joe or Joseph Bell, a resident of Hannibal, Missouri at the beginning of the Civil War, was born in Ralls County, Missouri, on January 2, 1835. He joined the 3rd Battalion, 2nd Division, MSG, as Battalion Commissary on March 22, 1862. He transferred to the Confederate Service at Camp Anderson, Arkansas, being commissioned Chief Surgeon, 10th Missouri Infantry on October 25, 1862. He married Virginia R. Hagan in 1864 while stationed in Arkansas and was also made Chief Surgeon of Parsons's Missouri Division the same year. Bell survived the war and returned to Hannibal, where he died on January 25, 1867, just shy of his 32nd birthday. Eakin, *Confederate Records*, 1:79; Harrell, *Arkansas, Confederate Military History*, 383; Peterson, 99; Pitcock, 354–355; Schnetzer, *Men of the Tenth*, 2.

57. When reporting his losses, General Holmes made two different accounts—on August 14, 1863, Holmes listed his losses as 173 killed, 687 wounded, with 776 missing—total 1,636. However, in an attached Addenda to his report Holmes listed his losses as 173 killed, 645 wounded, with 772 missing—total 1,590. I suspect that the latter figures are the true losses of the Confederates at Helena, with 4 of the missing returning, while 42 of the wounded were removed because of how slight their wounds were. Of the wounded, Federal sources reported capturing 357, of whom 212 were sent north to Union hospitals. However, see Appendix C for additional information on both the Confederate strength and losses at Helena. General Benjamin Prentiss, commanding the Union forces reported his losses as 57 killed, 146 wounded and 36 missing—total 239. *O.R.*, vol. 22, pt. 1:389, 391, 411–412; *O.R.*, series 2, vol. 6:96; "The Victory At Helena," *State Record*, July 22, 1863.

58. The Federal forces at Helena numbered 3,128 infantry, 831 cavalry and 170 artillerymen—total 4,129. *O.R.*, vol. 22, pt. 1:389.

59. At this point in his article, McNamara lists the officers in Parsons's Brigade who were killed at Helena on July 4, 1863. However, McNamara failed to mention Captain B. N. Cooke of the 7th (16th) Missouri Infantry. See Appendix A, for the list of those officers killed in Parsons's Brigade at the Battle of Helena, with brief biographies, and General Parsons's official order announcing their loss. *O.R.*, vol. 22, pt. 1:412.

60. James A. Kelly of St. Louis was the son of Colonel Joseph Kelly, who served on General Parsons's

time. I was fortunate enough to be taken charge of by Dr. Herndon of Parsons's Brigade, when I was pushed over the parapet into the outer ditch. The doctor had me taken into the timber out of the range of the shells, and with his skill and his probe and his hospital brandy left me quite comfortable behind a stump. This is the Dr. Herndon who criticized my estimate of our force at Prairie Grove so sharply. I can stand a great deal of adverse criticism from the good doctor before I'd be mad with him.

Young Kelly died in a Federal hospital at Memphis on the 13th of the same month (July, 1863). An old school mate of his, Maj. John P. McGrath of the Federal Army, was with him faithfully in his last moments and received his last message.

The Good Citizens of Memphis,

who turned out en masse, took charge of his burial and made it an impressive pageant. The hearse was drawn by eight white horses after a requiem high mass at St. Patrick's cathedral. He was buried, by the request of the mayor of the city—the Honorable Michael McGivney—in his own lot in the Catholic cemetery. Maj. McGrath, who furnished a beautiful metallic casket and otherwise took an active and friendly part in the burial, was made the subject of a complaint to Secretary [Edwin] Stanton.[61] The complaint stated that the major did more for the rebel officer than he would do for a Union officer. The Secretary of War referred it back to Maj. McGrath for an explanation. The explanation was straight and simple, that he and the young Kelly were college mates and companions at the breaking out of the war and that he did no more for Lieut. Kelly that he knew would be done for him were their positions reversed. Thus ended the matter.

When I landed in Memphis in June, 1865, a paroled prisoner, the same Maj.

---

staff. James was born about 1840, and prior to the Civil War he was a member of the Washington Blues, St. Louis Missouri Militia. He later joined his father in the MSG. He was in the Battles of Boonville, Carthage and Wilson's Creek, where he was wounded in the shoulder. After leaving the army he was detained in Gratiot Street Prison until October 12, 1862, when he posted a bond and took the oath of allegiance to the United States. He later joined what became Company C, 12th Missouri Infantry (CSA), where he was promoted to lieutenant on April 24, 1863. Kelly took a bullet in the thigh at Helena and was subsequently transported to Memphis, aboard the hospital steamer *R. C. Wood*. He was admitted to the Memphis hospital on July 7, where he died six days later. *O.R.S.*, pt. 2, vol. 38:624; "The Washington Blues," W. R. Babcock Collection, Missouri Volunteer Militia Scrapbook, page 3 of unnumbered pages, Missouri Historical Society; Bell, July 6, 1863; Eakin, *Missouri Prisoners of War*, "Kelly, James A." entry; National Archives, Record Group M322 (roll no. 163), Confederate Compiled Service Records, 12th Missouri Infantry; Schnetzer, *More Forgotten Men*, 130.

61. Edwin M. Stanton was born on December 19, 1814, in Steubenville, Ohio. He was a lawyer by profession and had an undistinguished career prior to the Civil War, though he briefly held the post of Attorney General under President Buchanan. Stanton became Abraham Lincoln's Secretary of War, replacing Simon Cameron on January 15, 1862. Stanton was a capable administrator throughout the war and continued on as the Secretary of War under President Andrew Johnson. As a bitter opponent of President Johnson, Stanton was forced to resign on May 26, 1868. Stanton died on December 24, 1869, four days after he was confirmed by the U. S. Senate to the U.S. Supreme Court. Faust, 712–713; Sifakis, *Who Was Who in the Union*, 386–387; Boatner, 792.

McGrath was the first old friend to take me by the cemetery to visit the grave of our "companion of other days." At that early day of "reconstruction" the war was over with us.

Back on the same very route, the defeated column marched till it passed Bayou de View, when it headed to the left passing through Cotton Plant and camping on the Cache River. Here the news of the fall of Vicksburg reached us, which intelligence had a worse effect on the morale of the troops than our own contemporary defeat.

On the second day of the retreat Gen. Price, surrounded by his staff, was sitting on the ground resting, when one of Parsons's men, as the column was passing, stepped out of the ranks and unfurling a captured Federal flag, spreading it on the ground, invited the general to rest on it. Price smiled and raised his slouched hat to the private and the whole column raised a shout for the gallantry of the soldier.

To help his brigade through the swamps Parsons had issued

Fifty-Seven Gallons of Whiskey.

The steamer Tom Suggs and a fleet of flatboats carried the brigade down Cache to "Surrounded Hill," an island formed by the Cache and White Rivers. Across the island the troops marched, tediously crossing White River to Des Arc, where we for a third time camped.[62] The prisoners captured at Helena were sent under Capt. [Elizahm or Elijah H.] Magoffin, Tenth Regiment to Little Rock.[63] In this camp hospitals were established for the worst cases of the wounded and sick, who were faithfully and skillfully attended to by Surgeons Herndon, Bell and [Godfrey N.]

---

62. On the morning of July 5, the defeated Confederates retreated the way they had come; however, in the course of the march General Holmes detached McRae's Brigade from Price's Division and ordered them back to Jacksonport, while Fagan's was attached to Price's command. Price's destination was Des Arc, on the White River. The army made Moro by the evening of July 6, crossed Bayou De View on July 9, and passed through Cotton Plant, "an inland village" which contained "about 200 inhabitants." The command, appears to have split at Cotton Plant, with McRae taking the road to Jacksonport, while Price's Division went into camp on the Cache River for several days to allow flat boats and the steamer *Tom Suggs* to convey the division to Des Arc. Parsons's Brigade crossed over first to Des Arc beginning on July 14, followed by Fagan's command. The division would remain in Des Arc for eleven days before it was ordered back to Little Rock. *O.R.*, vol. 22, pt. 2:942; *O.R.S.*, pt. 2 vol. 38:607; Bell, July 4, 9, 12–16, 1863; Hoskin, July 5–July 16, 1863; Pitcock, 40; Wallace, July 4, 15–16, 1863.
63. At the time Magoffin commanded Company B, 10th Missouri Infantry and would be promoted to major on December 2, 1863. He has been previously discussed. Following the battle, General Prentiss reported 36 men as "captured or missing." *O.R.*, vol. 22, pt. 1:390–391; Schnetzer, *Men of the Tenth*, 16.

Beaumont.[64] Chief Surgeon Baer and Surgeon [Andrew N.] Kincannon[65] were left behind to attend to our wounded on the field. The lighter cases found comfortable quarters in the hospitable homes of the little town. The sick of the prisoners receiving the same attention as our own...[66]

On the 25th the division struck tents taking up the line of march for the Arkansas River. A few days brought us into Camp Bayou Meto, twelve miles below Little Rock, where we enjoyed the luxuries of the season—peaches and "roasting ears." In honor of the dead Missourian, the camp was named "Camp Martin Green."[67] In this camp we received the news of the Battle of Gettysburg.

Gen. Parsons received leave of absence on the 29th, Col. A. C. Pickett taking command of the brigade. Gen. Price was now in command of the district, Gen. Holmes being sick.[68]

In this camp all the drills and ordinary duties of the soldier were resumed,

---

64. Godfrey Nash [or N. or W.] Beaumont (in *More Forgotten Men*, Beaumont is listed as "Nance G.") was born in Virginia about 1835, moved to Missouri, and was a resident of Camden Point, Platte County at the beginning of the Civil War. He joined a cavalry regiment in the MSG and transferred to the Confederate Service, being appointed a surgeon on September 26, 1862, in the 11th Missouri Infantry. Following the Battle of Helena, Beaumont was the Surgeon-in-Charge of the main Confederate hospital, located at Trenton, Arkansas. On December 29, 1863, he was assigned to duty in the 8th Missouri Cavalry, where he completed his military service. Surgeons Herndon and Bell have been previously covered. *O.R.S.*, pt. 2, vol. 38:231; Pitcock, 41; Schnetzer, *Men of the Eleventh*, 6; Schnetzer, *More Forgotten Men, 19.*

65. Andrew N. Kincannon was born in Virginia about 1822, and was living in St. Joseph, Buchanan County, Missouri, at the beginning of the Civil War. He was commissioned on October 8, 1862, as an assistant surgeon in Pindall's Sharpshooters and assigned to duty on January 31, 1863 (Harrell has the date as November 24, 1864), as surgeon of the battalion. Kincannon survived the war and was paroled at Shreveport, Louisiana on June 7, 1865. Surgeon Baer has been previously addressed. Bartels, *Bravest of the Brave*, 79; Harrell, *Arkansas, Confederate Military History*, 382; National Archives, Record Group M322, (roll no. 149), Confederate Compiled Service Records, 9th Battalion Missouri Sharpshooters.

66. At this point in his narrative McNamara inserts General Parsons's order announcing the death the brigade officers at the Battle of Helena. See Appendix A, for General Order No. 86.

67. On July 25, Holmes's army, now commanded by Sterling Price, completed its march to the Little Rock area, arriving at Bayou Meto on July 27. Fagan's Brigade arrived on July 28, while McRae's command staggered in between July 28–29, 1863, having been recalled from Jacksonport. *O.R.*, vol. 22, pt. 2:942; *O.R.S.*, pt. 2, vol. 2:752, 755, 758, 793, 807; *O.R.S.*, pt. 2 vol. 38:607, 614, 617–618; Bell, July 25, 27, 1863; Hoskin, July 25–July 27, 1863; Lotspeich, July 25–27, 1863; Wallace, July 25–27, 1863.

68. "If there was a positive result of the Battle of Helena," wrote Mark K. Christ, "for the Trans-Mississippi Confederacy, it was the loss of Theophilus Holmes as head of the District of Arkansas. The dithering general—hard of hearing, irresolute, and possibly suffering from arteriosclerosis" gave up his command to Sterling Price, effective July 23. Holmes, at the urging of Governor Thomas Reynolds of Missouri, never returned to command troops in the field. After Price assumed command of the District, General Fagan became the commander of Price's old division. As to General Parsons, his leave was temporary, as he had returned to command his brigade by August 8, when he inspected the troops. Following the Little Rock Campaign, Holmes was reinstated as commander of the District on September 25, but never led another combat mission for the Confederate Army. *O.R.*, vol. 22, pt. 1: 522; *O.R.*, vol. 22, pt. 2:942; Christ, 146; Hoskin, August 8, 1863; Lotspeich, August 8, 1863; Schultz, 95.

and the brigade thoroughly inspected in all its departments and the troops again equipped for campaign duty. Some important

Works Were Thrown Up

on rumors of the advance of the enemy.[69] More formidable works were then in course of construction, nearer Little Rock.[70]

For some days the enemy's cavalry were feeling their way and skirmishing with Marmaduke's.[71]

While in this camp Parsons had Col. [Robert] Lawthor [Lawther],[72] Capt.

---

69. General John W. Davidson's Union cavalry division began the Little Rock Campaign from Witts-burg, Arkansas (about 15 miles north of Madison, on the St. Francis River) on August 1, 1863. On August 8, the cavalry reached Clarendon, on the White River, followed by Frederick Steele's infantry from Helena, which began arriving on August 15, 1863. Davidson's cavalry command crossed the White River on August 18 and established "Camp Advance" 4 miles from Clarendon to protect the rest of the command while they crossed up river at DeVall's Bluff. On August 22, the Federal Army continued its advance on Little Rock, as Davidson's men led the way. Meanwhile, the Confederates prepared for the Federals while recovering from the Helena debacle. Inspections were held on August 8, 10 and 16. The men were "drilled four hours each day and then dress parade in the evening at re-treat." But all that ended on August 23, when the grayclads broke camp on Bayou Meto and moved to within a mile of Little Rock. At that time the Unionists were reported as being within 18 miles of the Confederate position. Brigades were assigned their positions in the main defenses: Parsons's Brigade had the center; John B. Clark's Missouri Brigade, from Pine Bluff, was to the left of Parsons; Fagan's Brigade was on the right next to the river; McRae's command was on the extreme left adjacent to Clark's Brigade; and Tappan's Brigade, lately arrived from Louisiana was held in reserve on the south side of the river. *O.R.*, vol. 22, pt. 1: 475, 483–484, 543; *O.R.*, vol. 22, pt. 2:978; Banasik, *Reluctant Cannoneer*, 171, 176, 178, 180; Banasik, *Serving With Honor*, 102; Christ, 150–151, 157, 160; Harrell, *Arkansas, Confederate Military History*, 207–209; Hoskin, August 28, 1863; Lotspeich, August 8, 10, 16, 23–27; Wallace, August 8–9, 23.

70. The Confederates had two set of works, protecting Little Rock. The first was constructed on Bayou Meto, about 12 miles from the city on the north side of the Arkansas River, while the second, and more formidable works, were but within three miles of the city. Of the closer work, one Missourian recorded that it was "almost impregnable, the walls being about ten feet broad, the outside ditch being five feet deeper about the same in breadth. A man can stand behind the works and load his gun without being in danger of being hit." Lotspeich, August 27, 1863.

71. Shortly after the campaign began, active skirmishing commenced between the two forces. A river expedition up the White and then the Little Red River netted the Union forces the Confederate steam-ers the *Tom Sugg* and the *Kaskaskia*, which were captured on August 14, followed by a skirmish at West Point that same afternoon. On August 16, Davidson's cavalry engaged rebel pickets at Harrison Landing, with but little effect to either side. The following day, four companies of the 13th Illinois Cavalry attacked the 5th Arkansas Cavalry and "routed them" according to their official report. Addi-tional accounts stated that some rebels were captured, but rebel statements acknowledged that no men were killed or wounded; however, "some of our boys could not stand it and gave way, while others retreated." On August 23, when the Confederate infantry gave up the Bayou Meto line, Davidson's cavalry were on a scout to Deadman's Lake near Brownsville, setting the stage for the most active engagements of the campaign. *O.R.*, vol. 22, pt. 1:468, 475, 483; *O.R.S.*, pt. 2, vol. 8:133, 138; *O.N.R.*, vol. 25:354–356, 876; Christ, 154; Leo E. Huff, "The Union Expedition Against Little Rock, August–September, 1863," *Arkansas Historical Quarterly* 22 (Autumn, 1963), 228-229, hereafter cited as Huff, "Union Expedition"; Lotspeich, August 23, 1863.

72. Robert R. Lawther was born in Kittanning, Pennsylvania, and was living in Jefferson City, Mis-souri at the beginning of the Civil War. He joined the 6th Division MSG, on A. E. Steen's staff and

[Henry A.] Peabody,[73] Lieuts. [Henry] Burt,[74] [J. F. H.] Ledbetter,[75] [Aaron] Rob-

---

later was elected major of the 1st Missouri Cavalry Regiment (CSA) when the regiment was organized on December 30, 1861. During the summer of 1862, Lawther organized a Partisan Ranger Regiment. Captured in Osage County on September 1, 1862, Lawther was sent to Gratiot Street Prison and then to Camp Chase, Ohio. He was later exchanged, and during the Little Rock Campaign Lawther commanded a "Temporary Regiment of Dismounted Cavalry." On April 24, 1864, he was elected colonel of the 10th Missouri Cavalry Regiment, to rank from December 12, 1863. He resigned on February 27, 1865, with a surgeon's Certificate of Disability and was paroled at Galveston, Texas, on June 20, 1865. After the war he eventually settled in Texas and was elected as a alderman of Dallas, where he died on October 1, 1911. See Appendix B for a complete biography. *O.R.*, vol. 22, pt. 1:731–732; *O.R.*, vol. 34, pt. 1:781; *O.R.*, vol. 41, pt. 1:698; *O.R.S.*,, pt. 2, vol. 38:253; Allardice, *Confederate Colonels*, 233; R. S. Bevier, *History of the First and Second Missouri Confederate Brigades 1861-1865. And From Wakarusa to Appomattox, A Military Anagraph* (St. Louis, 1879), 77, hereafter cited as Bevier; Crute, 203; Eakin & Hale, 261; James E. McGhee, *Letter and Order Book Missouri State Guard 1861–1862* (Independence, MO, 2001), unnumbered page 29 (entry pages 56–57); John S. Marmaduke, *Confederate States Trans-Mississippi Order and Letter Book* (Carolyn M. Bartels, ed.; Independence, MO, 2000) 239–240, hereafter cited as Marmaduke, *Order and Letter Book*; National Archives, Record Group M322, (roll no. 57), Confederate Compiled Service Records, 10th Missouri Cavalry Regiment; Peterson, 174.

73. Henry A. Peabody, a resident of Jefferson City at the beginning of the Civil War, joined the MSG at the outbreak of hostilities. He fought at Carthage, Drywood, Wilson's Creek and Lexington and later joined the 1st Partisan Ranger Regiment, commanding Company A. Captured 25 miles south of Jefferson City, at "Stevensburgh" on September 1, 1862, Peabody was first sent to Gratiot Street Prison and then to Alton Prison on October 24, 1862. After being forwarded to Johnson Island, on Lake Erie, Peabody was exchanged on December 8, 1862, at Vicksburg, Mississippi, and returned to the Trans-Mississippi Department. In August 1863, he commanded a company in Lawther's "Temporary Regiment," after which his name disappears from the rolls. *O.R.*, vol. 13, 264; Eakin, *Missouri Prisoners of War*, "Peabody, A. H." entry; Marmaduke, *Letter and Order Book*, 239-240; National Archives, Record Group M322 (roll no. 71), Confederate Compiled Service Records, 10th Missouri Cavalry; Schnetzer, *More Forgotten Men*, 180.

74. Henry Burt [or Bart] was born about 1831, in Callaway County, near Williamsburg, Missouri. When the war began he joined Company B, 2nd Cavalry Battalion, 2nd Division, MSG, as an orderly sergeant, then second lieutenant, and was elected captain on January 1, 1862. After he left the Guard, he joined the Confederate Service on June 20, 1862, at Musgrove, Cherokee Nation, Indian Territory (modern-day Oklahoma). He was elected 1st Lieutenant of his company on September 13, 1862, when the unit was organized and was promoted to captain of Company K, 6th Missouri Cavalry on December 18, 1863. Burt fought at Lone Jack in August 1862 and lost his horse at the Battle of Helena in July 1863. Detailed to command a temporary company of dismounted cavalry under Colonel Lawther, on August 6, 1863, Burt participated in "one-hundred and two battles, including such as that fought at Lexington, Pea Ridge, etc." Burt never received a wound of any type during the war, after which he went to Mexico for a time, but then returned to Nine Mile Prairie Township, in Callaway County. He married after the war and had six children. He moved to Danville and then Montgomery City, where he died on November 13, 1898, of heart disease. *O.R.S.*, pt. 2, vol. 38:218; Author anonymous, *The Gallant Breed: The 6th Missouri Cavalry, A Roster of the Men Who Rode Under the Flag of Shelby's Iron Brigade* (Carolyn M. Bartels and James E. McGhee, eds.; Independence, MO, 2009), 131, hereafter cited as Anonymous, *6th Missouri Cavalry*; Bartels, *Trans-Mississippi Men*, 42; Mark K. Douglas, *Soldiers, Secesh and Civilians Compiled Records of Callawegians In the War of the Rebellion, Etc.* (Montgomery, MO, 2001), 19–20; Joane C. Eakin, *Battle of Lone Jack August 16, 1862* (Independence, MO, 2001), 226, hereafter cited as Eakin, *Battle of Lone Jack*; Marmaduke, *Order and Letter Book*, 239–240; Peterson, 93.

75. J. [w/wo] Fuller Hendricks Ledbetter [or J. R. or F. Ledbetter] was a resident of Jackson County, Missouri, when he enlisted in what became Company I, 12th Missouri Cavalry (CSA) on August 12, 1862. He was a second lieutenant in the unit, being promoted on July 16, 1863. Ten days after his

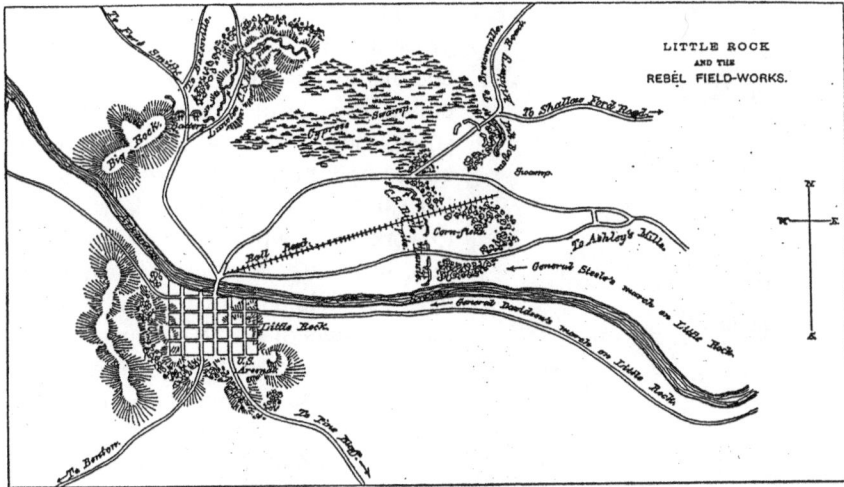

Approaches to Little Rock (August–September 1863)

erts[76] and Weir of Lawthor's Regiment, dismounted cavalry, placed under arrest for disobedience of orders and mutiny, they having refused to be disciplined and drilled as infantry. This was a very disagreeable duty to Parsons, for they were all brave cavalrymen, who had a strong antipathy to the "webfeet." They were soon released on indications of an early battle and resumed command of their companies and regiment.[77]

---

promotion Ledbetter was declared a "non-effective and dismounted" man, having lost his horse and assigned to duty in Lawther's Temporary Regiment. He was later remounted, returned to duty and survived the war. He was paroled out of the service on June 7, 1865, at Shreveport, Louisiana as a captain. *O.R.S.*, pt. 2, vol. 38:262; Author anonymous, *The Gallant Breed the 12th Missouri Cavalry: A Roster of the Men Who Rode Under the Flag of Shelby's Iron Brigade* (Carolyn M. Bartels and James E. McGhee, eds.; Independence, MO, 2009), 87, hereafter cited as Anonymous, *12th Missouri Cavalry*; Eakin, *Confederate Records*, 5:48–49; Marmaduke, *Order and Letter Book*, 239–240; National Archives, Record Group M322 (roll no. 60), Confederate Compiled Service Records, 12th Missouri Cavalry.

76. Aaron Roberts was born about 1838 and lived in Platte County, Missouri, at the beginning of the Civil War. He joined Lawther's Partisan Rangers in the summer of 1862, as a lieutenant, and was captured on September 7 in Osage County. Imprisoned first in Gratiot Street Prison, he was sent to Alton Prison on September 20, 1862, and to Johnson Island on Lake Erie on November 14, 1862. Roberts was forwarded to Ft. Delaware from a hospital in St. Louis on April 22, 1863, and was later exchanged. Returning to the Trans-Mississippi, he first joined Lawther's Temporary Regiment of dismounted Cavalry, and was later incorporated into the 11th Battalion, Missouri Cavalry (CSA), which then became Company C, 10th Missouri Cavalry. Final disposition unknown. *O.R.S.*, pt. 2, vol. 38:255; Eakin, *Missouri Prisoners of War*, "Roberts, Aaron," entry; Marmaduke, *Order and Letter Book*, 239–240; National Archives, Record Group M322 (roll no. 58), Confederate Compiled Service Records, 10th Missouri Cavalry Regiment.

77. On August 1, 1863, General Price issued Special Order No. 125, establishing "Lawthers Temporary Regiment of Dismounted Cavalry" with Colonel Lawther appointed its commander. Seven officers were assigned to the command, having previously lost their horses—Captains Henry A. Peabody and W. D. Sappington; Lieutenants Charles Berry, Henry Burt, Thomas Keithly, J. F. H. Ledbetter, and

John S. Marmaduke

On the 23d the baggage trains were ordered to the south side of the Arkansas, and the infantry into the ditches, constructed within sight of Little Rock. This was a strong line of earthworks, running right angles from the river for two miles across a flat, till it struck the hills. Each brigade went to work with a will to strength its own position. In front of Parsons's Brigade was an open cornfield about half a mile wide, and three-quarters of a mile in length. The men bent down the corn stalks at the height of a horse's knee so tangling them that it would be very difficult for either cavalry or infantry to charge through there. Immediately outside the ditch for the whole front of the brigade line, and for a hundred yards out, they constructed a sort of abatis of their own—by driving stakes into the ground at an angle of forty-five degrees and sharpening the points with their knives. This, the men said, "was for the benefit of Merrill's Cavalry."[78] One thousand pikes were distributed, to be used when the enemy attempted to climb the parapet. Our guns were in embrasures. In this position the troops waited for the enemy with forty rounds of cartridges and four day's cooked rations.

Aaron Roberts. There was no Lieutenant Wier or Weer found within the known records. All the men assigned to the regiment, including the officers, could rejoin their former commands upon remounting themselves. The unit was assigned to duty under General Parsons. Seven days later, General Parsons, addressed the 400 dismounted cavalrymen, who were encamped near his brigade on Bayou Meto. According to William Hoskin, Parsons "delivered a short address to the marmadukers & told them what was what—they didn't like his way of talking eny [sic] too well—he told them that they could transfird [sic] from the cavalry to the infantry & artillery in his Brig.—or if they would dissert [sic]—to do it tonight." Hoskin, August 8, 1863; Marmaduke, *Order and Letter Book*, 239–240.

78. "Merrill's Horse cavalry" was the 2nd Missouri Cavalry (Union). It was organized by Lewis Merrill in the summer of 1861. It served principally in the Trans-Mississippi, but in December 1864 it was ordered to the east side, to report to the Army of the Cumberland, where the regiment completed its military service. It was part of the Union Army that was advancing on Little Rock in the summer of 1863. The unit was also know as the "White Horse" cavalry regiment as the command were all mounted on white steeds. Many Missourians despised the 2nd Missouri Cavalry. John Edwards, Adjutant of Shelby's Brigade noted that the Unionists "had acquired much fame in chasing citizens over the country in Missouri," proving themselves "expert at this bastard kind of Cassock warfare." *O.R.S.*, pt. 2, vol. 34:559–560; *O.R.*, vol. 22, pt. 1:470; Burford, 12; Christ, 164; John Newman Edwards, *Shelby and His Men or the War in the West* (Cincinnati, OH, 1867; reprint ed., Waverly, MO, 1993), 174, hereafter cited as Edwards, *Shelby and His Men*; *The Union Army A History of Military Affairs in the Loyal United States 1861-18675—Records of the Regiments in the Union Army—Cyclopedia of Battles—Memoirs of Commanders and Soldiers*, 8 vols. (New York, 1908; reprint ed., Wilmington, NC, 1998), 4:273.

A Fatal Duel.

Daily skirmishing between Marmaduke's and the enemy's cavalry continued up to the 9th of September.[79] On that day troops were thrown into a state of great excitement on learning that Gens. Marmaduke and Walker, Arkansas cavalry, had fought a duel. Walker was the challenger, and was mortally wounded. He died on the 8th. Gen. Marmaduke was immediately placed under arrest by Gen. Price. But he was forced to release him in a few days for the cavalry refused to operate against the enemy unless they were lead by "our Marmaduke."[80]

On the morning of the 10th the enemy succeeded in crossing the Arkansas on pontoons five miles below Little Rock, thereby flanking the Confederate position. Marmaduke immediately engaged the enemy on the south of the river, whilst the infantry was withdrawn from the trenches. They crossed on a pontoon bridge and

---

79. After the Confederate infantry fell back to their main defenses nearer Little Rock a total of six major skirmishes or engagements took place before September 9, 1863. On August 25, the Federal advance drove back Marmaduke's Cavalry Division at Brownsville, capturing in the process Colonel John Q. Burbridge. The following day, the Federal advance again encountered rebel cavalry just east of Bayou Meto, with only light skirmishing taking place. After the main body of the Confederate cavalry crossed the Bayou Meto, Marmaduke's Brigade (formerly Greene's Brigade) withdrew to the west side of the bayou with the rest of the command. August 27 saw the Unionists trying to force their way across Bayou Meto at Reed's Bridge. After successfully driving the rebels from the eastern bank of the bayou, General Davidson ordered the 1st Iowa Cavalry to capture Reed's Bridge, to prevent the bridge from being destroyed, but they failed in their attempt. On August 30, at about 9:00 a.m. a series of skirmishes broke out in the vicinity of Shallow ford, over the Bayou Meto, between Davidson's Reserve Brigade under Colonel John Ritter and R. C. Newton's 5th Arkansas Cavalry. Things then remained quiet until September 2 when some "light skirmishing" occurred at Shallow ford between Shelby's Brigade and Davidson's cavalry. On September 7, the Federal cavalry again pressed Newton's command, now located at Ashly Mill. By noon on September 7, the skirmish had ended and the rebels were forced across the Arkansas River, setting the stage for the capture of Little Rock. *O.R.*, vol. 22, Pt. 1:468, 484–485, 521, 526–528, 530–532, 536–538; Banasik, *Reluctant Cannoneer*, 182; Burford, 23, 55–57, 127, 149, 153; Huff, "Union Expedition," 231–232; Sellmeyer, 120.

80. On September 2, 1863, General Walker sent a letter to Marmaduke, in which Walker asked Marmaduke to clarify a statement that Marmaduke supposedly made, calling Walker a coward for his lack of action at Reed's Bridge on August 27. Over the course of the next several days the two generals wrote several pieces of correspondence concerning Walker's abilities or lack thereof. Walker used Colonel Robert Crockett, of Texas (grandson of Davy Crockett), to convey his messages and to serve as his second in the forthcoming duel, while Captain John C. Moore of St. Louis acted on behalf of General Marmaduke. On September 4, Walker issued the challenge and the next day Marmaduke accepted. "Terms of Agreement" for the duel were cemented on September 5, setting the date for the duel the following day. When General Price heard of the pending duel he ordered both parties to remain in their headquarters for twenty-four hours. Marmaduke ignored the order, fought the duel at 5:40 a.m. on September 6, and mortally wounded Walker. General Price ordered Marmaduke's arrest but suspended the order because of the impending Federal advance on Little Rock. Marmaduke never faced a court martial for his actions on September 6. See Appendix A for the correspondence surrounding the Walker-Marmaduke Duel. *O.R.*, vol. 22, pt. 1:525–526; "Correspondence," Concerning Walker-Marmaduke Duel, *Washington Telegraph*, October 21, 1863; Burford, 141; Edwards, *Shelby and His Men*, 181-182; Harrell, *Arkansas, Confederate Military History*, 220–222; Huff, "Last Duel," 453–455; Huff, "Union Expedition," 232; Watts, 44–45.

formed in line in the main street of Little Rock, and so remained till the trains had a good start.[81]

The retreat began in the afternoon.[82] As the columns of infantry turned southward, Parsons at the head of his brigade counter marched to meet the enemy, with fifes and drums playing "The Bonnie Blue Flag," cheered by the whole column.

Parsons formed in line of battle in the rear of St. John's College, east of town, and there awaited the expected engagement.

Price seeing his trains safely on the road and his column fairly in motion, recalled Parsons. But Parsons

Remained in Line

to gratify his men with a brush with the enemy. A preemptory order from Price for Parsons to withdraw put the brigade in motion. As the sun went down the column headed southward.[83] Before leaving his position he visited the hospital in St. John's College and shook the hands of all his sick. It was an affecting scene to look upon these emaciated convalescents crowding around Parsons to shake his hand, and hear the "Good-bye men" "Good-bye, General" interrupted by bursting

81. On September 10, 1863, the Federals selected a horseshoe bend to cross the Arkansas River just north of Bearskin Lake, and about eight miles south of Little Rock—at Terry's Ferry or Terry's Ford. The Unionists placed batteries on the sides of the river bend to protect the crossing. The rebels opposed the crossing with Chamber B. Etter's four gun battery and some dismounted cavalry from Archibold Dobbin's Brigade, commanded by Major John Bull. In the ensuing action, at Bayou Fourche, the Confederate cavalry fought a delaying action to allow time for the remainder of the Confederate Army to evacuate Little Rock. The Federals lost 18 killed, 118 wounded, and 1 captured in their almost bloodless effort to take Little Rock. The Confederates lost 12 killed, 34 wounded and 18 missing. A more detailed look at this engagement will be found in the letters following. *O.R.*, vol. 22, pt. 1:476, 482, 522, 539; "Fall of Little Rock," *Washington Telegraph*, September 16, 1863; Huff, "Union Expedition," 233–235.

82. At about 11:00 a.m., on September 10, General Price ordered that the works on the north side of the Arkansas River be abandoned. Parsons's Brigade was by most accounts the last unit over the bridge, departing its works about 2:00 p.m. and crossing the bridge to the south side, after which the bridge was burnt. In the city, General Price closed his headquarters about 3:30 p.m. and joined the retreat southward. The last units out of Little Rock were reported by various sources to be either Parsons's Brigade, Fagan's Brigade or Tappan's command. S. C. Turnbo, from Tappan's Brigade, stated that his regiment was directed "to sweep the streets of stragglers." and that his regiment, the 27th Arkansas was the last to leave the city; clearly leaving the honor of the last Confederate unit in Little Rock to come from Tappan's Brigade. Turnbo also relates, while stopped at the "old fair ground," that General Price passed on by and when asked why "ain't we going to fight the yankees?" Price replied: "They are too many for us." By 5:00 p.m. the last of the Confederate troops had given up Little Rock and a short time later Federal troops entered the city from the south. The rebel cavalry, under a reinstated General Marmaduke, served as the rear guard of the army as they plodded along southward. *O.R.*, vol. 22, pt. 1:522; Burford, 187, 194; "Fall of Little Rock," *Washington Telegraph*, September 16, 1863; Huff, "Union Expedition," 234–235; Lotspeich, September 6–13, 1863; Turnbo, 292, 295–296; Quesenberry, September 10, 1863; Wallace, September 10, 1863.

83. John Quesenberry, of the 11th Missouri Infantry generally supports McNamara's account of Parsons's action, but differs in one important part. "As soon as the train was fairly under way, we took up the line of march for Arkadelphia," Quesenberry recorded. There was no delay in the brigade movement as implied by McNamara. Quesenberry, September 10, 1863.

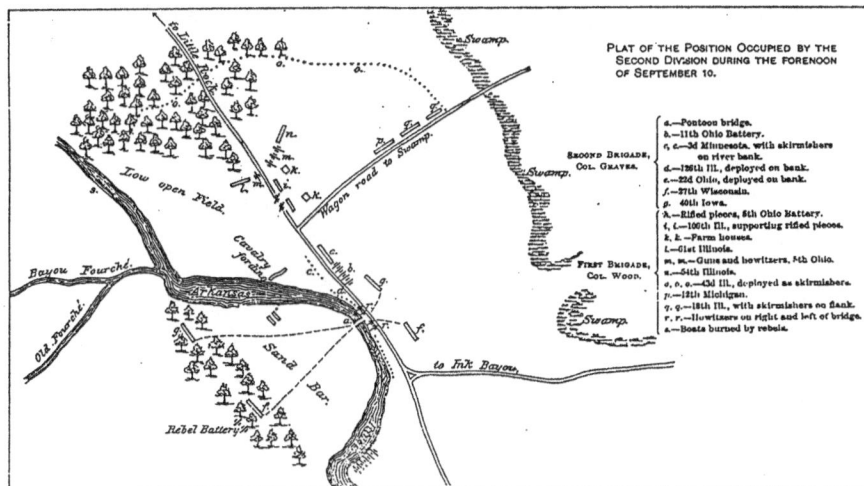

PLAT OF THE POSITION OCCUPIED BY THE
SECOND DIVISION DURING THE FORENOON
OF SEPTEMBER 10.

a.—Pontoon bridge.
b.—11th Ohio Battery.
c, c.—3d Minnesota, with skirmishers
on river bank.
d.—126th Ill., deployed on bank.
e.—22d Ohio, deployed on bank.
f.—27th Wisconsin.
g.—40th Iowa.
h.—Rifled pieces, 5th Ohio Battery.
i, i.—106th Ill., supporting rifled pieces.
k, k.—Farm houses.
l.—51st Illinois.
m, m.—Guns and howitzers, 5th Ohio.
n.—54th Illinois.
o, o, o.—43d Ill., deployed as skirmishers.
p.—12th Michigan.
q, q.—18th Ill., with skirmishers on flank.
r, r.—Howitzers on right and left of bridge.
s.—Boats burned by rebels.

Crossing the Arkansas River at Terry's Ferry (September 10, 1863)

of the enemy's shells. The enemy was reported 13,000 strong. The whole affected force under Price was 7,000.[84] In the skirmishing before Little Rock the Confederate loss was forty killed and wounded—all cavalry.[85]

Before the brigade got through the town many of the frame structures were on fire from the enemy's shells. While the column was passing the "Anthony House" a negro was seen at an upper story window plating a violin. A St. Louis wag in the battery, pointed up, shouted out, "Nero fiddled while Rome burned," which created a laugh, and was followed by a witticism from every other man in the column at the expense of the musical darky.

Price's Division bivouacked that night eight miles from Little Rock, and the next night the Saline River. All of this second day Marmaduke, who covered the retreat, skirmished with the emmy's cavalry, alternating charging him and repulsing his charges.[86] On the 13th we struck the Washita at Rockport, marching up that

---

84. When the Federal Army began the Little Rock Campaign it numbered 12,182 men and received an additional 2,000-man reinforcement during the course of the campaign. By the time the city had fallen Steele's command was down to 10,480 men of all types. General Price, for his part, reported that he "had barely 8,000 men of all arms" at the end of August 1863, and received no additional men after that date. However, by the end of the campaign General E. Kirby Smith reported that there were "not over 9,000 effective" men to oppose Steele on September 11, the day after the city fell. Additionally, Smith also reported that Price's command contained 2,000 unarmed men. On September 30, 1863, the District of Arkansas reported 8,436 officers and men present for duty, having lost 1,300 deserters during the retreat. *O.R.*, vol. 22, pt. 1:521; *O.R.*, vol. 22, pt. 2: 989, 1003, 1010, 1029; Banasik, *Reluctant Cannoneer*, 302–303; Banasik, *Serving With Honor*, 111.

85. On September 10, 1863, General Price reported the loss of 6 killed, 17 wounded, with 13 captured or missing—total 36. General Steele reported losing 7 killed, 64 wounded, with 1 man missing or captured—total 72. *O.R.*, vol. 22, pt. 1:482, 523.

86. After the fall of Little Rock, the Union Army conducted a half-hearted effort in its pursuit of the Confederates. Colonel Lewis Merrill was placed in command of a two-brigade division, composed

stream, going into camp at Arkadelphia on the 15th, where we remained till the 1st of October. The enemy now occupied Little Rock.[87]

* * * * * *

---

especially for the pursuit, with 12 pieces of artillery. Owing to the character of the terrain, the pursuit proved to be "exceedingly difficult," according to Colonel Merrill. After two days of light skirmishing that cost Merrill 1 man wounded he gave up the chase, "the weariness of the men and horses… rendered rapid pursuit impossible." Having failed to bag the retreating Confederates, Merrill did report capturing a large number of Confederates, mostly deserters, to the number of between 200–300. Merrill returned to Little Rock, reaching the city at sunset on September 12. *Ibid.*, 496–499.

87. When the Confederate troops left Little Rock they did so with mixed feelings. "We came off in good order, and if it had not been for a number of *cowardly desertions* we would not have been worsted" recorded one Arkansas soldier. Another from the same state noted that his command was "dishearted." Missourians presented a different tale—one recorded that the "boys are all cheerful and determined," while another recorded of his command: "The men were not despondent. Some of them had gotten used to fighting and falling back…I think that we did not dread pursuit, it was too hot for us to care much, and I think the enemy considered prudence the better part of valor." The retreat was not hurried, the army making 18 miles on September 11, as they passed through Benton, camping near General Fagan's residence. The men ate "scrumptiously," compliments of General Fagan and the Confederate Commissary, as pork, bacon, "muscatine" grapes and coffee were on the menu for the day. They rested until 10:00 a.m. the next morning and made 10 miles on each of the next two days, camping near Rockport on September 13. If there was any complaint on the march it was of the hot dusty conditions and the lack of good drinking water. The army made 13 miles and the Saline River on September 14. Another 13 miles on the 15th brought them to Arkadelphia where they crossed the river and went into camp the same day. By September 16, the whole army was camped at Arkadelphia. The men then licked their wounds, bathed in the Ouchita River, and for now, the retreat was over, but the toll in desertions was great. The Arkansas infantry brigades reported the loss of 1,272 deserters by October 8, while the two Missouri brigades numbered only 28 men gone. Banasik, *Serving With Honor*, 103–105, 111; Flanagan, 44; Hoskin, September 11–15, 1863; Quesenberry, September 10–13, 1863; Turnbo, 297–298, 302; Wallace, September 11–16, 1863; Waterman, 143.

Item: Crossing the Arkansas River (September 10, 1863) and the Engagement of Bayou Fourche September 10, 1863), by Henry C. Luttrell, Hindman Escort, Company G, 10th Missouri Cavalry (CSA).[88]

Published: May 15, 1886.

Fight On A Sandbar.

Editor *Republican*

Some considerable cavalry fighting took place on the river below the city of Little Rock on the morning of the 10th of September, 1863.

O. F. Blake in his "Great Rebellion," in speaking of the fierce encounter, endeavoring to cover up the rough handling of the Federals by intimating that the rebels were in greatly superior numbers to the Union forces, and in one instance he claims that the Union forces were ambushed. He also tells about the launching of a pontoon bridge, and how a certain Union officer who superintended the affair and worked with such vigor digging down the river bank was so overcome by his exertions that he fainted just as he pronounced the work complete.[89] Then again he tells us how a certain force on the river road was besmeared with the blood and brains of the rebel cavalry as they ran the gauntlet of the Union batteries posted on the north bank of the river. For a full account of this bloody day for the rebels, I simply refer the reader to "The Great Rebellion." What a pity that all this brave historian has told us is not true.[90]

---

88. Henry C. Luttrell was enlisted by Colonel John C. Tracy in what became Company G, 10th Missouri Cavalry (CSA) on August 10, 1862. He fought at Lone Jack on August 16, 1862, shortly after he joined the army and was in the Little Rock Campaign of 1863, Pine Bluff, Arkansas, and Price's 1864 Missouri Raid. He survived the war and was paroled at Shreveport, Louisiana, on June 8, 1865. After the war Luttrell wrote a series of articles on his wartime experiences, which appeared periodically in the *Missouri Republican* (these articles have appeared in Part Two of this series and will also be found in Part Four). Eakin, *Battle of Lone Jack*, 166; National Archives, Record Group M322 (roll no. 57), Confederate Compiled Service Records, 10th Missouri Cavalry; War Echoes, *Missouri Republican*, October 31, 1885.

89. General Davidson credits three men of his staff for the successful crossing of the Arkansas River: Lieutenant Colonel Henry Caldwell, Chief of Staff; Captain Julius L. Hadley, Chief of Artillery; and Captain Anton Gerster, Chief Engineer. The man, noted by Luttrell who collapsed, was Gerster. A reporter, who was with the expedition, supports Blake's comment on the incident surrounding the captain. He wrote:

At 10 o'clock the bridge was completed and in readiness for crossing. Capt. Gerster, the engineer who had worked so faithfully, in its construction, had become literally exhausted by his labors, and, pronouncing his work finished, sank to the ground with sun-stroke induced by over-exertion. He was borne to the shade and proper restoration immediately applied. To his promptness and skill is largely due to the success of Gen. Davidson's movements.

O.R., vol. 22, pt. 1:485–487, 490; Omaha, "The Battle Before Little Rock," *Chicago Tribune*, September 25, 1863.

90. This second comment came about as a result of the artillery fire that was covering Terry's Ford as the 5th Arkansas Cavalry withdrew toward Little Rock. Another Union account posted by a period reporter stated: "The rebels must have suffered severely in running the gauntlet of our batteries, as one or two of our shells, which did not explode, were found directly on the road along which they passed, while trees and fences gave abundant proof of the accuracy of the fire." Still another reporter recorded

As to the condition of the patriotic officer above alluded to we don't know, for we were not present, but we feel certain that he never died; they hardly ever do from such sudden attacks. We certainly excuse him for his prostration. We would also have gladly excused half of Gen. Steele's army at the same time and upon the same plea.[91]

And again, in "The Great Rebellion" we note where a certain Union officer, while defending his guns on the sand-bar near the above mentioned pontoon bridge

Receives A Severe Wound

while engaged in personal encounter with the rebel chieftain, and as the Union officer went down he fired a last shot at his adversary which laid him low upon the sand.[92] But all the rebels were not killed in those sanguinary battles.

On the morning of the 10th of September '63, Lieut.-Col. [M. L.] Young's Battalion—afterwards the Tenth Missouri Regiment—then composed of five companies and numbering about 320 effective men, was doing outpost picket duty, some eight to ten miles north of Little Rock, on, we think, the Caddo Gap Road, or the upper river road.[93]

---

of the same incident that "blood was found in several places upon the grass at the edge of the road, and marching in close columns the rebels must have suffered severe loss in running the gauntlet of our batteries." However, not mentioned in either account was the fact that blood could have come from the horses that the rebels rode. The Confederates, for their part, noted that the 5th Arkansas lost 4 wounded and 7 missing or captured on September 10, including the ensuing engagement at Bayou Fourche. *O.R.*, vol. 22, pt. 1:523, 539; Burford, 172; "From Little Rock," *Chicago Times*, September 23, 1863; Omaha, "Battle Before Little Rock," *Chicago Times*, September 25, 1863. Luttrell is probably referring to *Pictorial History of the Great Rebellion* (1866), by William O. Blake.

91. According to "Omaha," by September 13, 1863, Captain Gerster had nearly recovered. The captain would later fully recover and continue service in the Trans-Mississippi, as an Assistant Engineer, Department of Missouri. In March 1864 he was at Fort Smith, Arkansas, improving the fortifications, and in August 1864 he inspected Fort Davidson, at Pilot Knob as a prelude to improving those works. *O.R.*, vol. 34, pt. 2:791; *O.R.*, vol. 41, pt. 2:805–806; Omaha, "Battle Before Little Rock," *Chicago Times*, September 23, 1863.

92. During the engagement at Bayou Fourche, a section of Lovejoy's Battery of mountain howitzers was in the advance, of the Union forces and poorly supported by two companies of the 10th Illinois Cavalry. A charge by the 11th Missouri Cavalry Battalion (CSA) caused a panic in the 10th Illinois, leaving Lovejoy unsupported. Two of the guns were subsequently captured, with Lovejoy being wounded in the leg and foot. According to period newspapers, Lovejoy "drew his pistol, and was seen to have shot, the man who had wounded him." The 11th Missouri took no casualties, according to official accounts on September 10 at Bayou Fourche. *O.R.*, vol. 22, pt. 1:523, 534; Burford, 176; Omaha, "Battle Before Little Rock," *Chicago Times*, September 23, 1863.

93. Merrit L. Young was born in Shelby County, Kentucky, in about 1825, and came to Missouri at a young age. At the beginning of the Civil War he was a resident of Weston, Missouri, and joined the 1st Rifle Regiment, 6th Division, MSG under John S. Marmaduke in August 1861. He later entered the Confederate Service, serving under Emmett MacDonald as a major (May 16, 1862) and on January 8, 1863, was appointed a lieutenant colonel in MacDonald's command to rank from November 16, 1862. Young was noted for his "daring chivilary" at the Battle of Prairie Grove, where he commanded MacDonald's Regiment. He also participated in Marmaduke's Second Missouri Raid (April–May, 1863) and at Pine Bluff, Arkansas in October. On October 22, 1864, Young was wounded at Indepen-

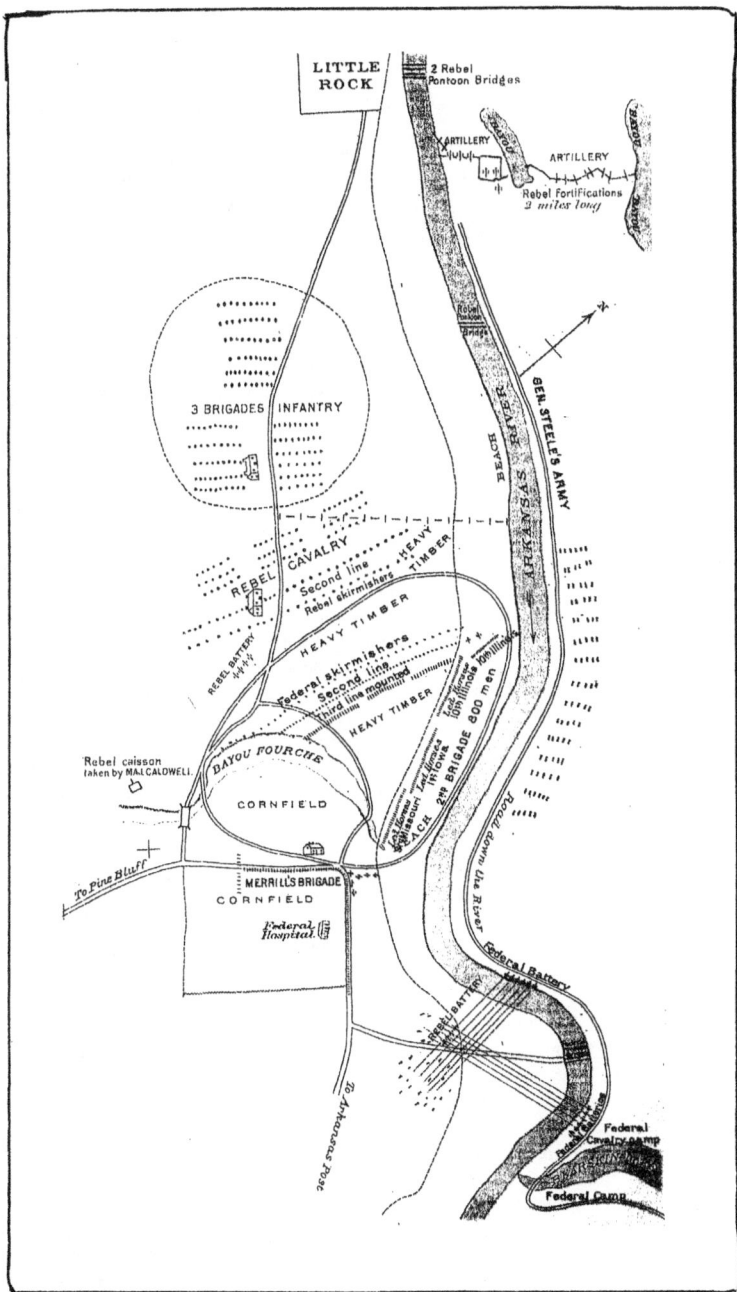

Engagement at Bayou Fourche, Arkansas (September 10, 1863)

A day or two previous, perhaps the 8th or 9th, the Federal cavalry made a demonstration in our front, but after slight skirmishing retired. But with the coming of day on the 10th came the boom of cannon from the southeast, and about the same time a courier, mounted on a foaming, panting charger, galloped into camp. "Boots and Saddles" sounded. In a trice the pickets were called in. But before they arrived we were in the saddle and moving in a fierce gallop for the scene of the conflict.[94] As we galloped down the river bank, north of the city and across the pontoon bridge, we saw the flames rising from the two Confederate ironclad steamers the *Tahlequah* and the *Arkansas*.[95]

And farther down the river we could see the white smoke of battle as it rose from the batteries. Gaining the south bank of the river, we sped down the river road at the same furious speed, passing other troops moving in the same direction, but at a more leisurely pace.

Now we can see cavalry forming in the eastern edge of a large plantation that reaches from the city to the borders of a cypress swamp; think this troop is the

---

dence, Missouri and was captured the following day. He died a short time thereafter. *O.R.*, vol. 22, pt. 1:156–157, 303, 732; *O.R.*, vol. 41, pt. 1:347, 360, 699; Eakin & Hale, 484; John S. Marmaduke Letters (December 4, 1862), Peter W. Alexander Collection, Columbia University; National Archives, Record Group M322 (roll no. 58), Confederate Compiled Service Records, 10th Missouri Cavalry.
The 10th Missouri Cavalry was originally commanded by Emmett MacDonald and consisted of three companies with two more added forming the "regiment" on December 1, 1862. The unit at that time was known as MacDonald's Regiment, even though it only contained five companies. MacDonald's command eventually joined with the 11th Missouri Battalion (CSA), paroled returnees from the First Missouri Brigade captured at Vicksburg, and Lawther's Temporary Cavalry Regiment (dismounted) to form the 10th Missouri Cavalry Regiment (CSA) in December 1863. *O.R.*, vol. 22, pt. 1:156; *O.R.*, vol. 22, pt. 2:781; *O.R.S.*, pt. 2, vol. 38:253–259; Crute, 203; National Archives, Record Group 109, Inspector General Report, in Confederate Muster Rolls, 10th Missouri Cavalry; National Archives, Record Group M322 (roll no. 57) Confederate Compiled Service Records, 10th Missouri Cavalry.
94. On the morning of September 10, the 11th Missouri Battalion (CSA) was bivouacked, with the rest of Marmaduke's Brigade, at the intersection of the Brownsville-Shallow Ford Road—or just east of the main rebel defenses and on the far left of their main defenses, while Shelby's Brigade was to the north of Little Rock, covering the Van Buren-Batesville Road to the left of the cypress swamp near "Big Rock"; and Dobbin's Brigade covered the south side of the Arkansas River. At about 9:50 a.m., General Marmaduke, who had been reinstated to his command a short time before, and placed in command of all the Confederate cavalry, ordered his brigade to march southward, via the lower pontoon bridge, to take up a position at Bayou Fourche. Meanwhile, messengers were sent to Shelby's Brigade to order them to Marmaduke's support. Unfortunately, Shelby's Brigade remained in place awaiting orders and would not join the main defenses at Bayou Fourche until about three hours later, as the courier delivering the marching orders got lost. *O.R.*, vol. 22, pt. 1:532–534; Burford, 171–172; Edwards, *Shelby and His Men*, 183; Huff, "Union Expedition," map between 232–233; Sellmeyer, 120–122.
95. The *Arkansas* and the *Tahlequah*, were both transport steamers that ferried men and supplies on the Arkansas River for the Confederate Army. The *Arkansas* had been captured at Van Buren, on December 28, 1863, burned but later recovered (See notes no. 31 and 39, Chapter 1). About 9:30 a.m., as the bridge was nearing completion, the Confederates fired the two steamers, to cover their retreat from Terry's Ferry or Ford. To the Federals at the ford. "It was an omen of good fortune..., showing that the rebels had abandoned all hope of preventing" Union troops from crossing the river. "From Little Rock," *Chicago Times*, September 23, 1863; Omaha, "Battle Before Little Rock," *Chicago Times*, September 25, 1863.

Eighth Regiment (Burbridge's).[96] Between this plantation and the river is a strip of heavy forest which reaches up the river for perhaps a mile; then it narrows down to only a fringe of trees. Here the road runs between the river bank and the plantation fence and is in full view of the north bank of the river.[97]

Just at the east edge of the plantation is

A Large Levee

or embankment, across a deep ravine—perhaps this ravine was once the original drain of the above mentioned cypress swamp. At this embankment the wagon road crossed the ravine, and just above, west of the ravine, we found one section of a battery posted, shelling the enemy.[98] We filed into the wood to the left of the battery. Here we met Gen. Marmaduke, who gave Col. Young his orders, and, as we swept past him, he said: "Men of Missouri, there is heavy work to do today, and I expect every man to do his whole duty. You have never failed me yet, and I pledge the greatest confidence in your courage and valor."

---

96. Burbridge's Regiment was the 4th Missouri Cavalry (CSA). It was organized on November 14, 1862, at Yellville, Arkansas, though it didn't add its last company until January 1863. The regiment fought at Clark's Mill (November 7, 1862) and Beaver Creek (November 24, 1862), both in Missouri, as their first two engagements. They were also in both of Marmaduke's Missouri Raids in 1863, the 1863 Campaign for Little Rock and the Battle of Pine Bluff. In 1864, the regiment was in the Camden Expedition and participated in Price's 1864 Missouri Raid. *O.R.*, vol. 22, pt. 1:199, 288, 527, 731; *O.R.*, vol. 34, pt. 1:785; *O.R.*, vol. 41, pt. 1:678; *O.R.S.*, pt. 1, vol. 4:24; *O.R.S.*, pt. 2, vol. 38:200; Carolyn Bartels, *Civil War Stories of Missouri* (Shawnee Mission, KS, 1995), 244; John Q. Burbridge Letters (November 10, 1862), Peter W. Alexander Collection, Columbia University.
John Q. Burbridge was born on May 21, 1830, in Pike County, Missouri. At the beginning of the Civil War, he lived in Louisiana, Missouri, as a banker, and was elected a captain in the 1st Infantry Regiment, 3rd Division, MSG, and then colonel of his regiment on July 3, 1861. During the course of the war, he led troops in the MSG and commanded regular Confederate troops, serving mostly in the Trans-Mississippi. He was captured at Brownsville, Arkansas, during the Little Rock Campaign and was later exchanged. After the war he ended up in Jacksonville, Florida, where he was elected mayor in 1887. He died on November 14, 1892, in Tucson, Arizona. For his complete military service record see Banasik, *Serving With Honor*, 378–380. Allardice, *Confederate Colonels*, 82; Eakin, *Confederate Records*, 2:186; Peterson, 113, 115.
97. After the Confederates abandoned their defense of Terry's Ford, they formed a battle line at Bayou Fourche. Marmaduke's Brigade, under Colonel William Jeffers, arrived on the scene first, at about 11:00 a.m. and was deployed, by the recently reinstated General Marmaduke. Young's Battalion anchored the left in a band of timber by the Arkansas River; Colton Greene's Regiment, under Major L. A. Campbell was on the right, with the 8th Missouri, under Lieutenant Colonel S. J. Ward and Burbridge's 4th Missouri under Lieutenant Colonel W. J. Preston occupying the center of the brigade. Meanwhile, Dobbin's Brigade, which fought a running battle with the pursuing bluecoats from Terry's Ford, finally arrived at Bayou Fourche. In an ensuing discussion with General Marmaduke, Dobbins refused to take orders from General Marmaduke and was immediately relieved of his command, and his brigade placed under R. C. Newton. Newton's Brigade was then placed to the right of Jeffer's command, along with two batteries of artillery. By noon the initial Confederate defense of Bayou Fourche was in place. *O.R.*, vol. 22, pt. 1:534, 539; Burford, 172; Christ, 179–180; Sellmeyer, 122.
98. The battery section belonged to Chamber B. Etter's Arkansas command and consisted of 2 10-pound rifled parrot guns. *O.R.*, vol. 22, pt. 1:539; Burford, 173; Letter (July 7, 1862), Newton to Dodge, Copy Letter Book No. 1.

A deafening cheer, cut in twain by the crash of guns on our right, greeted him. And he saluted us, hat in hand. Then someone shouted, "Hurrah for hell, damn a man that will not praise his own country." Gen. Marmaduke smiled and bowed as we swept past him "by companies to the left into line." Here we dismounted, reformed and at a "right shoulder shift" we "double-quicked" to the river bank. And this is what we saw on the sand-bar. Two companies of Federal cavalry moving in battle line upon the sand-bar with a section of mountain howitzers between them. And just in their rear is a support of four other guns and a regiment of cavalry.[99] And yet again in their rear is a column of infantry deploying into line from the newly launched pontoon bridge. The north bank of the river is thronged with blue coated infantry and artillery.

Without checking our "double-quick" we break column by companies to the right into line, and pour a scorching volley into the advancing enemy. The advance companies instantly stampeded, falling back in confusion upon the support.[100]

But we follow them up at a double-quick with a ringing fire. the yellow sand is soon dotted over with the dead and wounded. Artillery horses lay in heaps where they stood; cavalry horses rear and plunge about in the deep sand. Now the cavalry support breaks in disorder and falls back upon the advancing infantry, throwing them in confusion and we pounce upon the artillerymen, who stand to their guns and

---

99. The two squadrons of cavalry belonged to the 10th Illinois Cavalry Regiment—Companies B and H—and were the immediate support for the 2 artillery pieces. The two guns were part of Lovejoy's Missouri Battery of Mountain Howitzers from the 2nd Missouri Cavalry Regiment (Union). The guns were subsequently captured by Young's 11th Missouri Battalion (CSA) and not Shelby's Brigade as previously noted in my book *Reluctant Cannoneer*. Immediately behind Lovejoy's came 4 mountain guns, from Captain Gustave Stange's Battery M, 2nd Missouri Artillery Regiment. When the two companies of the 10th Illinois broke they sent waves of panic in the rest of the regiment, which retreated in disorder, along with Stange's guns. *O.R.*, vol. 22, pt. 1:489, 504–507, 925, 992; Banasik, *Reluctant Cannoneer*, 196 (n. 48); Christ 182–183.

100. Following the completion of the pontoon bridge at Terry's Ford, the 40th Iowa and 27th Wisconsin Infantries advanced across the bridge to secure the southern side of the bridge. With Davidson's command safely over the river, the infantry moved back to the north side of the Arkansas River and joined the advance in that quarter, except for the Iowans, who secured the bridge. With the bridge secure, Davidson's Second Brigade, under J. M. Glover, led the Union advance with Stange's Battery of four mountain howitzers and two of Lovejoy's guns. At about 1:00 p.m. (Burford has the time as noon) they reached Bayou Fourche. With little apparent resistance, Glover continued advancing his command in column with two mounted companies of the 10th Illinois Cavalry entering the wooded area next to the Arkansas River. A short time later, the advance units of the 10th Illinois were greeted with several vollies of fire on their flank. Disorder followed as they retreated in panic and in turn took the remainder of the regiment with them to the rear. Lovejoy, with two guns refused orders to withdraw, and was finally overrun. In the meantime, Glover, with the assistance of General Davidson, finally rallied his command, but failed to recapture the guns, giving the Confederate one of their few successes during the Little Rock Campaign. *O.R.*, vol. 22, pt. 1:503–505, 514; Burford, 174–176; "From Little Rock," *Chicago Times*, September 23, 1863; Ohama, "Battle Before Little Rock," *Chicago Times*, September 25, 1863; "War In Arkansas," *Chicago Tribune*, September 23, 1863.

Fight Like Turks.

They disregard our challenge to surrender, and fight to the bitter end. One falls with the lanyard in hand in the act of firing his piece; another in the act of inserting a shell, and another while swabbing his gun.[101] A Federal officer goes down under the close fire of Private Hillary Thistle's[102] pistol, and he in turn falls almost at the same instant, having tripped on his spur. But he rises the next moment, rifle in hand, and applies himself to the confused cavalry in the water's edge. So you see the Federal officer was mistaken as to the rank of his antagonist, and also mistaken as to the killing.

Now the artillerymen seeing themselves abandoned by their support are fleeing down the river to the surging, struggling masses near the pontoon. As they recede before us the scene changes. Now the Federal batteries upon the north bank of the river open up a tremendous fire. The battery of howitzers stand black mouthed, grim and silent in the yellow sand, but the horses are either killed or have run away. Now the men turn their attention to the guns. They seize them and attempt to drag them off by hand. But the sand is so deep they soon tire in the toilsome work. The two guns nearest the south bank were, however, removed, notwithstanding the heavy rain of iron ball poured upon us from the batteries from the north bank.[103] So there is the story of the "ambush" which took place upon an open sand-bar, and under the nose of Steele's army massed on the north bank of the river, and also in the presence of a Confederate battery that had been shelling them all morning. Our next position was in the east end of the plantation near the cypress swamp. We had been in position but a few moments when someone came

---

101. The soldier who was inserting the shell was John Roth or Rath, a member of Company I, 2nd Missouri Cavalry (Union). Rath had been assigned to duty with the battery on June 13, 1863. He was a resident of Ann Arbor, Michigan and born about 1839. Rath was later found dead, shot in the heart, while still holding the round he was attempting to load. In addition to Rath, R. L. Fricklin and George Kimball, were both mortally wounded while defending the battery. Lieutenant Lovejoy was wounded in the leg and foot and survived the engagement by crawling away after the battery was taken. National Archives, Record Group M405 (roll no. 46), Union Compiled Service Records, 2nd Missouri Cavalry; Omaha, "Battle Before Little Rock," *Chicago Times*, September 25, 1863; "War In Arkansas," *Chicago Tribune*, September 23, 1863.

102. Lewis H. "Hillary" Thistle enlisted in what became Company G, 10th Missouri Cavalry Regiment on August 10, 1862, in Johnson County. National Archives, Record Group M322 (roll no. 58), Confederate Compiled Service Records, 10th Missouri Cavalry Regiment.

103. As part of the overall Union strategy on September 10, while Davidson's cavalry advanced along the south side of the Arkansas River toward Little Rock, General Steele, with the infantry, moved along the north side of the river. In support of Davidson's troopers, Union artillery on the north side proved of "infinite service" to the Union cavalryman as they slowly pushed Marmaduke's horsemen back toward Little Rock. T. F. Vaughn's Battery A, 3rd Illinois Artillery Regiment provided the main support from the north side of the Arkansas River, coming into action opposite Bayou Fourche at about 2:30 p.m. By the time the battery was done for the day they had fired 314 rounds. To aid in the coordination of his advance, General Davidson used a lieutenant from his staff, carrying a guidon, on the south bank of the Arkansas River, to mark the advance of his division. *O.R.*, vol. 22, pt. 1:477, 487, 519; Burford, 182; Ohama, "Battle Before Little Rock," *Chicago Times*, September 25, 1863.

galloping up from the front through the tall corn-stalks and shouted: "Get out of this! The enemy is flanking us on the right! Get out of this, I say for God's sake!" Who he was we don't know. But in less than two seconds the battalion was galloping to the rear in hot haste, and Col. Young was just furious in his exclamation of wrath.

We again took position to the left and a little to the rear of the Eighth Regiment. Here we stood a heavy shelling, the other regiments maneuvering farther to the south as the enemy kept flanking us. Finally we passed back up the river road at a gallop, under a heavy artillery fire from the north side. But the road was intensely dusty, and the enemy's fire being directed at the dust cloud, mostly passed over us. Our loss was, perhaps, half a dozen horses and two or three men slightly wounded by shell. We skirmished with the enemy near the suburbs of the city, and as night closed in, the flash of our guns glittered on the surroundings of the old fair grounds.[104]

Henry C. Luttrell
Hindman Escort, Co. G, Tenth Missouri Cavalry.

* * * * * *

---

104. The Battle of Bayou Fourche and the defense of Terry's Ford had cost the Confederates but little in loses—Shelby's Brigade lost 3 killed, 2 Wounded and 2 missing; Marmaduke's Brigade (Jeffer's) lost 1 killed and 7 wounded; Dobbin's Brigade (Newton's) lost 2 killed, 10 wounded and 11 missing—grand total 6 killed, 19 wounded and 13 missing. Additionally, the official report for Young's Battalion has no losses recorded for September 10, which is clearly not correct according to the writer of this article. However, its also not uncommon for official casualties to leave out men who are slightly wounded as indicated by the author of the article. It should also be said that the *Official Records* noted the record of losses was "incomplete" for the Little Rock Campaign. *O.R.*, vol. 22, pt. 1:523.

Item: A response to John Decker of Company A, Third Missouri Cavalry (Union) on the Engagement at Bayou Fourche (September 10, 1863), by Henry C. Luttrell, Company G, Tenth Missouri Cavalry (CSA). **Published:** July 17, 1886.

Same Old Sandbar.

St. Louis, July 16.

Editor *Republican*

At the solemn admonition of Mr. John Decker,[105] we take our pen in hand, etc., etc., to rehearse a certain fight on a certain sandbar on a certain river down in Arkansaw [Arkansas]. Taking it for granted that Mr. Decker will allow us the same broad scope for assumption and supposition that he has occupied in his criticism, we will go on with the work in hand. From personal observation we have long since learned that it very seldom happens that two men standing side by side can watch a dog fight or even a man fight, and then both give a straightforward, close-cut narration of the affair that exactly coincides. Inasmuch as we occupied one place on this field and Mr. Decker occupied another, it is reasonable to suppose that he is a little off in his inferences and suppositions, although he says he "saw it with his own eyes." After telling us he belonged to Co. A, Third Missouri Cavalry,[106] Federal, he says: "Our regiment came up as a battalion of the Tenth Il-

---

105. John Decker joined Company A, 3rd Missouri Cavalry (Union) on September 23, 1861, at La Grange, Missouri. He was captured near Little Rock on February 26, 1864, sent to Camp Groce, Texas, where he was paroled on December 5, 1864 and later exchanged. After returning to his unit, Decker, now a member of Company I, was mustered out of the service on January 23, 1865. After the war he wrote a short response to Luttrell's description of the "Sandbar Fight" in the *Missouri Republican*, which was published on June 5, 1886. Decker's piece will be fully covered in the *Union Tales of the War*. See Appendix D for a copy of Decker's piece on the Battle of Bayou Fourche. John Decker, "That Sandbar Fight," *Missouri Republican*, June 5, 1886; National Archives, Record Group M405 (roll no. 69), Union Compiled Service Records, 3rd Missouri Cavalry Regiment; A. W. M. Petty, *A History of the Third Missouri Cavalry From Its Organization At Palmyra, Missouri, 1861 Up To November Sixth, 1864 With An Appendix and Recapitulation* (Little Rock, AR, 1865; reprint ed., Albany, MO, 1997), 114, hereafter cited as Petty.

106. The 3rd Missouri Cavalry Regiment (Union) was recruited and organized at Palmyra, Missouri, beginning in June 1861, with an organization date of November 26, 1861. Though designated a Missouri regiment, many of the troops came from Illinois, with one veteran asserting that the regiment should rightly be credited to the State of Illinois. Company A was commanded by Captain James Holand and made up of "able-bodied-men," whom one member noted with pride "that no company in the service can boast a better set of men." The regiment, including Company A, served primarily in the Trans-Mississippi, being engaged in guerrilla type operations in 1861–1862. In 1863, the unit operated against Confederate cavalry raids in Missouri and then took part in the 1863 Little Rock Campaign, where it was part of the Second Brigade of Davidson's Cavalry Division. The regiment also participated in the Camden Expedition of 1864. Toward the end of the war, the regiment was consolidated into five companies and on July 27, 1865, it was mustered out of the service. To Colonel John Glover, the 3rd Missouri held no equal, as he recorded: "We started out as the finest drilled and most efficient cavalry in the United States...Not only have we become artillerists, but have become more efficient than infantry...We have causewayed miles of swamp, built fortifications, bridged rivers, fought and always vanquished the enemy." *O.R.*, vol. 22, pt. 1:460; *O.R.S.*, pt. 2, vol. 34:681; J. M. Glover, "Highly

linois Cavalry[107] was falling back, having lost the guns." Now it is fair to suppose from the above statement that Mr. Decker never saw the fight that we described, for he emphatically says the guns were lost before his regiment got into position. He again says: "We dismounted and formed into line. The guns to our right were limbered up and dashed away to the left." Again we infer that these guns that he has alluded to were the ones we left on the bar, possibly,

Scampering to the Rear,

as to the left was the most available route. In all human possibility Mr. Decker did see and participate in the fighting that immediately followed the capture of these two guns he so much laments. But of the fighting that took place on the bar after we retired with the guns we don't know, for, as we stated before, the battalion was again mounted and their next position was in the east end of the plantation on the west side of the cypress swamp, which position we precipitately abandoned because of a false report some one started that we were flanked on our right. But let us follow our anxious friend a littler farther and see if our inference and suppositions, based upon his own statements, are not entitled to some consideration. He says: "It was all quiet in our front. Gen. [John W.] Davidson and Col. [John M.] Glover[108] rode forward perhaps about thirty yards, our line being across the

---

Interesting Letter From Col. Glover," *The Canton Weekly Press* (Canton, MO), October 15, 1863; Petty, 5–6; *Union Army*, 4:273–274; Volunteer, "The Third Cavalry Ordered South," *North Missouri Courier* (Hannibal, MO), March 12, 1863.

107. The 10th Illinois Cavalry was organized at Camp Butler, near Springfield, Illinois, in September 1861, and was mustered into the service on November 25, 1861. The regiment contained twelve squadrons or companies and was commanded by Colonel Dudly Wickersham, who led the regiment until his resignation on May 10, 1864, when James Stuart was made colonel of the unit. After its organization, the regiment began its training at Camp Wood, near Quincy, Illinois, in January 1862. The regiment next moved to Benton Barracks, in St. Louis, in March 1862, and continued its service in the Trans-Mississippi throughout its time in the army. From July 1862–July 1863, the First Battalion operated separately from the other two battalions of the regiment, reuniting for the 1863 Little Rock Campaign. Its major engagements included Prairie Grove and the 1863 Little Rock Campaign. The veterans of the regiment were on furlough during the Camden Expedition, while the non-veterans participated in the ill-fated expedition. When the veterans returned to Little Rock, they performed garrison duty in Arkansas until ordered to New Orleans, and then completed their service in Louisiana and Texas. The regiment was mustered out on November 22, 1865, at San Antonio, Texas, following a general period of "idleness" in "lengthy expeditions" chasing after Indians. The regiment finally reached Chicago on January 1, 1866, and following the receipt of their final pay the men were discharged. *O.R.S.*, pt. 2, vol. 8:3, 6–9; J. N. Reece, *Report of the Adjutant General of the State of Illinois* 9 vols. (Springfield, IL, 1900-1902), 9:254-257; *Union Army*, 3:353-354.

108. John Wynn Davidson came from a long line of military officers, including his grandfather who had been a general officer in the Revolutionary War. He was born in Fairfax County, Virginia, on August 18, 1824, and graduated from West Point in 1845 (number 27 of 41). Serving in the Mexican War, Davidson also fought Indians in the pre-Civil War days. Davidson was offered a commission in the Confederate Army, but refused it, and was subsequently appointed a Union brigadier general on February 3, 1862. He served in the East until August 1862, when he was posted to Missouri, where he commanded the District of Missouri (August 6–November 13, 1862) and the District of Southeast Missouri (November 13, 1862–February 23, 1863). During the Little Rock Campaign, he commanded

lower point of some timber into which the Tenth had been firing." We learn by this statement that the Tenth Illinois had done some fighting earlier in the day, and it is just possible and this firing, which Mr. Decker says was into the timber, was the firing they did when they lost their guns. However, let us go on with Mr. Decker's story. He says: "The timber was very large cottonwoods, with many trees lying on the ground. Gen. Davidson said to the colonel, as they rode back: 'Move you men forward. There is not a damned rebel in these woods.' He then rode to the left and the colonel took us in. We had advanced about fifty yards when the rebels opened with infantry and artillery from a concealed position." Now we infer from this that the fight was

John W. Davidson

Not on a Sandbar,

but in the timber. That your colonel led you into the timber and there you came upon the enemy whose lines were concealed by what? Trees and bush and the uneven nature of the ground. To prove that Mr. Decker's regiment was in the timber we will quote him further: "We were ordered to take shelter, and Steele's heavy guns immediately opened a cross-fire in front of our line from the north bank." Again we naturally infer that you took shelter behind the logs and trees which you

---

Steele's cavalry division. He left Arkansas on January 30, 1864, and was assigned to duty in the Cavalry Bureau, stationed in St. Louis. In June 1864 the War Department reassigned Davidson to duty as Chief of Cavalry in the Military Division of West Mississippi, where he completed his military service on the east side of the Mississippi River. After the war Davidson remained in the army, was injured when he fell from his horse in 1881, and died at St. Paul, Minnesota, on June 26, 1881. *O.R.*, vol. 34, pt. 2:187; *O.R.*, vol. 34, pt. 4: 240–241, 531; Boatner, 223; Warner, *Generals in Blue*, 112.

John M. Glover, "a man of considerable popularity," was a farmer and politician from LaGrange, Lewis County, Missouri (Petty has Glover from Knox County). He was called into the service on August 5, 1861, and at the request of General John Frémont raised a regiment of cavalry. Glover was mustered into the U.S. Army on September 4, 1861, and then proceeded to raise the 3rd Missouri Cavalry Regiment at Palmyra, Missouri in the Fall of 1861. He was officially commissioned the colonel of the 3rd on May 27, 1862, (Petty has the date as November 26, 1861) to date from September 4, 1861. During the war, Glover commanded the District of Northeast Missouri (March 12-November 1, 1862), the District of Rolla (November 2, 1862-June 5, 1863), and led the Second Brigade (June 5, 1863–March 13, 1864) of Davidson's Cavalry Division during the Little Rock Expedition. He tendered his resignation on February 23, 1864, for health reasons (meningitis) and was discharged March 13. *O.R.*, vol. 13:777; *O.R.*, vol. 22, pt. 2:47; *O.R.*, vol. 53:515, 559; National Archives, Record Group M405 (roll no. 70), Union Compiled Service Records, 3rd Missouri Cavalry; Petty, 5-6, 98, 102; *Union Army*, 4:273–274.

previously mentioned, "the Tenth having formed on foot came up and take position on our right, curving forward and getting a cross-fire. The enemy did not give up the whole woods until late and we took possession of the town about sunset; the Second Brigade camping in the western suburbs, while we camped in the pine grove in the city."[109] Now according to the above statement, this fight which you describe was made by dismounted cavalry, and, we suppose, without artillery, as you have failed to mention or its position. Neither do you mention the loss of any—but you can go on and camp the army in and about the city. Furthermore this fight took place in the woods, while the guns in question were captured on the open bar. We would now like to know how Mr. Decker is going to reconcile his two statements. For the first he says: "Our regiment came up as a battalion of the Tenth Illinois Cavalry was falling back, having lost the guns." Then he says: "The support was the Third Missouri Cavalry." How could the Third Missouri Cavalry support guns in a fight that took place before it came on the field? In conclusion, Mr. Decker makes assertions, draws inferences and asks questions all in the same breath. He makes the assertion that "the rebs did not stay on the bar five minutes," that, however, is

Not a Disputed Point.

We certainly never stated the length of time we were on the bar, but according to your statement we were there long enough to "push the Tenth away from the howitzers and drag them into the woods." Now if we would have been in the Tenth's place and the Tenth in our place, you would have said we skedaddled and we should have not got mad about it, either. You excuse yourself thus: "We could not fire for fear of hitting the men of the Tenth." And we of the Confederacy was well pleased at the situation, but if you were not in confusion why didn't you come on our side of the Tenth? That was the place to find glory. You say "there was not a dead horse on the sandbar next morning and there was no fighting in

---

109. The Second Brigade of Davidson's Division consisted of three cavalry regiments—10th Illinois, 1st Iowa, and 3rd Missouri. After Davidson's First and Second Brigades drove the Confederates back for several miles they were exhausted. With their horses of his First and Second Brigades to the rear and unable to pursue farther, Davidson ordered up John Ritter's Reserve Brigade and they made the final push into Little Rock, led by the 3rd Iowa Cavalry. At about 7:00 p.m. Mayor Charles P. Bertrand of Little Rock, formally surrendered the city.

Mayor's Office, Little Rock, Sept. 10, 1863
To the Officer commanding Federal Army,
The army of the Confederates has retreated and abandoned the defenses of this city. We are now powerless and ask your mercy. The city is now occupied, alone by women and children and non-combatants with, perhaps a few stragglers from the Confederate forces. May I ask of your protection for persons and property. I have been ill for some days and am unable to visit you in person.

Very respectfully,
C. P. Bertrand, Mayor.
O.R., vol. 22, pt. 1:487, 510; Omaha, "Battle Before Little Rock," *Chicago Times,* September 25, 1863; Ross, 413.

the water." So it was the next morning you visited the scene of the conflict. How do you know you was on the spot where the guns were captured? Besides, you never told us where all those contraband negroes and camp followers roosted the night after the battle. Are you sure they slept on empty stomachs? Did we tell you there was any fighting done in the water? Would you mind reading that little sketch again with a rest? If you would perhaps you would not jump to so many hasty conclusions. Come now; own up. Didn't that fight over the guns come off just before you got there? We won't feel a bit hurt if it did.[110]

Henry C. Luttrell.

* * * * * *

---

110. Luttrell is basically right in his assertions that Decker has his facts confused. The actions that Luttrell originally described throughout his piece on the engagement at Bayou Fourche occurred well before the 3rd Missouri Cavalry was deployed. This was further supported by official reports and period newspaper accounts. According to Colonel Glover, commanding the brigade, the 3rd Missouri was assigned to support the 1st Iowa Cavalry on the left, and it wasn't until the 10th Illinois had panicked and the guns were lost that Glover ordered the 3rd Missouri into action to support the right of his line. Dismounting the 3rd Missouri, along with the reformed 10th Illinois, Glover then began a long, drawn out process to drive the rebels out of their timbered area, which began about two hours after the howitzers were lost and lasted until near sunset. *O.R.*, vol. 22, pt. 1:504–506; Burford, 176, 182, 184; Omaha, "Battle Before Little Rock," *Chicago Times*, September 25, 1863.

Item: John S. Marmaduke's duel with Walker at Little Rock on September 6, 1863, by F. C. Bratlo, former member of Marmaduke's command. **Published:** August 8, 1885.

Note: This piece is extracted from an article entitled "Yanks and Yellers" by a special correspondent of the *Missouri Republican*, who was traveling to Texas, from St. Louis, for a Confederate reunion

Fort Worth, Tex. Aug. 6—(Special Correspondence):

Notables.

Old Missouri was well represented by her sons now in Texas, among those registered at the Missouri tent were Col. John L. Coffee, formerly of Dade County, now of Georgetown, Tex.; Col. J. M. Stemnions, also of Dade, now of Dallas; Col. S. P. Burns, formerly of Jasper, now of Brownwood; Col. D. A. Williams, formerly of Grundy, now of Dallas; Maj. A. K. Hulett of Boone County, now of Farmington, Tex.; Capt. David Pool, Formerly of Jackson, now of Colorado City; Capt. Tucker Hill, formerly of Lafayette County, now of McKinney; Lieut T. R. Fisher, formerly of Polk County, now of Dallas; John C. Richardson of Marion County, now of Fort Worth; Col. J. W. Murray of Johnson, now of Dallas; Capt. George W. Neally of Jasper County, now of Dallas; Dr. W. R. Trollinger of St. Clair County, now of Whitesboro; E. G. Bower of Marion County, now of Dallas; Capt. J. M. Strong of Bates County, now of Dallas; Maj. C. S. McNatt of Lawrence County, now of Bowie, as well as his brother, J. M. McNatt.[111] About

---

111. No attempt will be made to provide detailed information of these men, except for noting what unit they served in and the highest rank they obtained:
  Colonel John T. Coffee, 6th Missouri Cavalry
  Lieutenant Colonel John M. Stemmons, 16th Missouri Infantry
  Colonel S. P. Burns, 11th Missouri Infantry
  Colonel D. A. Williams, Williams's Missouri Cavalry
  Major or Captain A. K. Hulet, 4th Missouri Cavalry
  Captain Francis Marion "David" Pool, Quantrill's Guerrillas
  Private or Captain Tucker Hill, Quantrill's Guerrillas
  Lieutenant T. R. Fisher (No unit found.)
  Sergeant John C. Richardson, 10th Missouri Infantry
  Colonel J. W. Murray (No Colonel J. W. Murray found, however, the writer was probably referring to Lieutenant Colonel Thomas H. Murray of the 11th Missouri Infantry.)
  Captain George W. Neally [Neely], 10th Missouri Cavalry
  Captain William H. Trollinger, Commissary, 8th Division, MSG
  E. G. Bower, Company G, 5th Missouri Cavalry
  Lieutenant or Captain Jesse M. Strong, Pindall's Sharpshooters
  Major C. S. McNatt (No C. S. McNatt of any rank found.)
  J. M. McNatt (There were two James McNatts, one Sr. and one Jr. Both served in Company G, 16th Missouri Infantry.)
Allardice, *Confederate Colonels*, 84, 105, 397; Michael E. Banasik, *Cavaliers of the Brush: Quantrill and His Men* (Iowa City, IA, 2003), 145, 159; Bartels, *Bravest of the Brave*, 16; Janet B. Hewett, *The*

150 Missourians now living in Texas, who were in the Confederate Army have registered at headquarters.

The Marmaduke-Walker Duel

While in the Missouri tent this afternoon, I heard Mr. F. C. Bratlo tell the following story which will be of interest to St. Louisians.

"I was in Marmaduke's command." he said, "when he had his duel with Gen. Walker. A great many different stories have been told about that duel, but the truth of it is this: The trouble began at the Battle of Bayou Meta [Meto], five miles out of Little Rock. Gen Walker was the ranking officer of this field, but Gen. Marmaduke commanded in the field. In the report he made of the battle he mentioned that Gen. Walker's position was at the hospital.[112] When Gen. Walker saw this some days after he was very angry and said it amounted to accusing him of cowardice.[113] Marmaduke said he had no such meaning, but Walker challenged him. Marmaduke and his aid, John C. Moore,[114] I think it was, were the only men

---

Roster of Confederate Soldiers 1861–1865 16 vols. (Wilmington, NC, 1995–1996), vols. 2:240, 5:494–495, 11:12, 401–403, 451; Peterson, 129, 248, 280; Schnetzer, *Men of the Eleventh*, 6; Schnetzer, *Men of the Tenth*, 12.

112. Walker's Headquarters were located about one and a half miles from Marmaduke's position at Reed's bridge at the G. B. Gray house. The "home sat on a knoll, ensconced with a citadel of massive oaks. The farm-house overlooked fields to the south, cradled in a westward bend of the Military Road," which marked the main avenue of the Federal advance. Burford, 66.

113. There is no evidence that Walker ever saw the report that the writer described. However, General Marmaduke did write a report on the Action at Reed's Bridge, which was dated December, 1863. According to contemporary accounts leading up to the duel, a staff officer of Walker's command was informed of Marmaduke's comments on the affair at Reed's Bridge, by a member of Marmaduke's staff. An exchange of letters followed, clarifying the comments that Marmaduke made. In the end, General Walker demanded satisfaction on the matter and the duel was fought on September 6, 1863. *O.R.*, vol. 22, pt. 1:526–528; Marmaduke, *Order and Letter Book*, 426–427; Watts, 44.

114. John Courtney Moore was born August 18, 1834 (Eakin & Hale have the year as 1831), in Pulaski, Tennessee, and his family moved to St. Louis in 1840. Schooled at the University of Missouri, Columbia, Moore was admitted to the St. Louis bar and practiced law. In 1859 he moved to Colorado, searched for gold, and was elected the first mayor of Denver. With the beginning of the Civil War, Moore returned to Missouri and enlisted as a private in the MSG near Pinville, joining Emmett MacDonald's St. Louis Battery. Moore was promoted to sergeant on January 8, 1862, fought at Pea Ridge, and moved to Mississippi with the MSG in April 1863. When the battery reorganized for CSA service, Moore was elected captain of the battery, but later resigned and returned to Arkansas. He was elected 2nd Lieutenant in Company E, 27th Arkansas in August 1862, and then became an aid to Colonel Robert G. Shaver. Following the Battle of Prairie Grove, Moore joined General Marmaduke's staff as an assistant adjutant general on March 20, 1863. Moore was promoted to major on August 31, 1864, and in early 1865, Kirby Smith appointed Moore a colonel, with authority to raise a regiment in northern Arkansas. With the surrender of the Department by Kirby Smith, Moore went to Mexico, but returned to Kansas City in 1866. In the post Civil War era, Moore practiced law and founded the Kansas City *Times* (1868) and the Pueblo (Colorado) *Press*. He also authored the Missouri portion of the *Confederate Military History*. Moore died at his home in Excelsior Springs, Missouri, on October 27, 1915. *O.R.S.*, pt. 2, vol. 2:714; Allardice, *Confederate Colonels*, 278; Eakin, *Confederate Records*, 12; Eakin & Hale, 313; Marmaduke, *Order and Letter Book*, 105; Schnetzer, *More Forgotten Men*, 166; W. L. Webb, *Battles and Biographies of Missourians or the Civil War Period of Our State* (Kansas City,

in Marmaduke's command who knew anything about the trouble. They rode out to an open glade in the woods and met Walker and his second there.[115] Marmaduke told his second, 'I will not shoot to kill the first fire,' and he did not. His ball cut the hair of Walker's head. Marmaduke was the best pistol shot in the army. Walker insisted on a second shot and Marmaduke killed him.[116] He was suspended from his command for a day and a court-martial ordered, but we were being pressed by the Federals and no trial was held. A few days after the duel Little Rock fell, and that and other events prevented any trial. Marmaduke's services were too badly needed. I tell you Marmaduke was as brave a man as any that ever rode up to the music. He could have killed Walker on the first fire had he wished."

* * * * *

MO, 1900), 362–363.

115. Walker's second was Colonel Robert H. Crockett, the grandson of Davy Crockett of Alamo fame. Crockett gave an extensive account of the duel in the February 3, 1889, edition of the *Arkansas Gazette*. Watts, 35.

116. Not really true. The near-sighted Marmaduke was far from the "best pistol shot in the army." Further, prior to the duel the two parties agreed to the use of "regulation navy sixes" revolvers for the duel, and according to the rules of the duel "both parties shall fire at will at any time within five minutes or until all the loads of the pistol are exhausted, or one of the parties shall fall." There was never an insistence on a second firing—it was built into the rules. Following the first shots, both parties missed and Marmaduke fired again striking Walker in the side, while Walker hesitated; the bullet lodged in Walker's spine after passing through the kidneys. Walker died the next day and was buried with military honor the same day, in the Little Rock cemetery. Christ, 174; Marmaduke, *Order and Letter Book*, 429–430; "Terms of Agreement," *Washington Telegraph*, October 21, 1863; Turnbo, 289–290.

Item: Post Duty in Little Rock (August-September, 1863) and Retreat from the City, by Silas C. Turnbo, 27th Arkansas Infantry.[117]
Published: August 7, 1886.

The Fall of Little Rock.

Pro Tem, Mo., July 13.

Editor *Republican*

In the latter part of August, 1863, our army under Gen. Price had concentrated at Little Rock to oppose the threatened attack by Gen. Steele. The main body of the troops was posted at the works on the north side of the river a few miles from Little Rock. A severe battle was expected, with the enemy in superior force. The Missourians under Gen. Parsons were splendid troops and enthusiastic for their commander, who loved them like his own children. They had suffered terribly in some of the campaigns, but were always ready to march or fight. After sustaining considerable losses at Prairie Grove they endured the horrible exposure on that disastrous retreat to Little Rock, where they arrived nearly starved and frozen only to lose many more gallant fellows in the hospitals. But their spirit was not at all impaired, and even after taking a brilliant part in the bloody, unsuccessful attack on Helena they seemed as game as ever.[118] Our own regiment, the Twenty-seventh Arkansas, was doing post duty in the city. We had to guard the prisons, pontoon bridges and government property and preserve order.[119] The pontoon bridge was an excellent one, suited to the heaviest traffic. The guards had endless trouble and occasional fun. Gen. Price, the post commandant, and two or three other officers were the only ones allowed to pass the bridge without special authority. Orders were very strict. One day the writer had charge of the

Guard of Three Men

at the city end of the bridge when a drunken officer came up.[120] He was going right across to whip the Federal Army, but he had no pass. The guard stopped him and he was going to ride right over everything. While he was making a great noise

---

117. This version of the 27th's exploits during the 1863 Campaign for Little Rock is a shortened version of Turnbo's extensive history of the 27th Arkansas Regiment. Turnbo, 282–288, 292–299.

118. At Prairie Grove the Missouri Brigade lost 42 killed, 241 wounded, and 46 missing; at Helena the command lost 62 killed, 304 wounded, with 365 missing. Their losses during the winter of 1862–1863 are not known. See also Appendix C for the details of the brigade's losses at Helena. *O.R.*, vol. 22, pt. 1: 412; Banasik, *Embattled Arkansas*, 514.

119. Tappan's Brigade, to which the 27th Arkansas belonged, arrived in Little Rock on August 22, and was assigned as Provost Guard for the city. Colonel James Shaler was appointed Provost Marshall of Little Rock, while Lieutenant Hiram Ferril, previously of the MSG, was appointed the post adjutant. Ferril had been captured at Blackwater in December 1861, and was exchanged at Vicksburg, before reporting to duty in Little Rock. Eakin, *Confederate Records*, 3:40; Gaughan, 174; Peterson, 144; Turnbo, 282.

120. In his extended article on this incident Turnbo recorded that he commanded only three men and was in charge of the south end of the bridge. Turnbo, 283.

and the guard was trying to cool him down Gen. Price rode up. "Is that officer drunk?" said he. I replied that he was. "If he offers to impose on you in the least send him right to the guardhouse," said the general as he passed on. Then the fellow instead of wanting to whip the Federal Army, begged hard not to be put in the guardhouse. In another case a private cavalryman who had a pass wanted to trot his horse across the bridge and when the guard stopped him he spurred the horse into the river and swam ashore. He was bound to go on his own gait.[121] These are tame incidents, but they remind us of the difficulty of preserving discipline among the thousands of headstrong and heedless fellows who go to make up an army. One day I was detailed as sergeant of the guard at a large brick house which contained some prisoners of war. On going on duty I went among the prisoners to see how they were fixed when they immediately surrounded me, offering anything they had for something to eat and declaring they were starving. I could not believe it at first, but found that it was true. They had been shamefully neglected in some way. I reported to the Officer of the Guard, but as he would do nothing I went to the Post Commandant. He instantly accompanied me to the prison, and after investigating, had matters set right. I believe he found some crookedness, but what ever it was he had it rectified.[122] The old citizens of Little Rock had a company organized for the defense of the city.[123] They were all gray-beard men, and among them was a renowned ex-Gov. Elias N. Conway.[124] About the 5th of September occurred

---

121. In the extended version of the incident the errant cavalryman made it to the center of the bridge before he left. He then swam his horse to the north shore and departed the area. Ibid., 284–285.
122. In the extended version of the POW tale, Turnbo shed more light on the outcome, recording that the post commandant "went with me to the prison house and made an investigation and found some crookedness that had been done heretofore and had it straightened, but it was not quite so bad as the prisoners reported it to be." Ibid., 287.
123. On September 4, 1863, General Price issued an appeal to the citizens of Little Rock, "for every citizen capable of bearing arms, or ministering to the wants of the wounded," to come forth and support the army. They were urged to join any company of their choosing or organize themselves, "under the call of the governor." Among the notables who joined the call to defend Little Rock were William E. Woodruff, age 68, the founder of the *Arkansas Gazette*, and former Governor of Arkansas Henry M. Rector, as well as Rector's political enemy Robert W. Johnson, a former congressman and U.S. senator. Also found among the defenders was the "Bull Battery," organized by William E. Woodruff, Jr. The battery contained two pieces of artillery—one 12-pound Napoleon and one 24-pound howitzer. With no horses available the battery was pulled by oxen. Ferguson, 68; Sterling Price, Letter (September 4, 1863), *Columbia Missouri Statesman* (Columbia, MO), October 16, 1863; Ross, 384–385; Woodruff, W. E. *With the Light Guns in '61–'65 Reminiscences of Eleven Arkansas, Missouri and Texas Light Batteries, in the Civil War* (Little Rock, AR, 1903), 99, hereafter cited as Woodruff.
124. Elias Nelson Conway, a resident of Helena, began his political career as a Democrat, serving as the Arkansas State Auditor in 1835. In 1852 Conway was dubbed the "Dirt Road" candidate for governor and handily defeated his opponent by 3,028 votes from the 27,856 votes that were cast. Conway was overwhelmingly reelected in 1856, by almost 12,000 votes out of approximately 43,000 that were cast. Ferguson, 68; Ross, 130, 136, 291–292, 322–323.

The Duel

between Gens. Marmaduke and Walker, resulting in the death of the latter. His body was brought into town and our regiment assisted in the burial.[125] And now we come to the fall of Little Rock. I have seen several discussions in the *Republican* by some of Steele's men and by Mr. Luttrell on the Confederate side regarding that cavalry fight on the sandbar. I think all of them throw a little light on the events of that day as I remember hearing them described. Our regiment, however, was not in the fight. During the forenoon of September 10, we discovered that something was wrong. Couriers were flying about and trains were being loaded up in town. Then we learned that a portion of Steele's army had flanked us and were crossing some miles below the city, and soon Gen. Tappan's Brigade was ordered down that way. We marched down the south bank about four miles and we halted, taking position behind a fence with a pasture or stubble in front and a cornfield behind us.[126] We heard occasional firing and learned that our cavalry had already had a fight with the enemy. While we were in this position some Federal troops appeared on the north bank and a battery opened on us. We all hugged the ground, and, luckily, every shot went over the fence. The firing did not last long, and about the middle of the afternoon we were ordered back to Little Rock.[127] Part of the way we were in plain sight of Federal troops, marching in the same direction on the other side of the river. We had a good look at each other. On reaching the city we found our pontoon bridge in flames and the Federals looking at it from the north bank.[128] We soon drew off through the city and found that the whole army was falling back. I do not know whether ours was the last infantry regiment that

---

125. Of Walker's burial Turnbo wrote:
His body was enclosed in a nice coffin covered with black velvet. He was buried in the cemetery in Little Rock. The weather was clear and bright and as we marched with reversed arms and the tolling of the bells and the beating of the drums made us feel dismal. After the coffin was lowered into the vault we fired three volleys over the grave. Then we retired a few yards from the grave and the grave digger filled in the dirt and a little mound was formed over the dead commander who was brave and respected by his men.
Turnbo, 290.

126. The first infantry on the scene were from Tappan's Brigade, which arrived at Bayou Fourche at about 1:00 p.m. They took up their position immediately behind Marmaduke's troopers and never fired a shot during the entire engagement. Burford, 180–181; Woodruff, 101.

127. The Confederate retreat from Bayou Fourche, followed by the abandonment of Little Rock, began about 4:00 p.m. and continued until the rebels had successfully withdrawn from combat. By 5:00 p.m. Little Rock was abandoned and the Union Army occupied their prize shortly after 6:00 p.m., according to period newspaper reporters. Other accounts have the first elements of the Davidson's cavalry entering the city at 5:00 p.m. Banasik, *Reluctant Cannoneer*, 196; Burford, 189–190, 193; "From Little Rock," *Chicago Times*, September 23, 1863; Huff, "Union Expedition," 235; Hoskin, September 10, 1863; "War In Arkansas," *Chicago Tribune*, September 23, 1863.

128. Despite rebel efforts to destroy the pontoon bridges over the Arkansas River, two of the bridges were saved by the Federal troops, allowing Federal infantry to cross over into the city the next day, after minor repairs had been made. *O.R.*, vol. 22, pt. 1:477; "From Little Rock," *Chicago Times*, September 23, 1863; "War In Arkansas," *Chicago Tribune*, September 23, 1863.

passed through the city or not. The men grumbled at giving up the city, and we were halted in line, partly to stop the grumbling and partly to let the train get a start. Then we moved on with frequent halts, and night closed in upon us, only a short distance from the city, and we lay down supperless, only eight miles out. The men were most disheartened at the thought of another retreat.[129] We slept on a bed of pebbles and in the morning got up sore from head to foot.

We Had No Breakfast,

but Gen. Price had arrangements made at the front so food was cooked for us and when we reached the designated point we drew rations enough for a fair lunch. It is useless to deny that desertions that day were heavy among the northern Arkansas boys. They left publicly in squads of four and five. They were nether ashamed nor afraid. Our own regiment was greatly reduced. The boys that left were all good fellows, had always performed duty promptly and would have met the enemy bravely at Little Rock. But they had an idea that Price with his small force should have fought there to prevent the capture of the state capital, but here they were on another retreat as usual. After all their hardships they were disheartened and thought that they had done all they could. So away they went, some to surrender and some to join the cavalry, and some to their homes. I suppose that Gen. Price was right though. Gen. Steele's advance was skillful, his army large, brave and well organized. Price had not force enough to cope with him. A battle might have lost us our train and mules in addition to many hundred lives. As it was we got off in pretty fair shape for getting up and dusting again whenever necessary. That night we camped on the Saline river, two miles below Benton, near Gen. Fagan's home. The general had plenty of pretty fat hogs, and he gave the brigade permission to kill all they could eat, and for once we fared sumptuously. Gen. Marmaduke covered the retreat and we continued on to Arkadelphia, where we camped in the cane of the Ouachita bottom.

Silas C. Turnbo,
Twenty-seventh Arkansas Infantry.

---

129. As the 27th Arkansas was resting near the edge of Little Rock, General Price rode up, and one of the men queried him: "'General, ain't we going to fight the yankees?' and the old commander shook his head and said, 'No, boys, there are too many for us.' He looked like he was almost crying." Shortly thereafter the 27th turned southward, leaving the city at a "moderate gait." Overall there was a great deal of grumbling in the army as it retreated, but in hindsight one veteran recorded: "I think Price made a wise choice when he evacuated the city." Others were not so generous, with some accusing General Price of cowardice for not forcing the issue by defending the city. Arkansas soldiers were particularly incensed at Price's decision to give up Little Rock, causing large numbers of them to desert. However, the *Washington Telegraph* was very supportive of General Price following the fall of the city, recording: "We feel sure that when the whole matter comes to be investigated it will be found that Genl. Price acted with judgement and gallantry, and that his course saved the army." Unfortunately, Missouri Governor Thomas C. Reynolds, who unofficially investigated the matter, found that all the general officers under Price, save General Frost, wanted to hold the city. Reynolds wrote in his latter years, that Price admitted to him, that he had overestimated the number of Federal troops who opposed him, causing him to give up the city. "Fall of Little Rock," *Washington Telegraph*, September 16, 1863; Quesenberry, September 10, 1863; Schultz, 96–98; Turnbo, 295–296, 298.

Item: Life of the Confederate soldier serving in the Trans-Mississippi, including the 1863 Campaign for Little Rock, by Colonel Richard H. Musser.[130]
Published: September 19, 1885

The Confederate Soldier.

Following is the substance of a paper read by Col. R. H. Musser before the Southern Historical Society of St. Louis:

The future Montesquieu[131] who centuries hence shall discuss, not as the mere histories, but as the philosopher and jurist, the grandeur of the Americans, will find in the individual Confederate soldier the complete manhood and entirety of character which characterized the Roman soldier in the best days of the Latin race.

Called by the necessities of war into the field, engaged in a contest that he had not believed would be made, the Confederate soldier was as little fitted by his previous experiences and education for the duties and trials of a long war as could be imagined. Perhaps the only qualifications that he had for war were his high courage and knowledge of the use of firearms. Instruction in tactics and military evolutions he had none, for the ancient militia system had died out years before. The number of instructed soldiers were few in any state, fewer perhaps, than among any other people. The regular army of the United States, the result of the

---

130. Richard H. Musser was born on February 6, 1829, in Claysville, Kentucky, moved to Missouri in 1848, and settled in Brunswick, Chariton County. Admitted to the Missouri Bar in 1854, he was elected a Court of Appeals judge in 1855. Musser started the Brunswick *Gazette* newspaper and later bought the *Brunswicker*, which he combined with his previous newspaper to form the *Brunswicker and Gazette*. At the beginning of the Civil War Musser was appointed judge advocate general of the 3rd Division, MSG on June 23, 1861. He was at the Battles of Wilson's Creek and Lexington, where he served as aide to the division commander. At Pea Ridge, Musser had a horse shot out from under him while rallying some troops. Following Price to Mississippi, Musser spent a short time east of the Mississippi River, returned to the Trans-Mississippi Department and raised a battalion of infantry in late November 1862. His new command was known as Musser's Battalion or the 8th Missouri Infantry Battalion. On January 4, 1863, it united with Clark's and Mitchell's Missouri Infantries, and Ruffner's Missouri Battery to form John B. Clark's Missouri Infantry Brigade. On September 30, 1863, Musser's Battalion and Clark's Infantry were consolidated to form a new regiment. On December 15, 1863, per Special Order No. 177, Headquarters, Price's Division, the unit was designated the 9th Missouri Infantry, with Musser appointed colonel on January 1, 1864. Musser participated in the 1863 Campaign for Little Rock, the Red River Campaign (March 10–May 22, 1864) and the Camden Expedition (March 23–May 3, 1864). Following the war he relocated to St. Louis, practiced law in the city until 1877, when he returned to Brunswick, where he reestablished himself. He died at St. Joseph, Missouri, on November 24, 1898. *O.R.*, 8:320; *O.R.*, vol. 22, pt. 2:851; *O.R.* vol. 34, pt. 1:603, 812; *O.R.*, 53:423, 439, 824; Allardice, *Confederate Colonels*, 287; Banasik, *Serving With Honor*, 44–45, 93; *History of Howard and Chariton Counties, Missouri, Written and Compiled from the Most Authentic Official and Private Sources Including a History of Its Townships, Towns and Villages* (St. Louis, 1883), 761–764; National Archives, Record Group 109, Confederate Muster Rolls, 9th Missouri Infantry; Peterson, 108; Schnetzer, *More Forgotten Men*, 171.

131. Charles-Louis de Secondat, baron de La Brède et de Montesquieu, French political thinker and social commentator (1689–1755), best known for his theory of the separation of powers in governments.

jealousy of the people natural to all free republics, had always been ridiculously small, in comparisons with other nations, and outside a few holiday soldiers in the larger cities and a few hundred graduates of West Point, resigned from the regular army, there were no instructed soldiers in the South. It may be said the army was necessarily self-creative and self-instructive. Habits of discipline the Confederate

Had None,

yet he yielded, implicitly and with dignity, obedience to officers and authorities he placed over himself. The army was part of his own anatomy, and he who had studied politics and statesmanship in the newspapers and had been indoctrinated at the business, realized that the principles of government for which he took the field were not his hereditary birthright, but the result of his own honest convictions. He felt and claimed that he was in great part the state. This honest egotism of his patriotic head nerved him for every trial supplied him with patience in hardship and an unwavering fortitude in every labor and privation. He was sustained by honest pride, a pride based upon the conviction of right, and he learned the art of war impelled by his pride which preferred any sacrifice to submission other than to inevitable forces. It was due to this zeal that the hopes and expectations of the soldier during the long contest outran the confidence of the generals and officers. There was much to make the Confederate soldier dissatisfied because there was much to make him, sometimes unnecessarily, uncomfortable. But he was never known to complain of arrears of pay, the prolific source of trouble in mercenary armies, nor of the duration of the war as long as it would afford one more opportunity for battle. The rapidity with which he learned and the ready adaptation for military life will hereafter astound the historian and philosopher, but it will at the same time captivate and charm him. It was not alone the details of tactics, tedious and dull as they might be to men of mature years, but it was the habit of discipline, or that submitting with unquestioning readiness to the will and command of others that the Confederate had to learn. He who had theretofore only known peers and inferiors had now to learn superiors. He reconciled himself to the superior solely because he was "*magna pars*" of the government himself, and that in obeying others he was in a great part obeying himself. The theory led him shortly to that perfection of discipline that made him

Invincible.

When the Confederacy had gotten fairly into war; when the "on to Richmond" had been checked at Bull Run with crushing defeat; when Price and McCullough [McCulloch] had destroyed Lyon's columns at Wilson Creek, and Grant had been beaten at Belmont,[132] and inconsiderable but decisive advantages had crowned the

---

132. The Battle of Wilson's Creek as it was known by Federal forces, and Oak Hills by Confederate troops, was fought on August 10, 1861, near Springfield, Missouri. The Confederates were commanded by General Ben McCulloch and the Unionists were under General Nathaniel Lyon. The battle

Confederate armies along the whole line of battle in 1861, and the Congress of the United States had called for half a million men and voted four hundred millions of money, it was then, and then only, that it became evident to the belligerents that the war was serious and earnest.[133] Then, and then only, did it dawn upon the Confederate soldier that their statesmen had forgotten to provide for a contingency of a long war and that they were ill provided for the contest before them. It was in this emergency that the creative and adaptive powers of the Confederacy were first manifested.

The blockade on the seaboard, the blockade on the inland front of our line of battle made it apparent the supplies of arms and material of war were inadequate. The enemy's half million of men must be met. Of men we had enough, but where were the arms and the ammunition? Where the subsistence? Where the clothing? Just then and there it became apparent that the organization of the army was defective.[134] The men were the best who ever composed an army, but the officers, se-

---

was a Confederate victory and one of the first major battles of the war. The rebels lost 257 killed, 900 wounded, and 27 missing, while the Federals posted losses of 223 killed, 721 wounded, and 291 missing. Boatner, 932–935.

The Battle of Belmont, Missouri was fought on November 7, 1861, opposite Columbus, Kentucky. General U.S. Grant's Federal command consisted of two infantry brigades with some cavalry and a six gun battery. John A. McClernand and Henry Dougherty commanded brigades. The Confederates, though initially outnumbered moved additional troops from Columbus to Belmont to boost their strength to about 4,000 effective men. Generals Gideon Pillow and Benjamin F. Cheatham commanded the Confederates until Leoniadas Polk took command late in the contest. When the battle had ended the rebels controlled the field and claimed victory. Polk lost 105 killed, 419 wounded and 117 missing, while Grant lost 85 killed, 301 wounded and 99 missing out of 3,114 engaged. Of the Federal wounded, 125 were left as prisoners of war. *O.R.*, 3:266, 269, 271 308, 310; Boatner, 57–58.

133. During the course of the Civil War, President Lincoln issued twelve calls for troops or requests for militia, with the first occurring on April 15, 1861, when he asked for 75,000 militia for three months. Following this initial call for troops and the firing on Fort Sumter, Virginia, Tennessee, Arkansas and North Carolina seceded from the Union, placing all the states, save Kentucky on one side or the other. Kentucky would later join the Union side, when it was entered by rebel troops in September 1861. Missouri had a governor who supported secession and called for a legislative session at Neosho, Missouri, in October 1861, to vote for secession. The measure passed; however, there was not a proper quorum present to make the measure legally binding—as such Missouri remained in the Union. The call the writer was referring to, came on May 3, 1861, when the president requested 500,000 men. Congress finally approved the levy on August 6, 1861. From this last call 700,680 men were provided, with 657,808 being enlisted for three years, while the remainder were for shorter periods of time. Banasik, *Confederate "Tales of the War" 1862*, 15; H. Lee Cheek, Jr., "Secession," in *Encyclopedia of the Civil War*, 1718–1720; Lowell H. Harrison, "Kentucky," in *Encyclopedia of the Civil War*, 1117; Frederick Phisterer, *Statistical Record of the Armies of the United States* (New York, 1907), 3–9.

134. When the war began the Confederate States were at a clear disadvantage to their Northern cousins in terms of logistic capabilities. The South had but 18,026 "industrial establishments" to the Union's 110,274; the North was producing $2,200,000 worth of arms, while the Confederacy mustered production of $73,000, with the Tredegar Iron Works being the "only major rolling Mill" in the South at the beginning of the war; the South produced just 9 locomotives in the year prior to the war, while Northern mills turned out 451; 22,000 miles of railroad covered the North while the South had a mere 9,000 miles. In the area of draft animals Southern states had 2,500,000 to 4,700,000 for the North. And despite being a cotton producer, the South had difficulty providing clothing for its armies, having to frequently import cloth for the making of uniforms. Imports from foreign countries made up many of

lected hastily without practical knowledge of their fitness and ability were, many of them, high and low, inefficient and wanting in capacity. The evils that both armies suffered from worthless and incapable officers could be made the theme of a treatise and is out of the scope of this paper. These evils were unavoidable, because the best as well as the most inefficient solider did not know his own worth till tested by experience.

The Southern people rose with the occasion. They

Began to Create

what before the war they only knew how to consume. Their inventions had all the meritorious simplicity that had characterized all American inventions, whether of the North or the South. They took of necessity what was at hand and applied it to their most imperative uses. They began to manufacture arms and create material of war out of the simplest appliances of peace. They had used railroad iron for the armament of ships. They used hemp bales at Lexington,[135] not alone as Jackson used the cotton bales at New Orleans, but as moveable field works, capable of being transported before the soldier, and of infinite power of resistance when soaked full of water. The soldier's inventions extended to everything involving his personal comfort or safety.

[Line missing] of the campaign of 1862 arrayed in line of battle stretching almost across the continent, the North possessing more than twice the numerical strength of the South, white and black, with the advantage of the prestige of the national government in her favor and unbounded resources of men and money.[136] Not that alone, possessing a commercial navy as well as ships of war, with the whole world to draw from of men and material. The South had only their inter-

---

the Southern shortages, with sixty percent of their small arms, a third of their lead and two-thirds of their saltpeter coming by importation. Additionally, "uniforms, cloth, artillery pieces and ammunition, medicine, and great amounts of food" all were imported via blockade running. Boatner, 847; David A. Norris, "Blockade Running," in *Encyclopedia of the Civil War*, 243–245; David J. Ulbrich, "Logistics," in *Encyclopedia of the Civil War*, 1297.

135. Lexington was the county seat of Lafayette County, Missouri, and the site of a siege from September 13–20, 1861. Located about 300 miles from St. Louis on the Missouri River, Lexington's population at the beginning of the war was near 5,000 inhabitants, who participated primarily in the hemp growing and manufacturing industry. The city hosted two colleges. The Masonic College, which embraced some fifteen acres, served as the Federal defensive point during the siege in September 1861. In the final days of the siege, hemp bales were used as a moveable fortification to shelter the Confederate attackers, while they moved their lines ever closer to the Federal entrenchments, until the city finally fell. General Thomas A. Harris, commanding the 2nd Division, MSG was credited with the idea of using hemp bales to advance upon the Federal lines. *O.R.*, 3:171, 191; John McElroy, *The Struggle For Missouri* (Washington, DC, 1909), 206–207, hereafter cited as McElroy.

136. By March 31, 1862, Union muster rolls showed 637,127 men, while the Confederate forces for the same time period numbered 401,395 or about 63 percent of their foe. On January 1, 1863, Federal rolls contained 918,121 men while the Southern armies had 446,622 men or roughly 49 percent of the Union forces. Thomas L. Livermore, *Numbers & Losses in the Civil War in America: 1861–1865* (Bloomington, IN, 1957), 47.

nal agricultural resources, and such as her people could spontaneously create.[137] The grand emergency was the mother of invention and provider of undreamed resources. But first it gave use to that splendid system of autonomic discipline never seen in any other army. The institutions of the several sovereign states were democratic, so was the army. The officers of the companies and regiments were elected and

Were Vested with Authority

to command by the free choice of the commanded. We find the individual Confederate soldier the autonomic source of all power as vested in him, the people, and yet the disciplined an obedient subject of himself. He not only submitted to discipline and learning the drill, but he learned to endure privations and discomforts which were more severe trials of his patience, manhood and patriotism. If there was anything for which the South had a well established fame it was for an unrestricted hospitality and an abundance of fat things that makes life pleasant and independent. The wayfarer, though a fool, could, before the war, traverse the entire South without a purse or script, never enduring hunger or wanting the shelter of a roof at night, and would not have met from Texas to Missouri, or from Virginia to Louisiana, a hungry slate. It might be imagined that the Confederate would be impatient, when his food, at times, became worse than the husks the impoverished prodigal fed to the swine, or that he would be tempted to pine for the flesh-pots and abundance of his home in time of peace. This was an especial situation of the Missourians, for after 1862 he was an exile from his own state, and long after the last glimmering of hope of regaining his own country had died out he was the truest and most loyal to the Richmond government. He preferred poor beef—some of us can witness how poor it was—and corn bread, nakedness and hunger, privation, exposure and danger to flesh-pots he might have enjoyed for

---

137. Food production was yet another problem for the South, which had the acreage, but was more concerned with the production of cotton instead of foodstuffs to feed its population. The lack of food produced riots beginning in 1862, and it continued throughout the war. Every Confederate state was affected, and it made no difference whether the city was large or small. The large plantation owners simply refused to devote sufficient land to food production, electing instead to raise cotton for export. The government even enacted laws to support food production and distribution, but the "planters ignored the ill-enforced law and kept growing too much cotton. The result was continued hunger and rioting through the rest of the war." In the Trans-Mississippi, most of their critical needs for items such as cloth, uniforms, blankets, medicines, arms, shoes, and sheet iron came via blockade running. Money was habitually short in the Trans-Mississippi, making cotton the media of exchange for imported goods. The primary avenue of importation came via Matamoros, Mexico, into Brownsville, Texas. To better manage the supply shortages in the Trans-Mississippi the "Clothing Bureau" was formed in 1862, and the "Cotton Bureau" was established in 1863, functioning until the end of the war. Food problems were largely eliminated in the Trans-Mississippi region in 1864, when a "tithing system" was established, requiring one-tenth of the planters crops be delivered to the Confederate Government for distribution. James L. Nichols, *The Quartermaster in the Trans-Mississippi* (Austin, 1964), 28, 53, 58, 67, 81, 104–106; David Williams, "Class Conflict, C.S.A.," *Encyclopedia of the Civil War*, 443–445.

a parole of honor, which he regarded as involving dishonor and an abandonment of principles that a not too punctilious world would have excused.[138] Not alone, however, could he

Prefer to be Hungry

and naked and in "looped and windowed raggedness bide the pittings of the pitiless storm" of shelterless winter. He could sacrifice his patrimonial estate, could see the earnings and economies of his life wasted and destroyed, while he stayed by his colors and was true to his cause. It was also in loathsome prison, chafing in the indignity of restraint and the impatience of often wanton insult and wrong that his spirit was tried. Yet he could have bartered his manhood on easy terms for his liberation and given to his freeborn limbs their worried right to tread whither they would. The price of freedom was but the break of a parole or the abrogation of an oath. Yet that break was the value of a soul and its price to him was infamy and shame. How strong was the chivalric spirit of truth and loyalty in the Confederate soldier was attested by the plethoric repletion of Northern prisons where those who were taken in arms and as suspects of disloyalty were confined. The thousands of nameless prisoners' graves in Northern cemeteries, now decorated by a generous foe as often as the recurring year brings to the whole nation the flowers of May, attest the contrast devotion of those martyrs to a sacred but unfortunate cause.[139] The virtues which characterized the soldiers of the Confederacy are the

---

138. Rations varied from day-to-day for the Trans-Mississippi soldier. Normally in 1862 his ration consisted of "very poor beef...the coarsest of corn meal" with an occasional issue of bacon, sugar or coffee. In the latter part of 1862 one member of Parsons's Missouri Brigade recorded a general statement regarding food for the region. William Bull wrote:

> Food was very scarce with us at times not only with the soldiers but with the citizens also. We sometimes existed for days with nothing but horse corn to eat and even that was scarce and was issued in limited quantities to the men for food. When we had meat and bread, we had no salt—there was none to be had in the country. The citizens dug up the floors of their old smoke houses and boiled it to get the small amount of salt it contained.

By 1864 rations had improved considerably and rarely did you see complaints. The ration typically consisted of "fine fresh beef," cornbread and bacon. Banasik, *Missouri Brother in Gray*, 50; Banasik, *Serving With Honor*, 166, 177.

139. "About 215,000 Confederates...spent time as prisoners, of whom about 26,000 died." Early in the war, prisoners were regularly exchanged, but as the war progressed, disputes arose concerning the handling of black POWs from the Union Army. The Confederacy was going to treat them as "revolting slaves," and either execute them or return them to their masters; and thus ended all large scale exchanges in mid-1863. By early 1865, exchanges began again, but only after the Confederate Government had agreed to exchange captured black soldiers on an equal basis with white soldiers. However, the reinstated exchange program came too late for many a Confederate POW as Union authorities had cut rations to rebel prisoners to force the issue with the Richmond Government. "Consequently, tens of thousands of soldiers were doomed to death in Captivity." Thousands of rebels died in Union prisons and no Union official was ever held accountable for the losses, even though ample supplies were available to prevent the loss of life in Union prisons. Some of the more famous Union prisons were Johnson Island, in Lake Erie by Sandusky, Ohio; Camp Douglas in Chicago; Camp Chase in Columbus, Ohio; and Camp Morton in Indianapolis, Indiana. Douglas G. Gardner, "Prisons, U.S.A.," *Encyclopedia of the Civil War*, 1574–1575; James Gillispie, "Prisons, C.S.A.," *Encyclopedia of the Civil*

common heritage of the whole South. They are due to the simplicity and integrity of a people who were at the same time rich, chivalrous and honest, a people who were agricultural, and received from Almighty God in his sunshine and rain, in favorable season and fertile lands, all that they prized in the world. They were in a great measure unsullied and uncorrupted by the degrading influences of traffic and innocent of the courteous idolatry of usury and dishonest money-getting. They were an agricultural and uncommercial people and capable of highest patriotism, because patriotism was the law of the soil that bore and nurtured them.

In Actual Service

whether in bivouac or winter quarters, no Algerian Zouave ever made himself more comfortable under difficulties. It was a hard storm that ever made him damp and a cold day that his bivouac fire and blanket dog-house could not temper into tolerable comfort. Though he could not be brought to carry a knapsack or encumber himself with impediments, other than his blanket, rations and canteen, yet his ready invention supported him with comfort whenever he encamped. Perhaps the world has never seen a soldier less given to pillage. Though his government was never less than a year's pay in arrears and his Confederate money, when paid, was worth but a few cents to the dollar, he was but little given to marauding, and such was the moral *esprit de corps* of his company or his mess, that a soldier disgraced for marauding or known to be guilty of dishonest or indecent practices was shunned and despised. His chivalrous respect for ladies constituted a duty demanded not only by his own instincts and education, but imperatively by the moral sentiments of his race. Though of every variety of faith the soldiers required no constraints to pay decent respect to religious exercises no matter who was the chaplain; and in his treatment of prisoners of war, his humanity was only equalled by his gallantry in the field. War is always horribly inhuman, but it is to be doubled if, with all its carnage and suffering, there was ever known so humane a war as ours.

History will do us justice as a testament of prisoners. The worst phase of slavery was the first glimpse of civilization that alleviated

The Brutal Butchery

of victory by assigning to captivity those who were doomed to the sword. The captivity of prisoners[140] was accepted from considerations of cupidity and from no

---

War, 1573–1574.

140. Generally speaking both sides treated POWs with respect when caught on the battlefield. However, this statement is difficult to completely support given the Confederate treatment of black soldiers in the Battles of Fort Pillow, Tennessee, and Poison Springs, Arkansas. In both cases large numbers of surrendering black soldiers were allegedly executed on the spot. On a larger scale, the most infamous example of maltreatment of POWs occurred at Andersonville, Georgia, where 13,000 Northern soldiers died. Unfortunately, on the Union side, particularly in the Trans-Mississippi, atrocities were also frequent and a main cause for the "no quarter policy" adopted by both sides in the guerrilla warfare in

regard to humanity. The great master of the art of war, Julius Caesar, conquered all Gaul, Britain, Belgium, Germany and Helvetia, without ever incurring any debt or issuing any bond or greenback. The prisoners of war, made slaves, paid all expenses and enriched the soldiers besides, while the conquered provinces enriched the state.

He hath brought many captives home to Rome
Whose ransom hath the general coffers filled

is the panegyric of Marc Anthony at Caesar's death, but ours was a nation of people fighting without pay, almost without rations, and at a personal sacrifice of their estates individually because of a sentiment and a conviction that made their effort honorable even if it were conceded to be the effect of mistaken zeal. And yet the Confederate soldier did not resort to pillage to reimburse himself for his losses, nor was he cruel or vindictive to his prisoners. With him war was not private vengeance nor the rivalry of states degenerated into a private quarrel.

It has been said that Andersonville and Libby were prisons where inhuman neglect, want of food and medical treatment consigned many gallant and noble soldiers of our Northern brethren to untimely graves.[141] Let us concede it to be

---

the region. In the Trans-Mississippi, Federal authorities declared a no quarter policy on December 26, 1861, against anyone who burned a bridge, which made no differentiation as to whether the burner was a regularly enlisted soldier or not. The policy in part read: "Anyone caught in this act will be immediately shot, and anyone accused of this crime will be arrested and placed in close confinement until his case can be examined by a military commission, and, if found guilty, he also will suffer death." Union forces were also guilty of summary executions as seen by their operations against irregular Confederate forces in Missouri. This was particularly blatant at Palymra and Kirksville, where the local Union commander ordered executions with minimal or no judicial proceedings. There was no officially sanctioned response by the Confederate government to Federal actions in Missouri, although Confederate guerrillas also perpetrated summary executions, with the most famous being Lawrence, Kansas (August 1863) and Centralia, Missouri (September, 1864). *O.R.*, vol. 8:463–464; Banasik, *Cavaliers of the Brush*, 81–83, 186–193; Banasik, *Confederate "Tales of the War" 1862*, 116–117, 187–188; Boatner, 295–296; Faust, 588–590; Alicia Rodriguez, "Andersonville," *Encyclopedia of the Civil War*," 48, hereafter cited as Rodriguez.

141. The prison at Andersonville, Georgia, was officially known as Camp Sumter. Construction of the rectangular pine log enclosure began in January 1864, the first prisoners arrived on February 25, 1864, and the prison was closed on May 4, 1865. During its existence 45,613 men were housed there at one time or another, with the high point being reached in August 1864, when the camp held 33,000 men, though it was designed to hold only 10,000. The stockade embraced 16.5 acres and was loosely guarded by a minimum garrison, meant to hold the prisoners in the camp but not to regulate it. "Filth, vermin, disease, malnutrition, exposure to the elements, and a stench that was said to cause prisoners to vomit upon entering the grounds characterized," the prison. With General William Sherman's advance on Atlanta in the summer of 1864, most of the POWs were sent to other facilities in the south, and by December 1864, only 1,359 prisoners remained. Rodriguez, 48–51.

Libby Prison, in Richmond, Virginia, was opened in 1861, following the Battle of First Manassas or Bull Run and continued to operate throughout the war. At its height of operation, the former tobacco warehouse held 2,000 prisoners, and later in the war it was used strictly for housing Federal officers. After the war Union authorities used it to house high-ranking rebel prisoners until August 3, 1868, when it was closed. "Starvation and the lack of warm clothing" were the main problems with the prison, but this was also true of the general population of Richmond at the time it operated. Libby Prison was "perhaps the most notorious prison after Andersonville." Boatner, 482; Frank E. Deserino,

true; was it not the misfortune of the Federal government that there were no better rations, better medicines and better quarters for the Federal prisoners? And was it not the fault of Mr. Stanton, the United States Secretary of War, that Andersonville and Libby were not emptied by exchanges for the thousands of Confederates confined in the prisons of the North? It was a part of his

Cruel Strategy

to doom those gallant spirits to torture and to death in Southern prisons, because in the South there was no replacing our prisoners of war, while in the North all the world could send them recruits.

Prison is not a delightful place to dwell; and to be a prisoner, even under the most human palpitations, is not a situation to be sought or chosen. Yet, for every prisoner in Libby or Andersonville, Tyler, Tex.[142] or other place which the necessities of the great secretary's policy rendered unavoidable there was at least one Confederate prisoner confined at the North. Many of these prisoners could have escaped duress by a word or false oath. They could have subscribed to an oath, under circumstances which the duress of their situation would have gone far to excuse if not to justify [illegible] here, gentleman, mention what is in to-night—a circumstance alike honorable to the soldiers of both armies. During the Siege of Vicksburg, by a sort of common consent, and a result of no cartel between the commanders, the firing ceased at sunset and was resumed at sunrise. Our soldiers, grown, by familiarity, indifferent to the enemy's cannonade, were ensconced in their bombproofs, while Gen. Grant was industriously spading his way from the Yazoo side into our fortifications, and was by circumvallation slowly but surely gathering the doomed city into his meshes. There was a constant intercourse between the soldiers of the two armies. Speaking the same language, they gossiped across the giacts(?) of the fortifications. They interchanged news, indifferent to the war, exchanged newspapers and sent compliments of tobacco and whiskey. They even, in many instances, interchanged visits and spent convivial nights, always to return to their quarters before the firing resumed in the morning. This was a breech of discipline, yet there was no incident of perfidy or bad faith resulting from it.

"Libby Prison," *Encyclopedia of the Civil War*, 1178–1180.

142. Camp Ford, Texas, was established as an "open stockade" prison in August 1863, and was located four miles northwest of Tyler. A walled stockade eighteen feet high enclosed the camp which embraced ten acres. It was the largest of three POW camps in Texas, housing about 4,900 men in July 1864. The other camps were Camp Verde in Kerr County and Camp Groce by Hempstead, Texas. Camp Ford did not suffer the same problems as Andersonville, having a good supply of water and adequate rations to feed the inmates. The inmates had no shelter, but were given tools to make their own, which proved adequate for the men. Few men ever died at Camp Ford, with 232–286 being the estimated number of deaths. The camp existed for twenty-one months, being closed on May 17, 1865, and was burned upon occupation by Federal forces. Faust, 110; B. P. Gallaway, ed., *Texas the Dark Corner of the Confederacy: Contemporary Accounts of the Lone Star State in the Civil War* (Lincoln, NB, 1994), 192–193.

The Missourians

bore a particular relation toward the Confederate Army in which they served. They were precipitated into the war by sentiments of personal integrity rather than personal interests. Long after he ceased to have any tangible, material interest, the Missourian remained of the truest and most steadfast followers of the Confederate fortunes.

The state had been admitted into the Union in 1820, upon a compromise which was to be ever afterwards the source of agitation.[143] The citizens of the state had been the victims of constant discussions of the compromise as reenacted in 1850, and her material interest were retarded by the uncertainty of her domestic institutions. Her territory jutted out like an exposed peninsula into the North to the forty-first parallel, and she was almost entirely surrounded by non-slaveholding states. The descendants of Virginians and Southerners, Missourians had with them an identity of sentiment and sympathy the natural result of consanguinity, and the sentiment had been intensified by long and frequent agitations and embittered by the contests over the settlement and admission of Kansas. There was, excepting in large cities, almost unanimity of feeling and purpose throughout the state, not so much for secession as for the sovereignty of the state and withholding her hand from coercion.

Gov. [Claiborne F.] Jackson[144] undertook at first the impossible role of neutrality in the Union, which was construed by the Federal powers to be practically rebellion.

The capture of Gen. Frost's command of the state troops under the Federal flag, and the President's requisition on Missouri for her quota of 75,000 men for coercion produced a spontaneous response to Jackson's proclamation for 50,000

---

143. The Missouri Compromise was the first piece of legislation, from the U.S. Congress, which pitted "Slave-holding States" against "Free States." Crafted by Henry Clay of Kentucky, this 1820 Compromise allowed Missouri to enter the Union as a slave state while Maine entered the Union as a free state. The compromise further stated that slavery would not be extended into the Louisiana Purchase area, north of the southern boundary of Missouri. However, in 1854 the Congress passed the Kansas-Nebraska Act, which nullified the Missouri Compromise and brought the nation ever closer to civil war. As written, the act formed Kansas and Nebraska into territories and allowed them to vote on whether they entered the Union as free or slave states. This voting process was better known as "popular sovereignty." The Kansas-Nebraska Act led to years of violence on the Missouri-Kansas border in what became known as the "Bleeding Kansas" years (1854–1859), and proved to be the forerunner of the Civil War. Boatner, 69, 448, 556–557.

144. Claiborne F. Jackson was born on April 4, 1807, in Kentucky, moved to Missouri in 1826, and was independently wealthy by the age of thirty. Jackson was elected to the Missouri Legislature in 1836, and for the next several years maintained a high profile in Missouri politics. As a Democrat, Jackson supported slavery and believed in "States Rights." Elected Governor of Missouri on January 3, 1861, Jackson maintained his position throughout the Civil War, even after being driven from the state by Federal forces in late 1861. Jackson did not survive the war, dying on December 7, 1862, at Little Rock, Arkansas. See Banasik, *Missouri In 1861*, 350–352 for a complete biography; McElroy, 20, 25, 27.

Missourians for the service of the state.[145] The State Guards were attacked and dispersed at Boonville by Federal troops under Gen. Lyon.[146] They rallied and rendezvoused in the southwest, and by the aid of Confederates from Texas, Arkansas and Louisiana were

Bold Enough to Advance

and defeat the government's armies so as to regain the Missouri River at Lexington. This was war and meant prison or exile to many thousand of our people. In February, 1862, Gen. Price's army was compelled to retreat from Springfield into Arkansas.[147] His retreat was followed by thousands who were compromised

---

145. On April 15, 1861, President Abraham Lincoln issued a call for 75,000 militia troops, to serve three months. The troops were to "suppress" the rebellion and "cause the laws to be duly executed." Governor Claiborne F. Jackson refused to supply Missouri's portion of the call, noting in his judgment it was "illegal, unconstitutional and revolutionary in its object." On May 6, 1861, Jackson called for the Missouri Militia to assemble throughout the state for "instruction in military tactics." In St. Louis, Camp Jackson was established on the outskirts of St. Louis in Lindell Grove, bordered by Grand Avenue on the west, Compton Avenue on the east and Lindell on the north. On May 10, Union General Nathaniel Lyon captured the camp, without firing a shot. Lyon feared that the pro-secession governor was using the lawfully assembled Missouri Militia as a ploy to capture the St. Louis Arsenal, with its large store of weapons and ammunition. Following the capture of the Missouri Militia Brigade, the prisoners were marched off to the St. Louis Arsenal. En route, a mob attacked the Federal troops, who responded with musket fire, resulting in the killing of 25 civilian men, women and children along with 3 unarmed prisoners from Camp Jackson. This then became known as the "St. Louis or Camp Jackson Massacre" and propelled Missouri into the Civil War. The Missouri Legislature met late on the night of May 10, passed the Military Bill authorizing the MSG. Meanwhile, Governor Jackson attempted to forego a confrontation with Federal troops in Missouri, temporarily arranging a cease fire via the Price-Harney Agreement. On June 11, the agreement collapsed and the following day the Governor issued a call for 50,000 men to defend Missouri. *O.R.*, vol. 53:696–698; *O.R.*, Series 3, vol. 1:67–68, 82–83; Hans Christian Adamson, *Rebellion in Missouri: 1861 Nathaniel Lyon and His Army of the West* (Rahway, NJ, 1961), 62–64; Banasik, *Missouri Brothers in Gray*, 9–10, 12; Bevier, 24–25; "Governor's Proclamation—General Orders No. 7," *Missouri Republican*, May 2, 1861; William C. Winter, *The Civil War in St. Louis: A Guided Tour* (St. Louis, 1994), 34–35, hereafter cited as Winter.

146. Boonville was located in Cooper County, Missouri, on the south side of the Missouri River. It was the point to which Governor Claiborne F. Jackson fled from Jefferson City to avoid the advancing Federal troops under Nathaniel Lyon. On June 17, 1861, Lyon engaged the MSG at Boonville and easily dispersed them after a only a few minutes. During the engagement, Lyon lost 2 killed, 9 wounded (2 mortally) and 1 missing out of 1,700 men engaged. Lyon reported capturing 60 rebels, 500 arms, and 2 brass cannon. *O.R.*, 3:11–14, 809; Christopher Phillips, *Damned Yankee: The Life of General Nathaniel Lyon* (Columbia, MO, 1990), 217–220.

147. At dusk on February 12, Elijah Gates's 1st Missouri Cavalry attacked the advance pickets of the Federal Army to cover the rebel retreat from Springfield, which began shortly after midnight. By 10 a.m., on February 13, Federal troops had entered Springfield, followed by a vigorous pursuit, which did not abate until February 18. Of the fighting retreat General Price wrote: "Retreating and fighting all the way to the Cross Hollow, in this state [Arkansas], I am rejoiced to say my command, under the most exhausting fatigue all that time, with but little rest for either man or horse and no sleep, sustained themselves, and came through repulsing the enemy upon every occasion with great determination and gallantry." The final Federal attack occurred at Sugar Creek on February 17, with a loss 13 killed and 20 wounded, while the rebels lost 3 killed and 14 wounded. *O.R.*, 8:757; Michael E. Banasik, *Duty, Honor and Country: The Civil War Experiences of Captain William P. Black, Thirty-seventh Illinois Infantry* (Iowa City, IA, 2006), 73–75; Ephraim McD. Anderson, *Memoirs: Historical and Personal;*

by their zeal for the South, and who could not remain at home. The Missourians never found safe footing again in their state till the close of the war. Of the exiles many thousand combatants and non-combatants died.

Many of these brave exiles died in the first month of their service, for the heaviest casualties of war are in the military hospitals. And each recruit must go through the ordeal of a new infancy in the service. From croup to whooping-cough, measles and fever, diphtheria and such contagious afflictions, he is liable to be carried off, especially as any or all of them may be complicated with nostalgia in the earliest stages of military life. Homesickness is acute, but does not ordinarily last long, though it is sometimes incurable. It attacks mostly the rural recruits, the plough-boys and young farmers, who have bucolic tastes and habits. That intolerable and insatiate longing for and impatience to be with loved ones, however humble, a desire to be under the paternal.

Like all other Confederate soldiers our troops brought to the service with their healthy physiques an exhaustless fund of cheerfulness, wit and good humor, and after the first exodus had outlived their infantile diseases they formed a nucleus in both the Mississippi departments for all future accessions from the state.[148] They were able at once to teach the recruits by precept and example all the duties of the drill and the details of discipline. Many of these were graduates of various Northern prisons, and had either escaped or been exchanged.

In the Prisons

they had learned for their amusement and profit various arts and handicrafts which made them valuable accessions, and they were already veterans and seasoned to the constraints of duty. How many of our countrymen entered the Confederate service and were filtered through prisons and by escape or proscription from the brush, is an interesting question. There were not less than 50,000 seasoned veterans serving with the various corps of the Confederate Army and this 50,000 were the fittest survivors of probably 100,000 able-bodied exiles. At the close of the war there were twelve veteran regiments of infantry besides three battalions of light infantry. Those in the Trans-Mississippi were recruited up to their full strength. My own regiment was about 1,200 strong.[149] There was an average on

---

Including the Campaigns of the First Missouri Confederate Brigade (St. Louis, 1868; reprint ed. Dayton, OH, 2005), 140–141; Griffin Frost, *Camp and Prison Journal* (Quincy, IL, 1867; reprint ed., Iowa City, IA, 1994), 5.

148. In April 1862, General Van Dorn withdrew his Army of the West to the east side of the Mississippi River and never returned. The 1st and 2nd Missouri Brigades were part of Van Dorn's army. Banasik, *Embattled Arkansas*, 10.

149. Musser's regiment was the 9th Missouri Infantry. The unit was originally organized at Fort Smith, Arkansas, in November 1862, under the command of Colonel John B. Clark, Jr., with eight companies. On September 30, 1863, Musser's 8th Missouri Battalion and Clark's Infantry were consolidated to form a new ten-company regiment. On December 15, 1863, per Special Order No. 177, Headquarters, Price's Division, the unit was designated the Ninth Missouri Infantry. *O.R.S.*, pt. 2, vol. 38:585; National Archives, Record Group 109, Confederate Muster Rolls, 9th Missouri Infantry; Special Order

this side of the river 1,000 men each. The regiments in Cis-Mississippi were much depleted, but many efficient and intelligent men and officers had been promoted and transferred to other arms of the service and were serving with corps from other states. There were as many regiments of cavalry besides the companies of artillery, corps of sappers and miners, engineers and ordnance, aggregating not less than 35,000 men on duty at the time of the surrender, besides the immense number of Missourians not serving with their own corps at all, those who went to Virginia, in Texas and Louisiana and other states singly and took service there; besides those detailed in the bureau for the exportation of cotton and transportation of supplies from Mexico.

Though the drill and discipline of the Missourian was due originally to the lesson taught by Frost and [John S.] Bowen,[150] [James R.] Shaler and [Joseph] Kelly and others instructed in the state militia as it was organized before the war, yet much of the efficiency was due to the patience and diligence with which he studied and

Acquired All the Details

of tactics and conformed to the demands of discipline. He was personally cleanly to the extent that, though he often had almost no clothes, he never had anything but clean clothes. He was an incessant news gatherer and critic. His knowledge of military affairs was the result of study and contemplation. He became a student of history as well as a student of tactics and strategy, and he discussed army affairs and the matters of the nation fully and freely. His criticisms were made in no caviling and or mutinous spirit. Although many of them, corporals, sergeants and privates, were fully equal to the command of a brigade or an army, and some of them would have been glad to undertake so honorable a responsibility, they yielded unhesitatingly obedience to all commands and recognized authority of an officer. But each was a general officer in his own way. That is to say, he assumed to criticize the details of a campaign and suggest, as he saw fit, strictures on the inefficiency of the strategy or the inadequacy of the appliances in field or fortification to the end desired. This spirit of his criticism was the result of his intelligence and self-reliance his want from childhood. There are some, perhaps,

---

No. 38 (November 10, 1862), Special Order Book No. 1.

150. John S. Bowen was born at Bowen Creek, near Savannah, Georgia, on October 30, 1830. He was appointed to West Point in 1848, graduated in 1853 (number 13 of 51) and served three years before resigning. He moved to St. Louis in 1857, where he was an architect and joined the Missouri Militia as a colonel in 1861. Captured at Camp Jackson and paroled, Bowen went to Memphis where he organized the 1st Missouri Infantry Regiment. At the Battle of Shiloh, Bowen commanded a brigade as a brigadier general, was wounded, but recovered. At Corinth, in October 1862, Bowen again commanded a brigade. During the Vicksburg Campaign, Bowen successfully delayed Grant's army at the Battle of Port Gibson (May 1, 1863), earning a promotion to major general for his efforts. During the siege of Vicksburg, Bowen contacted dysentery and died on July 13, 1863, nine days after the surrender of the city. For complete biography see Banasik, *Missouri Brothers in Gray*, 135–136; Moore, *Missouri, Confederate Military History*, 205–206); Warner, *Generals in Gray*, 29–30.

here who will remember the siege of Little Rock, when the District of Arkansas, Trans-Mississippi Department, was commanded by Gen. Nathaniel [Theophilus] Holmes. He had in 1863 uncovered our front by an attack on Galena [Helena], exposed the weakness of the line of the Arkansas by an attempt to capture a town which was in itself of no strategic value if held and was untenable besides. This involved concentrating his whole force for the defense of Little Rock. The Missouri and Arkansas infantry were ordered to fortify a line of defenses on the north side of the Arkansas River, covering the town, and the work was done well. The lines were made impregnable if defended with spirit and well provided with a means of retreat over strong pontoon bridges connecting the fortifications with the city. We dug ditches and made earthworks, constructed banquettes and bastions and posted artillery in embrasure and barrette. Among the other means of defense we were required to make more chevaux de frise and abatis[151] in front of our parapet to prevent the enemy making a charge and carrying our works

By Assault.

On the right of my battalion was Gen. Fagan's brigade of infantry, and in front of us, i.e., Frost's brigade, was a large cornfield with stalks, all in confusion, the corn having been gathered for the use of our horses.[152] Gen. Fagan, who was a most efficient and dashing infantry commander, at the time, was noted for the grace of his horsemanship and his thorough discipline and perfect drill, had ordered the erection in front of his line of the required fortifications. Some of the regimental commanders had made a detail of soldiers to clean up the corn stalks preparatory to strewing the ground with abatis, and other obstacles to assault.

There was in my battalion a soldier by the named Gee—Jasper Newton Gee—from Randolph or Chariton County, not remarkable for the graces of his person—for he was lank and emaciated and very much bent in the shoulders.[153] Gee had

---

151. Chevaux de frise and abatis were two common means used in defensive positions to hinder enemy movements. The chevaux was commonly used to prevent cavalry charges or cause infantry to pause in their attack while they removed or worked their way around them. They were typically about nine feet in length and "studded with long pointed stakes." The abatis were simply felled trees with branches pointed outward to halt or discourage attacking enemy troops. Faust, 1, 136.

152. Frost's Brigade was commanded by John B. Clark, while D. M. Frost commanded the infantry of Price's command at Little Rock. By most period accounts, Parsons's Brigade was adjacent to Fagan's Brigade, which was next to the Arkansas River. Clark's Brigade then came next to Parson on his left. During the Little Rock Campaign, Clark's Brigade consisted of Clark's Missouri Infantry (9th), Mitchell's Missouri Infantry (8th), and Musser's Battalion (8th Battalion) with Ruffner's Missouri Battery. *O.R.*, vol. 22, pt. 2:781, 969, 976; Banasik, *Serving With Honor*, 104; Hoskin, August 27, 1863.

153. The only "Jasper Gee" discovered belonged to Wade's Missouri Battery. Gee was captured at Vicksburg, paroled and according to the Compiled Service Records, was surrendered in North Carolina, while still serving in Walsh's Battery, vice Wade's. However, it was not uncommon for soldiers on parole, after their exchange and being located in the Trans-Mississippi Department to be incorporated into a unit west of the river. Jasper Gee, according to the National Archives Records was a resident of Washington, Arkansas, and could have easily been at home when his exchange came through. National Archives, Record Group M322 (roll no. 91), Confederate Compiled Service Records, Walsh's

always been regarded as a more valuable adjunct to the subsistence department in eking out short and bad rations than as an efficient soldier. Like Senator [George G.] Vest,[154] he had a standing contract with the fish. In the Arkansas River the drum, bass, perch and cat, croppies and sucker came and hung themselves on his hook whenever they [line missing] He was a general and natural military engineer, for seeing Gen. Fagan's troops wasting their time and energy clearing off the corn-stalks, he ventured to mention to Capt. [John] Hanna,[155] his company commander, that the Arkansas troops were not only losing their labor but destroying an infinitely better abatis than by any amount of labor that could be placed there. He asserted that if the corn-stalks were only bruised, not broken, and strewed promiscuously across the furrows a dog could not catch the lamest rabbit among them, and that no organized body of infantry could move in ranks or even by the flank without disorder. Gee's strictures on Gen. Fagan's field-works being reported to me, I obtained permission to test his plan and ordered a company of infantry to the front of our parapet in command of a skillful officer with directions

To Charge Across

the corn-stalks arranged according to Gee's system. We found by experience they could make no progress, and had they been enemies could have been annihilated by our fire before reaching our works. I beg pardon for so long a story about Gee, but it illustrates the fact that with the Missouri and Confederate soldiers, nay, with the American soldier, the application of common sense and experience to the means of attack and defense had led to those inventions and discoveries in the art of war which has led to new appliances in field works and fortifications, as well as naval architecture the world over.

Missouri Battery.

154. George Graham Vest was born in Frankfurt, Kentucky, in 1830, was educated in Kentucky, and received a law degree from Transylvania University in Lexington, Kentucky, in 1853. He migrated to Pettis County, Missouri, the year of his graduation, and settled in Georgetown, the county seat. Vest married in 1854 and later became a resident of Cooper County, Missouri. At the beginning of the Civil War, Vest served as a colonel and Army Judge Advocate General for the MSG from September 20–November 20, 1861. During the Missouri legislative secession at Neosho in October 1861, Vest drafted the ordinance of secession for Missouri. He later became a congressman to the First and Second Confederate Congress, representing the Fifth Congressional District of Missouri, and in January 1865, Governor Thomas C. Reynolds appointed Vest the CSA Senator from Missouri. After the war George Vest served as a U.S. Senator (1879–1903) for twenty-four years, after which he retired. He died in August 1904 and was the "last surviving member of the Confederate Senate." Marcus J. Wright, *General Officers of the Confederate Army* (New York, 1911), 170, 180, hereafter cited as Wright; Eakin & Hale, 444; Manuel Irwin Kurr, "How George Vest Came to Missouri," *Missouri Historical Review* 59 (July, 1965), 424–427; Peterson, 35; Schlutz, 257, 265–266.

155. John Hanna was born in Pennsylvania in about 1832, and was living in Keyteville, Missouri, at the beginning of the Civil War. On January 4, 1863, he was elected captain of Company F, 8th Missouri Battalion, and upon forming the 9th Missouri his company became Company K. Hanna survived the war, being paroled at Shreveport, Louisiana, on June 7, 1865. *O.R.S.*, pt. 2, vol. 38:586, 591; National Archives, Record Group M322 (roll no. 147), Confederate Compiled Service Records, 9th Missouri Infantry.

It has been stated that a similar suggestion made by a Wisconsin logger as to the construction of a boom in Red River that had enabled Banks to save his fleet in 1864.[156] It was this insolent self-sufficiency of a British officer in repudiating the timely suggestion of a young American named Washington which lost Gen. Bradock his life and army.[157]

It ought to be said here that our fortified lines on the north side of the river at Little Rock did not, as works of military art, tempt the enemy to assault them. They forded the Arkansas below, turned our flank and threatened our rear. Gen. Holmes had neglected Fourche Bayou on the south side, and seemed to be the only man in the whole army who did not know that the river was fordable from Arkansas Post to Fort Smith.[158]

I have mentioned that the Missouri soldiers had many of them taken to useful and ornamental handicrafts in prison. This enabled him to make the most of every situation. Whenever he campaigned he was useful to the hospitable people who made him their welcome guest for he could repair or make whatever he needed from the clock to the plow and invent whatever was required for convenience or necessity. A regiment of Missouri infantry was a little kosmos [cosmos] of itself, self-reliant and self-sufficient for all the wants of civilization. It was possible to find someone who could make or do anything with the slenderest material and most inadequate appliances. This readiness and efficiency in everything made him welcome in every Southern home. He became domiciled with the people of the South and each was adopted into the family with whom he

---

156. During the Red River Expedition in the spring of 1864, the Federal fleet became trapped above the falls near Alexandria, Louisiana, on the Red River. Lieutenant Colonel Joseph Bailey of the 4th Wisconsin Infantry proposed saving the fleet by the use of "wing dams and a central boom." The plan worked and the Federal fleet was saved from destruction. Richard B. Irwin, "The Red River Campaign," *Battles and Leaders of the Civil War*, 4:358–360.

157. Musser is referring to General Edward Bradock (1695–1755), commander-in-chief of the North American forces during the early part of the French and Indian War. Bradock failed to listen to George Washington's suggestion on how to march and deploy his men when advancing into Indian county. At the Battle of Fort Duquesne, Bradock was mortally wounded and his command virtually destroyed by a combined French and Indian force. Norman Stone and J. P. Kenyon, *The Wordsworth Dictionary of British History* (Hertfordshire, England, 1994), 46.

158. General Holmes had departed the army for Hot Springs, to recover his health and was not responsible for the defense of the Little Rock. General Sterling Price was given the task of defending the city and recognized early on that it would be virtually impossible to do so as his defensive position on the north side of the river could be easily turned by crossing the river below the city. General Price in his official report of the campaign records his situation:

My only chance of meeting him [Steele] successfully lay in the possibility that he would attack me in my entrenchments. I would have given him battle confidently had he done this. But I had little hope that he would do this, as it was comparatively easy for him to turn my position by crossing the Arkansas below Little Rock. That river was at that time fordable in a great many places, and I could not guard it effectively without weakening my force within the trenches to a dangerous extent.

On September 10, when the Federals successfully crossed the river, Price also noted that the river was fordable in "twelve different places within 12 miles of Little Rock." *O.R.*, vol. 22, pt. 1:521–522; Gaughan, 175; Schultz, 94.

Spent His Furlough,

when the demand of the service allowed him occasion for absence from his command. From his Arkansas, Louisiana or Mississippi home he regularly received a supply of socks, clothing and domestic comforts, just as the patriotic housewives sent their own gallant sons in the field. It was at these homes by adoption that he was nursed in sickness and wounds, and to the noble hospitality of the good wives and daughters of these states is due the life and health of many now useful and honorable citizens, who would have perished for "Lack of woman's nursing and dearth of woman's tears."

It is due our compatriots to say that many of them remained South. Not a few, grateful to the hospitable hostess of Arkansas and Louisiana, adopted her for his mother-in-law and formed new and indissoluble ties with those they loved. And many were the instances where the soldier only returned home long enough to gather the fragments of his shattered patrimony together or settle his affairs and went back South to claim his bride. What effect the mixed generation of Arkansas, Texas, Louisiana, Mississippi and Missouri will have on the next war we shall perhaps not live to see.

In everything pertaining to his duties and trials to the Missouri soldier "Cheerfulness was the handmaid of his toil."

On the 13 of January 1863, caught in a fearful snow-storm at Crystal Hill, while marching to the relief of Arkansas Post and separated by swamps and swollen streams from his baggage, he spent the night in cheerfulness, if not in comfort, while mules perished of cold at their picket-ropes.[159] It there was anything particularly trying to him, it was when his fastidious palate and vigorous appetite were confronted with execrable rations. Beef from Texas

So Poor

that, like O'Detherann's pig, was only killed for food, to save its life, with musty cornmeal, without coffee, comprised at times the tedious variety of his daily menus. On one occasion the beef issued to my battalion was execrable, but the best that could be gotten. The soldiers formed a guard of honor around their rations when issued, and marched with reversed arms outside the camp and buried it with the honors of war. This was not mutinous or insubordinate, for they fasted without complaint till the next day.

Toward the time for the winter quarters each year, it was not an unusual thing for a jaded and attenuated train of oxen with a wagon containing the wife and children of a soldier to arrive in camp. Then it was that all contributed to the necessities of the destitute and helpless. Their ready skill and labor constructed the

---

159. See Chapter One of this book for detailed accounts of the Confederate Army's move from Ft. Smith to Little Rock in late December 1862 and early January 1863.

cabin and shanty, and of the economies of their daily rations the hungry mouths were fed.

But now was come the moment of our greatest trial, the time when those soldiers who, embodying in themselves the perfection of manly grace, the infantry worthy and capable of winning empires or sustaining the eagles of freedom, must lay down their arms. The star of the Confederacy had set at Appomattox and Gen. Lee had tendered his sword under the historical apple-tree to the great and generous soldier, who but so lately the whole world mourns. The Trans-Mississippi was still in arms when Joe Johnston's army surrendered in the Carolinas.[160] At Shreveport the Missourians, who had

Followed The Fortunes

of the flag long after there was a vestige of hope for regaining their own state, were the last to yield up their arms.[161] In their exile they had learned discipline and obedience. They maintained it to the end. The impatient troops of Louisiana and Arkansas and other states, after the war was particularly ended by the exhaustion of the South, eager to return to their desolate home and impoverished families, broke up in squads and hastened to their loved ones. The discipline of Missouri was superior to defeat. They remained by their colors, and when the last final hour came to surrender, they remained on duty until relived by the Federal troops. Their fatigue parties were relieved by the details from the enemy and the Confederate sentinel on guard received his relief at a port arms, gave him his instructions and then stacked his gun forever.

The exiles mostly returned home to Missouri on transportation and supplies furnished by the United States authorities, but others sought in exile, in Mexico principally, the occasion to re-establish their broken fortunes.

Into this exile went their chief. Gen. Price settled at Cordoba, Mexico. He was the idol of the Missouri troops in the Confederacy. His splendid presence and

---

160. General Robert E. Lee surrendered the Army of Northern Virginia on April 9, 1865, to U. S. Grant. General Joe Johnston surrendered his army on April 26, 1865, at Durham Station, just outside of Raleigh, North Carolina. The next major Confederate surrender came on May 4, 1865, when Richard Taylor surrendered the Department of East Louisiana, Mississippi, and Alabama to General E. R. S. Canby at Citronelle, Alabama. The Trans-Mississippi followed suit on June 2, 1865, when Kirby Smith surrendered his Department at Galveston, Texas, to General Canby. Boatner, 21–22, 770, 827–828; Faust, 114.

161. Parsons's Missouri Division was not the last major Confederate unit to give up its arms. That honor belonged to General Stand Watie, who surrendered the Indian troops in the Indian Territory on June 23, 1865. Parsons's command was the last major unit under arms in the Trans-Mississippi Army, commanded by E. Kirby Smith. When Smith surrendered the Department, Parson's Division was the last division to depart Shreveport, Louisiana, where they were bivouacked, departing on June 5, with the last of the division leaving on June 10. The lead elements of the command made Alexandria, Louisiana, on June 7, where the various company commanders filled out the parole rolls for their companies. On June 8 Parson's Division left Alexandria and headed back to Missouri, where they arrived at St. Louis on June 19, with the last boat arriving on June 21. Banasik, *Serving With Honor*, 227–230; Hoskin, June 10, 21, 1865; Quesenberry, June 5, 10, 21, 1865.

soldierly bearing attracted all hearts to him. All his instincts were manly and soldierly, and he possessed the magnetic power by which a great and brave soul can hold his soldiers under the heaviest and most deadly fire. This faculty is ascribed to but a few great men like Desaix. It is eminently the faculty possessed by those alone endowed with the highest courage, a power of infusing

His Own Great Soul

into an army and inspiring each man with "The big thoughts that make ambition virtue."

Insensible to peril, his faculties were only excited by the storm of battle and his judgement became calmer and cooler as the danger thickened and increased. Nor was he alone exalted and at home in victory. His faculties never failed him in reverse or defeat. On the retreat from Iuchea [Iuka], after disaster had befallen the Confederate arms, he deployed Col. Gate's brigade to hold the enemy at bay while he constructed over the Hatchie River a bridge on a mill dam and saved his last wagon. It was in this battle that Price swelled to his full stature as a soldier. His genius was executive and aggressive. In the administration of his command his great good heart shrunk from cruel punishments sometimes to the disparagement of discipline. But this gentleness endeared him the more to the brave people to whom he stood in the relation of chieftain. "For e'en his faults leaned onto virtue's side."

The followers of [Joseph O.] Shelby[162] went with their arms into Mexico. They witnessed their brave leader, as he crossed the Rio Grande, bury the unfurled battle-flag they had followed so many years in the water that divide the two republics. Many took service in Mexico as soldiers; others endeavored to form colonies and create new homes. But all, or nearly all, sooner or later, returned to the land of their birth, under the protection of

A Generous Government

which realized that men so gallant in battle could ill be spared from the country which produced them.

The songs of people are said to be more important than their laws. Our state had no folk-lore before the war, except that an Argonaut from Pike in 1849 had in this piacera(?) of California composed and sung "Joe Bowers." The genius of Missouri inspired the Confederate muse and hardly had the Camp Jackson prisoners been paroled and released till Joe Leddy composed the "Tenth of May"[163]

162. Brigadier General Joseph Shelby commanded a Missouri cavalry brigade in John S. Marmaduke's Fourth Division (Cavalry) of Thomas C.Hindman's First Corps Trans-Mississippi Army. A wealthy planter from Lafayette County, Missouri, Shelby joined the Missouri State Guard at the beginning of the Civil War and later the regular Confederate Army. He commanded companies to divisions before war's end and was the premier cavalryman in the Trans-Mississippi area. For a complete biography and photograph see Banasik, *Missouri Brothers in Gray*, 150–151.
163. Joseph Leddy was a resident of Saline County, Missouri, at the beginning of the Civil War, when

[line missing] of Confederate song, a wit particularly and essentially American and Western, a patches inspired by the tender and gental [gentle] affections so purely Southern, in the rudest duty which enlivened the camp-fire and mess-table, and the more dignified poetry of Harding's "Son Allen Held His Mule,"[164] there was a germ of a new school of Southern poesy. The spirit of poesy and song possessed the whole South. It inspired "All Quiet Along the Potomac To-night."[165] It produced the minstrelsy of Jake Connor that consoled the rough rider of Shelby's as he adjusted his johnny-cake to the clapboard or twined the snaky folds of his tough dough around the ramrod. Like the songs of the Swiss, the tenderest ballads were of home and its loved ones. The spirit of chivalric poesy awoke the Southern harp of the willows and produced [Alonzo] Slayback's "Burial of Shelby's Flag."[166] It has embalmed the banners of the lost cause in the sweetest numbers of the poet-priest, Father [Abram Joseph] Ryan,[167] and our colors are furled forever in the poesy that will never die.

R. H. Musser

* * * * * * *

he joined Captain Joseph Kelly's MSG unit. A poet, Leddy composed several pieces on the Civil War, with his most famous being "The Invasion of Camp Jackson by the Hessians," which he wrote in August 1861. The original poem, which was put into song, comprised thirteen verses, with a chorus. See Appendix E for the poem. Joe Leddy, "The Invasion of Camp Jackson by the Hessians," in Knapp Family Papers, Missouri Historical Society; Scott K. Williams, "The Capture of Camp Jackson," Internet site www.usgennet.org/usa/mo/county/stlouis/cj/campjack.htm.

164. See Appendix E for a portion of the song.

165. See Appendix E for the song.

166. Alonzo Slayback was born on July 4, 1838, at Plum Grove, in Marion County, Missouri, attended the Masonic College in Lexington, where he graduated in 1856. In the pre-war he was a teacher and was admitted to the bar just prior to the Civil War. Slayback was elected colonel of the 5th Infantry Regiment, 5th Division MSG, on September 23, 1861, and was the last commander of the 7th Division, MSG. As a Guard member he participated in the Battles of Drywood, Lexington, and Pea Ridge. He later entered the Confederate service, being appointed to John Marmaduke's staff as the Divisional Ordnance Officer. In 1864 he was appointed a lieutenant colonel and at the time of Price's raid he led a battalion of Missouri Cavalry, recruited from southeastern Missouri. After the war Slayback fled to Mexico and fought in Maximilian's army, but returned to St. Louis in August 1866, where he again practiced law and was involved in politics as part of the Democratic Party. On October 13, 1882, Slayback was killed when he confronted the editor of the St. Louis *Post-Dispatch*, after an article accused Slayback of being a coward. He was buried in St. Louis, but was later moved to Lexington, where he was reburied in Machpeleh Cemetery. See Appendix E for a copy of "The Burial of Shelby's Flag." *O.R.*, vol. 22, 1:148; Allardice, *Confederate Colonels*, 344; Eakin, *Confederate Records*, 7:39; Edwards, *Shelby and His Men*, 391; Hale, 296; Peterson, 165.

167. Farther Abram Joseph Ryan was a Confederate Chaplain and priest. He was born in Ireland in 1839 and moved to the United States during the Irish "Potato Famine." After his ordination he was assigned to a parish in Nashville, Tennessee, and was in Georgia at the beginning of the Civil War. After the war Ryan continued as a priest and wrote the "The Conquered Banner," which Alfred Nofi dubbed "among the best Southern poems on the war." Ryan died in 1886 at about age 57. See Appendix E for a copy of his poem. Albert A. Nofi, *A Civil War Treasury Being a Miscellany of Arms and Artillery, Facts and Figures, Legends and Lore, Muses and Mistrals, Personalities and People* (Conshohocken, PA, 1992; reprint ed., Edison, NJ, 2006), 411, hereafter cited as Nofi.

Item: Comments of an ex-Confederate on Colonel R. H. Musser's article on the "Confederate Soldier," by T. G. C. Davis[168]
Published: October 10, 1885.

An Acknowledgement to Col. Musser.

St. Louis, Mo., Oct. 5.
Col. R. H. Musser:

My Friend

I have just finished a careful reading of "The Confederate Soldier," published in the Missouri *Republican* of the 19th ult. I was much interested and pleased with it. The allusion to Montesquieu's "Grandeur of the Romans" in the first sentence is very fine, and cannot fail to arrest the attention of the well-informed reader. What you say of Gen. Price is due to his memory and you have neither heightened nor depressed—said neither too much nor too little in his praise. Your portraiture of the South is lifelike. You have not (as some) been timid in writing. A trembling hand cannot paint to the life. Nor can a timid soul rise to the heights of a true glory: Your Jasper Morton Gee is an original genius. His memory you have preserved, and for it accept my thanks. Tacitus[169] says: "*nam multos veterum relut in glorious it ignobiles, oblivio obruet.*" But Gee, of whom I never heard before I read your "Confederate Soldier," is rescued from oblivion by your pen.

You have truly characterized the poetry of the South—I mean the war poetry—and done yourself justice by mentioning Slayback's "Burial of Shelby's Flag." Many things die for want of a friend, and considering the brevity of human life, and the number of men engaged in getting money, it is truly wonderful that so many reminiscences are preserved. I met you a few days ago at a bar meeting in this city. Prompted by friendship you came from your present home in the

---

168. This was probably Thomas George Cosby Davis. He was born on February 4, 1814, in Hanover County, Virginia.
Davis was living in St. Louis at the beginning of the war and "made public speeches in favor of the South." A lawyer by profession, Davis was the "first lawyer in Missouri to argue against the 'Test Oath,' holding it invalid." Eakin, *Confederate Records*, 162.
169. Publius Cornelius Tacitus was a Roman historian who lived from about 55–117 A.D. Guralnik, 1447.

country, no short distance, to say a word in honor of a brave, honest man, the late Hon. Waldo P. Johnson.[170]

God bless you, sir. Your friend,

T. G. C. Davis

* * * * * * *

---

170. Waldo P. Johnson was born on September 16, 1817, in Bridgeport, Virginia (modern-day West Virginia). He studied law, being admitted to the Virginia bar in 1842. The following year he moved to Missouri, settling in Osceola, St. Clair County, where he lived in a simple clapboard house. He joined the Mexican War effort as a private in 1846. After the war, Johnson returned to his law practice, was elected to the Missouri Legislature, and later was elected a circuit judge in 1852, but resigned in 1854. Considered a strong Union man, Johnson was appointed to the Peace Conference in February 1861. As a Democrat, Johnson was elected a U.S. Senator by the Missouri Legislature on March 12, 1861, defeating James S. Green, and took his seat on March 17, 1861. After the war began, Johnson returned to Missouri, resigned from the U.S. Senate in August 1861 to join the MSG (The U.S. Senate would expel Johnson on January 10, 1862 for joining the Confederate Army). He fought at Pea Ridge, was wounded twice, and was also at Corinth, Mississippi. Johnson then returned to the Trans-Mississippi region and operated the recruiting service for Missouri troops while under Holmes's and Hindman's commands. With the death of Missouri senator Robert L. Y. Payton, Governor Reynolds appointed Johnson a Confederate Senator in December 1863, citing that, "It was a fixed rule in Missouri politics to distribute the Senators territorially, and that no one congressional district should have both the governor and a senator." Further, since the "late senator, Col. Peyton, was from the same section as" Johnson, who was previously a U.S. Senator, Reynolds appointed Johnson to the Confederate Senate. A confidential advisor to Jefferson Davis, Johnson returned to the Trans-Mississippi in March 1865, and at war's end fled to Canada. He returned to Osceola in 1866, again practiced law and died on August 14, 1885. *O.R.*, vol. 8:324, 326; *O.R.*, vol. 13:45, 880–881, 919; Hale, 166; Kathleen White Miles, *Bitter Ground: The Civil War in Missouri's Golden Valley Benton, Henry, and St. Clair Counties* (Warsaw, MO, 1971), 141, 150, 271; McElroy, 47; Sifakis, *Who Was Who In the Confederacy*, 150; Schultz, 105–106, 271; Snead, *Fight For Missouri*, 88–89.

Chapter 4

Fall 1863

Action at Pine Bluff
(October 25, 1863)

Item: The Battle of Pine Bluff, Arkansas (October 25, 1863), by Henry C. Luttrell, Company G, 10th Missouri Cavalry (CSA).
Published: November 13, 1886.

Young's Battalion at Pine Bluff.

Editor, *Republican*

After the occupation of Little Rock by Gen. Steele's army the Confederate cavalry maneuvered up and down the country trying to catch a detached portion of the enemy at a disadvantage, but few such opportunities presented themselves for our consideration until the middle of October. Then we learned that the Federals had occupied Pine Bluff.[1] After some desultory skirmishing in the near vicinity of Pine Bluff our commanders determined to dislodge the enemy.[2] So on the 23d the

---

1. Following the occupation of Little Rock on September 10, 1863, General Steele sent off various small groups of cavalry to protect his line of communications running from Little Rock to DeVall's Bluff. A few days later "a deputation of the most respectable citizens of Pine Bluff" arrived at Steele's headquarters, and requested a garrison to protect the city against rebel "depredations." On September 14, Steele dispatched a portion of the 5th Kansas Cavalry, under Lieutenant Colonel W. A. Jenkins to establish a garrison for Pine Bluff. Jenkins's men arrived at Pine Bluff in the late evening hours, the same day. On September 17, the remainder of the 5th Kansas arrived, followed by the 1st Indiana Cavalry, which arrived in mid-morning on September 26. *O.R.,* vol. 22, pt. 2:543-544; *O.R.S.,* pt. 2, vol. 15:181; *O.R.S.,* pt. 2, vol. 21:247, 257, 268; Edwin C. Bearss, "Marmaduke Attacks Pine Bluff," *Arkansas Historical Quarterly* 23 (Winter, 1964), 292, hereafter cited as Bearss, "Pine Bluff"; W. S. Burke, *Official Military History of Kansas Regiments During the War For the Suppression of the Great Rebellion* (Leavenworth, KS, 1870), 115, hereafter cited as Burke; DeBlack, 96; James W. Leslie, ed., "Arabella Lanktree Wilson's Civil War Latter," *Arkansas Historical Quarterly* 47 (Autumn, 1988), 261–262, hereafter cited as Leslie.
2. Following the successful Confederate retreat from Little Rock, General T. H. Holmes returned to command the District on September 25. He assigned General Marmaduke the responsibility "to cover the army," cautioning him that any offensive operation, should only be undertaken so as not to endanger the army. Marmaduke established pickets on all the road leading south, with one force under Colonel Archibold Dobbins located at Tulip, Arkansas. In an attempt to keep the Confederates off balance, Colonel Clayton Powell led a 300-man expedition, with 4 pieces of artillery, against Dobbins's camp at Tulip. The expedition, made up of detachments from the 1st Indiana Cavalry and the 5th Kansas Cavalry, departed Pine Bluff on October 10 and attacked Dobbins at 4:00 a.m. on October 11 (Dyer has the date as October 12 for the 1st Indiana Cavalry and October 10 for the 5th Kansas). An embarrassing rout followed in which Dobbins lost "all his camp and garrison equipment and trans-

battalion moves up to Tulip, and our pickets are thrown farther out to the north.[3] On the 24th the whole brigade under Col. [Colton] Greene moves up from Princeton.[4] After a twenty-five mile march a two-hours' halt is made. We feed our horses and then resume the march, which lasts all night. Daylight finds us dismounting near the southern suburbs of the city.[5] And as we form on foot and counting off by fours, I notice that Pope Fulkerson is No. 4 of the group to which I belong.[6] John [Joseph] Merser is No. 1, myself No. 2 and John Fisher No. 3. Pope's voice is firm and clear, and he sings out his number after the manner of a challenge. For be it known that Pope Fulkerson is a new recruit and this is his first battle.[7]

portation" along with "a number of prisoners and horses." Dobbins's force consisted of 200 men, with another 70 who were on picket duty at the time. Immediately following the incident at Tulip, Dobbins resigned from the service, pending Kirby Smith's approval. Further, on October 27th, Dobbins was Court Martialed for disobedience of orders during the engagement at Bayou Fourche on September 10, 1863. *O.R.,* vol. 22, pt. 1:674, 1042–1043; *O.R.S.,* pt. 2, vol. 15:181; *O.R.S.,* pt. 2, vol. 21:247; Burke, 115; Dyer, 680, 1104, 1182; Marmaduke, *Order and Letter Book,* 279, 281.

3. At the time of the Battle of Pine Bluff, Luttrell's command was the 11th Battalion, Missouri Cavalry. The battalion was incorporated with Lawther's Temporary Dismounted Cavalry Regiment and recently paroled POWs from the First Missouri Brigade, who had surrendered at Vicksburg, to form the 10th Missouri Cavalry. *O.R.S.,* pt. 2, vol. 38: 253–254; Crute, 203; Marmaduke, *Order and Letter Book,* 239–240; McGhee, Missouri Confederates, 67-69.

4. Greene's Brigade was actually Marmaduke's Brigade and for the Pine Bluff assault the brigade was divided into two parts— Colonel Robert Lawther led Greene's 3rd Missouri Cavalry, Kitchen's Missouri Cavalry Regiment, with Young's 11th Missouri Battalion and D. B. Griswold's Missouri 4-gun Missouri Battery; while Colonel W. J. Preston, led the other half of the brigade containing the 4th and 8th Missouri Cavalries, with S. T. Ruffner's 3-gun Missouri Battery—in all, Greene carried about 800 men into the battle. See Appendix C for a detailed look at the Confederate force at Pine Bluff. *O.R.,* vol. 22, pt. 1:730–732.

5. Marmaduke concentrated his command at Princeton on October 23, and issued orders to march for the following day. A little after 9:00 a.m. on the 24th, Robert C. Newton's command led out Marmaduke's force for the planned assault on Pine Bluff. Marmaduke's force made the Saline River about 6:00 p.m., and went into camp to make final preparations. Gathering his commanders together, Marmaduke laid out his plan of attack. The city would be attacked in three columns: entering the city from the southeast, via the Bayou Bartholomew Road would be R. C. Newton's force, consisting of Newton's Brigade, commanded by Major John P. Bull; Carter's Texas Brigade, under Major B. D. Chenoweth; and Major Robert C. Wood's Missouri Battalion. The center column, under Colton Greene would contain Marmaduke's Brigade and would approach the city by the Sulphur Springs Road; and James C. Monroe would lead the third column, approaching Pine Bluff from the Little Rock Road. Monroe commanded W. C. Cabell's Brigade, the "residue" of Shelby's Iron Brigade, under Colonel G. W. Thompson. (The remainder of the brigade, under Shelby was on a raid into Missouri at the time of the Battle of Pine Bluff.) *O.R.,* vol. 22, pt. 1:730–732; Bearss, "Pine Bluff," 294–295; Christ, 229, 231–232; Harrell, *Arkansas, Confederate Military History,* 223–225; Marmaduke, *Order and Letter Book,* 318; Wooster, 185, 188, 305.

6. James P. or "Pope" Fulkerson, enlisted in the Company G, 11th Missouri Battalion (CSA) on September 17, 1863, at Rockport, Arkansas. The Battle of Pine Bluff occurred a month after his enlistment. National Archives, Record Group M322 (roll no. 56), Confederate Compiled Service Records, 10th Missouri Cavalry Regiment.

7. Joseph Wayne [or S.] Mercer was born on February 25, 1845, in Platte County, Missouri. Educated in Lee's Summit, Mercer attended college at Chapel Hill at the age of 13. At the beginning of the Civil War he enlisted in Company H, 2nd Infantry Regiment, 8th Division, MSG on October 25, 1861. Prior to enlisting, Mercer took an active part in the Battle of Lexington in September 1861, was wounded

Much Fun

has been made at Pope's expense. For Pope was a bright, intelligent youth of about 18, and was wont to tell how, when he got the chance, he would smite the enemy hip and thigh. And John Fisher had always told him that he (John) would play a game of marbles upon the tail of his blouse while the smiting was going on. And Pope had always good naturedly replied that "You'll find me dangling to your old blouse, John, and if you run, I'll run, and if you fight I'll make a shadow for you to fight in." So today when he calls his number, he turns to Fisher and says in a jolly, bantering tone: "Oh, bless your life, I'm here. Where is your marbles John?"

We take position upon the left of the big dusty road.[8] Skirmishers are sent to the front and the line advances at a brisk walk. Crackling rifle shots ring out as the sharpshooters come into contact. The suburbs of the town are reached, and our skirmish line is brought to a stand by the enemy, who has a decided advantage, for

---

in the leg and incapacitated for several weeks. He enlisted in the Confederate Army on December 11, 1862, at Van Buren, Arkansas. In the course of the war, Mercer was at Elkhorn Tavern, Prairie Grove, Poison Springs and Pine Bluff, all in Arkansas. At the time of his wound, Mercer was a sergeant and was wounded in his right arm, which was later amputated. Mercer recovered from his wound and continued to serve in the army as a Commissary Captain. He survived the war and was paroled out of the service at McKinney, Texas, in 1865. Returning to Missouri, Mercer eventually settled in Independence, Missouri, married in 1870, and had six children with his wife Laura, of which four daughters survived. Following the war Mercer became a teacher, County Treasurer (1872), and in 1874 was elected State Treasurer. After one term in office, he became a banker, then a grocer, and was elected mayor of Independence, Missouri, in 1891. At the time of his death, in Independence on March 13, 1906, he was a Circuit Judge. Eakin, *Confederate Records*, 5:175; Eakin & Hale, 305–207; National Archives, Record Group M322 (roll no. 57), Confederate Compiled Service Records, 10th Missouri Cavalry; Peterson, 221, 225.

John W. Fisher, joined what became Company G, 10th Missouri Cavalry Regiment (CSA) on August 15, 1862, and was at the Battle of Lone Jack the following day. He survived the war and was paroled on June 8, 1865 at Shreveport, Louisiana. Eakin, *Lone Jack*, 153, 157; National Archives, Record Group M322 (roll no. 56), Confederate Compiled Service Records, 10th Missouri Cavalry.

8. Marmaduke's command arrived at Pine Bluff before 8:00 a.m. as the three columns took their assigned positions. By 8:00 all three columns were in place and awaiting a signal gun that was supposed to be fired from Greene's center column (Luttrell's brigade). Before assaulting the town, Colonel Robert Lawther, leading the center column, directed Major G. W. C. Bennett of the 11th Missouri Battalion to "reconnoiter the enemy's position" with Company F, 3rd Missouri Cavalry Regiment, under Captain Howard S. Randall and Company H of his own battalion under Captain William T. Barry. Shortly after 8:00, Bennett made contact with a 25-man Union forage patrol, with two wagons, under Lieutenant Milton F. Clark of the 5th Kansas that was moving down the Princeton or Sulphur Springs Road, when they came upon the advancing rebels. Shots were exchanged. Minutes later, Marmaduke advanced a flag of truce demanding the surrender of the Pine Bluff Garrison, to which Lieutenant Clark responded "Colonel Clayton never surrenders, but is always anxious for you to come and take him, and you must go back to your command immediately, or I will order my men to fire on you." The rebel parley party returned to their lines and both sides deployed for action. Lawther moved his detachment to the left side of the main road, while Preston's men were on his right. Meanwhile, back in Pine Bluff word had quickly reached Colonel Powell who deployed his men to meet the rebel threat. By 9:00, Marmaduke had made his final dispositions, and the signal gun was fired and the attack begun. *O.R.*, vol. 22, pt. 1:723, 732; *O.R.S.*, pt. 2, vol. 38:170, 257; Banasik, *Reluctant Cannoneer*, 309; Burke, 115–116; Christ, 232; DeBlack, 99–100; Marmaduke, *Order and Letter Book*, 318.

Battle of Pine Bluff, Arkansas
(October 25, 1863)

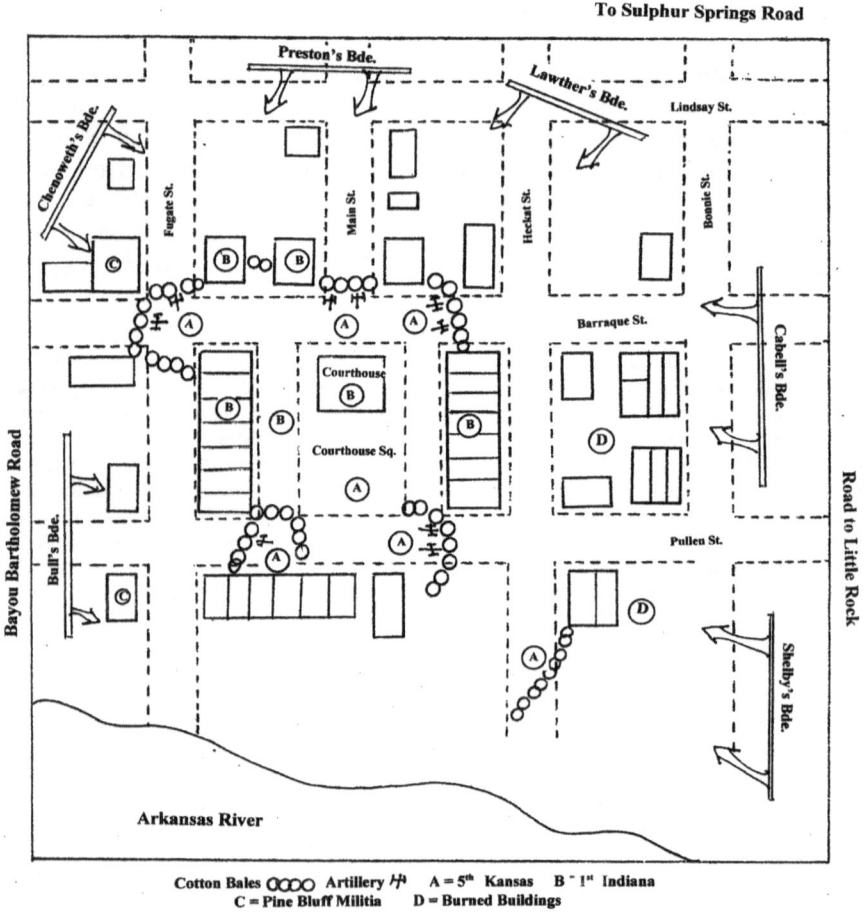

Cotton Bales ◯◯◯◯ Artillery A = 5ᵗʰ Kansas B = 1ˢᵗ Indiana
C = Pine Bluff Militia D = Burned Buildings

they occupy the buildings and take shelter under the fencings. As our battle line nears the edge of the a newly cleared piece of ground we are ordered to lie down.[9] Bullets are flying about at a lively rate. Already two or three men are wounded. The ground is level and we have been pushed up so near our skirmishers that we can see the smoke of the Federal rifles. Now a battery—I think it is Maj. Pratt's— comes into action in fine style.[10] The first few rounds are fired over us as we lie upon the ground.[11] Then we move forward again. This time an opening is left for each section of artillery and again the crash of canon drowns out the spattering of musketry.[12] Again we move forward, the artillerymen

---

9. Upon firing the signal gun, Marmaduke's command began a simultaneous advance from all quarters. Within an hour they had driven back the outlying Federal skirmishers and approached the main Federal defenses. Meanwhile, Colonel Clayton Powell had not been idle. When he heard that rebels were upon his city, he quickly directed Captain James B. Talbot, the "Superintendent of the Contrabands," to supply as many men as he could to barricade the courthouse square with cotton bales from Busby's warehouse, located on the west side of the square. Within a half hour, Talbot's 300 men completed the job, making the breastworks "2 bales deep," and "2 bales high," barricading the five routes into the courthouse square. The center position, Greene's command, far out-paced the other two columns causing Marmaduke to call a temporary halt to the advance to allow all elements to close up on the city. *O.R.,* vol. 22, pt. 1:723–724; Leslie, 266; Marmaduke, *Order and Letter Book,* 318.

10. Pratt's Texas Battery was organized by Joseph H. Pratt, an east Texas railroad man, with men from Harrison, Marion, and Cass Counties, Texas, in the sprig of 1861. However, the battery was not mustered into the Confederate Service until March 1, 1862, at Jefferson, Texas. It was then ordered to Little Rock in the spring of 1862, where it was assigned to duty with Parsons's Texas Cavalry Brigade. It participated in Marmaduke's Second Missouri Raid in 1863, was at Little Rock during the 1863 Campaign and participated in the assault on Pine Bluff as part of Carter's Texas Brigade. The battery continued in service of cavalry commands throughout its existence. It's guns were captured during Price's 1864 Missouri Raid, but the battery was reconstituted and completed its war service in the Trans-Mississippi Reserve Artillery Battalion. Joseph Pratt was promoted to major in the summer of 1865, and the battery was then commanded by H. C. Hynson. During its time in the service Pratt's Battery was considered one of the best batteries serving west of the Mississippi River, prompting an Inspector General of the army to record: the battery "is in very fine order, and a model command. Their discipline is very good. The men are well drilled." In June 1862 the battery was armed with four 6-lb iron guns, which were replaced with four new guns from Woodruff's Arkansas Battery (two 6-lb James Rifles) and Daniel's Texas Battery (two, 10-lb Parrots). *O.R.,* vol. 22, pt. 2:1051; *O.R.S.,* pt. 2, vol. 68:483; Banasik, *Embattled Arkansas,*520 (n. 3); Special Orders No. 29 (July 17, 1862), Special Order Book No. 1; Wooster, 304–305.

11. The artillery that came up to support Luttrell's battalion was S. T. Ruffner's 3-gun battery. At this time, the 11th Missouri Cavalry was about 300 yards from the main Federal defense, awaiting the orders to continue the advance. *O.R.,* vol. 22, pt. 1:731–732.

12. Once all three columns had linked up, Marmaduke ordered a second charge to drive the Federals back into the fortified courthouse square; some of the troops "charging up within twenty yards of the works, but the terribly effective fire of the enemy, both musketry and artillery compelled a halt and a retreat to cover." On the left of the Confederate line, Monroe's command dismounted, with Shelby's men on the left and Cabell's Brigade to the right. Hughey's Artillery took up a position near the river and to the left of Cabell's Brigade, shooting through some buildings in order to fire on the Federal position. For the remainder of the day Monroe's command did little more than fire artillery at the enemy, and "snipe" at the enemy as Monroe was not "able to effect anything with small arms." On the rebel right R. C. Newton advanced with Wood's Battalion on the left, the Texas Brigade on the right and Bull's command as a reserve. Easily pushing back the Union line, Newton came to a halt a block from the courthouse square and ordered Bull's troopers to the right of his line, while Pratt's Battery took its

Moving the Guns by Hand.

As we are moving across some open blocks, McDonald of Co. E is killed. He sinks quietly in his tracks as we move along.[13] Coming to a frame building, which is supported by brick pillars some four feet high, we crawl under it. When halfway through, Pope Fulkerson sings out cheerily: "I say, Fisher, somebody's been killed up above. Look at the blood."

"You blamed fool, that's molasses," exclaims Fisher, who is vigorously rubbing his hands in the dust, for they are covered with the precious sweets. Raising my eyes, I see the floor has been ripped three or four feet by cannon shot, and the red molasses is dripping in streams from the rent; also that half a dozen boys are holding their canteens to the streams, endeavoring to fill them. Emerging from under the house we assume an upright position and advance diagonally across the block to the northeast and take position, with our right resting across a cemetery. Here we are in easy range of the courthouse and would be in plain view, but for a mass of tall pines midway between. Our skirmishers are in the run of a small branch at the foot of the slope. Again our battery comes into action and again our line is advanced. The battery takes position at the church.[14] The battalion moves to the run of the branch and lies down in the mud where some pools of water have just dried up.[15]

---

position on the left next to Wood's Battalion. And like Monroe's column, they would remain in place for the rest of the battle. In the center, where Luttrell was, the second charge brought them to within 150 yards of the Federals, and like the other two, they halted, took cover and used "sharpshooters" to engage the enemy, allowing Ruffner's and Griswold's Artillery Companies to do the majority of the work against the Unionists. *O.R.,* vol. 22, pt. 1:733–735; Banasik, *Reluctant Cannoneer,* 311; Bearss, "Pine Bluff," 303–306; Alice L. Fry, *Following the Fifth Kansas Cavalry: The Letters* (Independence, MO, 1998), 56, hereafter cited as Fry; Marmaduke, *Order and Letter Book,* 318.

13. In Marmaduke's Official Report of the battle the only man listed as killed, in the 11th Battalion, was a sergeant Hall or Halley. There was no McDonald listed anywhere in Marmaduke's report as either killed, wounded, or missing. Additionally, the Compiled Service Records for the 10th Missouri listed no McDonalds or variations thereof. Marmaduke, *Order and Letter Book,* 319–321; National Archives, Record Group M322 (roll no. 57), Confederate Compiled Service Records, 10th Missouri Cavalry.

14. Ruffner's Battery came to rest at the Methodist Church, which became a focal point for the Confederate concentration of their artillery. As the day wore on Ruffner's Battery would be joined by Pratt's and both batteries would concentrate their fire on the courthouse, eventually driving the Federal sharpshooters out of the building. Griswold's Artillery was also present but to the left of Ruffner's command. *O.R.,* vol. 22, pt. 1:731; Bearss, "Pine Bluff," 305; Christ, 237–238.

15. The run that Luttrell described was to the immediate front of the graveyard and Methodist Church, which would put the 11th Missouri Battalion still in support of Griswold's Battery, which was to the left of Ruffner's artillery. Preston's command, of Greene's column, supported Ruffner's and Pratt's Batteries. The 4th Missouri Cavalry, of Preston's command, was located between the 8th Missouri Cavalry and Wood's Battalion of Newton's wing of Marmaduke's force. *O.R.,* vol. 22, pt. 1: 731; Bearss, "Pine Bluff," map between 312–313; Leslie, map between 262–263.

The Roar of the Battle Swells.

The artillery upon either side is in full play. The blocks from our guns tumble in upon us. Solid shot and shell are shrieking from both directions in the air above us. Grape and canister shot rip up the dust in every direction. The tops of the tall pines are toppling and crashing to earth, cut in twain by the cannon shot. The sides of the courthouse are perforated by solid shot. The cotton bales about the enemy's guns have repeatedly been set on fire.[16]

Under this storm of iron ball we lie expecting to charge the Federal position every moment. In the midst of this panorama a dog rushes from some building to our left near the enemy's battery. He runs headlong in our direction. When nearly half way he come in range of our guns as they discharge a round or grape and canister. As the dust rises about him, he turns about and runs in the other direction. Then a blast form the enemy's guns turns him back. Two other runs he makes of the same kind, and finally disappears in the branch to our right (east). Now the Federal sharpshooters got our range from some tall buildings to our left; minie balls are knocking up mud all about us.[17] "Whoop! this is too hot for me," exclaims John Mercer as a bullet splatters mud in his face, and he hustles out of the branch and takes shelter behind a small tree on the bank. We beg him to come back into line, for he is in plain view of the enemy. The bullets

Are Barking the Tree

rapidly, while John is lying flat upon the ground, resting his face on his hand, peeping out at his enemies. Suddenly, he cries out: "Oh! I'm shot, I'm killed!" and

---

16. Even as the fight became general, "fire had caught to the cotton bales" from the Union artillery, prompting Colonel Clayton to call upon Talbot's contrabands for assistance. Talbot formed a bucket brigade with about two hundred men and ferried water to the front, filling localized barrels and extinguishing the flames. On the Confederate side, Talbot's actions by the river had not gone unnoticed. Believing that the Unionists might be trying to escape, Colonel Newton ordered Major Bull's brigade to the riverbank at about 10:30 a.m. to extend his line and prevent the Federal escape. When Bull reached the river, he discovered the water brigade and quickly engaged them, killing one and wounding three others. Talbot's men initially panicked, but were quickly rallied, and put up a cotton barricade on the river bank to cover their operation. Additionally, fifteen of Talbot's men were armed and proceeded to protect the water bearers, even as the battle progressed. The contribution of Talbot's men as both barricade builders and water bearers was not overlooked by one period commentator who recorded—"Surely cotton" with Clayton's "ebony sceptre [sic] is king." A member of the 5th Kansas further summed up the importance of the contrabands in keeping the armed soldiers at their posts, instead of fighting fires. A. D. Brown wrote: "The contrabands relieved us from embarrassment. Barrels had been collected, and the blacks speedily filled them from the river...and thus our small force were all employed at their guns." *O.R.,* vol. 22, pt. 1:723–725, 735; Bearss, "Pine Bluff," 306–307; Christ, 236, 238–239; Fry, 56; Ralph Kaw, "The Battle of Pine Bluff, *Chicago Tribune,* November 17, 1863, hereafter cited as Kaw.

17. The principle antagonists in the quarter facing off against the 11th Missouri Battalion were Company K, 5th Kansas Cavalry, supported, and the three steel rifle cannons of the 1st Indiana Cavalry. *O.R.,* vol. 22, pt. 1:727.

he rolls over on his back and begins to kick his heels in the air. Adolf Wheatly,[18] an infirmary corps man, runs to his assistance. A shower of grape and canister rattles about them. A heavy shot ploughs up the ground under Mercer's back. "Hell and blue blazes!" he exclaims as he leaps to his feet and runs across the graves of the sleeping dead, while the bullets rattle and glance from the tombstones all about. I see his right arm is shattered near the shoulder, and is dangling about him as he runs. And Adolf Wheatly laughing at Mercer's flight and stampede goes back to shelter with the remark that "he got scared too late in the day." Now the roar of battle swells upon our left (west). Again it swells upon our right. A dark cloud of smoke arises from a cluster of buildings on our left near the Federal battery which is hurling shot and shell at us—the same buildings from which the enemy's sharp-shooters have so annoyed us. Soon the red flames are mounting the roofs.[19] Some of our troops are now falling back from the burning district. Is the heat too great for them, or does their retrograde movement mean retreat?

Now a cow comes lowing from the burning quarter. She

Runs the Gauntlet

of the artillery fire, lashing her sides with her tail, and finally takes shelter under a bridge that spans the branch which we lie to the eastward of. The fire of our battery weakens as the smoke of the burning building drifts across the Federal position. Presently the fire of our guns ceases, and I look back to see what the trouble is. The artillerymen are rolling the guns to the rear. They are black and begrimed

---

18. Adolphus or Adolph W. Wheatly joined the Confederate Service on November 12, 1862, at Camp Mulberry, in western Arkansas, near the Arkansas River. He was a resident of Johnson County and survived the war, being paroled at Shreveport, Louisiana, on June 8, 1865. National Archives, Record Group M322 (roll no. 58), Confederate Compiled Service Records, 10th Missouri Cavalry Regiment.
19. Between noon and 1:00 p.m., the Confederates set fire to some buildings on the west side of the courthouse square, near the camp of the 5th Kansas Cavalry. Within Shelby's Brigade, G. W. Thompson noted the fire had started somewhere in front of his command, "But by Whom," he didn't know. Cabell's Brigade, under J. C. Monroe appears to have set the fire to drive back the Federal troops, in the hope of finally capturing the town. Unfortunately the wind turned from the north, which favored the Confederates to the northeast which favored the entrenched Federals. Captain T. Fen Rieff and several of his men attempted to spread the fire after the winds changed; unfortunately he was hit by three bullets. "His men fled and left their captain to be plundered by the Kansans of 3 beautiful revolvers, one splendid gold watch, besides 3 to 400 dollars in money." Even while Rieff lay severely wounded, Federal troopers attempted to pull him away from the fire, but continued sharpshooting by the Confederate cavalry, forced them back. In the end Rieff was consumed in the fire. Meanwhile, Colonel Clayton, recognized the seriousness of the situation and put Talbot's contrabands back to work controlling the flames. One brave Kansan also stepped forward to assist in saving the courthouse square. Sergeant Jacob D. Orcutt, Company A, 5th Kansas "climbed upon the jail roof and drenched it with water to prevent that from catching fire; he then made his way on the top of a large two story and half house," also saving that house; all the while he was under fire from the rebel snipers. The actions of all concerned saved the town and preserved the Union position. There was little left for Marmaduke to do. If he wanted to take the town it would have to be by direct assault; an action that he was not going to take. O.R., vol. 22, pt. 1:723, 733; Banasik, *Reluctant Cannoneer*, 313; Bearss, "Pine Bluff," 207; Christ, 239; Fry, 51, 56–57; Kaw, "Battle of Pine Bluff"; Marmaduke, *Order and Letter Book*, 318.

by powder-stain, dirt and sweat; their uniforms are soiled and blackened from the same cause. The explosions from the Federal battery have almost subsided.

An orderly dashes up. In another minute the battalion is falling back, swinging over to the left (west). Crossing the big dusty road we form in line of battle along the north string of a pasture fence at the edge of town. "Oh! I'm here yet," says Pope Fulkerson as he dances around Fisher's elbow.[20]

"And you will see the elephant in just one minute by the watch, for I see the Yanks coming now," is Fisher's reply.

And so they were. They moved up and opened on us at about 200 yards. Bullets flew thick and fast, ripping the splinters from the fence and pattering against the trees.

"My gun won't shoot," yells Fulkerson.

"Why don't you load it?" admonishes Fisher.

"It is; I have, but it won't go."

"Then put a cap on it," again commands Fisher, working his gun with all his might. After trying several caps, Pope throws down the gun in disgust and humps down behind and old stump. The bark and rotten wood is flying from the old stump in a shower.

"Whoop! that stump is rotten!" exclaims Pope, as he jumps up and

Takes Shelter

behind a big tree about six feet in the rear of the line.

"Hold up, there! you're not going to run away, I hope" calls Fisher.

"Nary run. Give 'em the devil, Fisher! I'll count the dead! Just go to 'em, John Elia!" shouts Pope from behind the tree.

About this time the fire of the enemy dwindles down to a mere rattle, but I do not know whether they have retired or not, for there is enough smoke in the brush to prevent a clear observation. Then comes the order: "Attention! Right face! By fours into column! By right! Double quick! March!"[21]

---

20. At about 2:00 p.m. Marmaduke gave the word to withdraw, directing the various columns to leave the way they had come. By 2:30, the three columns were in motion, with Lawther's command, from Greene's center column providing the covering force for the overall retreat. Lawther's was the last to leave, departing the area at about 3:30 p.m. *O.R.*, vol. 22, pt., 1:723, 731–732, 735; Banasik, *Reluctant Cannoneer*, 309, 313; DeBlack, 101; Fry, 57.

21. With the Confederates withdrawing from the area, Colonel Clayton ordered a pursuit, with about 150 men from the 5th Kansas, who had their horses already saddled and ready. Major T. W. Scudder led the pursuit with Companies A, F, E and a portion of G, making contact a short distance outside of Pine Bluff. Following a fifteen minute exchange, Scudder returned to Pine Bluff, "not deeming further pursuit safe," thus allowing the rebel command to depart in peace. Even while the battle raged at Pine Bluff Colonel Clayton, directed Orderly Sergeant Lane, Company E, 5th Kansas to cross the Arkansas River, with an escort of ten men and ride for Little Rock for reinforcements. Two days later reinforcements arrived at Pine Bluff and did little more than ensure that the Confederates had withdrawn from the area. *O.R.*. vol. 22, pt. 1:727–29; "The Battle of Pine Bluff, Arkansas," *The Emporia News* (Emporia, KS), November 14, 1863; Bearss, "Pine Bluff," 309; Fry, 55, 57; Marmaduke, *Order and Letter Book*, 318.

Pope springs into line from his place behind the tree with the exclamation: "Wasn't that a dandy fight, John? and we whipped 'em, too, be gad!"

"Yes, like [hell] we did!" snorts Fisher.

By this time the head of the column is leaping the east string of the pasture fence at the great dusty road, and, the enemy opens up a lively fusillade. The fence is about waist high. I am loading my gun as I trot along. As I draw my ramrod from my gun I attempt to leap the fence. My right foot hangs on the top rail, and I fall headlong into the edge of the road with a fence-rail between my legs and the men pouring over the fence, tripping over the rail and falling upon me. "The poor devil is done for!" exclaims someone as I struggle in the dust. When the last of the battalion has passed over me I grasp the rail and try to throw it from me, but

It Hangs Fast,

and I see that a great splinter, as large as one's three fingers, has pierced my trousers leg near the knee, and it draws in so tight that I have to take both hands and break the splinter before I can get it loose. Then picking up my gun and grappling about in the dust I find my ramrod, and then I light out in quest of the battalion, which is out of sight. Passing a bunch of young trees and brush I come in sight of them forming on the east side of the road. The roar of musketry is filling the wood. I look back and see the Third Regiment[22] engaged at the clump of young timber mentioned above. I had passed them in a hurry without seeing them. Now a horseman rides out into the big road. Instantly both horse and rider go down. Running a short distance, I meet Capt. Tom Murry [Murray][23] and young Edmonson near the end of our line.

"Come down and help me carry my kinsman, who is wounded, from the field," cries Edmonson.

---

22. The 3rd Missouri Cavalry Regiment (CSA), also known as Greene's Regiment, was mustered into the Confederate service from August–November, 1862. The men came from southwestern Missouri, primarily from Springfield, Newtonia, and Polk County. Colton Greene was appointed the first colonel of the regiment on November 3, 1862, and either commanded the regiment or a brigade throughout his time in the Confederate Service. The regiment fought at Clark's Mill (November 7, 1862) and Beaver Creek (November 24, 1862), both in Missouri. They were also in both of Marmaduke's Missouri Raids in 1863, the 1863 Campaign for Little Rock, and the Battle of Pine Bluff. In 1864, the regiment was in the Camden Expedition and participated in Price's 1864 Missouri Raid. The 3rd was disbanded in the spring of 1865. *O.R.,* vol. 22, pt. 1:199, 288, 523, 731; *O.R.,* vol. 34, pt. 1:785; *O.R.,* vol. 41, pt. 1:678; *O.R.S.,* pt. 2, vol. 38:169–178; Allardice, Confederate Colonels, 173; Crute, 198.

23. Thomas Benton Murray was born on May 2, 1837, in Johnson County, Missouri. At the beginning of the Civil War he enlisted as a private in Company D, 16th Missouri Infantry. Murray was later promoted and transferred to Company G, 11th Missouri Cavalry Battalion, where he initially served as a second lieutenant (October 15, 1862) and later the unit's first lieutenant (May 10, 1863). By war's end he had been promoted to captain, commanding Company G, 10th Missouri Cavalry (CSA). Returning to Missouri, Murray married Calra Davenport, with whom he had two sons. Murray later remarried, a Lucretia Jane Wood, with whom he had four more children. Thomas Murray died in Empire, Montana, on July 4, 1893. Eakin, *Confederate Records,* 6:33-34; National Archives, Record Group M322 (roll no. 57), Confederate Compiled Service Records, 10th Missouri Cavalry Regiment.

"Shall I go?" I asked, turning to Capt. Murry.

"Do as you please about it." he said; "but I'd advise you both to let the job out, for you are both likely to get killed or captured. See! The Third Regiment is now falling back to a position on our right."

I handed my gun to the captain with the injunction to Edmonson "to lead out."

"There he is, where you see the dead horse," he says starting off at a double-quick. It was a good 150 yards to where he lay, and the bullets are flying about pretty lively. Horse and rider lay prone in the dusty road, the horse on one of the man's legs. He is an officer, Col. Green's adjutant [William B. Biser], name forgotten.[24] He is

Shot Through the Lungs

for he is spitting blood. We take him up between us and start back. He begs us to lay him down and let him die easy, but we keep on. Then he struggles frantically and we are obliged to let him down. Then we lock our hands under him and move on. The blood spurts from his mouth and it seems he is about to strangle. But he manages to blow the bloody foam from his mouth and is not yet dead when we put him in an ambulance, which drives to the rear at a furious rate of speed. Meantime, the rattle of musketry has subsided. There are no troops in sight, but I can see the dust rising upon either side and know that friend and foe are but a little way off. Getting upon a stump I look about for our horses. Yes, I see them, and the enemy, too. They are about as far beyond our horses as it is from us to our horses. We run for our horses, dodging in the brush to keep from being seen. Reaching them, we cut the halter-straps and slide into the saddle and strike a gallop just as the enemy spy us and sing out "Halt!" But we lie down on our horses necks and hold the rowels in their flanks and strike the road like a thunderbolt, soon raising such a dust that it spoiled the aim of the pursuing enemy. To our dismay the officer of the rear would not let us pass, but held us as "help," he thinking his command was

Not Sufficiently Strong,

to resist an onslaught of the enemy. But the next morning, when the new guard came on, we were set free. We find the brigade in camp six miles south of Pine Bluff. As we ride into camp we are greeted with cheers of welcome, and a general hand-shaking takes place about the mess-fire. Pope Fulkerson and John Fisher are

---

24. The Adjutant of Greene's 3rd Missouri Cavalry Regiment (CSA) was William D. or B. Biser. He entered the Confederate Service as a private on June 14, 1862, at Tupelo, Mississippi, after a tour in the MSG, and returned to Arkansas. On November 3, 1862, he was promoted to Colonel Green's staff as his adjutant general. At the time of his death, at Pine Bluff, he was listed as a lieutenant. He was born on February 6, 1831, in Maryland. Of his adjutant's death Colonel Greene wrote—Biser "fell at the close of the action. He was an efficient and useful officer and a gallant gentleman." *O.R.*, vol. 22, pt. 1:731; Eakin & Hale, 27; Marmaduke, *Order and Letter Book*, 320; National Archives, Record Group M322, (roll no. 22), Confederate Compiled Service Records, 3rd Missouri Cavalry Regiment.

yet sparring over yesterday's incident. Fisher swears that Polk shall never play second to him in another battle, and Pope declares he never could have stood the racket if it had not been for the assuring presence of Fisher's red banner (his hair). They are fast friends and jolly fellows well met, notwithstanding they at times rally each other to rudeness. The battalion is on the move before we have an opportunity to break our fast, but our messmates divide with us, and we manage to exist until we reach Princeton.[25]

Henry C. Luttrell,
Co. G, Tenth Missouri Cavalry.

* * * * * *

---

25. After Marmaduke's command rested on the evening of October 25, they returned to Princeton the following day, arriving at 7:00 p.m. Overall Marmaduke reported the loss of 18 dead, 67 wounded, with 16 missing—total 101. He also reported burning 1000 bales of cotton, capturing 300 horses and mules, and "brought off 100 Negroes," who were turned over to the Divisional Quartermaster. Union newspaper accounts scoffed at Marmaduke's claims, noting that no more than 50 bales of cotton were destroyed. However, Colonel Clayton admitted that at least one warehouse with over 250 bales was burned, while other first hand accounts put the losses in cotton at over 350 bales. One civilian witness to the battle even recorded that the rebels burned "2 or 3" warehouses of cotton, which would raise the total to between 700–1000 bales. Additionally, the 5th Kansas lost all their camp and garrison equipment and books and records, which were consumed in the ensuing fire. The contraband camp was also destroyed and many of the houses in the town sustained substantial damage. But the loss in life was relatively small as Federal losses amounted to 16 dead, 39 wounded, with 1 missing—total 56. Overall, despite the rosy picture that Marmaduke tried to paint on the Battle of Pine Bluff, the fact remains that he failed to take the city. General Holmes wrote Marmaduke on October 28, noting that Marmaduke's failure would probably make the Federals secure, prompting them to launch a raid of their own, which they eventually did. On November 10 a Federal expedition departed Benton, Arkansas, and conducted operations at Caddo Gap and Mt. Alba, before returning to Benton on November 18. *O.R.,* vol., 22, pt. 1:724–725, 752–754; Banasik, *Reluctant Cannoneer,* 313; "Battle of Pine Bluff," *Emporia News,* November 14, 1863; Fry, 59; Kaw, "Battle of Pine Bluff," *Chicago Tribune,* November 19, 1863; Leslie, 266–268; Marmaduke, *Order and Letter Book,* 289–290, 318–319.

Appendix A
Miscellaneous Correspondence, Orders and Proclamations

Item: The last known letter of Colonel Alexander Early Steen.[1]

Camp near Van Buren
Dec. 1st 1862

Dear Cousin,

The order of march has just been published. The army and the transportation is so reduced that it precludes all from carrying a trunk. So I take the liberty of sending my trunks to you for storage in some safe place—until our return or until I can send for them. Trusting in God that I may be spared to live to wear out all the good clothing. Contained there in also to cherish the many trifles which are dear to me cousin. I regret exceedingly I could not have seen more of you and all of my relatives in and near Van Buren and Ft. Smith—however such is war and the fate of a soldier. Excuse this scribble and the liberty I take with you. I am writing on my knee.

Affectionately
Your Cousin
A. E. Steen

Mrs Mary Walker
Van Buren, Arkansas

* * * * * * *

Item: Missouri Brigade Expresses Sorrow at the Loss of General Thomas C. Hindman as Commander of Their Division.[2]

Parson's Brigade, Mo. Vols.,
Hindman's Division, T.M.A.,
Camp Near Little Rock, March 3, 1863.

At a meeting of the commissioned officers of this Brigade, on the 3d day of March, 1863, the following proceedings were had:

On the motion of Col. Moore, "Steen's" regiment, Lieut. Col. Burns, "Hunter's" regiment, was appointed chairman, and Col. Austin M. Standish, secretary.

Lieut. Col. Lewis, "Caldwell's" regiment, explained the object of the meeting to be an expression, by the officers of the "Missouri Brigade," of their deep sorrow at parting with their commander, Maj. Gen. T. C. Hindman, who has been

---

1. Letter, Steen to Walker (December 1, 18672), Civil War Papers (Box 21–4), Missouri Historical Society.
2. Letter to the Editor (March 3, 1863), *True Democrat*, March 18, 1863.

relieved of the command of this division of the army. Col. Lewis recounted the trials and triumphs of Hindman's corps in the campaign of the north-west, paying a merited tribute to the genius and self-sacrificing patriotism of Gen. Hindman; the sentiments of which speech were greeted with applause.

On motion of Col. Lewis, the chairman appointed the following committee, with instructions to draft resolutions: Col. Lewis and Captain Bronaugh, "Caldwell's" regiment; Lieut. Colonel Moore and Capt. Mayoffice [Magoffin], "Steen's" regiment; Maj. Murray and Capt. Phillips, "Hunter's" regiment; Maj. Pindall and Capt. Coke [Cake], of "Pindall's Sharpshooters;" Lieut. Col. Stanford, of White's regiment.

After a short absence, the committee reported the following preamble and resolutions:

WHEREAS, We have learned, with profound regret, that Maj. Gen. Hindman, commanding this division, has been relieved of command among us; and to give expression to the sorrow caused in this, our "Missouri Brigade," by his removal, be it unanimously

Resolved, That in Maj. Gen. Hindman's removal from this command we have lost one of the leaders that we had hoped to see in the army now marshalling to redeem our State, and give back our friends and families in Missouri the happiness and freedom, wrested from them by the ruthless foe now holding that beloved State under brutal and despotic rule.

Resolved, That we recognize in Gen. Hindman the patriotic leader who looks neither to the right hand nor to the left for the powers or favors of public opinion—who has only one great object in view: the independence and welfare of his country.

Resolved, That as a mark of the high esteem in which Maj. Gen. Hindman is held by the officers and men of this brigade, that we adjourn, en masse, to the residence of Gen. Hindman, and greet him with as complimentary serenade.

Resolved, That a copy of these proceedings be sent to Maj. Gen. Hindman, and to the Little Rock "True Democrat" newspaper.

The resolutions were unanimously adopted, and the meeting adjourned.

S.P. Burns, Lt. Col. and Ch'n.
Austin M. Standish, A.A.G. and Sec'y.

* * * * * *

Item: General Order detailing the use of Negro labor in the Department of the Gulf, with the President Lincoln's Proclamation implementing the Emancipation Proclamation.[3]

General Orders No. 12

Hdqrs. Department of the Gulf,
New Orleans, January 12, 1863.

The proclamation of the President of the United States, dated January 1, 1863, is published in general orders for the information and government of the officers and soldiers of this command and all persons acting under their authority. It designates portions of the State of Louisiana which are not to be affected by its provisions. The laws of the United States, however, forbid officers of the Army and Navy to return slaves to their owners or to decide upon the claims of any person to the service or labor of another, and the inevitable conditions of a state of war unavoidably deprive all classes of citizens of much of that absolute freedom of action and control of property which local law and the continued peace of the country guaranteed and secured to them. The forcible seizure of fugitives from service or labor by their owners is inconsistent with these laws and conditions, inasmuch as it leads to personal violence and the disturbance of the public peace and it cannot be permitted. Officers and soldiers will not encourage or assist slaves to leave their employers, but they cannot compel or authorize their return by force.

The public interest peremptorily demands that all persons without other means of support be required to maintain themselves by labor. Negroes are not exempt from this law. Those who leave their employers will be compelled to support themselves and families by labor upon the public works. Under no circumstances whatever can they be maintained in idleness, or allowed to wander through the parishes and cities of the States without employment. Vagrancy and crime will be suppressed by enforced and constant occupation and employment.

Upon every consideration labor is entitled to some equitable proportion of the crops it produces. To secure the objects both of capital and labor the sequestration commission is hereby authorized and directed, upon conference with planters and other parties, to propose and establish a yearly system of negro labor, which shall provide for the food, clothing, proper treatment, and just compensation for the negroes, at fixed rates or an equitable proportion of the yearly crop, as may be deemed advisable. It should be just, but not exorbitant or onerous. When accepted by the planter or other parties all the conditions of continuous and faithful service, respectful deportment, correct discipline, and perfect subordination shall be enforced on the part of the negroes by the officers of the Government. To secure their payment the wages of labor will constitute a lien upon its products.

This may not be the best, but it is now the only practicable system. Wise men will do what they can when they cannot do what they would. It is the law of suc-

---

3. *O.R.*, vol. 15: 666–669.

cess. In three years from the restoration of peace, under this voluntary system of labor, the State of Louisiana will produce threefold the product of its most prosperous year in the past.

The quartermaster department is charged with the duty of harvesting corn on deserted fields and cultivating abandoned estates. Unemployed negroes will be engaged in this service under the control of suitable agents or planters, with a just compensation in food, clothing, and money, consistent with the terms agreed upon by the commission, and under such regulations as will tend to keep families together, to impart self-supporting habits to the negroes, and protect the best interest of the people and the Government.

By command of Major-General Banks:

Rich'd B. Irwin,
Lieutenant -Colonel, Assistant Adjutant-General.

By The President Of The United States.
A Proclamation.

Whereas on the twenty-second day of September, in the year of our Lord one thousand eight hundred and sixty-two, a proclamation was issued by the President of the United States containing, among other things, the following, to wit:

That on the first day of January, in the year of our Lord one thousand eight hundred and sixty-three, all persons held as slaves within any State or designated part of a State, the people whereof shall then be in rebellion against the United States, shall be then, thenceforward, and forever free; and the executive government of the United States, including the military and naval authority thereof, will recognize and maintain the freedom of such persons, and will do no act or acts to repress such persons, or any of them, in any efforts they make for their actual freedom.

That the Executive will, on the first day of January aforesaid, by proclamation, designate the States and parts of States, if any, in which the people thereof respectively shall then be in rebellion against the United States; and the fact that any State or people thereof shall on that day be in good faith represented in the Congress of the United States by members chosen thereto at elections wherein a majority of the qualified voters of such States shall have participated shall, in the absence of strong countervailing testimony, be deemed conclusive evidence that such State and the people thereof are not then in rebellion against the United States.

Now therefore I, Abraham Lincoln, President of the United States, by virtue of the power in me vested, as Commander-in-Chief of the Army and Navy of the United States in time of actual armed rebellion against the authority and Government of the United States, and as a fit and necessary war measure for suppressing said rebellion, do, on the first day of January, in the year of our Lord one thousand eight hundred and sixty-three, and in accordance with my purpose so to do, publicly proclaimed for the full period of one hundred days, from the first day above mentioned, order and designate as the States and parts of States wherein the people thereof respectively are this day in rebellion against the United States the following, to wit:

Arkansas, Texas, Louisiana (except the parishes of Saint Bernard, Plaquemines, Jefferson, Saint John, Saint Charles, Saint James, Ascension, Assumption, Terre Bonne, La Fourche, Saint Marie, Saint Martin and Orleans, including the city of New Orleans), Mississippi, Alabama, Florida, Georgia, South Carolina, North Carolina, and Virginia (except the forty-eight counties designated as West Virginia, and also the counties of Berkeley, Accomac, Northampton, Elizabeth City, York, Princess Ann, and Norfolk, including the cities of Norfolk and Portsmouth), and which excepted parts are for the present left precisely as if this proclamation were not issued.

And by virtue of the power, and for the purpose aforesaid, I do order and declare that all persons held as slaves within said designated States and parts of States are and henceforward shall be free; and that the executive government of the United States, including the military and naval authorities thereof, will recognize and maintain the freedom of said persons.

And I hereby enjoin upon the people so declared to be free to abstain from all violence except in necessary self-defense; and I recommend to them that in all cases, when allowed, they labor faithfully for reasonable wages.

And I further declare and make known that such persons, of suitable conditions, will be received into the armed service of the United States, to garrison forts, positions, stations, and other places, and to man vessels of all sorts in said service.

And upon this act, sincerely believed to be an act of justice, warranted by the Constitution, upon military necessity, I invoke the considerate judgement of mankind and the gracious favor of Almighty God.

In testimony whereof I have hereunto set my name and caused the seal of the United States to be affixed.

Done at the city of Washington this first day of January, in the year of our Lord one thousand eight hundred and sixty-three, and of the Independence of the United States the eighty-seventh.

Abraham Lincoln

By the President:
William H. Seward,
Secretary of State.

* * * * * * *

Item: The loss of officers in Parsons's Missouri Brigade at Helena, Arkansas, on July 4, 1863, as recorded by Captain James H. McNamarra.[4]

James McNamarra's List of Officers Killed At Helena, Arkansas (July 4, 1863)

"With the hundreds of brave privates who were killed, were the following officers of Parsons's Brigade: Maj. T. B. Stafford [Sanford], Ninth Regiment; Capt. [D. T.] Lanners [Lanius], Ninth Regiment; Lieut. Richard Spencer, Ninth Regiment; Lieut. W. E. Kerr, Ninth Regiment; Capt. G. W. Perry, Seventh Regiment; Lieut. [Robert] Austin, Seventh Regiment; Lieut A. P. Foster, Eighth Regiment...."[5]

Brief Biographies of the Officers Lost in Parson's Brigade:

[Note: McNamara's list was not complete and one additional name was added for that oversight—Lieutenant James J. Farley 7th (11th) Missouri Infantry (CSA).][6]

Robert A. Austin was born in Kentucky about 1833, and was a resident of Saline County at the beginning of the Civil War, when he joined Company A, 2nd Infantry Regiment, 4th Division MSG. He was wounded at Blue Mills, Missouri, on September 17, 1861, recovered and was captured at Blackwater or Milford, Missouri, on December 19, 1861. Sent to Alton Prison, Austin was probably exchanged with the other prisoners from Milford in the spring or summer of 1862. He then joined what became Company A, 16th Missouri Infantry on June 18 and was elected a lieutenant on August 18, 1862. Mortally wounded at Helena, on July 4, Austin was sent to Memphis on the hospital steamer the *R. C. Wood*, where he was admitted to the hospital on July 7. He died on July 15, 1863 at Memphis.[7]

James J. Farley was born in Virginia in about 1831, and was a resident of Polk

---

4. This was originally part of McNamara's article in the *Missouri Republican* entitled "Missouri Confederates," published on December 5, 1886.

5. This part was extracted from McNamara's original article as noted in his piece in Chapter Two of this book.

6. In his official report on the battle, General Holmes listed both Captain W. J. Lillard and B. N. Cocke as killed at the battle. J. F. H. in his letter also lists Captain Cocke as killed at Helena. However, W. J. Lillard of the 8th (11th) Missouri was a corporal in Company C and not an officer. Benjamin N. Cocke was the captain of Company B, 7th (16th) Missouri Infantry, but was not killed at Helena. Cocke was captured, sent to Alton Prison and forwarded on to Johnson Island. Cocke was later exchanged, was promoted to major by war's end, and survived the war. Additionally, J.F.H. in his letter on the battle has Lieutenant James J. Farley of the 8th (11th) Missouri listed as killed in the battle, where Holmes does not list the name—Farley was actually mortally wounded and died at Memphis on December 5, 1863. Farley has been added to the list as officers killed at Helena in Parsons's Brigade. *O.R.*, vol. 22, pt. 1:412; *O.R.S.*, pt. 2, vol. 38: 638; Eakin, *Confederate Records*, 2:76; Eakin, *Missouri Prisoners of War*, "Cocke, B. N.," entry; Eakin & Hale, 82; J. F. H. Letter; Miles, 314; Schnetzer, *Men of the Eleventh*, 75.

7. *O.R.S.*, pt. 2, vol. 38:638; Bartels, *Forgotten Men*, 8; Bartels, *Trans-Mississippi Men*, 231; Eakin, *Missouri Prisoners of War*, "Austin, Robt A." entry; National Archives, Record Group M322 (roll no. 166), Confederate Compiled Service Records, 16th Missouri Infantry.

County, Missouri, when he joined the Confederate service on August 10, 1862. When his command was organized on August 31, 1862, Farley was elected second lieutenant of what became Company G, 11th Missouri Infantry (CSA). His company was at the Battle of Lone Jack on August 16, 1862, though it unclear as to Farley's status. At Helena Farley was mortally wounded, taking a bullet in the left thigh, which was subsequently amputated. He was transported to Memphis on board the hospital steamship the *R. C. Wood* and was admitted to the hospital on July 7, 1863, where he lingered for several months. He died in the Memphis hospital on December 5, 1863.[8]

A. P. Foster was born in Tennessee in about 1831, and was a resident of Hickory or Henry County, Missouri, when he joined the 12th Cavalry Regiment, 8th Division MSG as captain of the unit on October 3, 1861. He was discharged on January 1, 1862, but rejoined the Confederate Army at Fayetteville, Arkansas, on July 4 or 6, 1862. Upon organization of Company D, 11th Missouri Infantry, Foster was elected first lieutenant on August 31, 1862, a position he was holding when he was killed at Helena on July 4, 1863.[9]

William E. Kerr was born about 1821 in Georgia and was a resident of West Plain, Missouri, when he joined Company C, 2nd Infantry Regiment, 7th Division MSG. After serving his six months in the Guard, he left the army as a sergeant and later joined what became Company A, 12th Missouri Infantry on July 26, 1862, as a corporal. Kerr was elected second lieutenant on October 24, 1862, was wounded at Helena, and was subsequently paroled at the Polk Plantation on July 7. Kerr survived the war and was living in Hannibal, Missouri in 1914, age 83. (Note: The National Archives has Kerr dying at Memphis on July 20, 1863.)[10]

Daniel T. Lanius [or Lonneus or Lanier] was born in Hydesburg, Missouri, about 1841, and enlisted in the 12th Missouri Infantry on August 2, 1862, as a private. He was subsequently elected first lieutenant of Company F, 12th Missouri Infantry (CSA), on August 15, 1862. Following the death of Thomas D. Lashley, Lanius was promoted to captain, to rank from March 2, 1863.[11]

---

8. *O.R.S.*, pt. 2, vol. 38:611; National Archives, Record Group M322 (roll no. 157), Confederate Compiled Service Records, 11th Missouri Infantry; National Archives, Record Group M861 (roll no. 36), Records of Confederate Movements and Activities, 11th Missouri Infantry; Schnetzer, *Men of the Eleventh*, 75.

9. Bartels, *Forgotten Men*, 116; National Archives, Record Group M322 (roll no. 157), Confederate Compiled Service Records, 11th Missouri Infantry; Schnetzer, *Men of the Eleventh*, 41.

10. *O.R.S.*, pt. 2, vol. 38:624; Bartels, *Trans-Mississippi Men*, 210; J. F. H. Letter; National Archives, Record Group M322 (roll no. 163), Confederate Compiled Service Records, 12th Missouri Infantry; Schnetzer, *More Forgotten Men*, 131.

11. *O.R.*, vol. 22, pt. 1:412; *O.R.S.*, pt. 2, vol. 38:625; Eakin, *Confederate Records*, 5:40; J. F. H. Letter; National Archives, Record Group M322 (roll no. 164), Confederate Compiled Service Records, 12th Missouri Infantry.

George W. Perry was born in Alabama, about 1824. He joined the Confederate Army as a private on July 8, 1862, was elected first lieutenant of Company C in J. Vard Cockrell's Cavalry Regiment, and participated in the Battle of Lone Jack, Missouri on August 15, 1862. On August 31, 1862, Perry was retained as a lieutenant in the recently organized Company C, 16th Missouri Infantry (CSA). Perry became captain of his company on May 24, 1863, upon the promotion of Jesse P. Harrell to major of the regiment and was killed at Helena on July 4.[12]

Thomas B. Sanford was born in New York about 1836, and joined Company A, 3rd Cavalry Regiment, 1st Division MSG, as second lieutenant on August 1, 1861. He served until December 27, when he was commissioned a captain and Assistant Division Commissary officer. Upon organization of the 12th Missouri Infantry, at Yellville, Arkansas, he was elected major of the unit on October 22, 1862. He was killed at Helena while charging the Union encampment at the bottom of Graveyard Hill.[13]

Richard Spencer was born in Missouri about 1839, and joined the Confederate Service as a private. He was elected first lieutenant of Company E, 12th Missouri Infantry (CSA) on August 6, 1862, and resigned on April 24, 1863, for health reasons (chronic diarrhea). The Confederate War Department approved his resignation on June 8, 1863; however the paperwork never reached his command before the Battle of Helena. Spencer participated in the Battle of Helena, pending approval of his resignation, where he was killed on July 4.[14]

* * * * * * *

General Order No. 86 (July 24, 1863)
Fourth Brigade, Price's Division15
[The following order announces the death of the officers of the brigade above mentioned]

Headquarters Fourth Brigade, Price's Division, July 24, 1863.
(General Order No. 86.)

    The brigadier general commanding is pained to announce to the troops under

---

12. *O.R.S.*, pt. 2, vol. 38:638; Eakin, *Lone Jack*, 153; National Archives, Record Group M322 (roll no. 170), Confederate Compiled Service Records, 16th Missouri Infantry.

13. *O.R.S.*, pt. 2, vol. 38:292, 623; Bartels, *Forgotten Men*, 320; J. F. H. Letter; Peterson, 41; National Archives, Record Group M322 (roll no. 165), Confederate Compiled Service Records, 12th Missouri Infantry.

14. *O.R.S.*, pt. 2, vol. 38:625; National Archives, Record Group M322 (roll no. 165), Confederate Compiled Service Records, 12th Missouri Infantry.

15. The following was extracted from James McNamara's Article, "Missouri Confederates" as published in the *Missouri Republican*, December 5, 1885.

his command the death of the following officers of this brigade. They fell as brave men should fall—with their front to the foe—at Helena, in the recent action of the 4th. (Names above mentioned). While we mourn the loss of our comrades, let us endeavor to emulate their gallant bearing. By order of

Brig. Gen. Parsons
Austin M. Standish, A.A.G.

* * * * * * *

Item: Official correspondence concerning the Walker-Marmaduke Duel, held at Little Rock, Arkansas on September 6, 1863.[16]

[Note No. 1.]

From Gen. Walker to Gen. Marmaduke.
Sept. 2, 1863,
General—I am informed that you have pronounced me a coward, and that I so acted in the fight at Reed's Bridge. You will please inform me whether you have been correctly reported.
This will be handed to you by Co. R. H. Crockett.

Yours respectively,
L. M. Walker.

To Gen. Marmaduke.—Present.

[No. 2.]

From Gen. Marmaduke to Gen. Walker.
Camp near Little Rock, Ark.,
Sept. 2, 1863.
General—I received your note dated Sept. 2, 1863, per Col. R. H. Crockett at 9 a.m., this morning, stating that it had been "reported" to you that I had "pronounced me (you) a coward" in the fight at Reed's Bridge.

I do not recognize the right of yourself or any one else to call for "explanations" when your information is based upon nameless "reporters." In this case, however, I will waive it.

I have not pronounced you a coward but I desire to inform you that your conduct as commander of the cavalry, not only at Reed's Bridge, but during the late retreat from Brownsville was such that I determined no longer to serve under you, and in consequence I informed Major Snead, Adjt. Gen. Dist. of Ark., that he must either order me from under your command or relieve me from the command of my own troops.

16. "Correspondence," Concerning the Walker-Marmaduke Duel, *Washington Telegraph*, October 21, 1863.

Your note would have received earlier attention, but official duties—having to visit my advanced outposts—prevented.

My friend, Captain Jno. C. Moore, will hand you this, and is authorized to further act in my behalf.

Yours respectively,
J. S. Marmaduke

To Gen. L. M. Walker.—Present.

[No. 3.]

From Gen. Walker to Gen. Marmaduke
Camp near Terry's Ferry.
Ark. River, Sept. 3, 1863.

General—Your note; through your friend Capt. J. C. Moore, was received this afternoon at 5 p.m., and is so far satisfactory in what relates in the questions contained in my note of the 2d, "but," you say, "I desire to inform you (me) that your (my) conduct as commander of cavalry, not only at Reed's Bridge, but during the late retreat from Brownsville, was such that I determined no longer to serve under you (me)."

The above language is capable of many different constructions, and I therefore demand an *explicit explanation* of your meaning.

This will be handed you by my friend, Col. R. H. Crockett.

Respectively,
L. M. Walker.

To Gen. J. S. Marmaduke.

[No. 4.]

From Capt. Moore to Col. Crockett
Little Rock, Ark., Sept. 4, 1863.

Colonel—I have the honor to acknowledge the receipt of Gen. L. M. Walker's letter to Gen. J. S. Marmaduke, dated Sept. 3, 1863, in which Gen. Walker acknowledges the reception of Gen. Marmaduke's note of Sept. 2, 1863, and says that though the first portion of the note is entirely satisfactory, yet that he demands an "*explicit explanation*" of the words of the latter portion.

Though Gen. Marmaduke disclaims the use of the specific term "coward" in relation to Gen. Walker, still for the inferences of such a nature that may be drawn from the statements contained in the last portion of the note, he holds himself responsible. And wishing to be entirely frank in regard to this whole matter, Gen. Marmaduke freely avows that the statements referred to were predicated upon the something more than scrupulous care with which Gen. Walker avoided all positions of danger during the retreat of the cavalry from Brownsville to Bayou Metre

[Meto], and the fact of his refusal to make his appearance upon the field of battle, though requested by Gen. Marmaduke to do so.

I have the honor, Colonel to be,
Very respectively, your ob't serv't.
Jno. C. Moore.

To Col. R. H. Crockett.—Present.

[No. 5.]

From Col. Crockett to Capt. Moore.
Little Rock, Ark., Sept. 4, 1863.

Captain—Your note of today in answer to one of yesterday from Gen. Walker to Gen. Marmaduke has been received.

It presents but one alternative. As the friend of Gen. Walker, and without consultation with him, I demand in his behalf of Gen. Marmaduke the satisfaction due to a gentleman.

You will please to confer with me at your earliest convenience, so that proper preliminary arrangements can be made for a meeting at once.

Very respectively, your ob't serv't.
R. H. Crockett.

Capt. J. C. Moore.—Present.

[No. 6.]

From Capt. Moore to Col. Crockett.
Little Rock, Ark., Sept. 5, 1863,

Colonel—Your note of Sept. 4th I have the honor to acknowledge. It affords me pleasure, as the friend of Gen. Marmaduke, to accord to the demand of satisfaction made therein.

I shall be pleased to meet you at your earliest convenience, and arrange the necessary terms, &c.

Very respectively, your ob't serv't;
Jno. C. Moore.

To Col. R. H. Crockett.—Present.

[No. 7.]
Terms of Agreement.
Little Rock, Ark., Sept. 5, 1863.

Gen. Marmaduke agrees to meet Gen. Walker on the following terms:

1st. The place of meeting shall be the old Godfrey LeFevre place, seven miles below Little Rock, on the north side of the Arkansas river. The time shall be 6 o'clock a.m., tomorrow. Position and the order shall be determined by chance.

2d. Either party shall be accompanied by his second, his advising friend and two surgeons.

3d. The weapons shall be what is known as *Colt's Navy Revolver*, all the barrels of which shall be loaded. The distance shall be *fifteen paces*, to be stepped by the mutual friends of the parties in company.

4th. The pistols of both parties shall be loaded on the ground, and shall be charged with the "round ball."

5th. The word shall be "are you ready?" The reply shall be "ready" or "not ready" within ten seconds by each party. Both parties having replied "ready," the word shall be given to "fire." After which both parties shall fire at will at any time within five minutes or until all the loads of the pistol are exhausted, or one of the parties shall fall. At the end of five minutes, or upon the falling of either party, the word shall be given "stop," when both parties shall cease firing. Neither party shall in the meantime leave his position.

6th. The pistols shall be placed in the hands of the principals already cocked, and shall be held with the muzzle downward at an angle not exceeding ten degrees from the foot, or upward at the same angle from the head.

7th. The seconds and advising friends of both parties shall wear their side arms only; and any attempt to violate these terms shall subject the party, whether principal, second or friend, to be shot upon the spot.

Jno. C. Moore,
On part Gen. Marmaduke
R. H. Crockett,
On part Gen. Walker.

[Note: The following correspondence was not part of the original pieces published in the *Washington Telegraph*, but is germane to the subject, being General Walker's deathbed correspondence to General Marmaduke.][17]

[No. 8]

General J. S. Marmaduke

Sir, General Walker, before his death, requested me to see you in person, and reassure you that before taking the last sacrament, he sincerely forgave you for his death, and desired his friends and relatives also to forgive you and neither to persecute nor prosecute you. You will readily understand, General, why I have taken this method of conveying General Walker's last message to you in preference to a personal interview.

I have the honor, etc.,
R. H. Crockett

---

17. Marmaduke, *Order and Letter Book*, 430; Watts, 48.

Appendix B
Selected Biographies

Thomas J. Churchill

Thomas James Churchill was born on March 10, 1824, on a farm near Louisville, Kentucky. He graduated from St. Mary's College in 1844, and then studied law at Transylvania University in Lexington, Kentucky. At the beginning of the Mexican War Churchill joined the 1st Kentucky Mounted Rifles and was appointed to the rank of first lieutenant. He was captured in January 1847 and not released until Mexico surrendered, after which he moved to Little Rock, Arkansas, where he married in 1848 and operated a plantation near the city.

At the beginning of the Civil War, Churchill, who at the time was postmaster of Little Rock, organized the 1st Arkansas Mounted Rifles at Ft. Smith, of which he was elected colonel on June 9, 1861. He fought at Wilson's Creek, where General McCulloch recorded that Churchill led his regiment "into action with the greatest coolness and bravery, always in front of his men, cheering them on." At Pea Ridge he was noted for his "conspicuous" and gallant service. After he returned to Van Buren, Arkansas, following the Battle of Pea Ridge, Churchill was informed that he had been promoted to brigadier general on March 6, to rank from March 4.

Churchill served briefly on the east side of the Mississippi River, where he commanded a division and played an important role in the Battle of Richmond, Kentucky, on August 30, 1862. In the latter part of 1862 he returned to Arkansas where he was given command of Arkansas Post in December. He surrendered Arkansas Post in January 1863, and was exchanged in April 1863. After a short stay with the Army of Tennessee, Churchill was ordered back to Arkansas on August 18, 1863, where he commanded an Arkansas division. He subsequently participated in the Red River and Camden campaigns and was promoted to major general on March 18, 1865.

The men under his command generally liked Churchill, with one soldier calling him a "good officer," though with a "self-satisfied sanctimonious look." Still another recorded that "Arkansas men esteemed General Churchill very highly and had great confidence in him as an honest and skilful officer, and knew that he was brave and had much respect for the private soldier." When Churchill was promoted to major general

Thomas James Churchill

some in his command felt that he was "worthy" of the promotion, while others disagreed.

As to his physical appearance, a member of the 15th Texas Cavalry wrote: "He is a tall, fine looking man, with a thin visage, a fine eye, & wears no beard—is much older than he looks to be at a distance, is probably forty years old—is an intelligent & polished gentleman; pleasant in conversation."

After the war Churchill returned to Arkansas, was elected state treasurer in 1874 and reelected in 1876 and 1878. He was elected governor in 1880, served one term and retired amid a scandal over something that happened during his term as treasurer. Retiring to his farm outside Little Rock, Churchill never again entered politics and died in Little Rock on May 14, 1905.[1]

* * * * * * *

Robert Ralston Lawther

Robert Ralston Lawther was born in Kittanning, Pennsylvania, on January 21, 1836. Prior to the war he was living in Muscatine, Iowa, where he was a business man and served as the treasurer of a local Presbyterian Church. Lawther left Iowa after running afoul of the local police for "cheating his business partner" and defrauding his church and the city,

At the beginning of the war, Lawther was a grocer living in Jefferson City, Missouri, when he joined the 6th Division, MSG, as a volunteer aid-de-camp on A. E. Steen's staff and later as the colonel of the 1st Cavalry Regiment, 6th Division, MSG. With the organization of the 1st Missouri Cavalry Regiment (CSA) on December 30, 1861, Lawther was elected major of that unit.

Lawther departed the 1st Missouri Cavalry on June 12, 1862 (Allardice has the date as June 2), and with the permission of President Jefferson Davis organized the 1st Regiment, Missouri Partisan Rangers (CSA) during the summer of 1862. Cap-

PARALYSIS CAUSES DEATH OF WELL-KNOWN CITIZEN.

Col. R. R. Lawther.

---

1. *O.R.*, 3:106; *O.R.*, 8:780; *O.R.*, vol. 22, pt. 1:902; *O.R.*, vol. 34, pt. 1:785; *O.R.*, Series 2, 5:477; Bailey, "Thomas James Churchill," *Confederate General*, 1:186–187; Boatner, 697–698; Crute, 42; Chambers, 3; Faust, 141; Gaughan, 99, 102, 233; Harrell, *Arkansas, Confederate Military History*, 394–396; Heitman, 2:47; Sifakis, *Who Was Who in the Confederacy*, 53; Turnbo, 329, 363; Warner, *Generals in Gray*, 49–50; Wiley, 143.

tured in Osage County on September 1, 1862, Lawther was sent to Gratiot Street Prison and transferred to Camp Chase, Ohio, on January 30, 1863. He was later exchanged and returned to the Trans-Mississippi.

During the Little Rock Campaign Lawther was given command of a "Temporary Regiment of Dismounted Cavalry," which later, after his command was re-mounted, was incorporated into the 10th Missouri Cavalry, with Lawther elected the colonel of the regiment on April 20, 1864, to rank from December 12, 1863. Lawther led his command until he resigned on February 27, 1865 (service record has the date as January 10), with a surgeon's Certificate of Disability.

During the war, Lawther participated in the Arkansas engagements at Pea Ridge, Pine Bluff (October 25, 1863), the Camden Expedition (March–May 1864) and Price's 1864 Missouri Raid. He was paroled at Galveston, Texas on June 20, 1865.

After the war, Lawther tried at first, to return to his native Pennsylvania, but was not welcomed and went back instead to Galveston, where he took up farming. He later moved to Dallas, where he was elected alderman. Lawther died in Dallas on October 1, 1911. General James F. Fagan, whom Lawther served under during Price's 1864 Missouri Expedition, recalled that Lawther was "a gallant and competent officer."[2]

* * * * * * *

Levin Major Lewis

Levin Major Lewis was born in Maryland on January 6, 1832, attended the Maryland Military Academy (1848–1849) in Washington, DC, and Wesleyan University (1850–1851) in Middletown, Connecticut. He moved to Missouri about 1854, settling in Liberty where he practiced law, was a Methodist preacher, and then a school teacher.

When the Civil War began, Lewis was a captain of the "Washington Guards," and shortly thereafter was appointed colonel of the 3rd Infantry Regiment, 3rd Division, MSG, by Governor C. F. Jackson. He served as an aid to General Van Dorn at the Battle of Pea Ridge, for which he received the praise of Van Dorn for the "courage and intelligence" that he displayed during the engagement. Shortly thereafter Lewis joined the Confederate Army as a captain of a cavalry company on June 18, 1862, which eventually became Company A, 16th Missouri Infantry (CSA).

Lewis received four wounds at Lone Jack, Missouri (August 16). He was pro-

---

2. *O.R.*, vol. 22, pt. 1:731–732; *O.R.*, vol. 34, pt. 1:781; *O.R.*, vol. 41, pt. 1:698; *O.R.S.*, pt. 2, vol. 38:253; Allardice, *Confederate Colonels*, 233; Bevier, 77; Crute, 203; Eakin, *Missouri Prisoners of War*, "Lawther, Robt. R." entry; Eakin & Hale, 261; "The 'Invader,'" *Muscatine Daily Journal* (Muscatine, IA), May 28, 1863; McGhee, *Letter and Order Book*, unnumbered page 29 (entry pages 56–57); Marmaduke, *Order and Letter Book*, 239–240; National Archives, Record Group M322, (roll no. 57), Confederate Compiled Service Records, 10th Missouri Cavalry Regiment; Peterson, 174.

moted to major of his regiment following the resignation of S. D. Jackman in the fall of 1862, to lieutenant colonel effective December 4, 1862, and colonel regiment on March 24, 1863. Lewis was captured at Helena, Arkansas, on July 4, 1863, and sent to prison at Johnson Island, Ohio. While in prison, Lewis was offered the position of Confederate senator from Missouri in early 1864, by then Governor Thomas Reynolds; however, political expediency caused George Vest to assume the position. Lewis was exchanged in September 1864, at the request of Jefferson Davis, via a "Special Exchange." Lewis subsequently refused Davis's offer of a special appointment, "saying that the President could find a suitable man for the proffered place, who was incapacitated for field services by reasons of wounds or other causes and that he preferred to return to his regiment." Lewis returned to the Trans-Mississippi Department and rejoined his command. Kirby Smith appointed him a brigadier general on May 16, 1865, just days before the surrender; however, he was never confirmed by the Confederate Congress.

Levin Major Lewis

After the war Lewis served as a preacher in Shreveport, Louisiana, also in Galveston, Texas, and then moved back to Missouri for his health in 1869. In 1874 he became the president of the Arkansas Female College in Little Rock, and moved again to Texas in 1878, where he became a professor of English at Texas A & M University in 1878. He later returned to preaching in Dallas and went to California for his health, where he died at Los Angeles on May 28, 1886. His body was returned to Dallas, Texas, where he was buried.

Summing up Lewis's life one biographer described him as "a profound scholar, 'popular and attractive, humorous and magnetic.'"[3]

* * * * * * *

3. *O.R.*, 8:286; Allardice, *Confederate Colonels*, 238; Allardice, *More Generals in Gray*, 142–143; Arthur W. Bergeron, Jr., "Levin M. Lewis," *Confederate General*, 6:188–189; T. W. Cassell, Letter (February 12, 1911), Skaggs Collection; Castel, 169–170; Moore, Skaggs Collection; National Archives, Record Group M322 (roll no. 169), Confederate Service Records, 16th Missouri Infantry; Schultz, 105 113; Wight, 165, 175.

Henry Eustace McCulloch

The younger brother of General Ben McCulloch, Henry McCulloch was born on December 6, 1816, in Rutherford County, Tennessee, where he received his early education. He moved to Guadalupe County, Texas, in 1837, was elected sheriff in 1843, and commanded a company during the Mexican War in Bell's Texas Volunteers. Following the war, McCulloch was elected to the Texas Legislature (1853), the Texas Senate (1855) and prior to the Civil War was appointed the U.S. Marshal for the Eastern District of Texas by President James Buchanan. Henry McCulloch served as a representative to the Texas Secession Convention in February 1861, after which he entered the military. On April 15, 1861, he was appointed colonel of the 1st Texas Mounted Riflemen and played a leading role in the surrender of Federal troops in Texas in 1861. McCulloch was made a brigadier general on March 14, 1862, and as a result was given command of East Texas on June 12, 1862. During the summer of 1862, he forwarded some "six brigades" of troops to Arkansas, and in August he was reassigned to Little Rock. Arriving in the Arkansas capital in late August, McCulloch was given command of a division on September 6, that would form the core of what became Walker's Texas Division. With the assignment of John G. Walker to command the division, McCulloch was given command of the Third Brigade.

McCulloch's one battle of note was Milliken's Bend, Louisiana (June 7, 1863), during the relief efforts for Vicksburg. On July 22, McCulloch departed Walker's Division, and three days later he was officially relieved of command and ordered to General John B. Magruder in Texas, no doubt for his lack of success at Milliken's Bend. In reporting on McCulloch's failure, General Richard Taylor wrote: "General McCulloch appears to have shown great personal bravery, but no capacity for handling the masses." Taylor had no confidence in McCulloch. In August 1863, McCulloch returned to command the Military District of Texas, New Mexico and Arizona, a post he "fulfilled... with honor to himself and his adopted state, until the close of the war."

To his men, McCulloch was a "plain and simple" general, who "could not [be] distinguished from a private soldier...He was considered a fine commander and his men esteemed him highly."

Following the war, McCulloch returned to farming in Texas, earning the praise of one biographer who wrote: "In civil life, his gentle manliness and adhesion to right

Henry Eustace McCulloch

and justice won for him success in his undertakings and love and admiration of those who knew him." McCulloch died in Rockport, Texas, on March 12, 1895.[4]

* * * * * * *

Dandridge McRae

Dandridge McRae was born on October 10, 1829, in Baldwin County, Alabama, where he was tutored at the family plantation until he attended the University of South Carolina. He graduated in 1849, and moved to White County, Arkansas, with his mother, who purchased a plantation in the Little Red River Township. Trained in plantation management, McRae oversaw the operation of his mother's holdings, and in 1853 he moved to Searcy where he took up permanent residence. The following year, after studying law, he was admitted to the Arkansas bar, and in January 1855 he married. In 1856 McRae was elected county and circuit clerk of White County, and served in the post for six years, even after entering the army.

At the beginning of the Civil War, even before Arkansas seceded from the Union, McRae organized the 47-man Border Rangers Company on April 29, 1861. On May 22, Governor H. M. Rector appointed him "special mustering officer" to receive volunteers into the army in the Searcy area. McRae was known to be "zealous for the cause, and showed great ability in recruiting, organizing and training soldiers for the service." However, McRae was also "indifferent to military protocol," though he seemed to be able to shape up his men "into good soldiers."

On July 15, 1861, McRae's 3rd Arkansas Battalion was organized, and he was elected lieutenant colonel of the unit. He led the unit at Wilson's Creek and received praise from General Ben McCulloch for "coolness and bravery," being "always in front of his men, cheering them on." On December 3, 1861, his battalion was organized as a regiment, being designated at times either the 15th or 21st Arkansas Infantry, and McRae was elected colonel of the unit. At Pea Ridge,

Dandridge MacRae

4. O.R., vol. 9:718; O.R., vol. 24, pt. 2:459, 465; O.R., vol. 26, pt. 2:121; Blessington, 37, 127–128; Faust, 458–459; Heitman, 2:60; Letter (August 27, 1862), Holmes to Hindman, Theophilus H. Holmes Letters, Peter W. Alexander Collection, Columbia University; Lowe, 113; Roberts, Texas, Confederate Military History, 36, 244–245; Sifakis, Who Was Who in the Confederacy, 183; Turnbo, 255–256; Warner, Generals in Gray, 201.

McRae was again noted by the commanding general for his good conduct during the battle.

His command was transferred to the east side of the Mississippi River in April 1862, and on May 8, 1862, the regiment was reorganized. McRae elected not to run for colonel, but preferred returning to Arkansas, where he thought it "likely to have stirring times."

After his arrival in Little Rock in early June, General Hindman assigned McRae to command the Middle District of Arkansas, with authority to raise a regiment of infantry for service. Within a short time, McRae organized what became the 36th Arkansas Infantry. McRae commanded his new regiment for but a short time and was quickly elevated to brigade command. At the Battle of Prairie Grove McRae commanded a brigade and earned the praise of his division commander.

By the time that McRae was promoted to brigadier general on November 5, 1862, he had become disgusted with the service and offered his resignation, but he was refused. On December 10, the day of an army review, General Holmes stopped at McRae's Brigade and remarked to McRae: "Colonel allow me to congratulate you upon your promotion! you have won it upon a bloody field and you are entitled to it. It affords me infinite pleasure to announce it in the presence of your command!" Shocked by the announcement, McRae learned that it had been approved two months earlier, and for some reason the announcement had been delayed.

McRae next led a brigade at Helena and during the Little Rock Campaign. In early October 1863, Kirby Smith relieved McRae of his command, after which General Price assigned McRae to command in northeast Arkansas in November 1863, a post he held until early 1864. Returning to the main army, McRae participated in the Camden and Red River Expeditions and in June 1864 a Court of Enquiry was held, at McRae's request, concerning his performance at Helena in July 1863. Following the court's decision in late December 1864, an exonerated McRae resigned from the service, returned to Searcy, and resumed his law practice in 1865.

After the war, McRae was elected the Arkansas Deputy Secretary of State in 1881, served four years, and then represented Arkansas at the New Orleans's Worlds Fair from 1885–1886. He was the "vice President of the Bureau of Emigration for Arkansas" in 1887. The following year he was working for the U.S. Treasury Department as an "expert for gathering information." McRae was also an active Mason. He died at home in Searcy on April 23, 1899, where he was buried.[5]

---

5. *O.R.*, 3:106; *O.R.*, 8:285; *O.R.*, vol. 22, pt. 2:1035; *O.R.*, 53:688, 691; *O.R.S.*, pt.1, vol. 4:61; *O.R.S.*, pt. 2, 14:557, 563, 570; Anne Bailey, "Dandridge McRae," *Confederate General*, 4:134–135; Banasik, *Embattled Arkansas*, 513; Crute, 51; Faust, 466–477; Harrell, *Arkansas, Confederate Military History*, 407–408; Letter, (June 5, 1862), Newton to McRae, Copy Letter Book no. 1; Letter fragment (no date), McRae Papers (box 1, folders 2, 19), Arkansas History Commission; McRae Letters (October 17, 30, November 3, 16 and December 23, 1862); Freeman K. Mobley, *Making Sense of the Civil War*

James Camp Tappan

James Camp Tappan was born in Franklin, Tennessee, on September 9, 1825, was educated in New Hampshire, then at Yale University (class of 1845), and studied law in Vicksburg, Mississippi. After passing the bar, Tappan relocated to Helena, Arkansas, opened a law office and was subsequently elected to the Arkansas Legislature in 1851, where he served two terms, including one as the Speaker of the House.

At the beginning of the Civil War Tappan was a circuit judge when he organized and outfitted the 13th Arkansas Infantry in May 1861, at Harrisburg, Arkansas, using primarily his own funds. The men came from southeastern Arkansas, principally from Phillips, Arkansas, and Monroe Counties. Even though he possessed no military training, Tappan was elected colonel of the regiment, and was commissioned on May 11, 1861. The unit was mustered into the Confederate service in July.

Tappan led his regiment in the fight at Belmont, Missouri (November 7, 1861), for which he was praised by General Leonidas Polk. Tappan then moved his command east of the Mississippi, where they fought gallantly at Shiloh, though Tappan was sick and not present until the second day of the battle. Tappan remained in the Western Theater, until after Bragg's Kentucky invasion, when he was promoted to brigadier general on November 5, 1862, and returned to the Trans-Mississippi Department.

James Camp Tappan

General T. H. Holmes assigned Tappan to command Shaver's Arkansas Brigade on February 28, 1863, and on April 10 he assumed command. He subsequently fought at Pleasant Hill and Jenkins' Ferry, where he earned the praises of both Generals Sterling Price and Thomas Churchill. Tappan was also was part of Price's 1864 Missouri Raid.

"Tappan was a stranger on his arrival" to command his new brigade. The men "rather dreaded him" because they "had heard that he was 'hell on the field of battle.'" In time the men found him to be "gentlemanly to all the privates as well as the officers." Tappan was declared a "noble" general, by a mem

in Batesville-Jacksonport and Northeast Arkansas 1861–1874, (Batesville, AR, 2005), 144, 169–170; "Roster of the Border Rangers of the Second Division of the Arkansas Volunteers—1861," in White County Heritage Civil War Collection Volume 1–25 (Searcy, AR, nd), vol. 1, No. 4:22; Special Orders No. 22 (June 27, 1862), Special Order Book No. 1; Faye O. Strother, "Dandridge McRae An Arkansas General," in White County Heritage Civil War Collection Volume 1–25 (Searcy, AR, nd), vol. 1, No. 4:4–6; Warner, Generals in Gray, 206.

ber of the 27th Arkansas Infantry and one who took care of his men, "and was never threatening to have any" of them shot.

After the war Tappan returned to Helena, practiced law, was again elected to the Arkansas Legislature and twice declined the Democratic Party nomination for Governor of Arkansas. He was a representative to the Democratic National Convention in 1884 and was appointed to the West Point Board of Visitors in 1885. Tappan was the Dean of the Arkansas Bar when he died in Helena, on March 19, 1906.[6]

* * * * * * *

John G. Walker

John George Walker was born in Cole County, Missouri, on July 22, 1822, and attended the Jesuit College in St. Louis (today known as St. Louis University). Upon graduation from college, President James Polk appointed him a first lieutenant in Company K, 1st Mounted Rifles of the U.S. Army on May 27, 1846. He served in the Mexican War, was wounded at the Battle of Molino del Rey, and cited for "gallant and meritorious conduct in that affair at San Juan de los Lianos." On August 1, 1847, Walker was breveted a captain and upon the close of the war remained in the U.S. Army. Prior to the Civil War, Walker served in the western territories or states and received his permanent promotion to captain on June 30, 1851. Walker also took time, in the pre-civil War days, to tour several of the capitals of Europe—London, Paris and Rome—with Senator Stephen Douglas of Illinois.

With the outbreak of the Civil War, Walker resigned his commission on July 31, 1861, while stationed at Fort Union, New Mexico Territory. He journeyed to Richmond, Virginia, where was promoted to major in the Regular Confederate Cavalry on December 21, 1861, to rank from

John George Walker

6. *O.R.*, 3:309; *O.R.*, vol. 10, pt. 1:429–430; *O.R.*, vol. 22, pt. 2:793; *O.R.*, vol. 34, pt. 1:783, 800; *O.R.*, 53: 478; Crute, 50; Faust, 742; Harrell, *Arkansas, Confederate Military History*, 416–417; Nathaniel Cheairs Hughes, Jr., *The Battle of Belmont: Grant Strikes South* (Chapel Hill, NC, 1991), 73; Terry L. Jones, "James Camp Tappan," in *Confederate General*, 6:26–27: Charles Edward Nash, *Biographical Sketches of Gen. Pat Cleburne and Gen. T. C. Hindman Together With Humorous Anecdotes and Reminiscences of the Late Civil War* (Little Rock, AR, 1895; reprint ed., Dayton, OH, 1977), 110; Sifakis, *Who Was Who in the Confederacy*, 275; Turnbo, 221, 233, 270, 274–275; Warner, *Generals in Gray*, 298–299.

March 31, 1861 (Note: According to Norman D. Brown, this John G. Walker is not the same one who is noted as being in the 8th Texas Cavalry. However, the editors of the *Supplement to the Official Records* say that the John G. Walker who commanded Company K, 8th Texas Cavalry was General John G. Walker, the subject of this sketch.)

During the early part of Civil War Walker served in Virginia and North Carolina. He was promoted to brigadier general on January 9, 1862, and earned his promotion to major general on November 8, 1862, for his performance during the Antietam Campaign. He was then transferred to the Trans-Mississippi on November 11, 1862.

After Walker arrived in Little Rock General Holmes assigned him to command of a Texas division on December 23, 1862. Walker took command on the day after Christmas and led the division, which became famously known as "Walker's Texas Division." After successful campaigns in northeast Louisiana (1863), the Red River and Camden Expeditions (1864), Walker replaced General Richard Taylor as commander of the District of Western Louisiana in June, 1864. He completed his Civil War service commanding the District of Texas, New Mexico, and Arizona, being assigned to command in August 1864, and briefly commanding a cavalry corps in April 1865.

As a commander, "none could surpass him," wrote one veteran. "Devoid of ambition, incapable of envy, he was brave, gallant and just." A staff officer of Walker's noted that "the Genl. is the most popular General in the Trans-Mississippi & has acquired his popularity by gallant service in the field." A captain in the 19th Texas Infantry recorded that Walker "was the best Gen. on this side of the Miss. sure treats his men best." Local newspapers "reported 'his unbounded popularity with his men.'" Still another periodical recorded of the general: "We have never heard an officer or private from General Walker's old Division but spoke of him in terms of admiration and attachment."

Physically, Walker was described as "a small man, weight about 140 lbs., height about 5 ft.,10 in., auburn hair, very large blue eyes, long bunch of beard upon his chin, and a mustache, in all a handsome man."

Following the surrender, Walker moved briefly to Mexico and then to London, England. He returned to the United States in the latter part of the 1860s, settling in Winchester, Virginia, where he dabbled in mining and railroad interests. In 1887 President Grover Cleveland appointed Walker as a diplomat to Bogota, Colombia. Walker died on July 20, 1893, in Washington and was buried in Winchester, Virginia.[7]

---

7. *O.R.*, vol. 34, pt. 1:7; *O.R.S.*, pt. 2, vol. 67:786, 798; *O.R.S.*, Index, 5:5415; Blessington, 65, 72–74; Brown, 188 (n. 79); Norman D. Brown, "John George Walker," in *Confederate General*, 6:88–89; Faust, 797; Heitman, 1:996; Lowe, 61–63; Moore, *Missouri, Confederate Military History*, 223–225; Sifakis, *Who Was Who in the Confederacy*, 293; Warner, *Generals in Gray*, 224, 319–320.

Appendix C
Organization of Selected Confederate Units

Abbreviations:
Bat. = Battery
Bn. = Battalion
Brig. Gen. = Brigadier General
Capt. = Captain
Col. = Colonel
Dmtd. = dismounted
EFF = Effectives
(E) = Estimated
Fld. = Field
Gen. = General
K = Killed
K/MW = Killed/ Mortally Wounded

Lieut. = Lieutenant
Lt. Col. = Lieutenant-Colonel
How. howitzer
M = Missing
MSG = Missouri State Guard
Mtd. = mounted
POW = Prisoner of War
SB = smoothbore
ukn. or ? = unknown
unorg. = unorganized
WIA = Wounded In Action
[ ] = Losses

Parsons's Missouri Brigade
Selected Biographies and Organizational
Information of Principle Units

Brigade Organization:
    Roberts Cavalry Company (General Parsons's Escort, Co. I, 4th Missouri Cavalry)
    10th Missouri Infantry (Steen's, Picket's or Moore's)
    11th Missouri (8th, Hunter's, Gunter's, or Burn's)
    12th Missouri (9th, White's or Ponder's)
    16th Missouri (7th, Jackman's, Caldwell's, or Lewis's)
    9th Battalion Missouri Sharpshooters (Pindall's)
    3rd Missouri Field Artillery (Gorham's, Tilden's, Lesueur's)

Roberts Cavalry Company

At the beginning of the Civil War, Leroy D. Roberts organized a cavalry company in Camden County, Missouri, which became Company I, 1st Cavalry Regiment, 6th Division, MSG. His company subsequently fought at all the primary battles in western Missouri in 1861, and at Pea Ridge. In early 1862, Roberts organized Company A for John H. Winston's Regiment, which was dismounted in April 1862 and moved to the east side of the Mississippi River. After Roberts returned with his company in July 1862, General M. M. Parsons requested permission to remount Roberts's command. Meanwhile, Roberts's men procured horses on their own accord and subsequently became the escort company for Parsons's Missouri Brigade on November 9, 1862, with an organization date of September 24. With the departure of General Hindman in March 1863, Roberts's Company was transferred to the 4th Missouri Cavalry Regiment (CSA), where it became Company I. Roberts was later praised by his brigade commander during the Camden Expedition for his performance of duty, recording that he "behaved with marked and distinguished courage." Roberts was wounded and captured at the Battle of Pilot Knob (September 17, 1864), sent to Gratiot and Myrtle Street Prisons in St. Louis, and on November 28 he was transferred to Johnson Island. Final disposition was unknown.[1]

9th Battalion Missouri Sharpshooters (CSA)

Commanded by Lebeus Pindall, the sharpshooter battalion was organized on December 2, 1862, with the appointment of Pindall as unit commander. At Prairie Grove the battalion contained three companies, adding a fourth company on June 7, 1863, just prior to the Battle of Helena. Companies E and F were added on December 15, 1864, from recruits obtained during Price's 1864 Missouri Raid. These last two companies were commanded by a Captain Majors and Samuel M. Morrison.

Pindall was born in Virginia in about 1832 and later moved to Missouri. In early 1861, Pindall was appointed the provost marshall of the 2nd Division, MSG. He was knocked off his horse at the Siege of Lexington by a cannonball, but recovered. Commissioned a lieutenant colonel on January 23, 1862, Pindall led the 3rd Battalion, 2nd Division, MSG, at Pea Ridge. On April 30, 1862, he was made a major in the Confederate service and in May 1862, he was elected lieutenant colonel of J. W. Priest's MSG Regiment at Memphis, Tennessee. Pindall returned to the Trans-Mississippi with Priest's MSG Regiment, in the summer of 1862, and actively recruited for Missourians, which eventually led to his receiving command of the sharpshooter battalion. Pindall, as a Confederate major, fought at Prairie Grove, Helena, and all other engagements in which Parsons's Brigade participated during its service in the Civil War. He was promoted to lieutenant colonel, effective December 15, 1864, after his command added its fifth and sixth companies. After the war, Pindall settled in Desha County, Arkansas. He died while visiting Mexico, Missouri, in July 1885.[2]

10th Missouri Infantry (CSA)

The 10th Missouri Infantry, also known as Steen's of Picket's Regiment, was organized on November 10, 1862, on Mulberry Creek between Van Buren and Clarksville, Arkansas. The regiment was composed of portions of the MSG

1. *O.R.*. vol. 34, pt. 1:830; *O.R.*, vol. 41, pt. 4:8; *O.R.S.*. pt. 2, vol. 38:194, 200, 660; Eakin, *Missouri Prisoners of War*, "Roberts, L. D.," entry; Marmaduke, *Order and Letter Book*, 113; Parsons letters, September 27 and October 17, 1862; Peterson, 176-177; Special Orders No. 38 (November 9, 1862), Special Order Book No. 1.
2. *O.R.*, vol. 3:193; *O.R.*, vol. 8:315; *O.R.*, vol. 13:45; *O.R.*, vol. 53:458, 460; George W. Calvert Letter (November 4, 1913), Skaggs Collection; Bartels, *Bravest of the Brave*, 15, 104; McGhee, *Missouri Confederates*, 110-111; Moore, Skaggs Collection; National Archives, Record Group 109, Confederate Muster Rolls, 9th Battalion Missouri Sharpshooters; Peterson, 82, 99; Wallace, June 7, 1863 and December 15, 1864.

regiments of John W. Priest and John H. Winston, with elements of William O. Coleman's Missouri Cavalry Regiment and contained an initial strength of 1,164 officers and men. The majority of the men were from the Ozarks of southern Missouri and northern Arkansas, while Companies B and I were from the St. Louis area and Companies A and B were from northern Missouri. The regiment served throughout the war and surrendered at Shreveport in June 1865.[3]

Alexander Early Steen, the first commander of the 10th, was born in 1828, in St. Louis. His father, Enoch Steen, was a colonel in the U.S. Army and remained loyal to the Union at the outbreak of the Civil War. The younger Steen served during the Mexican War, receiving a brevet for "gallant and meritorious conduct in the battles of Contreras and Churubusco." Steen mustered out of the army in 1848, but reentered the service in 1852, only to resign on May 10, 1861, upon the capture of Camp Jackson. Joining the MSG, Steen rose to the rank of brigadier general, commanding the 5th Division, MSG. He fought at Wilson's Creek and was present at Lexington, though ill at the time. Steen was absent from his command during Pea Ridge, being in Richmond, Virginia, where he was attempting to secure a generalship in the Confederate Army. On November 10, 1862, Steen was appointed a Confederate colonel and given command of the 10th Missouri Infantry. Steen was killed at Prairie Grove on December 7.[4]

Following Prairie Grove and the death of both the colonel and lieutenant colonel, Alexander Corbin Pickett was made colonel of the 10th. Picket was born on April 11, 1821, in Limestone County, Alabama. A Mexican War veteran, Picket moved to Arkansas, settling in Jacksonport. A lawyer by profession, Pickett helped organize Company G (Jackson Guards), 1st Arkansas Infantry in late April 1861, and was elected captain of the unit on May 19. Following the unit's reorganization, Pickett was not retained, and he returned to Arkansas to organize a battalion of infantry which was incorporated into 10th Missouri Infantry, with Picket as the major of the regiment. Following the death of Colonel Steen and Lieutenant Colonel Chappell at Prairie Grove, Picket was appointed colonel and led his regiment at Helena in July 1863 and during the Campaign for Little Rock in September 1863. Following an election on December 2, 1863, Pickett was relieved of command. After the war Pickett lived in Augusta, Arkansas, serving as a lawyer and judge. He died on January 17, 1883, in Augusta, Arkansas, where he was buried.[5]

William M. Moore next commanded the 10th. He was born on September 30, 1837, in Harrison County, Kentucky, and moved to Missouri in 1839. He gradu-

3. *O.R.*, vol. 22, pt. 2:1057; *O.R.S.*, pt. 2, vol. 38: 596; National Archives, Record Group 109, Confederate Musters Rolls, 10th Missouri Infantry; Moore, Skaggs Collection; Newton to Parsons (November 9, 1862), Copy Letter Book No. 1; Schnetzer, *Men of the Tenth*, ii-iii.

4. *O.R.*, 8:321; *O.R.*, 53:444; Allardice, *More Generals In Gray*, 215-216; Banasik, *Missouri Brothers in Gray*, 155; Heitman, 1:919.

5. *O.R.S.*, pt. 2, vol. 2:273; Allardice, *Confederate Colonels*, 306-307; National Archives, Record Group 109, Confederate Muster Rolls, 10th Missouri Infantry; National Archives, Record Group M311 (roll no. 154), Confederate Compiled Service Records, 10th Missouri Infantry; Moore, Skaggs Collection; Schnetzer, *Men of the Tenth*, 1.

174 / Confederate Tales of the War in the Trans-Mississippi

ated from the University of Missouri and entered the MSG in 1861 as a private in Company B, 1st Cavalry Regiment, 2nd Division, MSG. Appointed the adjutant of the 1st Cavalry and later of the 5th Cavalry Regiment of his division, Moore was wounded in the arm at Lexington in September 1861. Following Pea Ridge, Moore was appointed lieutenant colonel of the 1st Cavalry Regiment. He entered Confederate service on September 1, 1862, as captain of what became Company A, 10th Missouri Infantry (CSA) on November 10. Moore was promoted to lieutenant colonel of the 10th effective December 7, 1862, following the death of William C. Chappell at Prairie Grove. Wounded at Helena on July 4, 1863, Moore was promoted to colonel on December 2, 1863, and was again wounded at the Battle of Jenkins Ferry on April 30, 1864. Following a six-month recovery he took command of Parsons's old brigade, which he led until the end of the war. One old veteran noted that Colonel Moore rode a very intelligent horse that he named "Sneezewood" and further that Colonel Moore was "the most perfect model of a soldier" that he had ever seen. After the war Moore returned to Lewis County, farmed and was elected county sheriff. Moore served in the Missouri Legislature, as both a member and Speaker of the House and moved to Kentucky in 1882, where he served in the Kentucky Legislature (1889–1892). He died at the home of one of his three daughters, in Cynthiana, Kentucky, on December 25, 1927. "Colonel Moore was a gallant soldier, an honorable gentleman, a good citizen, and a sincere Christian…He was honored and respected by the whole community and loved by his friends and Confederate comrades."[6]

11th Missouri Infantry (CSA)

The 11th was organized on Sugar Creek, near the Pea Ridge battlefield on September 15, 1862. The regiment was composed of D. C. Hunter's Cavalry Battalion of seven companies, which had been dismounted on August 31, with an additional three companies that had previously been organized in northwest Arkansas. The initial strength of the regiment was 1,248 officers and men. The men of the regiment came from southwest Missouri counties of Barry, Cass, Cedar, Jasper, Lawrence, Polk, and Vernon, with Company H being raised from Ray County in north Missouri. The regiment served throughout the war and surrendered at Shreveport on June 8, 1865.[7]

DeWitt Clinton Hunter, the first commander of the 11th Missouri, was born on August 2, 1830, in Manchester, Illinois. Prior to the Civil War he prospected

---

6. *O.R.*, vol. 34, pt. 1:815; Allardice, *Confederate Colonels*, 279-280; "Col. W. M. Moore," *Confederate Veteran* 36 (January, 1928), 64; Eakin, *Confederate Records*, 6:14; Flanagan, 48, 57; Moore, *Missouri, Confederate Military History, Extended*, 372-373; Moore, Skaggs Collection; National Archives, Record Group M322, Confederate Service Record, 10th Missouri Infantry; Peterson, 84, 94; Schnetzer, *Men of the Tenth*, 1, 3.

7. *O.R.*, vol. 22, pt. 2: 1057; *O.R.S.*, pt. 2, vol. 38: 609; National Archives, Record Group 109, Confederate Muster Rolls, 11th Missouri Infantry; National Archives, Record Group M861 (roll No. 36), Records of Confederate Movements, 11th Missouri Infantry (CSA); Quesenberry, September 8-15, 1862; Schnetzer, *Men of the Eleventh*, 2,5.

for gold in California and returned east to become a leading citizen of Nevada, Missouri. A lawyer by profession, Hunter surveyed and built the first house of Nevada. At the beginning of the Civil War Hunter was the circuit and country clerk for his home county. He was elected colonel of the 7th Cavalry, 8th Division, MSG on July 10, 1861, and resigned on December 10. While serving in the Guard, Hunter fought in only one battle—Wilson's Creek. Hunter reentered the service as a Confederate major and was sent into Missouri on July 11, 1862, to recruit a regiment of infantry. Hunter organized a cavalry battalion on August 31, 1862, which formed the nucleus of 11th Missouri, which was organized on September 15. Hunter led his command at Prairie Grove on December 7, 1862, after which he resigned on February 4, 1863, though the resignation was not accepted until March 24. Hunter again raised a cavalry regiment in the spring of 1864, and led that command at Marks' Mill, Arkansas (April 25, 1864) and on Price's 1864 Missouri Raid. Following the war Hunter returned to Nevada where he again practiced law. He moved to Oklahoma in the 1880s and died on October 3, 1904, in Checotah.[8]

Thomas M. Gunter, of the 34th Arkansas, briefly commanded the regiment from February 4–March 24, while awaiting the approval of Hunter's resignation and the appointment of a permanent commander.[9]

Simon Pierce Burns, the next permanent commander of the 11th Missouri, was born on January 1, 1834, in Logan County, Ohio, raised in Iowa, then moved to western Missouri and settled in Carthage, Jasper County. At the beginning of the Civil War he was elected second lieutenant of Company D, 5th Cavalry Regiment, 8th Division, MSG and went on to command the company. Burns resigned from the Guard on December 5, 1861, and later enlisted in Dewitt C. Hunter's cavalry battalion as a private on July 21, 1862. He was elected major of Hunter's command on September 1, 1862, and lieutenant colonel on September 15. When Hunter resigned on March 24, 1863, Burns was promoted to colonel by the Confederate Congress on January 8, 1864, to rank from March 24, 1863. On March 25, 1864, Burns was given command of the First Brigade in M. M. Parsons's Missouri Division. As senior colonel in Parsons's Missouri command, Burns expected to be promoted to brigadier general, but instead L. M. Lewis got the nod, causing Burns to leave his command "in a huff & never returned." G. G. Lindsey, a lieutenant in the regiment, supported the reason for Burns's non-promotion, recording that Burns was "lazy in action" and showed "no initiative." After the war Burns moved to Brownwood, Texas, where he took up farming and later served in the Texas Legislature. He died on April 8, 1898, and was buried near his home

8. *O.R.S.*, pt. 2, vol. 38:273-274, 609; Allardice, *Confederate Colonels*, 207; Bartels, *Forgotten Men*, 178; Crute, 208; Hale, 152-153; National Archives, Record Group 109, Confederate Muster Rolls, 11th Missouri Infantry; Snead, 269; Special Orders No. 28 (July 11, 1862), Special Order Book No. 1.
9. *O.R.S.*, pt. 1, vol. 4:71; National Archives, Record Group 109, Confederate Muster Rolls, 11th Missouri Infantry.

town. Sidney Jackman would eulogize Burns, calling him "an excellent [man]... none better."[10]

12th Missouri Infantry (CSA)

The 12th Missouri Infantry (also known as the 9th Missouri, White's, or Ponder's Regiment) was organized on October 22, 1862, at Yellville, Arkansas, just prior to departing the area for the main Confederate Army encamped at Mulberry Creek. The unit served throughout the war.[11]

James Daniel White, the first commander of the regiment, was born on October 23, 1834, in South Carolina and settled in Morley, Scott County, Missouri (Jerry Ponder has White as a resident of Fredericktown, Madison County) prior to the Civil War. A civil engineer by profession, White was commissioned a captain in the 1st Division, MSG, on May 5, 1861, and was elected colonel of the 3rd Cavalry Regiment on October 5, but mustered out in December 1861. General Hindman appointed White commander of a Missouri regiment on August 29, 1862. White led his regiment in only one battle—Helena—at which time he was wounded. Not popular with his command, White resigned from the service on February 13, 1863, departing his regiment on August 28, 1863, and went on to become the Provost Marshal of the Second Arkansas District, which encompassed the lower Arkansas River. Paroled in June 1865, White fled briefly to Mexico, returned to Missouri, settling in Acadia. A post-war contractor for the Iron Mountain Railroad, White died on October 13, 1873, in Lafayette County, Arkansas, of malaria and was returned to Acadia for burial.[12]

The last major commander of the 12th Missouri was Willis M. Ponder. Born in Hickman County, Tennessee, near Bon Aqua Springs on October 12, 1823, Ponder moved to Ripley County, Missouri, in 1843. A farmer and sawmill operator by profession, Ponder also served as the county tax assessor and clerk. At the beginning of the Civil War, he joined the 1st Division, MSG, in early 1861 as a private and then sergeant, being elected major of the 3rd Infantry Regiment on July 8, 1861 for "gallantry" at the Battle of Fredericktown, Missouri. He resigned from the Guard on January 8, 1862, returned to Ripley Country where he organized what became Company A, 12th Missouri in July 1862. When the regiment was organized on October 22, 1862, Ponder was made lieutenant colonel and became colonel of the command when Colonel White departed on August 28, 1863. Ponder was captured on April 18, 1864, near Cotton Plant, Arkansas, and exchanged

---

10. Allardice, *Confederate Colonels*, 84; Bartels, *Forgotten Men*, 13, 42; Lindsey Letter (May 22, 1922), Skaggs Collection; Moore, Skaggs Collection; National Archives, Record Group M322 (roll no. 156), Confederate Service Record, 11th Missouri Infantry; Peterson, 262; Wallace, March 25, 1864.

11. *O.R.*, vol. 22, pt. 2:1057; National Archives, Record Group 109, Confederate Muster Rolls, 12th Missouri Infantry.

12. This short biography corrects one that I wrote on James White in Volume Seven, Part Two of this series. *O.R.*, vol. 48:249; Allardice, *Confederate Colonels*, 391-392; Banasik, *Embattled Arkansas*, 514; Bartels, *Forgotten Men*, 387; Hale, 346-347; National Archives, Record Group 109, Confederate Muster Rolls, 12th Missouri Infantry; Peterson, 53-54.

on January 23, 1865 (National Archives has the exchange date as February 26, 1865). Following the war, Ponder returned to his former profession and was later elected to the state legislature. He died on April 9, 1904, at Walnut Ridge, Lawrence County, Missouri, and was buried in a local cemetery. "Men who knew him and saw him upon the field of battle, and his old comrades all bear witness to the fact, that no braver man ever lived."[13]

16th Missouri Infantry (CSA)

The 16th Missouri Infantry was organized on August 31, 1862, at Camp Hindman, Arkansas, with an initial muster roll of 1267 officers and men. The regiment served throughout the remainder of the war, disbanding just prior to surrender in May 1865.[14]

The first colonel, of what became the 16th Missouri Infantry, was Sidney D. Jackman. He was born on March 7, 1826, in Kentucky, moved to Howard County, Missouri, in 1830, and settled in Bates County, Missouri in 1855. At the beginning of the Civil War, Jackman was a farmer and teacher. Jackman raised a company in Bates County and was elected captain of the unit, which became part of the 9th Cavalry Regiment, 8th Division, MSG. Operating behind enemy lines, Jackman raised two regiments during the war; the first was organized in the fall of 1862, and the second was raised in late spring of 1864. During the war, Jackman was basically a guerrilla leader, participating in only two major engagements: Lone Jack (August 16, 1862) and Westport (October 22–23, 1864). Jackman fled to Mexico at the close of the war, but soon moved to Texas, settling in Hays County. As a Texan, Jackman served in the legislature and was a U.S. marshall. He died at his Texas ranch on June 2, 1886.[15]

Josiah Hatcher Caldwell followed Jackman in command of the 16th. He was born on September 30, 1822, in Green County, Kentucky. Trained as a doctor at the University of Louisville Medical School, Caldwell was a practicing physician in Warrensburg, Missouri, at the beginning of the Civil War. On June 30, 1861, he was elected first lieutenant of Company G, 3rd Infantry Regiment, 8th Division, MSG, but resigned on October 21 (Allardice has the date as October 23). Governor C. F. Jackson appointed Caldwell a member of the MSG Medical Examining Board, a position he held until the Guard was disbanded. Caldwell later

---

13. *O.R.S.*, pt. 2, vol. 50:623, 627; Allardice, *Confederate Colonels*, 309; "Col. W. M. Ponder," Newspaper Clipping File, Skaggs Collection; Crute, 204; National Archives, Record Group 109, Confederate Muster Rolls, 12th Missouri Infantry; National Archives, Record Group M322 (roll no. 164), Compiled Service Records, 12th Missouri Infantry (CSA); Peterson, 65.

14. *O.R.*, vol. 22, pt. 2:1057; *O.R.S.*. pt. 2, vol. 38:646; Crute, 205; National Archives, Record Group 109, Confederate Muster Rolls, 16th Missouri Infantry.

15. See Volume 7, Part Two of this series for a complete biography. Allardice, *Confederate Colonels*, 210-211; Allardice, *More Generals In Gray*, 133-135; Crute, 201, 208; Mrs. Mary Jackman Mullins, "Sketch of Col. Sidney D. Jackman," in *Missouri During the Sixties* (Jefferson City, MO, 1911), 93-96; Richard L. Norton, *Behind Enemy Lines: The Memoirs and Writings of Brigadier General Sidney Drake Jackman* (Springfield, MO, 1997), v, 3-9, 19.

joined the Confederate service, being elected lieutenant colonel of what became the 16th Missouri Infantry on September 1, 1862. Following the resignation of S. D. Jackman on October 23, 1862, Caldwell was made colonel of the regiment with an effective date of December 4. Caldwell fought with "confidence" at Prairie Grove, on December 7, 1862, and was worthy of his commission, according to his brigade commander. However, his men had a lesser opinion of Caldwell, with one soldier calling him "the meanest Col. now that I have ever been under." Caldwell, himself admitted "that he was deficient in tactics and could do more good as a physician." He tendered his resignation on January 21, 1863, which was accepted March 24, 1863. He moved to Texas following the war and died at Waco on September 29, 1896.[16]

The last colonel of the 16th was Levin Major Lewis, who was born in Maryland on January 6, 1832. He attended school in Washington, D.C., the Maryland Military Academy, and Wesleyan University in Middletown, Connecticut. He moved to Clay County, Missouri, about 1854, becoming a lawyer, preacher, and then a school teacher. When the Civil War began, Lewis was elected colonel of the 3rd Infantry Regiment, 3rd Division, MSG. He later joined the Confederate Army, as the colonel of the 16th Missouri Infantry. Lewis was captured at Helena on July 4, 1863, and exchanged in September 1864. Kirby Smith appointed Lewis a brigadier general on May 16, 1865, but he was never confirmed by the Confederate Congress. He died in 1886, and was buried in Dallas, Texas.[17]

3rd Missouri Field Artillery (CSA)

This Missouri battery had its roots in Gorham's MSG Battery, having obtained its guns from Henry Guibor's MSG Battery, which was disbanded in October 1861. It was part of the 6th Division, MSG, and initially contained four 6-pound iron smoothbore guns. By Prairie Grove the battery contained two 6-pound smoothbores and two 12-pound howitzers, which it carried through the remainder of the war. James C. Gorham, who commanded the battery, was from Marshall, Saline County, Missouri, and remained with the battery until General Thomas C. Hindman replaced him with Charles B. Tilden on November 10, 1862.

Charles B. "Buck" Tilden was born in Maryland in about 1835, and lived in St. Louis at the beginning of the Civil War. He was first elected second lieutenant of the "Plattin Rangers Company," 1st Division, MSG, and then first lieutenant of Gorham's MSG Battery. After Pea Ridge Tilden entered Confederate service and was appointed first lieutenant of Gorham's reorganized battery on September 24, 1862. On November 10, 1862, Thomas C. Hindman (National Archives has Parsons making the appointment) appointed Tilden commander of Gorham's Battery, which was renamed "Tilden's Battery." Tilden was at Prairie Grove, but elected

---

16. *O.R.*, 53:461; *O.R.S.*, pt. 2, vol. 38:646; Allardice, *Confederate Colonels*, 87; Bartels, *Trans-Mississippi Men*, 233-234; Lotspeich, February 2, 1863; Schnetzer, *More Forgotten Men*, 39.
17. See Appendix B for a complete biography. Allardice, *Confederate Colonels*, 238; Allardice, *More Generals In Gray*, 142-143; Turnbo, 384.

not to lead his battery at Helena. He was thrown out as battery commander on December 18, 1863, in part for being an inefficient officer, but more specifically because of his failure to lead his company at Helena.

Alexander Lesueur, the next and last commander of the battery, was born in St. Louis in 1842 and graduated from St. Louis University in 1858. He joined Joseph Kelly's St. Louis Volunteer Militia Company prior to the Civil War and avoided capture at Camp Jackson on May 10, 1861. Prior to joining the artillery, Lesueur rose to the grade of sergeant major in Kelly's 1st Regiment, 6th Division, MSG. He was elected second lieutenant of Gorham's MSG Battery in late September 1861. As a Guard member, Lesueur fought in all the early battles in Missouri and was wounded at Wilson's Creek. When his battery entered Confederate service in September 1862, Lesueur remained with the unit, ascending to the rank of first lieutenant on November 10, 1862. Lesueur was elected captain of the battery in December 1863, in part because his leadership at Helena. Lesueur also participated in the Red River and Camden Campaigns of 1864. Following the war Lesueur settled for a time in Lexington, where he edited the *Lexington Intelligencer*. He was a member of the state legislature and served three terms as the Missouri secretary of state, prior to 1896. Lesueur died on January 16, 1924, in Burbank, California.[18]

* * * * * * *

Organization of Walker's Texas Division[19]
(December 26, 1862)

Walker's Texas Division was initially organized on September 28, 1862, with two brigades. Upon the death of Allison Nelson, who commanded another division, on October 7, 1862, Walker's command was increased to three brigades. Deshler's 4th Brigade was later added to the division, but was detached and ordered to Arkansas Post on November 22, 1862, leaving the division with three brigades as shown below. Henry McCulloch, brother of Ben McCulloch, initially commanded the division, and on December 23, 1863, T. H. Holmes appointed Walker commander of what became known as "Walker's Texas Division." Three

18. *O.R.*, vol. 22, pt. 1:421; *O.R.*, vol. 34, pt. 1:816; *O.R.*, vol. 53:461; Banasik, *Missouri Brothers In Gray*, 27, 43, 55; Eakin, *Confederate Records*, 5:56; Hoskins, December 18, 1863; Moore, *Missouri, Confederate Military History, Extended*, 338-339; National Archives, Record Group M322 (roll no. 85), Confederate Compiled Service Records, 3rd Field Battery Missouri Artillery; Jeffery Patrick, ed. "Remembering the Missouri Campaign of 1861: The Memoirs of Lieutenant William P. Barlow, Guibor's Battery, Missouri State Guard," *A Journal of the American Civil War* 5 (No. 4, 1997), 49-50; Peterson, 56, 192.

19. The initial structure of the division is based upon Blessington's account of the division and adjusted by the other references as needed. *O.R.*, 13:884-885, 928; *O.R.*, vol. 22, pt. 1:904; *O.R.*, vol. 34, pt. 1:314; Blessington, 46, 50, 54, 64-65, 77, 164-165; Brown, 188 (n. 79); Crute, 331; Lowe, 41-42, 81, 160, 249-252, 255; Wooster, 127-128, 224-226, 251, 291-292, 302-303.

days later, Walker was announced as the commander of the division, during a dress parade, and on January 1, 1863, he assumed command. On April 24, 1863, the division left its camp at Pine Bluff and marched off to Louisiana, there to participate in assorted operations including Operations to Relieve Vicksburg (June–July 1863), Bayou Bourbeau (November 3, 1863), Red River Campaign (1864) and Camden Expedition (1864). In March 1865 the division returned to Texas where it slowly fell apart, being disbanded in May 1865, near Hempstead, Texas.

1st Brigade—Colonel Overton Young (Sept. 28, 1862–April 24, 1863); Brig. Gen. J. M. Hawes (April 25–Feb. 1864; relieved); Brig. Gen. T. N. Waul (Feb. 1864–end)
>   12th Texas Infantry (Lt. Col. B. A. Philpot)
>   18th Texas Infantry (Col. W. B. Ochiltree)
>   22nd Texas Infantry (Col. R. B. Hubbard)
>   13th Texas Cavalry (Dmtd., Col. J. H. Burnett)
>   4th Texas Fld. Art. (Capt. Horace Halderman)
>   4 guns: two 12-lb how. & two 6-lb SB

NOTE: The 12th Infantry was also known as the 8th Texas Infantry.

2nd Brigade—Colonel Horace Randal
>   11th Texas Infantry (Col. O. M. Roberts)
>   14th Texas Infantry (Col. Edward Clarke)
>   28th Texas Cavalry (Dmtd., Lt. Col. E. H. Baxter)
>   Gould's or 23rd Texas Cavalry (Dmtd., Major Robert S. Gould)
>   9th Texas Fld. Battery (Lamar Battery; Capt. James Daniels)
>   4 guns: two 12-lb how. & two 6-lb SB

NOTE: The 15th Texas Infantry served briefly in this brigade but was transferred on December 16, 1862, for service in the Indian Territory.

3rd Brigade—Brig. Gen. H. E. McCulloch (Reassigned, Aug. 1863); Colonel George Flournoy.
>   16th Texas Infantry (Lt. Col. J. Shepard)
>   17th Texas Infantry (Col. R. T. P. Allen)
>   19th Texas Infantry (Col. R. Waterhouse)
>   16th Texas Cavalry (Dmtd., Col. William Fitzhugh)
>   1st Texas Fld. Battery (Alamo Battery; Capt. William M. Edgar)
>   6 guns: one 12-lb how. & five 6-lb SB

* * * * * * *

Organization of Confederate Forces at Helena, Arkansas
(July 4, 1863)

Introduction:

It appears from various accounts, the men in the artillery companies who served as infantry were counted in the effective totals of the units that they were assigned to; however those that worked the artillery pieces were not counted as effective men. See comment under Fagan's Brigade for details.

Also, by the time of the battle, escort companies for the various brigade, division, or army commanders had disappeared. However every brigade, division, or army commander had staff with them at the battle, some of whom were casualties, like Major George Gallagher, Assistant Adjutant General of Holmes's staff. To the overall Confederate strength it would be safe to add 12 men for Marmaduke's staff, as division commanders, as well as the same amount for Holmes as the army commander. Price for his part, listed 17 members of his staff who participated in the battle. The assorted brigade commanders could be counted on for about 6 staff members each, unless otherwise known—this would account for aides, commissaries, ordnance personnel, etc., for more than 36 additional effectives. Parsons, for his part, listed 6 members of his staff who assisted in the battle, but also implied there were others. General Fagan listed his staff as 8 members, who took part in the battle. Overall Holmes's command probably carried more men into the battle than he actually reported, with the assorted staff adding at least another 79 men to his reported 7,646 engaged or 7,725.[20]

There are also indications that Holmes, as well as the other commanders, only listed men as their effectives. See the 9th & 10th Missouri Infantry, Parsons's Brigade for a comment on this. However, as the evidence is scant, the number as reported by Holmes and his commanders is generally used, except as noted above and in the individual units, where applicable.

General references:

1. *O.R.*, vol. 22, pt. 1:412, 422–423, 438.
2. *Battles and Leaders of the Civil War*, 3:461.
3. Bearss, "Battle of Helena," 295–297.

* * * * * * *

Confederate Forces (Lieut. Gen. T. H. Holmes):
    Staff: EFF = 12 (E) [0 K, 1 WIA, 0 M]
Price's Division (Maj. Gen. Sterling Price):
    Staff: EFF = 17 [0 K, 0 WIA, 0 M][21]

---

20. *O.R.*, vol. 22, pt. 1:411, 416-17, 423, 427; "Additional From Helena," *Arkansas State Gazette*, July 11, 1863; "Attack On Helena," *Arkansas State Gazette*, July 11, 1863; "The Battle of Helena," *Tri-Weekly Telegraph*, August 12, 1863.
21. General Price in his official Report of the battle noted the presence of 17 staff members while

McRae's Brigade (Brig. Gen. Dandridge McRae):
  Staff: EFF = 6 (E) [0 K, 0 WIA, 0 M]
  Sharpshooters, Co. B, 39th Ark. Inf. (Capt. C. N. Biscoe)
    EFF = See 39th Ark. [1 K, 3 WIA, 2 M][22]
  32nd Ark. Inf. (Col. Lucian C. Gause)
    EFF = 391 [17 K, 46 WIA, 26 M][23]
  36th Ark. Inf. (Col. John E. Glenn)
    EFF = 451 [21 K, 70 WIA, 68 M][24]
  39th Ark. Inf. (or 30th Ark.; Col. Robert A. Hart, WIA, POW; Lieut. Col. James W. Rogan)
    EFF = 349 [7 K, 43 WIA, 37 M][25]
  Marshall's Ark. Bat. (Capt. John G. Marshall)
    EFF = 36 [0 K, 6 WIA, 0 M][26]
  McRae's Brigade Total = 1,233 EFF[27]
  Brigade Losses = [46 K, 168 WIA, 133 M][28]
    Brigade Total Losses = 347 K/WIA/M

Parsons's Brigade (Brig. Gen. Mosby M. Parsons):[29]

---

another 2 were absent. *O.R.*, vol. 22, pt. 1:416-417.

22. During the battle, the company was attached to Pindall's Missouri Sharpshooters. *O.R.*, vol. 22, pt. 1:421; *O.R.S.*, pt. 2, vol. 2:729.

23. The 32nd Arkansas showed an effective strength of 391 on May 31, 1863. There would have been little change in their strength from that date until the battle on July 4. National Archives, Record Group 109, Confederate Muster Rolls, 32nd Arkansas Infantry.

24. The strength of the 36th is calculated based on the stated strength of McRae's Brigade and the values of the other units. *O.R.*, vol. 22, pt. 1:413; National Archives, Record Group 109, Confederate Muster Rolls, 32nd and 30th/39th Arkansas Infantry; Young, 114.

25. The regiment was also known as the 30th Arkansas, Hart's Regiment or the 5th Trans-Mississippi Regiment. The regiment became the 39th after April 1863. The losses suffered by Company B have been extracted from the regiment and are embraced under the Sharpshooter Company for the Brigade. *O.R.*, vol. 22, pt. 1:412, 417; *O.R.S.*, pt. 2, vol. 2:723, 727; Crute, 56; National Archives, Record Group 109, Confederate Muster Rolls, 30th/39th Arkansas Infantry.

26. Captain Marshall left his artillery behind and ordered his men armed with muskets to participate in the assault as infantry, per directions from division headquarters. Additionally, if the situation should arise, his men were to man captured artillery and turn them on the enemy. As too strength, Robert E. Young, of Tilden's Battery also in Price's Division, recorded that orders were issued from headquarters, stating that his battery was to detail 35 men and one lieutenant to serve as sharpshooters. Since Marshall's Battery and Tilden's were both four gun batteries and both served in the same division, it seems reasonable that both commands would have provided the same size detachment. *O.R.*, vol. 22, pt. 1:413, 418; Young, 114.

27. *O.R.*, vol. 22, pt. 1:413.

28. *Ibid.*, 412, 420.

29. The effective strength of the various regiments was calculated using the known effective strength of all the regiments on July 6. The men lost as either killed or missing on July 4 are then added to the values as reported as effective on July 6. This method yields 1,708 effectives, leaving 160 men unaccounted for based upon the stated brigade effective strength of 1,868 on July 4. From the 160, Lesueur's Detachment of 36 is subtracted to account for the men of the Tilden's Battery who served as infantry, leaving 124 still unaccounted for. The remaining men would have come from those listed as wounded on July 4. The total wounded, excluding Tilden's Battery were 296 men. This total is then

Staff: EFF = 6 [0 K, 0 WIA, O M]
Pindall's Sharpshooters (Maj. L. A. Pindall)
   EFF = 185 [9 K, 26 WIA, 8 M]
7th (16th) Missouri Inf. (Col. Levin M. Lewis, POW)
   EFF = 444 [16 K, 124 WIA, 53 M]
8th (11th) Missouri Inf. (Col. Simon P. Burns)
   EFF = 525 [14K, 78 WIA, 66 M]
9th (12th) Missouri Inf. (Col. James D. White, WIA)
   EFF = 199 [12 K, 27 WIA, 15 M][30]
10th Missouri Inf. (Col. Alexander C. Pickett)
   EFF = 479 [10 K, 41 WIA, 220 M][31]
Tilden's Missouri Battery (Lt. L. L. Lesueur)
   EFF = 36 [1 K, 8 WIA, 3 M][32]
Parsons' Brigade Total = 1,874 EFF[33]

---

divided into the wounded from each individual regiment to get the percentage of wounded that they contributed to the overall loss in the brigade as follows:

Unit	WIA Loss	% of Bde Loss	Proportion of 124	Total EFF
7th Inf.	124	42%	52	444
8th Inf.	78	26%	32	525
9th Inf.	27	9%	11	199
10th Inf.	41	14%	18	479
Pindall's SS	26	9%	11	185
Lesueur's Det	--	--	--	36
Brigade Totals	296	100%	124	1868

O.R., vol. 22, pt. 1:412, 423; Young, 114.

30. Of the 10 companies in the regiment 8 have known strengths for the Battle of Helena: A (47), B (?), C (15), D (20), E (29), F (23), G (?), H (7), I (18), K (12); for a total of 171 "men." Of the two companies, "B" and "G," which have no stated strength, it appears that they carried few if any men into the battle, in a similar vein as the rest of the companies. My number of 199 would appear to be a good number, though this number may include both "officers and men." *O.R.S.*, pt. 2, vol. 38:628-637.

31. Of the 10 companies in the regiment 8 have a known strength at Helena: A (80), B (67), C (30), D (57), E (40), F (?), G (37), H (30), I (45), K (?); total = 386. Further, Lieutenant M. C. Helterbrand, of Company I, noted that "nearly 500...went into the engagement." This would seem to support my figure of 479 as being "men" who were in the battle from the 10th Missouri Infantry, and did not include officers. *Ibid.*, 600, 602-608.

32. The number of men in the detachment varied from 30, as reported by General Parsons to 36 as recorded by Robert Young. William Bull put the number at 32. In this case Young's numbers were used because of his statement, which read—"we received orders from headquarters to equip thirty-five men as sharpshooters with one lieutenant and report them to Major Pindall." *O.R.*, vol. 22, pt. 1:413, 421; Banasik, *Missouri Brothers in Gray*, 55, 60; Young, 114.

33. In reporting the strength of the brigade at Helena, it's unclear as to whether the total included officers and men or just "men" as stated by General Price. In recalling the battle one veteran noted that the brigade carried 2,200 "officers and men" into the battle, "leaving only 1,300 to answer the roll call [the] next day." In his after action report Parsons listed his "effective aggregate"—which would be

Brigade Losses = [62 Killed, 304 WIA, 362 M]
Brigade Total Losses = 728 K/WIA/M
Price's Division Total = 3,124 EFF
Total Division Losses = [108 K, 472 WIA, 495 M;
Division Total Losses = 1,075 K/WIA/M[34]

* * * * * * *

Fagan's Independent Brigade (Brig. Gen. James F. Fagan):[35]
Staff: EFF = 8 [0 K, 0 W, 0 M]
Hawthorn's Ark. Regt. (Col. Alexander T. Hawthorn)
EFF = 453 (E) [17 K, 53 WIA, 67 M]
Bell's Ark. Regt. (37th; Col. Samuel S. Bell)
EFF = 432 [14 K, 17 WIA, 191 M][36]
King's Ark. Regt. (35th; Col. James P. King)
EFF = 454 (E) [16 K, 44 WIA, 15 M]
Brigade Total = 1,347 EFF
Brigade Losses = [47 K, 114 WIA, 273 M]
Brigade Total Losses = 434 K/WIA/M

Detached (Col. William H. Brooks):[37]
3 Cos. of Cav. (Capt. W. B. Denson)
EFF = 129 (E) [0 K, 3 WIA, 0 M][38]

---

men—as 1,359 on July 6, which given the losses of 728 seems to support Robert Young's comment as to the brigade's strength at Helena. *O.R.*, vol. 22, pt. 1:413, 421; Young, 118.

34. The losses and strength are those reported by General Price and differ from those recorded by T. H. Holmes, who reported 108 killed, 472 wounded and 498 missing for a total of 1078. General Holmes report was written a month after Price's report, which would suggest that corrections had been made to the losses that Price suffered. *O.R.*, vol. 22, pt. 1:408, 412-413, 415, 422.

35. The *Arkansas State Gazette*, reported that Fagan's Brigade had "500 men detached from it, including Capt. Blocker's [Blocher's] battery." Fagan reported that he had 1,339 men "engaged against Fort Hindman." Thomas L. Snead has Fagan's Brigade at 1,770 effectives, including the 34th Arkansas infantry—this would give the 34th 431 effectives. Subtracting 431 from 500, as reported in the *Gazette*, would give Etter's Section of Artillery and Blocher's Battery, 69 men or 11.5 men per gun. Of the three infantry units, in Fagan's Brigade, which assaulted Battery D, only Bell's Regiment has a known strength of 432 effectives. The other two regiments are estimated by subtracting the 432 from 1,339 (the known strength of Fagan's three regiments), leaving 907 men or 453.5 men per regiment. The staff for the brigade was 8 men. *O.R.*, vol. 22., pt. 1:426-427, 433; "Attack On Helena," *Arkansas State Gazette*, July 11, 1863; "The Battle of Helena," *Tri-Weekly Telegraph*, August 12, 1863; Snead, "Conquest of Arkansas," 3:456.

36. *O.R.*, vol. 22, pt. 1:433.

37. See note no. 35 above for details on the detachment.

38. Denson's Louisiana Calvary Company shows a strength of 53 "present for duty" on April 30, 1863; using this as the basis for the three companies that Denson commanded at Helena would give his command 159 present for duty. To determine the effectives in the command I used Marmaduke's Cavalry Division, which has a known effective strength at Helena of 1,750 "men"—this may not include officers; however I will treat it as including both officers and men. The "present for duty" strength of Marmaduke's two brigades that were at Helena was 2,152 on May 20, 1863. The 1,750 effectives represent 81 % of those present on May 20; 44 days before the battle. There's no reason to

Brooks' Ark. Regt. (34th; Col. William H. Brooks)
    EFF= 431 [O K, 1 WIA, 0 M]
Blocher's Ark. Art. (Capt. William D. Blocher) 2 12-lb How.; 2 6-lb SB[39]
    EFF = 46 [0 K, 0 WIA, 0 M]
Etter's Ark. Art., Sec. (Lt. J. C. Arnett) 2 10-lb parrots[40]
    EFF = 23 [0 K, 0 WIA, 0 M]
    Detachment Total = 629 EFF
    Detachment Losses = [0 K, 4 WIA, 0 M]
        Detachment Total Losses = 4 K/WIA/M
Fagan's Brigade EFF = 1,976
Fagan's Losses = [47 K, 118 W, 273 M]
    Brigade Total Losses = 438 K/WIA/M

Marmaduke's Division (Brig. Gen. John S. Marmaduke):
    Staff: EFF = 12 [1 K, 0 W, 0 M]
    Greene's Brigade (Col. Colton Green):[41]
        Staff: EFF = 6 (E) [0 K, 0 WIA, 0 M]
        3rd Mo. Cav. (Lt. Col. L.C. Campbell)
            EFF = 262 (E) [3 K, 6 WIA, 0 M]
        8th Mo. Cav. (Col. W.L. Jeffers)
            EFF = 263 (E) [1 K, 0 WIA, 0 M]
        Kitchen's Mo. Cav. Bn. (Lt. Col. Solomon G. Kitchen)[42]
            EFF = 131 (E) [0 K, 0 WIA, 0 M]
        Young's Mo. Cav. Bn. (Lt. Col. M. L.Young)
            EFF = 131 (E) [1 K, 1 WIA, 0 M]
        Greene's Brigade EFF = 787[43]

---

suspect that Denson's command would be much different from the other cavalry in the area. As such, 81 % of 159 men in Denson's Battalion would yield 129 effectives. *O.R.*, vol. 22, pt. 1:412, 430, 436; *O.R.*, vol. 22, pt. 2:832, 845.

39. Banasik, *Embattled Arkansas*, 513.

40. *O.R.*, vol. 22, pt. 1:430; *O.N.R.*, 25:229; Bearss, "Battle of Helena," 273; Letter (July 7, 1862), Newton to Dodge, Copy Letter Book No. 1.

41. The strength of the various units was prorated based upon and equal division of the troops among the various elements, with a battalion being counted as 1/2 of a regiment or 131 per battalion or 262 men per regiment. Also see note concerning Kitchen's Battalion for some added strength to the brigade.

42. Crute identified the battalion as being in Shelby's Brigade and present at Helena, with the losses as stated. However, its clear from Marmaduke's Order Book, that Kitchen's Battalion was part of Colton Greene's Brigade, being assigned to duty on June 3, 1863. Green's Brigade was ordered from Wittsburg on June 23 and there is no reason to expect that Greene would have left the battalion behind, as John Q. Burbridge's command was tasked with picketing northeast Arkansas, while Green's command was absent at Helena. Crute, 208-209; Marmaduke, *Order and Letter Book*), 192; Sellmeyer, 105.

43. The staff figures have been added to the brigade total, which increases the strength of the brigade as reported by General Marmaduke. Additionally, as it appears that Kitchen's Battalion was never engaged in the battle, Marmaduke probably did not included those men as part of his force at the battle. Additionally, Marmaduke, stated that his "mounted command" include 650 men of Greene's Brigade at the battle. Does this mean that their were dismounted men who were present and serving

Greene's Brigade Losses = [5 K, 7 WIA, 0 M][44]
Brigade Total Losses = 12 K/WIA/M

Shelby's Brigade (Col. Joseph O. Shelby, WIA; Col. G. W. Thompson):[45]
Staff: EFF = 6(E) [0 K, 2 WIA, 0 M]
5th Mo. Cav. Regt. (Lt. Col. B. F. Gordon)
EFF = 344 (E) [3 K, 11 WIA, 0 M]
6th Mo. Cav. Regt. (Col. G. W. Thompson; Lt. Col. J. C. Hooper)
EFF = 344 (E) [1 K, 17 WIA, 1 M]
Jean's Mo. Cav. Regt. (Col. B. G. Jeans)
EFF = 343 (E) [3 K, 9 WIA, 0 M]
Elliot's Mo. Bn. (Maj. Benjamin Elliot)[46]
EFF = 69 (E) [0 K, 0 WIA, 0 M]
Bledsoe's Mo. Bat. (Capt. Joseph Bledsoe)[47] 2 10-lb parrots; 1 6-lb Brass; 1 6-lb iron
EFF = 46 (E) [1 K, 6 WIA, 0 M]
Shelby's Brigade EFF = 1,152[48]
Shelby's Brigade Losses = [8 K, 45 WIA, 1 M]
Brigade Total Losses = 54 K/WIA/M
Marmaduke's Division = 1,951 EFF
Marmaduke's Division Losses = [14 K, 52 WIA, 1 M]
Division Total Losses = 67 K/WIA/M

Walker's Cavalry Brigade (Brig. Gen. Lucius M. Walker):[49]
Staff: EFF = 6 [0 K, 0 WIA, 0 M]
5th Ark. Cav. (Col. Robert C. Newton)

---

at the battle? As such, and additional 131 men were added to Greene's total to reflect the presence of Kitchen's Battalion at the battle. *O.R.*, vol. 22, pt. 1:434, 436; Crute, 208-209.

44. This differs from Holmes' Official Report as Kitchen's Battalion has been added in, where Holmes never mentioned it in his report, though clearly the battalion was in the battle. *O.R.*, vol. 22, pt. 1:412, 438; Crute, 209.

45. The various commanders come from Bearss' account of the battle. The strength of the various units are estimated based on a prorated basis, with 10 companies per regiment, with 2 companies for Elliot's Battalion, for a total of 32 companies or 34.38 men per. *O.R.S.*, pt. 2, vol. 38:201-204, 216-218, 252, 260-262; Bearss, "Battle of Helena," 296; R. P. Marshall Letter (January 29, 1912), Skaggs Collection.

46. Though not listed under either Marmaduke's or Holmes's Order of Battle, it appears that Elliot was present with his command. *O.R.*, vol. 22, pt. 1:412, 436, 438.

47. Effective men present is based upon 11.5 men per gun as seen under Blocker and Etter's Arkansas Batteries. Battery composition the same as the brigade had on their raid in April-May 1863. *O.R.*, vol. 22, pt. 1:289; Banasik, *Missouri Brothers in Gray*, 111.

48. The staff figures and Bledsoe's men have been added to the brigade total, which increases the strength of the brigade as reported by General Marmaduke. Additionally, Marmaduke, stated that his "mounted command" include 1,100 men of Shelby's Brigade at the battle. Does this mean that their were dismounted men who were present and serving at the battle? *O.R.*, vol. 22, pt. 1:434, 436.

49. Snead places the combined strength of Walker's and Marmaduke's commands at 2781 men. Marmaduke listed his command with 1,750 effectives; this would leave 1,031 men for Walker's Brigade. *O.R.*, vol. 22, pt. 1:436; Snead, "Conquest of Arkansas," 3:456.

EFF = 581 [8 K & WIA][50]
Dobbin's Ark. Cav. (Col. Archibold Dobbin)
   EFF = 450 [4 K, 8 WIA, 0 M][51]
Griswold's Mo. Battery (Capt. Daniel B. Griswold)[52] 4 12-lb Mt. How.
   EFF = 46 (E) [ukn]
Walker's Cavalry Brigade EFF = 1,083[53]
Walker's Losses (incomplete)= [4 K, 8 WIA, 0 M; + 8 K & WIA]
   Brigade Total Losses (incomplete) = 20 K/WIA/M
Total Confederate Effectives = 8,146
Total Confederate Losses = [173 K, 651 WIA, 769 M][54]
   Grand Total Confederate Losses = 1,593[55]

---

50. The strength of Newton's Regiment was calculated by subtracting the known value of Dobbin's Regiment from the overall brigade total, leaving the 5th Arkansas with 581, effectives. The losses come from Major John Bull, who wrote a personal letter regarding the battle as recorded in *Missouri Brothers in Gray*. *O.R.*, vol. 22, pt. 1:436; Banasik, *Missouri Brothers in Gray*, 112; Crute, 60; Snead, "Conquest of Arkansas," 3:456.

51. Crute, 208-209.

52. Though not listed on Holmes's Order of Battle it was clear from the official reports of both R. C. Newton and A. S. Dobbin, that Walker's command contained a four gun battery. A review of the Official Records and the National Archives Records, shows that Griswold's Missouri Battery was "attached" to Kitchen's Missouri Cavalry Battalion and Crute's *Units of the Confederate Army* places Kitchen's Battalion at Helena, where they took an active part. There's no reason to believe that Kitchen would have left his battery back in Greene County, Arkansas, when ordered to join Marmaduke's Division for their movement on Helena. The strength of the battery was based upon Blocher's Arkansas Battery as it was also a 4 gun battery. Bearss in his Order of Battle has Bell's Missouri Artillery as part of Walker's command—which I suspect was because the Hamilton's or Bell's Battery was part of Green's Brigade while at Jacksonport in May 1863. Also, the National Archives has Bell's or Hamilton Battery listed as a "2 gun" battery. That said, Hamilton's/Bell's and Griswold's Batteries could have been combined for the Battle of Helena, thus producing a 4 gun battery. By the Battle of Pine Bluff, Hamilton's/Bell's Battery had disappeared from the records and Griswold's command was listed as a 4 gun "mountain" battery. *O.R.*, vol. 22, pt. 1:412, 433-435; *O.R.*, vol. 22, pt. 2: 943, 1054; Bartels, *Forgotten Men*, 137; Bearss, "Battle of Helena," 297; Crute, 208-209; National Archives, Record Group M322 (roll no. 83), Confederate Compiled Service Records, 13th Missouri Battery (Griswold's); National Archives, Record Group M322 (roll no. 88), Confederate Compiled Service Records, Hamilton's Missouri Battery (also known as Bell's Battery).

53. Strength also includes the men of the battery and staff as shown under previous notes.

54. The losses reflect those reported by Holmes on August 14, as noted in his Addenda, with additional figures added for units that he missed, including; Major George A. Gallagher of his staff who was wounded; and 3 wounded from Denson's Cavalry Squadron. Also, according to an Official Record note, concerning Parsons' Brigade, it was clear that the figures listed on Holmes' Addenda seems to be the correctly reported figures for the Confederate losses at Helena. The Addenda also noted that the 5th Arkansas Cavalry's report of losses was missing—An additional 8 men Killed and Wounded should be added to the overall losses, based upon a personal letter recorded by Major John P. Bull of said command. *O.R.*, vol. 22, pt. 1:422, 430; Banasik, *Missouri Brothers In Gray*, 112; "The Battle of Helena," *Washington Telegraph*, July 15, 1863.

55. Note—8 additional K/WIA/M should be added to the overall total to reflect those losses from the 5th Arkansas Cavalry, of Walker's Brigade, that are not known as to whether they were K or WIA. The new overall total would then be 1,601 K/WIA/M. See note no. 50 for details.

Confederate Order of Battle
Pine Bluff, Arkansas (October 25, 1862)

Introduction:

Determining the strength of Marmaduke's command at Pine Bluff should be relatively easy, given an official monthly return from his division, dated October 31, 1863, and the by name casualty report that Marmaduke submitted with his official report on the battle. The return listed the number of officers and men present for duty, including the number of artillery pieces in each brigade. Overall, Confederate effective strength is based upon the number of enlisted men present for duty, excluding officers as seen by a note attached to an "Abstract From Return" for December 31, 1863. By adding in the officer strength, this process would yield 3,575 as Marmaduke's effective strength at Pine Bluff (excluding the dismounted cavalry regiment which was not present at the battle), with 18 pieces of artillery. These figures are then adjusted by adding in 72 for those men killed or wounded (excluding slightly wounded personnel), at Pine Bluff, giving the division strength of 3,647 officers and men that should have been at Pine Bluff. Additionally as a cavalry unit, to be effective, a sufficient amount of horses must be available to mount the command. On October 31, 6450 serviceable horses were noted as in Marmaduke's command; so a sufficient number of horses were available for both the men and the artillery that they would have taken on the raid.

However, for the Battle of Pine Bluff, Marmaduke listed his strength as "twenty-three hundred (2300) men and twelve (12) pieces of artillery;" a far cry from what he had as effective for October 31. With scant information available as to the actual number at the battle, save Marmaduke's report, a best guess is used to determine the assorted brigade strength at the battle as shown below.

The only command that had a reported strength at the battle was Greene's Division, made up of Lawther's and Preston's detachments or demi-brigades. Greene reported an "effective aggregate of 800." Using Greene's present for duty total of 1,269, on October 31, adjusted by another 15 for losses of enlisted men at the battle, and his stated effectives of 800 in the battle, we can determine that the 800 represent 62.3 percent (rounded to 63) of the total present enlisted men on October 31; using the same calculation yields 88 effective officers out of 139 present, for a total strength of 888 officers and men in Greene's Division for the battle. This 63 percent figure is then applied to all the known strengths from various units that were reported on October 31, 1863. To the final numbers of the unknown units are added the known killed, wounded and missing, while excluding the slightly wounded.

The artillery is equally puzzling, as on October 31 Marmaduke clearly shows that he had 18 pieces of artillery available, though by December 31, 1863, that number was 16. This would suggest that 2 of the guns were unserviceable, which would still leave him 16 guns for the battle. From various accounts we know that Griswold's, Pratt's, Hughey's and Ruffner's Batteries were present at the battle.

Of those present we know that Ruffner's had three guns and Pratt had four. However we also know that from past practices, the Confederate command in the Trans-Mississippi, for some reason did not count "mountain guns" as artillery as seen in the Prairie Grove Campaign, where General Hindman reported having 22 artillery pieces when he actually had 29; he excluded the mountain guns that were present (See *O.R.*, vol. 22, pt. 1:138; *Embattled Arkansas*, 526, n. 8g). With the exception of Ruffner's Battery, the guns listed below reflect those that the various commands had prior to the battle and I believe were present.[56]

Marmaduke's Cavalry Command (Brig. Gen. John S. Marmaduke).
    Newton's Division (Col. Robert C. Newton).[57]
        Wood's Mo. Cav. Bn. (Major Robert C.)
            EFF = 138 [1 K, 1 WIA, 0 M]
        Newton's Arkansas Brigade (Maj. John. P. Bull):[58]
            5th Ark. Cav. Regt. (Cdr—Ukn.) [1 K, 0 WIA, 0 M]
            Dobbins' Ark. Regt. (Capt. William B.) [0 K, 0 WIA, 0 M][59]
            Denson's La. Cav. Co. (Capt. W. B. Denson) [0 K, 2 WIA, 0 M][60]
                Newton's Bde. = 280 EFF
                Newton's Bde. Losses = [1 K, 2 WIA, 0 M]

        Carter's Texas Brigade (Maj. B. D. Chenoweth):[61]
            21st Texas Cav. Regt. (Maj. B. D. Chenoweth) [3 K, 2 WIA, 1 M]
            McKie's Texas Cav. Co. (Capt. B. D. Mckie) [0 K, 2 WIA, 1 M]
            Morgan's Texas Cav. Co. (Capt. C. L. Morgan)
            Pratt's Texas Battery (Capt. Joseph H. Pratt) 4-guns; 2 6-lb James Rifles, 2 10-lb Parrot Rifles[62] [2 K, 4 WIA, 0 M][63]
                Carter's Bde. = 203 EFF

---

56. *O.R.*, vol. 22, pt. 2:1054, 1127; Banasik, *Reluctant Cannoneer*, 309; Bearss, "Pine Bluff," 296; Marmaduke, *Order and Letter Book*, 318-321.
57. *O.R.*, Vol. 22, pt. 1:734-736.
58. *Ibid.*, 737-738.
59. *Ibid.*, 736.
60. *Ibid.*
61. *Ibid.*, 738-739; Banasik, *Reluctant Cannoneer*, 312.
62. In his July 1863, letter to the *Galveston Tri-Weekly News*, Leon refers to Pratt's Battery as containing "two twelve-pound Parrot" guns. The 10-pound Parrot was commonly referred to as both a 10-pound or 12-pound Parrot, according to Warren Ripley. Leon, Letter (June 25, 1863), *Galveston Tri-Weekly News* (Galveston, TX), July 8, 1863; Leon, "Texans Making A Raid Into Missouri, Under Gen. Marmaduke, and Col. G. W. Carter," *Galveston Tri-Weekly News*, June 2, 1863; Warren Ripley, *Artillery and Ammunition of the Civil War* (New York, 1970), 110.
63. In Marmaduke's report he lists his total losses as 101 with 18 killed, 67 wounded and 16 missing. He also provides a by name list, which encompasses 16 killed, 62 wounded and 16 missing, with a note that says that Pratt's Battery left several wounded in the Division Hospital. The difference in the two numbers would reflect the losses in Pratt's command, less the losses in Shelby's Brigade, which were not listed in Marmaduke's report. *O.R.*, vol. 22, pt. 1:733; Marmaduke, *Letter and Order Book*, 318-321.

Carter's Bde. Losses = [5 K, 6 WIA, 2 MIA]
Newton's Division = 633 EFF
Newton's Division Losses = [7 killed, 10 WIA, 2 MIA]
Newton's Total Division losses = 19 K/WIA/M

Greene's Division (Col. Colton Greene):[64]
Kitchen's Mo. Cav. Regt. (Col. S. G. Kitchen)
1st Detachment—Left Wing (Col. R. Lawther).
11th Mo. Cav. Bn. (Lt. Col. Col. M. L. Young) [1 K, 7 WIA, 0 M]
3rd Mo. Cav. Regt. (Maj. L. A. Campbell) [3 K, 7 WIA, 0 M]
Griswold's Mo. Battery (D. B. Griswold) 4-guns; 4 12-lb Mt. How.[65] [1 K, 0 WIA, 0 M]
Lawther's Detachment Losses = [5 K, 14 WIA, 0 M][66]
2nd Detachment—Right Wing (Lt. Col. W. J. Preston)
4th Mo. Cav. Regt. (Cdr—Ukn) [0 K, 4 WIA, 0 M]
8th Mo. Cav. Regt. (Cdr—Ukn) [2 K, 3 WIA, 0 M]
Ruffner's Mo. Battery (S. T. Ruffner) 3-guns; 2 12-lb James Rifles and 1 6-lb SB[67] [0 K, 0 WIA, 0 M]
Preston's Detachment Total Losses = [2 K, 7 WIA, 0 M]
Greene's Division = 888 EFF
Greene's Division Losses = [7 K, 21 WIA, 0 M]
Greene's Division Total Losses = 27 K/WIA/M

Monroe's Division (Col. James C. Monroe):[68]

---

64. "Greene's Division" was actually Marmaduke's Cavalry Brigade divided into two detachments, commanded by Colonel Robert R. Lawther and Lieutenant Colonel W. J. Preston. Additionally, Colonel S. G. Kitchen's Regiment was also part of Greene's command but remained under direct control of Greene during the battle. The losses reflected in the various units comes from Marmaduke's by name list of losses in the battle, which is supported by Greene's Official Report of the battle. *O.R.*, vol. 22, pt. 1:730-732; Marmaduke, *Letter and Order Book*, 319-321.

65. Griswold's Battery has a sketchy history, being linked to Hamilton's/Bell's and Harris' Missouri Batteries—and it appears that all four were one in the same battery, though at times labeled as Hamilton's, Bell's or Griswold's or Harris' Battery, depending on who commanded at the time. Griswold's Battery was organized in the Summer of 1863 as part of Colton Green's Cavalry Brigade. C. H. Hamilton was noted as in command in May 1863 (resigned November 7, 1863); Griswold was given command of the battery in June 1863; C. O. Bell led the unit during Little Rock Campaign (He was killed at Reed's Bridge on August 27, 1863); and Griswold led the unit at Pine Bluff. By February 1864, Griswold had departed the command and Captain S. S. Harris was appointed commander of the unit. The battery contained 4 12-lb mountain howitzers. *O.R.*, vol. 22, pt. 1:533; *O.R.*, vol. 22, pt. 2:846, 1054; *O.R.S.*, pt. 2, vol. 38:345-346, 348, 355; Marmaduke, *Letter and Order Book*, 203, 301, 375, 399.

66. In his Official Report, Lawther reported 4 killed with 13 wounded. He clearly did not count the one man from Griswold's Battery who was also killed and probably left out one of the slightly wounded men. *O.R.*, vol. 22, pt. 1:732.

67. Banasik, *Embattled Arkansas*, 515, 524 (n. 6); Crute, 209.

68. *O.R.*, vol. 22, pt. 1:733-734; Allardice, *Confederate Colonels*, 195; Bearss, "Pine Bluff," 301 (n. 29); Marmaduke, *Order and Letter Book*, 319-320.

Cabell's Cav. Brigade (Col. James C. Monroe).[69]

    1st Ark. Regt. (Lt. Col. J. M. O'Neil)[70] [3 K, 12 WIA, 1 M]

    Carroll's Ark. Regt. (Lt. Col. Anderson Gordon)[71] [1 K, 10 WIA, 6 M]

    Crawford's Ark. Bn. (17th Ark.; Lt. Col. W. A.Crawford)[72] Losses = [0 K, 0 WIA, 0 M]

    Hill's Ark. Regt. (7th Ark.; John F. Hill)[73] [1 K, 7 WIA, 4 M]

    Witherspoon's Ark. Bn. (16th Ark. Bn.; James L. Witherspoon) [0 K, 3 WIA, 4 M]

    Woosley's Ark. Bn. (CDR—Ukn) [0 K, 2 WIA, 0 M]

    Hughey's Ark. Battery (Capt. W. M.) 4-guns; 6-lb, iron[74] [0 K, 0 WIA, 0 M]

    Cabell's Brigade = 548 EFF

    Cabell's Brigade Losses = [5 K, 34 WIA, 15 M][75]

        Cabell's Brigade Total losses = 54 K/WIA/M

Shelby's Missouri Brigade (Col. G. W. Thompson):[76]

    5th Cav. Regt. (Cdr—Ukn) [0 K, 0 WIA, 0 M]

    6th Mo. Cav. Regt. (Cdr—Ukn) [0 K, 0 WIA, 0 M]

    12th Mo. Cav. Regt. (Cdr—Ukn) [0 K, 1 WIA, 0 M]

---

69. Cabell's Brigade was ordered to Little Rock on September 10, with less than 900 men, "and nothing could prevent the men from deserting." Hill's Crawford's and Woosley's command were all composed of "deserters and jayhawkers, who had been lying in the mountains and forced into service." Cabell's command arrived too late to help out in Little Rock, as the city had fallen on the same day that they were ordered to join the main army. Instead, they joined the army as it was retreating from the area. On September 21, 1863, Cabell's Brigade was attached to Marmaduke's Division. *O.R.*, vol. 22, pt. 1:604; Marmaduke, *Letter and Order Book*, 265.

70. With Monroe commanding the brigade, O'Neil would have been the commander of the regiment. *O.R.*, vol. 22, pt. 1:607.

71. Lee L. Thomsom commanded Carroll's Regiment until he was dropped from the rolls on September 14, 1863. The next colonel of the regiment was Anderson Gordon, who was a lieutenant colonel and commanded at Pine Bluff. Anderson was subsequently wounded, in the leg at Pine Bluff. *O.R.S.*, pt. 2, vol. 2:240-241; Marmaduke, *Order and Letter Book*, 319.

72. *O.R.S.*, pt. 2, vol. 2:253.

73. The majority of Hill's Regiment was not present at the Battle of Pine Bluff. It appears that only Companies C, D and E were present at the battle; Companies E, G, K, L, and M were absent, either scouting or on recruiting service north of the Arkansas River; Companies A, B and H could have been at Pine Bluff, though their is not sufficient information to make that determination. *Ibib.*, 234-237.

74. *O.R.*, vol. 22, pt. 1:604.

75. Of the 15 men listed as missing, all were supposed to have been killed. This seems to be supported by one Kansan who noted that following the battle they had buried 30 Confederates. Fry, 59; Marmaduke, *Order and Letter Book*, 320.

76. Prior to the Battle of Pine Bluff, Colonel J. O. Shelby departed the main army and moved to Missouri on a raid, that was also meant to recruit for his command. Shelby took detachments from his brigade, numbering 600 men (John N. Edwards puts the number at 800, including 200 men from each f Shelby's three regiments, Elliot's scouts at 100 men, an advance party of 50 men and a section of artillery for the final 50). Shelby Departed on September 22 and did not return to Washington, Arkansas until November 3. Those men remaining behind were commanded by Colonel Gideon W. Thompson. Edwards, *Shelby and His Men*, 196-197; *O.R.*, vol. 22, pt. 1:671, 677.

Shelby's Brigade = 193 EFF
Shelby's Brigade Losses = [0 K, 1 WIA, 0 M][77]
    Shelby's Bde. Total Losses = 1 K/WIA/M
Monroe's Division = 783 EFF
Monroe's Division Losses = [5 K, 35 WIA, 15 M
    Monroe's Division Total Losses = 55 K/WIA/M
Marmaduke's Command = 2,304 EFF
Marmaduke's Losses = [19 K, 66 WIA, 17 M]
    Marmaduke's Total Losses = 102 K/WIA/M

---

77. *O.R.*, vol. 22, pt. 1:733.

Appendix D
Battle of Bayou Fourche (September 10, 1863)

Item: A Union Account of the Battle of Bayou Fourche, September 10, 1863; by John Decker.[1]

That Sandbar Fight

Savannah, I. T. [Indian Territory], May 24
Editor, *Republican*

I notice that Henry C. Luttrell of Hindman's escort tells about the fight on the sandbar below Little Rock. He has made some mistakes, and as I belonged to Co. A, Third Missouri cavalry, I will say a word in reply. Gen. Davidson commanded the cavalry division, Col. John M. Glover of the Third Missouri commanded our brigade. Our regiment came up as a battalion of the Tenth Illinois cavalry was falling back, having lost the guns. We dismounted and formed in line. The guns to our right were limbered up and dashed away to the left. The bayou where the road crossed was a dry sandbar to the right, while to the left of the crossing it held a large body of water. It was all quiet in our front, Gen. Davidson and Col. Glover rode forward perhaps thirty yards, our line being across the lower point of some timber into which the Tenth had been firing. The timber was very large cotton-woods, with many trees lying on the ground. Gen. Davidson said to the colonel as they rode back: "Move your men forward. There is not a damned rebel in these woods" He then rode to the left and the colonel

Took Us In.

We had advanced about fifty yards when the rebels opened with infantry and artillery from a concealed position. We were ordered to take shelter and Steel's heavy guns immediately opened a cross fire in front of our line from the north bank, the Tenth having formed on foot, come up and taken position on our right, curving forward and getting a cross fire. The enemy did not give up the whole wood till late and we took possession of the town about sunset, the Second Brigade camping in the western suburbs while we camped in a pine grove in the city. Now as to Mr. Luttrell's statements. He says: "We see two companies of federal cavalry with a section of mountain howitzers between them and just in their rear is a support of four other guns and a regiment of cavalry." This is all very well only it was two guns instead of four. The support was the Third Missouri cavalry. The rebs did not stay

---

1. This piece is presented without comment and will be fully covered in the Union Tales of the War in this series of books at a later date. John Decker, "That Sandbar Fight," Missouri Republican, June 5, 1886.

On The Bar

five minutes. They pushed the Tenth away from the howitzers and drugged the guns into the woods and stayed there. I was there on the bar and saw this with my own eyes. We could not fire for fear of hitting the men of the Tenth. Neither he nor any other confederate passed below the mouth of that bayou that day after that unless he went as a prisoner. I should like to ask Mr. Luttrell how it was that they left one of their dead comrades just above the bayou in plain sight if they went below, stampeding our cavalry supports and infantry, of which there was none on the field, and there was not a dead horse on the sandbar the next morning and there was no fighting in the water. The bar where the howitzers were lost was about as wide as the river, about 260 yards. The confederates also used the fences along the bayou to make breastworks, while our center fought in an open cornfield.

John Decker

Appendix E
Songs and Poetry of the Civil War

Item: "The Invasion of Camp Jackson," by Joseph Leddy.[1] This is the original version as penned by Leddy on May 30, 1861, at Camp Frost in Jefferson City. There are other versions of this poem and song, most of which are abbreviated, leaving out verses 3, 7–13 and changing some of the words, spellings, or combining verses or adding other verses.

Verse No. 1:

> It was on the Tenth of May, Kelly's men were all away,
> When the Dutch surrounded Camp Jackson,
> Lyon was there, with Boerstein and Blair,
> To take our men from the Happy Land of Canaan.

Chorus (repeated after every verse):

> Oh! Oh! Oh! Ah! Ah! Ah! Ah!
> The time of our glory is a-coming.
> We yet will see the time, when all of us will shine,
> And drive the Hessians from our Happy Land of Canaan.

Verse No. 2:

> Lyon came into camp with such a pompous tramp,
> And said, Frost, you'll have to surrender,
> One-half hour I will give, that is if you want to live,
> To get out of this Happy Land of Canaan.

Chorus:

Verse No. 3:

> The filthy dirty hogs pounced upon our boys like dogs,
> And after taking all our ammunition,
> In double quick time they marched us into line,
> To take us to their filthy Land of Canaan.

Chorus:

---

1. Joe Leddy, "The Invasion of Camp Jackson by the Hessians," in Knapp Family Payers, Missouri Historical Society.

Verse No. 4:

> Our men looked so neat, when they formed upon thestreet,
> You could tell that sour kraut was not their feeding;
> Our men were straight and tall, the Dutch were thin and small,
> And a disgrace to our Happy Land of Canaan.

Chorus:

Verse No. 5:

> The people gave three cheers for Davis and the Volunteers,
> Which raised the Hessians' indignation,
> Who fired upon our brothers, killing sisters, wives and mothers!
> But we'll avenge them in this Happy Land of Canaan.

Chorus:

Verse No. 6:

> With Captain Kelly at our head, we will fight till we are dead;
> Wherever he goes we will sustain him;
> If he had been Frost not a musket would have been lost,
> For we would have them in our Happy Land of Canaan.

Chorus:

Verse No. 7:

> Our boys went to Gasconade and raised a barricade,
> And swore to protect it from the Hessians;
> The Engineer came and tried to pass his train,
> But we stopped him in the Happy Land of Canaan.

Chorus:

Verse No. 8:

> Our boys were then engaged to come up to Osage,
> For they heard that Blair was coming,
> So a battery they erected, and well did they protect it
> From the Dutch in the Happy Land of Canaan.

Chorus:

Verse No. 9:
> You all have heard tell of the Agent called Joel,
> Who came to Osage as a spy man,
> But he was nicely plucked, and in the river ducked,
> And then driven from the Happy Land of Canaan.

Chorus:

Verse No. 10:
> Now I'll take my rhyme way back to ancient time,
> When this country was invaded by the Britons,
> But Freedom's noble son, our brave George Washington,
> Made them git from this Happy Land of Canaan.

Chorus:

Verse No. 11:
> Now I'll bring my lay down to present day
> And St, Louis is invaded by the Hessians,
> But with Kelly, Duke and Green, we can give them pork and beans,
> If we catch them in our Happy Land of Canaan.

Chorus:

Verse No. 12:
> The upper country volunteers come down to join us here,
> And Captain Kelly's men took and trained them;
> The boys were rough and tough, and made of the right stuff
> To keep the Dutch from their Happy Land of Canaan.

Chorus:

Verse No. 13:
> The boys are all gone home, and we are left alone,
> But we hope again soon to meet them;
> Thank God, we are all well, and can give the Dutchmen hell,
> If we catch them in our Happy Land of Canaan.

Chorus:

Verse No. 14:[2]

> Twas just three months that day, since the gloomy 10th of
> May,
> When Lyon once again had us surrounded.
> But we were fighting for State-Rights, and we proved it in the
> fight,
> For we shot him in this Happy Land of Canaan.

Chorus:

* * * * * *

Item: Excerpts of "Son of Allen Held His Mule," by Colonel James Harding.[3]

> It was in March, first month of spring,
> An army brave and strong.
> At Elkhorn made the welkin ring
> With shouts both loud and long
> And while the battle raged so hot,
> And fighting was the rain.
> In what was thought a sheltered spot,
> Llewellyn held his mule.
> He did not hold a mule alone,
> For that was duty light.
> He also held a noble roan
> Whose master shared the fight.

* * * * * *

Item: Originally published as "The Picket Guard" on November 30, 1861, "All Quiet Along the Potomac" was later put to song by a Confederate officer, John H. Hewitt. Hewitt claimed he got the words of the song from Lamar Fontaine of Texas, but Fontaine's credibility is suspect. The real author of the poem turned into a song was Ethel Lynn Eliot Beers, from New York. Beers was inspired to do the poem following her frequent reading of newspapers which bore the headline of "All Quiet Along the Potomac."[4]

---

2. This fourteenth verse was not part of Leddy's original prose and was found on an Internet site listed below. As to whether Leddy added it at a later date is not known. However, there are indications that there were 15 verses to the poem. Scott K. Williams, "The Capture of Camp Jackson," Internet site www.usgennet.org/usa/mo/county/stlouis/cj/campjack.htm.

3. Banasik, *"Tales of the War" Part Two 1862,* 65.

4. Nofi, 126–128.

All Quiet Along the Potomac
Lyrics by Ethel Lynn Eliot Beers
Song by Lamar H. Hewitt

"All quiet along the Potomac to-night!"
　　Except here and there a stray picket
Is shot, as he walks on his beat, to and fro,
　　By a rifleman hid in the thicket.
'Tis nothing! a private or two now and then
　　Will not count in the news of a battle;
Not an officer lost! only one of the men
　　Moaning out, all alone, the death rattle.
All quiet on the Potomac to-night!
　　Where the soldiers lie peacefully dreaming;
And their tents in the rays of the clear autumn moon,
　　And the light of their camp-fires are gleaming.
A tremendous sight, as a gentle night-wind
　　Through the forest leaves slowly is creeping;
While the stars up above, with their glittering eyes,
　　Keep guard o'er the army sleeping.
There's only the sound of the lone sentry's tread,
　　As he tramps from the rock to the fountain,
And thinks of the two on the low trundle bed,
　　Far away, in the cot on the mountain.
His musket falls slack, his face, dark and grim.
　　Grows gentle with memories tender,
As he mutters a prayer for the children asleep,
　　And their mother—"may heaven defend her!"
The moon seems to shine forth as brightly as then—
　　That night, when the love, yet unspoken,
Leaped up to his lips, and when low-murmured vows
　　Were pledged ever to be unbroken.
Then drawing his sleeve roughly over his eyes,
　　He dashes off the tears that are welling;
And gathers the gun closer to his breast,
　　As if to keep down his heart's swelling.
He passes the fountain, the blasted pine-tree,
　　And his footstep is lagging and weary;
Yet onward he goes, through the broad belt of light,
　　Towards the shades of the forest so dreary.
Hark! was it the night-wind that rustled the leaves?
　　Was it moonlight so wondrously flashing?
It looked like a rifle: "Ha! Mary, good-by!"

And his life-blood is ebbing and splashing.
"All quiet along the Potomac to-night!"
No sound save the rush of the river;
While soft falls the dew on the face of the dead,
And the picket's off duty forever!

* * * * * * *

Item: On July 4, 1865, General Joe Shelby and about 500 of his men were crossing over into Mexico. The day was sunny, they were in sight of the El Paso del Aquilar Mountains, and in a solemn ceremony, Shelby "buried" his flag and his famed plume in the Rio Grande River. Before the deed was done "Colonels Elliot, Williams, Gordon, Slayback and Blackwell, held it up for a few brief moments…and at last, with not a dry eye among all five hundred stern soldiers, the Battle Flag of Shelby's division was lowered slowly and sadly beneath the water. In later years Colonel Alonzo Slayback immortalized that moment in the following poem:

The Burial of Shelby's Flag.
by Colonel Alonzo Slayback.[5]

A July sun, in torrid clime, gleamed on exile band
  Who, in suits of gray,
  Stood in mute array
On the banks of the Rio Grande.
They were dusty and faint with their long, drear ride,
And they passed when they came near the river side,
  For its wavelets divide,
  With their flowing tide
Their own dear land, of youth, hope, pride,
And comrades' graves who in vain had died,
From the stranger's home in a land untried.

Above them waved the Confederate flag, with its fatal cross of
stars,
  That had always been
  In the battle's din,
Like a pennon of potent Mars.
And there curved from the crest of their leader's plume,
That the brave had followed in joy and gloom,
  That was ever in sight

---

5. Edwards, 548–549.

In the hottest fight
A flaunting dare for a soldier's tomb,
For the marksman's aim and the cannon's boom,
But it bore a charm from the hand of doom.

Forth stepped that leader then and said to the faithful few
around,
   "This tattered rag
   Is the only flag
That floats on Dixie found.
And this plume that I tear from the hat I wear
Of all my spoils is my only share;
   And brave men! I swear
   That no foe shall dare
To lay his hand on our standard there.
Its folds were braided by fingers fair;
'Tis emblem now of their deep despair.

"Its cause is lost. And the men it led on many a glorious
field,
   In disputing the tread
   Of invaders dread,
Have been forced at last to yield.
But this banner and plume have not been to blame,
No exulting eye shall beheld their shame;
   And these relics so dear
   In the waters here
Before we cross shall burial claim;
And while yon mountains may bear a name
They shall stand as monuments of our fame."

Tears stood in eyes that had looked on death in every awful
form
   Without dismay,
   But the scene that day
Was sublimer than mountain storm!
'Tis easy to touch the veteran's heart
With the finger of nature, but not of art.
   While the noble of soul
   Lose self-control,
When called on with flag, home and country to part,
Base bosoms are ever too callous to start,
With feelings that generous natures can smart.

They buried then that flag and plume in the river's rushing
tide,
    Ere that gallant few
    On the tried and true
Had been scattered far and wide.
And that group of Missouri's valiant throng,
Who had fought for the weak against the strong—
    Who had charged and bled
    Where Shelby led,
Were the last who held above the wave
The glorious flag of the vanquished brave,
No more to rise from its watery grave!

* * * * * *

Item: "The Conquered Banner." A mainstay of Southern history of the Civil War, the poem is "a lament for the defeat of the Confederacy." The poem is frequently recited in southern schools and has since been "performed on stage as a pantomime."[6]

The Conquered Banner
by Father Abram Joseph Ryan

Furl that Banner, for 'tis weary;
Round its staff 'tis drooping dreary;
Furl it, fold it, it is best;
For there's not a man to wave it,
And there's not a sword to save it,
And there's no one left to love it,
In the blood which heroes gave it
And its foes now scorn and brave it:
Furl it, hide it—let it rest!
Take the Banner down! 'tis tattered;
Broken is the staff and shattered.
And the valiant hearts are scattered
Over home it floated high.
Oh! 'tis hard for us to fold it;
Hard to think there's none to hold it;
Hard that those who once unrolled it
Now must furl it with a sigh.

---

6. Nofi, 410–411.

Furl the banner furl it sadly!
Once ten thousands hailed it gladly,
And ten thousands wildly, madly
Swore that foeman's sword should never
Hearts like theirs entwined discover
Till that flag should float forever
O'er their freedom or their grave!
Furl it! for the hands that grasped it
And the hearts that fondly clasped it,
Cold and dead are lying low.
And that Banner—it is trailing!
While around it sounds the wailing
Of its people in their woe.
For, though conquered, they adore it!
Weep for those who trailed and tore it!
But, oh!, wildly they deplore it.
Now who furl and fold it so.
Furl the Banner! True, 'tis glory
And 'twill live in song and story
Though its folds are in the dust;
For its fame and highest pages,
Penned by poets and by sages,
Shall go sounding down the ages—
Furl its folds though we must.
Furl that Banner, softly, slowly!
Treat it gently—it is holy—
For it droops above the dead.
Touch it not—unfold it never,
Let it droop there, furled forever,
For its people's hopes are dead.

* * * * * *

Appendix F
Confederate Pieces Not Used, 1863

Item: "Gen. Johnston disagrees with Jefferson Davis," by unknown reporter. General Joe Johnston's comments on his operations in Mississippi in 1863.
Published: December 4, 1886.

Item: "An Old Letter," by Thomas J. Portis. Letter (January 13, 1863) addressed to Thomas L. Snead, regarding clothing provided for Sterling Price's troops while stationed in Mississippi by the ladies of Dallas County, Alabama.
Published: July 3, 1886.

Item: "Women's Lot in War Time," by E. H. The experiences of a Confederate women and her family living in the Shenandoah Valley, a short distance from Winchester in 1863.
Published: June 12, 1886.

Item: "Guibor's Battery as Heavy Artillery," by W. P. Barlow. Guibor's Missouri Battery (CSA) at Grand Gulf, Mississippi (April 29, 1863), during the siege of Vicksburg, Mississippi (May 19–July 4, 1863); and its conversion from light guns to heavy artillery.
Published: July 17, 1886.

Item: "The Death of Stonewall Jackson," by Capt. James Power Smith. The death of Stonewall Jackson at Chancellorsville, Virginia, by one who was there. Excepts from the original published in the October 1886 issue of the *Century Magazine.*
Published: October 9, 1886.

Item: "Capture of the *Maple Leaf*," by A. E. Asbury. Capture of the steamer *Maple Leaf* (June 13, 1863), in Chesapeake Bay, by captured Confederate officers en route to Fort Delaware from New Orleans and Fort Norfolk, Virginia.
Published: March 13, 1885.

Item: "Incidents and Camp and Field," by William W. Gibson, 6th Arkansas Infantry, Govan's Brigade. Assorted incidents of camp life in Govan's Brigade from the Battle of Liberty Gap, Tennessee (June 25, 1863), near Murfreesboro.
Published: March 20, 1886.

Item: "Disputed Points," by John B. Smith. Archer's Brigade at Gettysburg (July 1–3, 1863). Archer's command style in always leading from the front and describing his capture.
Published: May 29, 1886.

Item: "Archer's Brigade at Gettysburg," by J. B. Smith. Archer's Brigade at Gettysburg (July 1–3, 1863); corrections made to a piece (in the March 13, 1886 newspaper) by Loyd G. Harris, of the Iron Brigade, by a Confederate in Archer's Brigade. Also includes a brief history of the 1st, 4th and 7th Tennessee Infantries.
Published: April 24, 1886.

Item: "Archer's Brigade," by W. P. Davis, Company K, 14th Tennessee Infantry. Archer's Brigade at Gettysburg; another account.
Published: June 19, 1886.

Item: "Colors Gracefully Surrendered," by John B. Smith. The new flag of the 2nd Mississippi Infantry Regiment; the original being captured at Gettysburg on July 1, 1863.
Published: June 12, 1886.

Item: "The Charge at Gettysburg," by J. B. Smith. Pickett's charge; giving recognition to the other troops who participated in the charge.
Published: March 5, 1887.

Item: "Reunion of Pickett's Division," by Robert McCulloch of St. Louis. Formation of an organization to honor the survivors of Pickett's Division.
Published: March 19, 1887.

Item: "Confederate Monument at Gettysburg," by unknown. Dedication of the first Confederate monument at Gettysburg, honoring the 1st Maryland Battalion, Lieutenant Colonel James R. Herbert. Includes monument inscription and brief history of the battalion.
Published: November 27, 1886.

Item: "A Tough Old Reb," by Adam C. Johnson, correspondent. An old Arkansas Confederate, John Clement, relates the tale of his wounding at Gettysburg as well as other incidents of the battle.
Published: November 27, 1886.

Item: "The Last Shots at Vicksburg," by Captain W. T. DeWitt. The last shots fired at Vicksburg, Mississippi on July 3, 1863, by Company C, 1st Missouri Infantry, Confederate.

Published: March 13, 1886.

Item: "The 'Barren Victory' of Chickamauga" and "Gen. Bragg at Chickamauga," by D. H. Hill. The Battle of Chickamauga (September 19–20, 1863). Excerpt for D. H. Hill's account previously published in the *Century Magazine*.
Published: March 26 and April 2, 1887.

Item: "Gen. Morgan's Escape," by Thomas W. Bullitt. General John H. Morgan's escape from prison in November 1863.
Published: July 4, 1885.

Item: "Rear Guard Fighting at Ringgold," by William W. Gibson, 6th and 7th Arkansas Regiment, Govan's Brigade, Cleburne's Division. Covering the Confederate retreat from Missionary Ridge, in November 1863.
Published: October 17, 1885.

Item: "Smith's Brigade at Mission Ridge," by Leon Fremon, 6th Texas Infantry Regiment, Smith's Brigade. The Battle of Missionary Ridge.
Published: October 31, 1885.

Item: "Refreshing Memories of Mission Ridge," by William W. Gibson, Company D, 6th Arkansas Infantry, Govan's Brigade. The retreat from Missionary Ridge, in response to Leon Fremon's piece above.
Published: December 12, 1885.

Bibliography

Books/Pamphlets/Articles

Adamson, Hans Christian. *Rebellion in Missouri: 1861 Nathaniel Lyon and His Army of the West*. Rahway, NJ: Quinn & Boden Company, 1961.

Allardice, Bruce S. *Confederate Colonels: A Biographical Register*. Columbia, MO: University of Missouri Press, 2008.

————. *More Generals In Gray*. Baton Rouge, LA: Louisiana State University Press, 1995.

Anderson, Ephraim McD. *Memoirs: Historical and Personal; Including the Campaigns of the First Missouri Confederate Brigade*. St. Louis: Times Printing Co., 1868. Reprint. Dayton, OH: Morningside Bookshop, 2005.

Ankesheiln, Wade. *The Last Guardsmen*. Independence, MO: Two Trails Publishing, 2008.

Anonymous. Bartels, Carolyn M. and James E. McGhee, eds. *The Gallant Breed: The 6th Missouri Cavalry, A Roster of the Men Who Rode Under the Flag of Shelby's Iron Brigade*. Independence, MO: Two Trails Publishing, 2009.

————. Bartels, Carolyn M. and James E. McGhee, eds. *The Gallant Breed the 12th Missouri Cavalry: A Roster of the Men Who Rode Under the Flag of Shelby's Iron Brigade*. Independence, MO: Two Trails Publishing, 2009.

Bailey, Anne J. *Between the Enemy and Texas: Parsons's Texas Cavalry in the Civil War*. Fort Worth, TX: Texas Christian University Press, 1989.

Banasik, Michael E. *Cavaliers of the Brush: Quantrill and His Men*. Unwritten Chapters of the Civil War West of the River Volume V. Iowa City, IA: Camp Pope Publishing, 2003.

————. *Confederate "Tales of the War" In the Trans-Mississippi, Part Two: 1862*. Unwritten Chapters of the Civil War West of the River Volume VII. Iowa City, IA: Camp Pope Publishing, 2011.

————. *Duty, Honor and Country: The Civil War Experiences of Captain William*

P. Black, Thirty-seventh Illinois Infantry. Unwritten Chapters of the Civil War West of the River Volume VI. Iowa City, IA: Camp Pope Publishing, 2006

———. *Embattled Arkansas: The Prairie Grove Campaign of 1862*. Wilmington, NC: Broadfoot Publishing Company, 1996.

———. *Missouri Brothers in Gray: The Reminiscences and Letters of William J. Bull and John P. Bull*. Unwritten Chapters of the Civil War West of the River Volume I. Iowa City, IA: Camp Pope Publishing, 1998.

———. *Missouri in 1861: The Civil War Letters of Franc B. Wilkie, Newspaper Correspondent*. Unwritten Chapters of the Civil War West of the River Volume IV. Iowa City, IA: Camp Pope Publishing, 2001.

———. *Reluctant Cannoneer: The Diary of Robert T. McMahan of the Twenty-fifth Independent Ohio Light Artillery*. Unwritten Chapters of the Civil War West of the River Volume III. Iowa City, IA: Camp Pope Publishing, 2000.

———. *Serving With Honor: The Diary of Captain Eathan Allen Pinnell of the Eighth Missouri Infantry (Confederate)*. Unwritten Chapters of the Civil War West of the River Volume II. Iowa City, IA: Camp Pope Publishing, 1999.

Barr, Alyn. "Confederate Artillery in Arkansas." *Arkansas Historical Quarterly* 22 (Autumn 1963): 238–272.

Bartels, Carolyn M. *The Bravest of the Brave Pindall's 9th Missouri Battalion of Sharpshooters*. Independence, MO: Two Trails Publishing, 2001.

———. *Civil War Stories of Missouri*. Shawnee Mission, KS: Two Trails Publishing, 1995.

———. *The Forgotten Men: Missouri State Guard*. Shawnee Mission, KS: Two Trails Publishing, 1995.

———. *Trans-Mississippi Men at War, Volume I: Missouri C.S.A.* Independence, MO: Two Trails Publishing, 1998.

Bartlett, Napier. *Military Record of Louisiana Including Biographical and Historical Papers Relating to the Military Organizations of the State*. New Orleans:

L. Graham and Company, 1875. Reprint. Baton Rouge, LA: Louisiana State University Press, 1964.

Bearss, Edwin C. "The Battle of Helena, July 4, 1863." *Arkansas Historical Quarterly* 20 (Autumn 1961): 256–297.

———. "The Battle of the Post of Arkansas." *Arkansas Historical Quarterly* 18 (Autumn 1959): 237–279.

———. "The Federals Raid Van Buren and Threaten Fort Smith." *Arkansas Historical Quarterly* 26 (Summer 1967): 123–142.

———. "Marmaduke Attacks Pine Bluff." *Arkansas Historical Quarterly* 23 (Winter 1964): 291–313.

Bevier, R. S. *History of the First and Second Missouri Confederate Brigades 1861–1865. And From Wakarusa to Appomattox, A Military Anagraph.* St. Louis: Bryan, Brand & Company, 1879.

Blessington, Joseph Palmer. *The Campaigns of Walker's Texas Division.* New York: Lange, Little & Co., Printers, 1875.

Boatner III, Mark Mayo. *The Civil War Dictionary.* New York: David McKay Company, Inc., 1959.

Britton, Wiley. *The Civil War on the Border A Narrative of Military Operations in Missouri, Kansas, Arkansas, and the Indian Territory, During the Years 1861-1862, Based Upon Official Reports of the Federal Commanders Lyon, Sigel, Sturgis, Frémont, Halleck, Curtis, Schofield, Blunt, Herron and Totten and of the Confederate Commanders McCulloch, Price, Van Dorn, Hindman, Marmaduke and Shelby.* New York: G. P. Putnam's Sons, 1899.

Brock, R. A. Ed. *Southern Historical Society Papers.* 52 vols. Richmond, VA: Southern Historical Society, 1876–1959. Reprint. Wilmington, NC: Broadfoot Publishing Company, 1990–1992.

Brown, Norman D. *Journey to Pleasant Hill: The Civil War Letters of Elijah P. Petty Walker's Texas Division C.S.A.* San Antonio, TX: The University of Texas, 1982.

Burford, Timothy Wayne and Stephanie Gail McBride. *The Division: Defending Little Rock: August 25–September 10, 1863.* Jacksonville, AR: Wire Storm Publishing, 1999.

Burke, W. S. *Official Military History of Kansas Regiments During the War For the Suppression of the Great Rebellion.* Leavenworth, KS: W. S. Burke, 1870.

Castel, Albert. *General Sterling Price and the Civil War in the West.* Baton Rouge, LA: Louisiana State University Press, 1968.

Christ, Mark K. *Civil War Arkansas 1863: The Battle for a State.* Norman, OK: University of Oklahoma Press, 2010.

———, ed. *Rugged and Sublime: The Civil War in Arkansas.* Fayetteville, AR: The University of Arkansas Press, 1994.

"Col. W. M. Moore." *Confederate Veteran* 36 (February 1928): 64.

Crute, Joseph H. *Units of the Confederate States Army.* Midlothian, VA: Derwent Books, 1987.

Davis, Edwin Adams. *Heroic Years Louisiana in the War for Southern Independence.* Baton Rouge, LA: Vail-Ballou Press, Inc. 1964.

Davis, William C. Ed. *The Confederate General.* 6 vols. Harrisburg, PA: National Historical Society, 1991.

Douglas, Mark K. *Soldiers, Secesh and Civilians: Compiled Records of Callawegians in the War of the Rebellion, Etc.* Montgomery, MO: Jones Republic Press, 2001.

Dyer, F. H. *A Compendium of the War of the Rebellion.* Des Moines, IA, 1908. Reprint. Dayton, OH: The Press of Morningside Bookshop, 1978.

Eakin, Joanne C. and Donald R. Hale. *Branded as Rebels: A List of Bushwhackers, Guerrillas, Partisan Rangers, Confederates and Southern Sympathizers from Missouri During the War Years.* Independence, MO: Wee Print, 1993.

Eakin, Joanne C. *Battle of Lone Jack August 16, 1862.* Independence, MO: Two Trails Publishing, 2001.

―――――. *Confederate Records From the United Daughters of the Confederacy Files*. 8 vols. Independence, MO: Two Trails Publishing, 1995-2001.

―――――. *Missouri Prisoners of War From Gratiot Prison & Myrtle Street Prison, St. Louis, Mo. and Alton Prison, Alton Illinois Including Citizens, Confederates, Bushwhackers and Guerrillas*. Independence, MO: Two Trails Publishing, 1995.

Edwards, John Newman. *Shelby and His Men or the War in the West*. Cincinnati, OH, 1867: Reprint. Waverly, MO: General Joseph Shelby Memorial Fund, 1993.

Edwards, William B. *Civil War Guns: The Complete Story of Federal and Confederate Small Arms: Design, Manufacture, Identification, Issue, Employment, Effectiveness, and Postwar Disposal*. Secaucus, NJ: Castle Books, 1962.

Evans, Clement A., ed. *Confederate Military History*. 13 vols. Atlanta, 1899. Reprint. Secaucus, NJ: Blue & Gray Press, 1974.

Evans, Clement A. and Robert S. Bridgers, eds. *Confederate Military History Extended Edition*. 19 vols. Atlanta, 1899. Reprint. Wilmington, NC: Broadfoot Publishing Company, 1987.

Faust, Patricia L., ed. *Historical Times Illustrated Encyclopedia of the Civil War*. New York: Harper Perennial, 1986.

Ferguson, John L. and J. H. Arkinson, *Historic Arkansas*. Little Rock, AR: Arkansas History Commission, 1966.

Foster, Samuel C. "We Are Prisoners of War." *Civil War Times Illustrated* 16 (May 1977): 24–33.

Frost, Griffin. *Camp and Prison Journal*. Quincy, IL: Quincy Herald Book and Job Shop, 1867. Reprint. Iowa City, IA: Press of the Camp Pope Bookshop, 1994.

Fry, Alice L. *Following the Fifth Kansas Cavalry: The Letters*. Independence, MO: Two Trails Publishing, 1998.

Gallaway, B. P. Ed. *Texas the Dark Corner of the Confederacy: Contemporary*

Accounts of the Lone Star State in the Civil War. Lincoln, NE: University of Nebraska Press, 1994.

Gaughan, T. J., ed. *Letters of a Confederate Surgeon.* Camden, AR: The Hurley Co., Inc., 1960.

Gibbons, Tony. *Warships and Naval Battles of the Civil War.* New York: W. H. Smith Publishers, Inc., 1989.

Guralnik, David B., ed. *Second College Edition Webster's New World Dictionary of the American Language.* New York: The World Publishing Company, 1972.

Hale, Donald R. *Branded as Rebels, Volume 2.* Independence, MO: Blue & Grey Book Shoppe, 2003.

Harrington, Fred Harvey. *Fighting Politician: Major General N. P. Banks.* Philadelphia, PA: University of Pennsylvania Press, 1948.

Hearn, Chester G. *Ellet's Brigade: The Strangest Outfit Of All.* Baton Rouge, LA: Louisiana State University Press, 2000.

Heidler, David S. and Jeanne T. Heidler, eds. *Encyclopedia of the American Civil War: A Political, Social, and Military History.* New York: W. W. Norton & Company, 2000.

Heitman, Francis B. *Historical Register and Dictionary of the United States Army From Its Organization, September 29, 1789, to March 2, 1903.* 2 vols. Washington: Government Printing Office, 1903. Reprint. Gaitherburg, MD: Old Soldiers Books Inc., 1988.

Hewett, Janet, ed. *The Roster of Confederate Soldiers 1861–1865.* 16 vols. Wilmington, NC: Broadfoot Publishing Company, 1995-1996.

Hewett, Janet, ed. *Supplement to the Official Records of the Union and Confederate Armies.* 100 vols. Wilmington, NC: Broadfoot Publishing Company, 1994–2001.

History of Buchanan County, Missouri, Containing a History of the County, Its Cities, Towns, Etc. St. Joseph, MO: St. Joseph Steam Printing Company, Printers, Binders, Etc., 1881.

History of Cole, Moniteau, Morgan, Benton, Miller, Maries and Osage Counties, Missouri, Etc. Chicago: The Good speed Publishing Co., 1886.

History of Howard and Cooper Counties, Missouri, Written and Complied From the Most Authentic Official and Private Sources, Etc. St. Louis: National Historical Company, 1883.

History of Howard and Chariton Counties, Missouri, Written and Compiled from the Most Authentic Official and Private Sources Including a History of Its Townships, Towns and Villages. St. Louis: National Historical Company, 1883.

Huff, Leo E. "The Marmaduke-Walker Duel: The Last Duel in Arkansas." *Missouri Historical Review* 58 (October 1964): 452–463.

———. "The Union Expedition Against Little Rock, August–September, 1863." *Arkansas Historical Quarterly* 22 (Autumn 1963): 224–237.

Hughes, Jr., Nathaniel Cheairs. *The Battle of Belmont: Grant Strikes South.* Chapel Hill, NC: The University of North Carolina Press, 1991.

Irwin, Richard B. "The Red River Campaign." *Battles and Leaders of the Civil War.* 4 vols. New York: Century Company, 1887–1888. 4:345–362.

Kuhr, Manuel Irwin. "How George Vest Came to Missouri." *Missouri Historical Review* 59 (July 1965): 424–427.

Leslie, James W. "Arabella Lanktree Wilson's Civil War Latter." *Arkansas Historical Quarterly.* 47 (Autumn 1988): 257–272.

Livermore, Thomas L. *Numbers & Losses in the Civil War in America: 1861–1865.* Bloomington, IN: Indiana University Press, 1957.

Lowe, Richard. *Walker's Texas Division C.S.A. Greyhounds of the Trans-Mississippi.* Baton Rouge, LA: Louisiana State University Press, 2004.

Marmaduke, John S. *Confederate States Trans-Mississippi Order and Letter Book.* Independence, MO: Two Trails Publishing Press, 2000.

McElroy, John. *The Struggle For Missouri.* Washington, DC: National Tribune Co., 1909.

McGhee, James E. *Letter and Order Book Missouri State Guard 1861–1862*. Independence, MO: Two Trails Publishing, 2001.

———. *Missouri Confederates: A Guide to Sources for Confederate Soldiers and Units 1861–1865*. Independence, MO: Two Trails Publishing, n.d.

McKechnie, Jean L. *Webster's New Universal Unabridged Dictionary Deluxe Second Edition*. New York: Simon & Schuster, 1979.

Miles, Kathleen White. *Bitter Ground: The Civil War in Missouri's Golden Valley Benton, Henry, and St. Clair Counties*. Warsaw, MO: The Printery, 1971.

Mobley, Freeman K. *Making Sense of the Civil War in Batesville-Jacksonport and Northeast Arkansas 1861–1874*. Batesville, AR: P. D. Printing, 2005.

Moore, Frank, ed. *The Rebellion Record: A Diary of American Events*. 12 vols. Vols. 1–6, New York: Putnam, 1861–1863. Vols. 7–12, New York: Van Nostrand, 1864–1868. Reprint ed. New York: Arno Press, 1977.

Mudd, Joseph A. "What I Saw At Wilson's Creek." *Missouri Historical Review* 7 (January 1913): 89–105.

———. *With Porter in North Missouri: A Chapter In the History of the War Between the States*. Washington: National Publishing Company, 1909.

Mullins, Mrs. Mary Jackman. "Sketch of Col. Sidney D. Jackman." In *Reminiscences of the Women of Missouri During the Sixties*, 93–96. Jefferson City, MO: Missouri Division, United Daughters of the Confederacy, 1911.

Nash, Charles Edward. *Biographical Sketches of Gen. Pat Cleburne and Gen. T. C. Hindman Together With Humorous Anecdotes and Reminiscences of the Late Civil War*. Little Rock, AR: Tunnah & Pittard, Printers, 1895. Reprint. Dayton, OH: Morningside Bookshop, 1977.

Neal, Diane and Thomas W. Kremm. *Lion of the South General Thomas C. Hindman*. Macon, GA: Mercer University Press, 1993.

Nichols, James L. *The Quartermaster in the Trans-Mississippi*. Austin, TX: University of Texas Press, 1964.

Nofi, Albert A. *A Civil War Treasury: Being a Miscellany of Arms and Artillery, Facts and Figures, Legends and Lore, Muses and Minstrels, Personalities and People.* Conshohocken, PA: Combined Books, 1992. Reprint. Edison, NJ: Castle Books, 2006.

Norton, Richard L. *Behind Enemy Lines: The Memoirs and Writings of Brigadier General Sidney Drake Jackman.* Springfield, MO: Oak Hills Publishing, 1997.

Oliphant Wm. J. "Arkansas Post." In *Southern Bivouac.* 4:736–739. Reprint ed. Wilmington, NC: Broadfoot Publishing Company, 1993.

Patrick, Jeffery. Ed. "Remembering the Missouri Campaign of 1861: The Memoirs of Lieutenant William P. Barlow, Guibor's Battery, Missouri State Guard." *Civil War Regiments: A Journal of the American Civil War* 5, no. 4 (1997): 20–66.

Peterson, Richard C., et al. *Sterling Price's Lieutenants: A Guide to the Officers and Organization of the Missouri State Guard.* Jefferson City, MO: Two Trails Publishing, 1995.

Petty, A. W. M. *A History of the Third Missouri Cavalry From Its Organization At Palmyra, Missouri, 1861 Up To November Sixth, 1864 With An Appendix and Recapitulation.* Little Rock, AR: J. Wm. Demby, Publisher 1865. Reprint. Albany, MO: Century Reprints, 1997.

Phillips, Christopher. *Damned Yankee: The Life of General Nathaniel Lyon.* Columbia, MO: University of Missouri Press, 1990.

Phisterer, Frederick. *Statistical Record of the Armies of the United States.* New York: Charles Scribner's Sons, 1907.

Pitcock, Cythia Dehaven and Bill J. Gurly. *I Acted Out of Principle: The Civil War Diary of Dr. William M. McPheeters, Confederate Surgeon in the Trans-Mississippi.* Fayetteville, AR: The University of Arkansas Press, 2002.

Pollard, Edward A. *The Lost Cause: A New Southern History of the War of the Confederates, etc.* New York: E. B. Treat & Co., Publishers, 1867. Reprint. New York: Bonanza, 1970.

Porter, David D. *Naval History of the Civil War.* New York: n.p., 1886. Reprint. Secaucus, NJ: Castle, 1984.

Reid, Thomas. *Spartan Band: Burnett's 13th Texas Cavalry in the Civil War*. Denton, TX: University of North Texas Press, 2005.

Ripley, Warren. *Artillery and Ammunition of the Civil War*. New York: Litton Educational Printing, Inc., 1970.

Ross, Margaret. *Arkansas Gazette: The Early Years 1819–1866*. Little Rock, AR: Arkansas Gazette Foundation, 1969.

Schnetzer, Wayne H. *Men of the Eleventh: A Roster of the Eleventh Missouri Infantry Confederate States of America*. Independence, MO: Two Trails Publishing, n.d.

———. *Men of the Tenth: A Roster of the Tenth Missouri Infantry Confederate States of America*. Independence, MO: Two Trails Publishing, n.d.

———. *More Forgotten Men: The Missouri State Guard*. Independence, MO: Two Trails Publishing, 2003.

Schultz, Robert G., ed. *General Sterling Price and the Confederacy*. St. Louis: Missouri History Museum, 2009.

Sears, Stephen W. *Chancellorsville*. Boston: Houghton-Mifflin Company, 1996.

Sellmeyer, Deryl P. *Jo Shelby's Iron Brigade*. Gretna, LA: Pelican Publishing Company, 2007.

Shea, William L. and Earl J. Hess. *Pea Ridge: Civil War Campaign in the West*. Chapel Hill, NC: University of North Carolina Press, 1992.

Sifakis, Stewart. *Who Was Who in the Confederacy: A Comprehensive, Illustrated Biographical Reference to More Than 1,000 of the Principal Confederacy Participants in the Civil War*. New York: Facts on File, 1988.

———. *Who Was Who in the Union: A Comprehensive, Illustrated Biographical Reference to More Than 1,500 of the Principal Union Participants in the Civil War*. New York: Facts on File, 1988.

Simons, Don R. *In Their Words: A Chronology of the Civil War in Chicot County, Arkansas and Adjacent Waters of the Mississippi River*. Sulphur, LA: Wise Publications, 1999.

Simpson, Harold B., ed. *The Bugle Softly Blows: The Confederate Diary of Benjamin M. Seaton*. Waco, TX: Texan Press, 1965.

———. *Texas in the War 1861–1865*. Hillsboro, TX: The Hill Junior College Press, 1965.

Snead, Thomas L. "The Conquest of Arkansas." In *Battles and Leaders of the Civil War*, 3:441–459. New York: Century Company, 1887–1888.

———. *The Fight For Missouri: From the Election of Lincoln to the Death of Lyon*. New York: Charles Scribner's Sons, 1866.

Stanton, Donal J., Goodwin F. Berquist, and Paul C. Bowers, eds. *The Civil War Reminiscences of General M. Jeff Thompson*. Dayton, OH: Morningside Bookshop, 1988.

Stone, Norman and J. P. Kenyon. *The Wordsworth Dictionary of British History*. Hertfordshire, England: Wordsworth Editions Ltd. 1994.

Taylor, Richard. *Destruction and Reconstruction: Personal Experiences of the Late War*. New York: D. Appleton and Co., 1879. Reprint. Nashville, TN: J. S. Sanders & Company, 1998.

The Union Army: A History of Military Affairs in the Loyal United States 1861–1865—Records of the Regiments in the Union Army—Cyclopedia of Battles—Memoirs of Commanders and Soldiers. 8 vols. Madison, WI: Federal Publishing Company, 1908. Reprint. Wilmington, NC: Broadfoot Pub. Co., 1998.

Warner, Ezra J. *Generals in Blue: Lives of the Union Commanders*. Baton Rouge, LA: Louisiana State University Press, 1964.

———. *Generals in Gray: Lives of the Confederate Commanders*. Baton Rouge, LA: Louisiana State University Press, 1959.

Waterman, Robert E. and Thomas Rothrock, eds. "The Earle-Buchanan Letters of 1861–1876" *Arkansas Historical Quarterly* 33 (Summer 1974): 99–174.

Watts, J. Carter. "Duel of Generals." *Confederate Veteran* 36 (January–February, 1988): 35, 44–45, 48.

Webb, W. L. *Battles and Biographies of Missourians, or the Civil War Period of Our State*. Kansas City, MO: Hudson-Kimberly Pub. Co., 1900.

Weddle, Robert S. *Plow-Horse Cavalry: The Caney Creek Boys of the Thirty-fourth Texas*. Austin, TX: Madrona Press, Inc., 1974.

White County Heritage Civil War Collection, Volume 1–25. Searcy, AR: White County Historical Society, nd.

Wiley, Bell Irwin. *Fourteen Hundred and 91 Days in the Confederate Army*. Wilmington, NC: Broadfoot Publishing Company, 1987.

Wills, Garry. *James Madison*. New York: Time Books, 2002.

Winter, William C. *The Civil War in St. Louis: A Guided Tour*. St. Louis: Missouri Historical Society Press, 1994.

Winters, John D. *The Civil War In Louisiana*. Baton Rouge, LA: Louisiana State University Press, 1963.

Woodruff, W. E. *With the Light Guns in '61–'65 Reminiscences of Eleven Arkansas, Missouri and Texas Light Batteries, in the Civil War*. Little Rock, AR: Central Printing Company, 1903.

Wooster, Ralph A. *Lone Star Regiments in Gray*. Austin, TX: Eakin Press, 2002.

Wright, Marcus J. *General Officers of the Confederate Army*. New York: The Neale Publishing Company, 1911.

Young, Dr. R. E. *Pioneers of High, Water, and Main: Reflections of Jefferson City*. Jefferson City, MO: Twelfth State, 1997.

Government Sources

Davis, George B., Leslie J. Perry, and Joseph W. Kirkley. *Atlas to Accompany the Official Records of the Union and Confederate Armies*. Washington, DC: Government Printing Office, 1891–1895.

National Archives. Record Group 109. Confederate Muster Rolls. Assorted units. Washington, DC.

———. Record Group M317. Confederate Compiled Service Records: Arkansas. Assorted rolls and units. Washington, DC.

———. Record Group M322. Confederate Compiled Service Records: Missouri. Assorted rolls and units. Washington, DC.

———. Record Group M405. Union Compiled Service Records: Missouri. Assorted rolls and units. Washington, DC.

———. Record Group M861. Records of Confederate Movements and Activities. Assorted rolls and units. Washington, DC.

Reece, J. N. *Report of the Adjutant General of the State of Illinois*. 9 vols. Springfield, IL: Journal Company, 1900–1902.

Naval History Division. Navy Department. *Civil War Naval Chronology, 1861–1865*. 6 vols. Washington, DC: Government Printing Office, 1971.

United States War Department. *The War of the Rebellion: A Compilation of the Official Records of the Union and Confederate Armies*. 70 volumes comprising 128 books. Washington, DC: U.S. Government Printing Office, 1880–1901. Reprint. Harrisburg, PA: National Historical Society, 1985.

———. *The War of the Rebellion: Official Records of the Union and Confederate Navies*. 31 volumes. Washington, DC: U.S.: Government Printing Office, 1894–1922.

Internet Sites

Christy, Dr. Robert J. "The Memoirs of Dr. Robert J. Christie." http://flanaganfamily.net/genealo/memoirs.htm

Snell, Daniel E. "Captain Samuel William McAllister." http://www.6thtx.org/mcallisterhistory.htm

Williams, Scott K. "The Capture of Camp Jackson: The First Major Action Bringing Civil War to Missouri." http://www.usgennet.org/usa/mo/county/stlouis/cj/campjack.htm

Manuscripts/Special Collections

Camden, AR. Camden Public Library.
    Smart, Lula Grinstead. "H. L.Grinstead." Confederate Scrapbook.

Carlisle, PA. U.S. Army Military History Institute.
    Civil War Times Illustrated Collection:
        John C. Williams memoirs.

Chapel Hill, NC. University of North Carolina.
    Southern Historical Collection.
        Wallace, James T. Diary (1862–1865)

Columbia, MO. State Historical Society of Missouri.
    Western Historical Manuscript Collection:
        Hoskins, William N. Civil War Diary.
        Quesenberry, John P. Manuscript Diary.

Indianapolis, IN. Indiana Historical Society.
    Bishop, S. C. Letters.
    Denny, Gilbert H. Letters.
    Hougland, James H. Civil War Diary.

Liberty, TX. Sam Houston Regional Library Research Center.
    Chambers, Thomas Jefferson. Arkansas Post Civil War Memorandum For 1863: Jan. 1–13, With Map.

Little Rock, AR. Arkansas History Commission.
    Lotspeich, C. B. Typescript Diary (January 17–September 26, 1863).
    McRae Papers.
    Skaggs Collection:
        Calvert. George W. Letter.
        Cassell, T. W. Letter.
        Lindsey, G. G. Letter.
        Marshall, R. P. Letter.
        Moore, W. M. Letters.
        Newspaper Clipping File.
    Wassell. Samuel Spotts. Collection.
        McRae, Dandridge. Letters.

Little Rock, AR. University of Arkansas.
    Turnbo, S. C. "History of the Twenty-seventh Arkansas Confederate Infantry With Many Interesting Accounts of the Counties Through Which it Passed

During the Civil War and Accurate Accounts of the Battles in which it Engaged."

New York. Columbia University.
    Peter W. Alexander Collection:
        Burbridge, John Q. Letters.
        Copy Letter Book, June 1–Dec. 18, 1862. Hindman's Command.
        Copy Letter Book, June 11–Dec. 30, 1862. Hindman's Command.
        Holmes, Theophilus H. Letters.
        Marmaduke, John S. Letters.
        Parsons, Mosby M. Letters.
        Miscellaneous Correspondence.
        Special Order Book, June 1–Dec. 18, 1862. Hindman's Command.
        Special Order Book, June 11–August 19, 1862. Army of the Southwest.
        Telegrams. Hindman's Command.

Rolla, MO. Missouri State Historical Society.
    Bradford, Moses Jasper. Letters (1861–1865).

St. Louis, MO. Missouri Historical Society.
    Babcock, W. R. Collection.
        Missouri Volunteer Militia Scrapbook.
    Civil War Papers.
        Steen, Alexander. Letter.
    Knapp Family Papers.
        Leddy, Joe. "The Invasion of Camp Jackson by the Hessians."
    Parsons, M. M. Collection.
        Bell, R. J. Diary.

Newspapers

Alabama:
    Mobile Advertiser and Register (Mobile)

Arkansas:
    Arkansas Patriot (Little Rock)
    Arkansas State Gazette (Little Rock)
    The Arkansas True Democrat (Little Rock)
    Washington Telegraph (Washington)

Illinois:
    Chicago Daily Tribune (Chicago)
    The Chicago Times (Chicago)

The Quincy Herald (Quincy)
Waukegan Weekly Gazette (Waukegan)

Indiana:
The Indianapolis Daily Journal (Indianapolis)

Iowa:
The Daily Gate City (Keokuck)
Home Journal (Mount Pleasant)
Muscatine Daily Journal (Muscatine)

Kansas:
The Emporia News (Emporia)
Daily Conservative (Leavenworth)
Freedoms Champion (Atchison)
Leavenworth Daily Times (Leavenworth)
The State Record (Topeka)

Missouri:
The Canton Weekly Press (Canton)
The Daily Missouri Democrat (St. Louis)
The Daily Missouri Republican (St. Louis)
North Missouri Courier (Hannibal)

Mississippi:
The Memphis Daily Appeal (Jackson)

Texas:
Bellville Countryman (Bellville)
Dallas Herald (Dallas)
Galveston Tri-Weekly News (Galveston)
Tri-Weekly Telegraph (Houston)

Credits

Photographs and Illustrations

Baton Rouge, LA. Louisiana State University: James F. Fagan.

Confederate Veteran 15 (August 1907): 346: Levin M. Lewis.

Dallas Morning News, October 2, 1911: Robert Ralston Lawther (courtesy of Bruce Allardice).

Little Rock, AR. University of Little Rock: James C. Tappan.

Moore, John C., *Missouri, Confederate Military History*, 9:216: John G. Walker.

Miller, Francis T. *The Photographic History of the Civil War in Ten Volumes*, 10:297: Lucius M. Walker.

Roberts, Oran M., *Texas, Confederate Military History*, 11: 252; Henry E. Mc-Culloch.

Searcy, AR. Dorothy D. Young Collection: Dandridge McRae.

Snead, Thomas L., "Conquest of Arkansas," *Battles and Leaders of the Civil War,* 3:450: Thomas J. Churchill.

St. Louis, MO. Missouri History Museum: Mosby M. Parsons (MHM FEIN 43-0654561).

The Union Army, 8:72: John W. Davidson.

Washington, DC. Library of Congress, Prints & Photographs Division:
Popular Graphic Arts Collection. LCUSZC2-1987: Bombardment of Arkansas Post.
Brady-Handy Collection. LC-USZ62-62368: Fort Curtis, Helena Arkansas.
Civil War Glass Negatives and Related Prints. LC-B8184-10523: Theophilus H. Holmes; LC-DIG-cwpb-06002: Gen. J.D. [*sic*] Marmaduke; LC-DIG-cwpb-07294: Maj. Gen. Frederick Steele.

Maps

Michael E. Banasik, Battle of Pine Bluff, October 25, 1863.

Michael E. Banasik, Operations In Northeast Louisiana (June–August 1863).

Battles and Leaders of the Civil War, 4:348: Area of Operations: Arkansas and Louisiana, modified and enhanced by Michael E. Banasik.

Davis, George B., et al. *Atlas of the Civil War*, plt. 23, no. 3: Engagement At Bayou Fourche, September 10, 1863.

O.R., vol. 22, 1:448: Approaches to Little Rock August–September, 1863.

O.R., vol. 17, 1:711: Arkansas Post.

O.R., vol. 22, 1:515: Crossing of the Arkansas River At Terry Ferry, September 10, 1863.

O.R., vol. 22, 1:515: Battle of Helena, July 4, 1863.

"Pine Bluff, Ark., Scene of the Battle," *Chicago Tribune*, November 17, 1863: Battle of Pine Bluff, enhanced and redrawn by Michael E. Banasik.

Index

www.ingramcontent.com/pod-product-compliance
Lightning Source LLC
Chambersburg PA
CBHW022015090426

42739CB00006BA/147